Harsh Justice

Harsh Justice

Criminal Punishment and the Widening Divide between America and Europe

JAMES Q. WHITMAN

OXFORD
UNIVERSITY PRESS

OXFORD
UNIVERSITY PRESS

Oxford New York
Auckland Bangkok Buenos Aires Cape Town Chennai
Dar es Salaam Delhi Hong Kong Istanbul Karachi Kolkata
Kuala Lumpur Madrid Melbourne Mexico City Mumbai Nairobi
São Paulo Shanghai Taipei Tokyo Toronto

First published in 2003 by Oxford University Press, Inc.,
198 Madison Avenue, New York, New York 10016

www.oup.com

First issued as an Oxford University Press paperback, 2005

Library of Congress Cataloging-in-Publication Data
Whitman, James Q.
Harsh justice : criminal punishment and the widening divide between
America and Europe / by Jame Q. Whitman.
p. cm.
Includes index.
ISBN 0-19-515525-4; 0-19-518260-X (pbk.)
1. Punishment—United States. 2. Punishment—France.
3. Punishment—Germany. 4. Punishment—Philosophy. I. Title.
K5103 .W48 2003
364.6′01—dc21 2002004838

1 3 5 7 9 8 6 4 2

Printed in the United States of America
on acid-free paper

In grateful memory of Edward Shils

Note and Acknowledgments

Since I closed the research for this book in 2001, there have been two developments that deserve at least a brief mention. One is the tough-talking law-and-order movement that entered French politics with the election of 2002. This may conceivably bring change to the French system of punishment, and readers familiar with the French scene will certainly think of it as they read this text. The impact of this newest law-and-order movement is something that I will address more directly in the French version of this book. Let me simply observe here that such developments have a long history in France and that they have yet to alter the fundamental drive toward dignity in punishment that is my topic. The other development of 2002 that deserves some mention is the string of American corporate scandals exemplified by Enron. These scandals have brought a considerable intensification of the assault on white-collar offenders that was already underway in our country during the previous decades. They have also been the occasion for some striking journalistic writings on the harsh treatment of imprisoned white-collar offenders, such as J. Senior, "You've Got Jail," at http://www.newyorkmetro.com/nymetro/news/crimelaw/features/6228/. An updated version of this book would have to take more account of both developments.

My thanks for comments and other help to Bruce Ackerman, Hans-Jörg Albrecht, Olivier Beaud, Mirjan Damaska, George Fletcher, Lawrence Friedman, Antoine Garapon, Dan Gordon, Dieter Grimm, Felix Herzog, Dan Kahan, Xavier Lameyre, Peter Landau, John Langbein, Christine Lazerges, Klaus

Marxen, Jörg Müller, Martha Nussbaum, Christoph Paulus, Pierrette Poncela, Kitty Preyer, Eric Rasmussen, Rainer Schröder, Thomas Weigand, Robert Weisberg, and Elisabeth Zoller. My thanks also for the welcome given to me by the administrations of prisons at Tegel, Stadlheim, and Fleury-Mérogis. I benefited from the hospitality of the Max Planck Institut für Ausländisches und Internationales Strafrecht, Freiburg im Breisgau. Parts of the text were presented at seminars at the European University Institute in Florence, the American Academy in Berlin; DEA seminars in philosophy of law and comparative law at the University of Paris II (Panthéon-Assas); the Colloque "Sens de la Peine" at the École d'Administration Pénitentiaire in Agen, November, 2000; and workshops at the law schools of Harvard, University of Michigan, and Yale. My thanks to participants at all these venues. I benefited from wonderful research assistance, especially from Gabi Friedman, Ginny Vander Jagt, and Willow Crystal. The research for this book was largely completed while I was a fellow in the matchless setting of the American Academy in Berlin, and a visiting professor at the Université de Paris II (Panthéon-Assas), from whose rich intellectual life I benefited immensely.

All translations are my own, unless otherwise noted.

Contents

Harsh Justice

Introduction

At the beginning of the twenty-first century, criminal punishment is harsh in America, and it has been getting harsher. In the year 2000, the incarcerated population reached the extraordinary level of 2 million, roughly quintupling since the mid-1970s.[1] America's per capita incarceration is now the highest in the world, approaching, and in some regions exceeding, ten times the rate in Western Europe. Large-scale incarceration is only part of the story, though. Juveniles have increasingly been tried "as adults"—something that Western Europeans find little less than shocking. New sorts of punishments have been invented over the last twenty-five years, from boot camps to electronic monitoring devices; and old sorts of punishments, from chain gangs to public shaming, have been revived. Some of the new harshness has involved matters almost everybody regards as momentous: in particular the death penalty, reintroduced in the United States at the very moment that it was definitively abolished in Western Europe. At the same time, some of the new harshness has involved almost laughably trivial matters: "quality of life" policing has landed people in jail—if only for a night—for offenses like smoking cigarettes in the New York subway;[2] and the Supreme Court has declared that police may jail persons for something as minor as driving without a seatbelt.[3] All of these developments, whether trivial or momentous, have been surrounded by a jarringly punitive rhetoric in American politics, perhaps best exemplified by the Phoenix sheriff who proudly declares that he runs "a very bad jail."[4]

None of this is news. Everyone who reads the newspapers knows that we have been in the midst of a kind of national get-tough movement, which has lasted for about the last twenty-five years. Still, Americans may not quite grasp how deeply isolated this period has left us in the Western world. Punishment in America is now, as Michael Tonry observes, "vastly harsher than in any other country to which the United States would ordinarily be compared."[5] There are certainly some parts of the world that have turned harsher over the last twenty-five years. This is true in particular of some Islamic countries.[6] But among Western nations, only England has followed our lead—and even England has followed us only up to certain point.[7] As for the countries of continental Western Europe, the contrast between their practices and ours has become stark indeed. The Western European media regularly runs pieces expressing shock at the extreme severity of American punishment.[8] Meanwhile, continental justice systems have come to treat America as something close to a rogue state, hesitating to extradite offenders to the United States.

To be sure, this era of American harshness will presumably not go on forever, and it may already have slowed.[9] Nevertheless, it is the disturbing truth that we now find ourselves in a strange place on the international scene. As a result of the last quarter century of deepening harshness, we are no longer clearly classified in the same categories as the other countries of the liberal West. Instead, by the measure of our punishment practices, we have edged into the company of troubled and violent places like Yemen and Nigeria (both of which, like many jurisdictions in the United States, execute people for crimes committed when they were minors—though Yemen has recently renounced the practice);[10] China and Russia (two societies that come close to rivaling our incarceration rates);[11] pre-2001 Afghanistan (where the Taliban, like American judges, reintroduced public shame sanctions);[12] and even Nazi Germany (which, like the contemporary United States, turned sharply toward retributivism and the permanent incapacitation of habitual offenders).[13]

What is going on in our country?

This is the question I want to approach in this book. This is a book about the cultural roots of harsh criminal punishment as it has emerged in contemporary America. Most especially, it is a book about the how harsh criminal punishment can develop in a society that belongs to the Western liberal tradition. America *is*, after all, a country that belongs to something it is fair to call the Western "liberal" tradition, elusive though the concept of liberalism may be. Certainly there are many aspects of American culture that seem manifestly to belong to a humane strain of liberalism. Ours, of all Western countries, is the one that is most consistently suspicious of state authority. Ours is the country with the inveterate attachment to the values of procedural fairness. Ours is the country that—unlike Germany or France—never succumbed to any variety of fascism or nazism. Why, then, is ours not the country with the mildest punishment practices? Certainly, in most respects, Americans define their values by opposition to *illiberal* societies—to the societies of places like China or the Afghanistan of the Taliban or Nazi Germany.

How could our patterns of punishment be bringing us closer to them than to the dominant polities of the contemporary European Union?

The answer this book will offer is drawn from history—a comparative history that reaches back to the eighteenth century, to a time before the French and American revolutions. In particular, it is drawn from a close comparative study of the United States, on the one hand, and the two dominant legal cultures of the European continent, France and Germany, on the other. There are good reasons to choose France and Germany for such a study. Of all the continental countries, these are the two that cry out most for close comparison with our own, in this era of American harshness. They are large and powerful industrial nations that have been strongholds of humane and democratic Western values since 1945. They are countries that have set the tone for all of the continent for many generations, and that continue to set much of the tone for the human rights jurisprudence of the European Union. Not least, they are the countries that we have measured ourselves against since the time of the American Revolution. Indeed, they are countries that, once upon a time, seemed precisely to lack the humane and democratic values that *America* stood for. France and Germany, as they exist today, are the descendants of the "despotic," state-heavy, hierarchical societies against which we defined ourselves two and half centuries ago. They are also countries that have had recurrent episodes of authoritarian government, from the nineteenth century through the horrific 1930s and 1940s. Yet at the end of the millennium, they are countries that punish far more mildly than ours does. Why?

There is one sort of answer that must be rejected out of hand. This is the sort of answer given by the high-theoretical literature on the sociology of punishment in "modern" society. Sociologists of punishment and "modern" society, from Durkheim to Foucault and beyond, are among the best-known intellectual figures of the day. Their books are widely assigned in college courses, and the sociology of "modernity" is probably the first thing that most educated people think of when the topic is punishment. But theirs is a sociology precisely about punishment in "modern" society in general. The sociology of "modernity" simply does not grapple with the question of how punishment practices can vary—let alone how sharp differences can exist between the "modern" societies of places like the United States, France, or Germany. The sort of "modernity" that Foucault and his followers talk about seems especially beside the point, and especially frustrating to read in the face of recent American developments. Foucault, in his famous *Discipline and Punish*, described modern punishment as the product of an ominous shift from disciplining the body to disciplining the soul. This makes for a dramatic, and sometimes fitting, description of continental punishment; and it also makes for a fitting description of *some* aspects of American punishment. But it tells us nothing about how punishment practices could diverge on the two sides of the Atlantic, with America striking off alone on the road to intensifying harshness. Much the same objection applies even to the most sensitive recent work on "modernity."[14] Of course large industrial countries share some "modern" features. But what they share can hardly explain how they have diverged; and these countries *have* diverged. How can any approach that starts by invoking "modernity" explain why?

This book will accordingly avoid talking much about "modernity." We cannot understand American punishment without understanding *America;* and the same goes for the rest of the "modern world." Sensible criminologists have always been ready to acknowledge that different cultures produce different forms of punishment—that, as one pre-Foucault textbook put it, "One learns to react punitively or in some other way just as learns to speak English, German or Japanese."[15] One does indeed. Like other wise scholars, I will accordingly focus on comparative culture:[16] there is something in the American idiom, something in American culture, that is driving us toward harsh punishment.

Of course, "American culture" is a vast topic, and I should emphasize from the outset that there are important aspects of American culture that I am not going to explore with any care. It is clear, for example, that American harshness has something to do with the strength of its religious tradition, and especially its Christian tradition. Part of what makes us harsher than continental Europeans is the presence of some distinctively fierce American Christian beliefs. It is also the case that American harshness has something to do with American racism—though, as we shall see, continental European race relations are not noticeably better than American. While I will touch on both of these issues repeatedly, I will not discuss either in any detail. Perhaps most important, it is clear that the relative harshness of American punishment has a great deal to do with the prevalence of violence in American society—both because Americans have higher rates of violent crime, and because American patterns of violence also make themselves felt in prisons, policing, and elsewhere.[17] The difference in patterns of violence matters immensely, and it certainly deserves attention beyond what I will give it in this book. Nevertheless, American violence is another problem that I leave for another day.

Instead, leaving race, Christianity, and violence to one side, this book will focus on two quite different aspects of American culture: on American patterns of *egalitarian social status* and on American patterns of *resistance to state power*. American society has a deeply rooted tradition of status egalitarianism: a strong dislike for social hierarchy runs throughout through American history. American society also displays a recurrent suspiciousness in the face of state power. These are both features of American life that are integral to the American style of liberalism. They are also features of American life that differentiate us unmistakably from the countries of continental Europe. Countries like France and Germany show much more tolerance for traditions of social hierarchy than we do, and much more tolerance for state power as well. And, as I am going to try to show, these most characteristically "liberal" features of American culture have contributed to making American punishment uniquely harsh in the West.

The bulk of this book will be about the American style of status equality. The notion that the peculiarities of American culture have to do with peculiar

American traditions of status equality is nothing new. Tocqueville, in particular, is famous for arguing that the forms of American culture grew out of our historic lack of social hierarchy—out of our lack of what he called the "aristocratic element." This has seemed critically important to many observers of American society ever since, from H. G. Wells to Louis Hartz and Seymour Martin Lipset,[18] and this book too is going to treat it as critically important.

But I am going to offer a very different argument from the kind that Tocqueville offered. To Tocqueville, the absence of an "aristocratic element" implied that America would have *mild* criminal punishment. "Societies become milder," he declared in his *Democracy in America*, "as conditions become more equal": after all, people who are equal can be expected to have more reciprocal empathy, and therefore to go easy on each another. America, he thus concluded in 1840, being the most egalitarian country, must inevitably have "the most benign criminal justice system."[19] Nor is Tocqueville the only observer to offer this sort of argument. A kindred idea appeared, a half-century later, in the sociology of Durkheim. To Durkheim, the harshness of punishment in a given society had something to do with its degree of "contractualization." To the extent that market-oriented, contractlike relations governed societies, Durkheim hypothesized, they would tend to have "restituitive" rather than "penal" regulation—they would tend to rely on civil remedies rather than on harsh criminal punishment. This Durkheimian claim had nothing to do with social status as such. Nevertheless, to the extent we associate market forms of social organization with rejection of status hierarchy, we can see real resemblances between Durkheim's arguments and those of Tocqueville.[20] Certainly Durkheim's arguments suggest the same conclusion about America as Tocqueville's: if Durkheim is right, we would expect to observe a link between American styles of market-oriented egalitarianism and mildness in criminal punishment.

Yet, of course, in America there is no such link. Americans display unmistakably deep-rooted patterns of status egalitarianism; Tocqueville was right about that. Yet our punishment is unmistakably harsh. As for market-orientation: it would be hard to point to any society that is more "contractualized," more market-oriented, than ours. Yet ours is the society of harsh punishment.

The main purpose of this book is to explain why—why the American style of status equality should produce results so thoroughly at odds with what these subtle and thoughtful French observers predicted.

The explanation I will offer involves a comparative legal history that reaches well back into the eighteenth century. The key to understanding how Tocqueville and Durkheim went wrong lies, I am going to argue, in understanding the link between traditions of social hierarchy and the dynamic of *degradation* in punishment. Contemporary American criminal punishment is more *degrading* than punishment in continental Europe. The susceptibility to degradation lies at the core of what makes American punishment harsh. And our susceptibility to degradation has to do precisely with our lack of an "aristocratic element."

The literal meaning of "to degrade" is to reduce another person in status, to treat another person as *inferior*; and it is that literal meaning that I will take as my point of departure. We all know intuitively that degradation, in this sense, often plays a significant role in punishment: part of what makes punishments effective is their power to degrade—their power to make the person punished feel diminished, lessened, lowered. Within the world of criminal punishment, such degradation is achieved in the widest variety of ways, from beatings to mutilation to day-glo orange prison uniforms.

Now, contemporary France and Germany are countries, I am going to show, with a deep commitment to the proposition that criminal offenders must not be degraded—that they must be accorded *respect* and *dignity*. The differences between continental and American practices can be little short of astonishing. Some of the most provocative examples come from continental prisons. Prison is a relatively rare sanction in continental Europe, by sharp contrast with the United States, and sentences are dramatically shorter. Nevertheless, there are continental prisons, and there are continental prisoners. But those comparatively few continental offenders who do wind up in prison are subjected to a regime markedly less degrading than that that prevails in the United States. Thus continental prisons are characterized by a large variety of practices intended to prevent the symbolic degradation of prison inmates. Prison uniforms have generally been abolished. Rules have been promulgated attempting to guarantee that inmates be addressed respectfully—as "Herr So-and-So" or "Monsieur So-and-So." Rules have also been promulgated protecting inmate privacy, through such measures as the elimination of barred doors. Most broadly, these measures include what in Germany is called "the principle of approximation" or "the principle of normalcy": the principle that life in prison should approximate life in the outside world as closely as possible. Like all ideals in the law of punishment, this one is sometimes realized only fitfully: to study norms of dignity in prison is often to study aspirations rather than realities. France in particular lags well behind Germany in implementing these practices, and life in French prisons can be very tough. Nevertheless, the "principle of approximation" does have real meaning, and indeed it has led to some practices that will seem astounding to Americans. German convicts, for example, are supposed to work at jobs that are *real* jobs, like jobs in the outside world. This means that they enjoy far-reaching protection against arbitrary discharge, and even four weeks per year of paid vacation (!). All of this is intended to dramatize a fact about their dignity. The lives of convicts are supposed to be, as far as possible, no different from the lives of ordinary German people. Convicts are not to be thought of as persons of a different and lower status than everybody else. As we shall see, these same ideas also pervade European political debate over prison policy. (These are also the continental ideas that most recently came to the fore in European protests over the treatment of the captured prisoners held in Guantanamo Bay after the American campaign in Afghanistan.)

Prisons are not the only places where this continental commitment to dignity shows itself. There are many examples that take us beyond life within prison walls. Thus in America we are far less bothered by public exposure for criminal offenders than Europeans are—whether those inmates are being kept behind barred prison doors that expose them to the view of all, or being shown on internet broadcasts, or being subjected to public shame sanctions, or having their records opened for public inspection. There are other examples, involving deprivation of civil and political rights. The oldest legal form of status degradation—automatic deprivation of rights of participation—still survives in America. Convicted American felons are frequently automatically deprived of civic rights—a practice of status degradation that has disenfranchised a substantial proportion of the African-American population in some regions. As we shall see, French and German prison systems, by contrast, have programs that encourage inmates to exercise their (almost always unimpaired) right to vote. On the deepest level, American criminal justice displays a resistance to considering the very personhood of offenders. This is a resistance that shows in the triumph of determinate sentencing in America, and it is a resistance that is absent in Western Europe.

These are differences of profound significance, I am going to argue, differences that take us a long way toward understanding how American punishment culture has come to differ so much from French and German. Cultures that systematically show respect for offenders are also cultures that are likely to punish with a mild hand; conversely, cultures (like our own) that have no commitment to respect for the offender are likely to show harshness. Where do these differences come from?

"Modernity" obviously has no answer to offer.

That does not mean that sociology has no answer to offer. On the contrary, these are differences we can only explain if we are grasp some deeply rooted differences in social values and social structure. But the sociology we need is a historical sociology. The continental commitment to "dignity" and "respect" in punishment is something that has grown very slowly since the eighteenth-century, and it is a commitment that offers striking evidence of a fundamental connection between degradation in punishment and traditions of social status. For at its core, as I want to demonstrate in this book, it is a commitment to *abolishing historically low-status treatment*.

To understand the differences that divide us from the French and the Germans, we must indeed begin in the eighteenth century. France and Germany are countries in which, two centuries or so ago, there were sharp distinctions between high-status people and low-status people. In particular, there were two classes of punishments: high-status punishments, and low-status punishments. Forms of execution are the most familiar example: nobles were traditionally beheaded; commoners were traditionally hanged. There are many other examples, too: low-status offenders were routinely mutilated, branded, flogged, and subjected to forced labor; all while being displayed before a raucous public, both before and after their deaths. High-status offenders were generally spared such treatment. Forms of imprisonment differed by status as well. Two and a half centuries ago, high-status continental convicts—who included such famous eighteenth-century prisoners as Voltaire or Mirabeau—

could expect certain kinds of privileged treatment. They were permitted a relatively normal and relatively comfortable existence, serving their time in "fortresses" rather than in prisons. Their "cells" were something like furnished apartments, where they received visitors and were supplied with books and writing materials. They were immune from forced labor and physical beatings. They were accorded easy and regular visitation privileges. They were permitted to wear their own clothing and to provide their own food; they were permitted to provide their own medical care as well. They were shielded from public exposure, and indeed from all forms of shame. Low-status prisoners by contrast were subjected to conditions of effective slavery, often resulting in horrifically high mortality.

The subsequent development of punishment in these countries can be captured, in its broadest outline, in a simple sociological formula: over the course of the last two centuries, in both Germany and France, and indeed throughout the continent of Europe, *the high-status punishments have slowly driven the low-status punishments out*. Gradually, over the last two hundred years, Europeans have come to see historically low-status punishments as unacceptable survivals of the inegalitarian status-order of the past. More and more offenders have been subjected to the relatively respectful treatment that was the privilege of a tiny stratum of high-status persons in the eighteenth century. In particular, what used to be the privilege of relatively respectful imprisonment has slowly been extended to every inmate. This is a generalization that can only be made in broad outline: I speak of tendencies that, while always present, are never fully realized. What has happened, has happened only within the limits of the possible. There is no way that every ordinary inmate can really be accorded all the accommodations and comforts that an imprisoned Voltaire or an imprisoned Mirabeau once enjoyed. It has happened, in part, only recently: the full-scale abolition of low-status punishments has occurred only over the last twenty-five years, and is indeed still in the process of occurring. Nevertheless, it has happened. The old "honorable" forms of imprisonment have driven the "dishonorable" forms out: within the limits of the possible, everyone in a continental prison is now treated in the way only aristocrats and the like were once treated, and norms of dignified and respectful treatment have become generalized. This is a development that is, moreover, entirely typical of continental European law: as I have argued elsewhere, in almost every area of the law, we see the same drive toward a kind of high-status egalitarianism—of an egalitarianism that aims to lift everyone up in social standing. These countries are the scene of a *leveling-up* egalitarianism—an egalitarianism whose aim is to raise every member of society up in social status.[21]

High social status for everybody: this is the drive in continental Europe. This drive has caught the attention of continental observers from Rudolf von Jhering in the nineteenth century to Norbert Elias and Pierre Bourdieu in the twentieth.[22] All of these continental authors see the same deep desire among their countrymen to eliminate the vestiges of low status and bring everyone up in social rank. It is a desire that has profoundly affected the continental approach to punishment. High social status for everybody has come to mean high social status even for criminal offenders.

Nothing of the kind has happened in the United States, by contrast; and this reflects the fact that the history of social status in the American world is very different. Our traditions of punishment do not begin the way continental traditions do: with an eighteenth-century practice of making sharp distinctions between high- and low-status punishment. The common-law world does not have the same long history of legally guaranteeing high-status treatment for some. In certain ways, in fact, English status-differentiation had already begun to break down in the later Middle Ages and sixteenth century. Certainly by the mid–eighteenth century the contrast between the continental and Anglo-American worlds was very striking: by around 1750, special high-status treatment had already begun to vanish in both the British colonies and in metropolitan England. Over the course of the nineteenth century, this historic tendency became consistently stronger in the United States, as special high-status treatment was regularly attacked. The consequence is that our large sociological tendency ran in a direction opposite from that of continental Europe. Where nineteenth-century continental Europeans slowly began to *generalize* high-status treatment, nineteenth-century Americans moved strongly to *abolish* high-status treatment. From a very early date, American showed instead, at least sporadically, a typical tendency to generalize norms of *low*-status treatment—to level down. The tale of this American development is, as we shall see, exceedingly complex. Most important, it is bound up with the history of American slavery in ways that have to be carefully traced and carefully weighed. What matters though, for my purposes in this book, is principally what did *not* happen. Americans never displayed the European tendency to maintain and generalize older high-status patterns of treatment.

In this, the law of punishment is, once again, simply typical of the law more broadly: Europeans live with the memory of an age of social hierarchy and feel a corresponding horror at historically low-status punishments. To tolerate the infliction of degrading punishments, for Europeans, is to tolerate a return to the bad old world of the ancien régime, when ordinary people had to fear flogging, mutilation, and worse. We do not live with memories of that kind in the United States (despite our history of slavery), and the European urge to replace low-status punishments with high-status ones is an urge that we do not feel. We can revive old-style public shaming, for example, without feeling any European qualms: humiliating and degrading offenders, for us, does not smack of social hierarchy: We have not learned to think of humiliation and degradation, in the way that Europeans do, as inegalitarian practices.

The connection between traditions of social hierarchy and degradation is my main topic, but it is not my only one. I will also spend some time on another aspect of American liberalism: our traditions of resistance to state power.

Here too, there is a long tradition of interpretation that seems simply wrong when tested against the American case. At least since Montesquieu, people have believed that harsh punishment is produced by strong states, with relatively unbridled power.[23] Durkheim stated it as nothing less than a "law": the intensity of punishment, he held, depended not only on the complexity of a society, but on the "absolute character" of its state power.[24] This is an idea that is still taken perfectly seriously by scholars,[25] and it is an idea that most ordinary Americans undoubtedly find completely congenial. Following this idea, one would imagine that the countries that punished harshly were what Montesquieu called the "despotic" ones. In particular, one would predict that America, home of a powerful antistatist tradition, would punish mildly. And indeed, most Americans assume that our traditions of resistance to state power, and especially our traditions of procedural protections against prosecution, make our country uniquely liberal in its criminal justice. Yet, despite our unmistakably libertarian traditions, ours, among Western countries, is the one with distinctively harsh punishment.

This too is a puzzle for any of us attached to the values of liberalism. Part of the solution to the puzzle is that Americans overestimate the distinctiveness of their traditions. Europeans have procedural protections too, as we shall see. Indeed, they have been actively extending their procedural protections over the last quarter century. (What is more, even the historical difference is not as sharp as Americans imagine: it has been argued, for example, that the privilege against self-incrimination, far from being an Anglo-American innovation, was borrowed from the continent.[26])

But the issue goes beyond procedural protections. It is my aim to show that traditions of state power can make for *mildness* in punishment, in ways that our scholarship has not fully grasped—ways that have to do primarily with two aspects of state power: the exercise of systematic mercy and the tendency toward bureaucratization.

Mercy is the most important of the aspects of state power that I will discuss. "Mercy" is complex concept. In part, it is concept that assumes, once again, relations of status hierarchy. Mercy comes de haut en bas: superiors accord it to inferiors. In this, mercy is akin to degradation: when we show a person mercy, we confirm his inferior status—more gently, but just as surely, as when we degrade him. A society with a strong tradition of acknowledging and enforcing status differences will thus often be a society with a tradition of mercy.

There is more to the concept of mercy than that, though. Mercy involves respecting individual differences. A merciful justice looks down on the offender, and asks: what is it that might entitle this offender to milder punishment than others who have committed the same offense? In this sense, mercy involves individualization of justice—a willingness to distinguish between more deserving and less deserving persons. The contrary of mercy, as understood in this sense, is formal equality: a system that operates by the principle of formal equality is a system that aims to treat all persons exactly alike, extending no special mercy to anyone. Kant is the most famous advocate of a species of formal equality that excludes mercy, and his best-known passage presents his view with a kind of Old Testament fury: "The law of punishment is a categorical imperative, and woe to him who creeps along the serpent paths of the theory of social welfare hoping to turn up some argument that makes it seem like good policy to release him from his punishment, or diminish it."[27] When we reject mercy, in the spirit of this slightly terrifying passage, we refuse to countenance any special treatment for any offender.

As we shall see, the values of mercy have shown themselves to be much stronger in French and German justice, over the last quarter-century, than in American justice. This is partly because practices of mercy that date back to the eighteenth century, and beyond, have never died in continental Europe: both France and Germany still dispense general amnesties, just as the royal and princely governments of the eighteenth century did. But it is not just a matter of the literal survival of ancien régime practices of mercy. It is also that a vaguer spirit of mercy pervades continental justice. Individualization of punishment, and a concern for individual deserts, run throughout both French and German law. American law, by contrast, is much more hesitant to individualize. To be sure, there is plenty of mercy in America, as we shall see. Nevertheless, the strong tendency of the last twenty-five years has been toward a formal equality of nearly Kantian severity, and there is no doubt that America differs dramatically from continental Europe by this measure. Unlike the French or the Germans, we display a powerful drive to hit every offender equally hard.

Why are the values of mercy so much stronger in continental Europe?

Part of the answer that I will give takes us back once more to the European history of status hierarchy. Mercy does indeed come de haut en bas; and a long continental tradition of condign grace can still be detected in the law of today. Moreover, traditions of status-oriented thinking have conditioned continental jurists to think in terms of distinctions between persons in a way that is relatively alien to American legal thought. Making distinctions between persons has been the stuff of continental law for centuries: French and German jurists have always resisted the idea that everybody is exactly alike. One consequence is that today both French and German justice are much readier than American justice to make individualizing distinctions among offenders. Formal equality is just not at home in continental Europe. Traditions of status are not the only source of the strength of the values of mercy in continental Europe, though. Those values have another taproot too, and one that is of fundamental importance for understanding the shape of continental criminal justice: France and Germany are countries with much stronger states than ours.

What we mean by a "strong" state is of course no simple matter; the proposition that France and Germany have stronger states calls for some real care in definition. For my purposes here, I will mean two things when I describe continental states as "strong": Germany and France have state apparatuses that are both relatively *powerful* and relatively *autonomous*. They are powerful in the sense that they are relatively free to intervene in civil society without losing political legitimacy. They are autonomous in the sense that they are steered by bureaucracies that are relatively immune to the vagaries of public opinion. The relative power and autonomy of these continental states, I am going to argue, has done a great deal to keep the values of mercy alive in continental society and to promote other forms of mildness in criminal punishment as well.

The connection between state power and mercy is clearest in the survival of amnesties, and in the various ways in which the old practice of pardoning has persisted in modern practices of "individualization." The power of the continental states has also produced another, especially important, form of mildness: both Germany and France display a notable tendency to define many acts, not as *mala in se*, but as *mala prohibita*—not as acts evil in themselves, but simply as acts the state may choose to prohibit through the exercise of its sovereign power. This capacity to define forbidden acts as merely forbidden, not evil, has been of great importance for the establishment of relatively mild orders of punishment in contemporary Europe. The contrast with the United States is stark: as I will try to show, contemporary American law has a strong tendency to define all offenses as inherently evil and consequently to punish them harshly. And as I will suggest, the capacity to define offenses merely as *mala prohibita* is a capacity that European states enjoy largely because the exercise of state power has much more untroubled legitimacy in continental Europe than it does in the United States.

State power, in short, has made for mildness, in continental punishment. This is a claim that will seem exceedingly paradoxical to Americans. We have a very long tradition of resisting state power, and many protections for offenders that involve guarantees of due process. (Indeed, in general Americans tend to have procedural protections where Europeans have substantive ones.) Moreover, it is certainly the case that state power does not always breed mildness in continental Europe. There are undeniably aspects of continental justice in which the application of state power comes down hard—most importantly in investigative custody, the preconviction form of imprisonment that is the focus of the worst problems in continental incarceration. But these differences do not alter the picture of the divergence of the last quarter century. If continental Europeans have a weaker tradition of procedural protections, it is nevertheless the case they have been working to improve their procedural protections over the last twenty-five years. In this too, the continental tale is a tale of a deep structural drive toward increased mildness. Indeed, even with the problems of investigative custody taken into account, the strength of continental states has, I am going to try to show, made the application of the power to punish far more sparing than it is here at home. State power has turned out, in northern continental Europe, to make for mild punishment.

Much mercy comes, in fact, from the *power* of continental states. Much mercy comes from their *autonomy* too. This is partly for a reason that is obvious—indeed, a reason that has captured the attention of every thoughtful commentator on the American punishment scene. American punishment practices are largely driven by a kind of mass politics that has not succeeded in capturing Western European state practices. We have, as many commentators observe, "popular justice," and indeed populist justice.[28] The harshness of American punishment is made in the volatile and often vicious currents of American democratic electioneering. Calling one's opponent "soft on crime" has become a staple of American campaigning—even in judgeship elections, whose candidates were longtime holdouts for norms of decorum; and this has had a powerful, often a spectacular, impact on the making of harsh criminal legislation in the United States. Even practices that have nothing directly to do with election campaigns are part of a momentous American pattern—a pattern in which public officials use garish punishments as a way of grabbing political publicity. Prosecutors in particular have been making political hay all over the country through actions such as leading Wall Street executives out of their offices in handcuffs or televising the names of the busted clients of prostitutes.

Politicians in continental Europe do sometimes try to play to the same public instincts that American politicians play to. For the most part, though, American-style politics has failed to exert an American-style influence on German or French criminal justice, as we shall see. Part of explaining why France and Germany are different involves explaining why this kind of politics has not made any headway in those countries; and that, in turn, involves exploring the relative autonomy of German and French state apparatuses. Manifestly, the weakness of the politics of harsh punishment in Germany and France reflects the autonomy of the state in both countries: what is at work in both countries is a basic tension identified long ago by Max Weber: the tension between democratic politics and bureaucratic control. In both Germany and France, bureaucrats have succeeded in keeping control of the punishment process, without becoming subject to decisive pressure from a stirred-up public. The success of bureaucratic control also has some other consequences for continental punishment, as we shall see: consequences such as the careful effort to define and train prison guards as civil servants.

There is, in fact, an intimate nexus between the politics of mass mobilization, unchecked by bureaucracy, and the making of harshness in criminal punishment; and that is a fact that should raise some uncomfortable questions for any of us who like to think of ourselves as committed to the values of democracy. Part of what I want to do, in this book, is to weigh those questions, and to ask how uncomfortable they should make us.

As this summary suggests, my argument will take some complex turns. Nevertheless, at the end of the day, my claim will be a simple one, and one that I think ought to have special resonance in America. Criminal punishment is milder in continental Europe today largely because Europeans have been shaped by social and political traditions that we in the United States have vigorously rejected. The continental Europe of today is recognizably descended from the continental Europe of the eighteenth, and even the seventeenth, centuries. It is a world of strong, condescending states, with a close historical connection to norms of social hierarchy.

It is, in short, the world whose values the traditions of the American

Revolution condemn. Americans already feared strong states and strong traditions of social hierarchy in the eighteenth century; and most of them undoubtedly still associate strong states and strong traditions of social hierarchy with all that is harsh and nasty in human relations. Yet in the long run, I am going to try to show, the traditions of the continent have developed into the milder traditions, at least in the law of punishment.

This is thus partly a book about the legacy of the American Revolution. I also hope it will be read as a book about the character of criminal punishment more broadly. Our parting of the ways with Europe, over the last twenty-five years, should force us to confront some fundamental, and hard, questions about the workings of criminal justice. Degradation matters, in ways that our philosophies of criminal punishment have neglected. There are unexpected facets of the exercise of state power that matter in neglected ways as well. Most of all, social and political traditions matter. Criminal punishment is not something that can be analyzed in abstract and general terms. It differs deeply from society to society, and it differs in ways that reflect fundamental divergences in social and political values.

One final preliminary word, and one methodological caveat, before I begin. The preliminary word: in making my argument, there is one seemingly obvious explanation for the differences between the United States and continental Europe that I will downplay. This is the explanation that holds that continental justice is milder today because the continental countries experienced fascism and nazism. German and French lawyers can often be heard making this claim: their countries, they say, learned the lesson of fascism in the 1930s and 1940s, and that is why they have turned to humane practices today. This claim is by no means entirely false, and I will try to do justice to it. Nevertheless, it is by no means entirely true either. The place of the fascist period in European development is much more ambiguous than this frequently repeated explanation would suggest. Moreover, the historical roots of the differences are far older than the fascist period, and indeed far older than the twentieth century.

The methodological caveat: the characterizations of both American and continental European systems that I offer in this book are not offered as true characterizations in the absolute sense. This is a study in *comparative* law, and accordingly my claims will be comparative ones, and not absolute. This is nothing to be apologetic about. It is precisely the capacity of comparative lawyers to identify relative differences that gives comparative law its special value. No absolute descriptive claim about any legal system is ever true. Human society is much too complex for that; there are always exceptions. If we make the absolute claim, for example, that American law is committed to the values of the free market, we are saying something false: there are many exceptions. On the other hand, if we claim that American law is *more* committed to the values of the free market than are most comparable legal systems, we are saying something that is both true and extremely important. As this example suggests, relative claims can be a good bit more revealing than absolute ones. Therein lies the unique strength of comparative law. It is precisely because they deal in relative claims that comparative lawyers can walk the high road to the understanding of human legal systems, as they have been trying to do since Montesquieu.

At the same time, comparative lawyers always run the risk of creating false impressions—of seeming to claim more than they should. Let me therefore emphasize that my claims in this book *are* relative ones. I do not mean to argue that American punishment is always and everywhere harsh and degrading; and I certainly do not mean to argue that German or French punishment is never degrading or never harsh. I do not mean to deny that there are regional differences in America—just as there are regional differences in Germany in France. What I mean to say is that American punishment is often more degrading and often harsher—and that where we find these relative differences, we can detect the intermittent strength of some real, if subterranean, differences in fundamental values that are widely shared in each of the three societies that I discuss.

1

Degradation, Harshness, and Mercy

American punishment is comparatively harsh, comparatively degrading, comparatively slow to show mercy. So I want to show. But what exactly do we mean by "degradation," "harshness," and "mercy"?

The Dynamic of Degradation

Degradation is at once one of the most obvious aspects of punishment, and one of the most neglected. It is clear that offenders feel punished partly because they feel degraded. It is clear that degradation has a complex interpersonal dynamic: when we punish someone in a degrading way, our relationship to that person changes. It is also clear that it has a complex social and political dynamic: the urge to degrade criminal offenders can have a powerful impact on the overall harshness of a criminal justice system, and it can play a dramatic role in the shaping of mass politics. Yet most of our philosophers of punishment, and too many of our sociologists of punishment, have little to say on the topic. Much of what I want to argue in this book is that this neglect of degradation has undermined our analysis of punishment. We miss too much of what is going on in the contemporary United States, in particular, if we do not think about what degradation is and how it works.

What, then, is "degradation"? The term is in very wide use in the law, especially in the literature of international human rights. Leading international conventions forbid "degradation," and there have been some famous decisions condemning particular acts of "degradation," notably at the European Court of Human Rights.[1] Nevertheless, it is not a term that has been carefully defined in the legal literature. Degradation is not coterminous with either violence or torture.[2] Degrading acts need hardly be violent. As for "torture," that term is best understood in its technical sense, as harsh treatment intended to coerce persons to cooperate or confess.[3] Torture, in this technical sense, can certainly be degrading. Indeed, many historical societies have restricted the use of torture to low-status persons such as slaves precisely because torture was viewed as degrading, and therefore inappropriate, for high-status persons.[4] Nevertheless, there is plenty of degrading treatment that has nothing to do with coercing cooperation or confession; torture and degradation are not same thing. But if degradation is neither violence nor torture, what is it, precisely? Courts and scholars have mostly been content to use the concept impressionistically; we do not have any secure definition.

To be sure, on one level, the definition is a simple one. As I suggested in the introduction, degradation is what its etymology says it is: it is treatment of others that make them feel *inferior, lessened, lowered.* Such treatment may include violence; but of course, it frequently does not. The notion that punishment often degrades offenders in this sense is entirely familiar. We all know that some quality of inferiority clings to punishment. As Heinrich Popitz says, "When somebody inflicts pain on us, we never experience it as 'merely physical.' . . . When you are subjected to physical punishment, you feel that you must submit to the power of your punisher. You feel that you are being subjugated in every aspect of your being."[5] And indeed, the forms of punishment often include dramatically degrading elements, such as the prone posture and bared buttocks of a person who is spanked or caned. Daily life and history are full of examples of degrading language and degrading practices in punishment. The language of criminal justice has sometimes given vent to an astonishing vocabulary of disgust when describing offenders.[6] Such institutions as Nazi concentration camps manifestly functioned partly by degrading inmates.[7] This is all the familiar stuff of everyday experience.

Nevertheless, if the fact of degradation is familiar to all of us, it is easy to miss how much it matters, and how many dangers it carries with it. Degradation is not just some incidental by-product of punishment. There are thoughtful social scientists and philosophers who have argued that it is *essential* to punishment—that punishment only works if it succeeds in making the punished person feel like an inferior. Thus the sociologist Harold Garfinkel analyzed the criminal trial as a "degradation ceremony," designed to ritually demean the offender.[8] Erving Goffman's famous *Asylums* traced the workings of the same sort of degradation in the daily life of imprisonment.[9] Both of these sociologists believe that punishment is effective partly because it ritually diminishes or demeans the offender. Kindred ideas are to be found in the anthropology of Mary Douglas. As Douglas sees it, social status is connected to pollution, in ways that are easiest to understand if we think about categories like "untouchability" in traditional Hindu society.[10] Low-status persons are polluted persons. Status and pollution in turn are connected to risk: things that we regard as "dirty" or "polluted" are, broadly, things that we regard as freighted with risk. Criminals, of course, are persons whom we regard as presenting us with risk, and it follows that we often tend to regard them as polluted. Criminals, to Douglas, are "risky," "dirty," status inferiors. Thus it is wholly unsurprising that criminal punishment should ritually degrade them. Punishment works by assigning the offender to the status of an inferior.

Social scientists are not alone in analyzing punishment this way. Many philosophers, both modern and ancient, have said the same thing—though is a striking fact that the philosophers have not always regarded treating offenders as inferiors as necessarily a *bad* thing. One of the most familiar is Nietzsche, who gave a characteristically disturbing account of the function of the horrific punishments of the Christian afterlife. What Aquinas and Tertullian promised individual Christians, according to Nietzsche, was the immense satisfaction of witnessing the torments of the damned, and being thereby confirmed in their own blessed superiority.[11] Punishment, as Nietzsche presented it, thus had to do partly with lording it over others, and indeed with the sheer pleasure of lording it over others. It is impossible to say whether Nietzsche thought this was good, bad, or simply inevitable; but other philosophers have painted a more unambiguously positive picture of the same phenomenon. Jean Hampton, for example, one of the most prominent of modern American punishment theorists, agrees with Nietzsche that punishment puts the offender down. But as she views it, this is a wholly appropriate response to the fact that the offender has improperly put himself *up*: "By victimizing me, the wrongdoer has declared himself elevated with respect to me, acting as a superior who is permitted to use me for his purposes."[12] Lording it over him, punishing him as an inferior, has the purpose of *expressing* the wrongness of this claim of superiority: "the retributive motive for inflicting suffering is to annul or counter the appearance of the wrongdoer's superiority and thus affirm the victim's real value."[13] Punishment aims at "resubjugating the subjugator."[14] There is thus, in Hampton's view, nothing inherently objectionable about treating offenders as inferiors. On the contrary, it is an indispensable practice.

This interesting notion, the notion that punishment *justifiably* slaps uppity offenders down, was widespread among ancient philosophers as well. For many ancient Greek authors, punishment was intended to penalize hubris—"the failure to behave as befits one's position in the social hierarchy."[15] Correspondingly, the Greeks often spoke of punishment as serving in part the laudable function of *kolasis*, the function of "teach[ing] people their proper place" in that hierarchy.[16] *Kolasis*, is often translated as "chastisement," and that translation nicely captures its sense. As K. J. Dover observes in an elegant essay on Greek attitudes, chastisement is the kind of corrective punishment that schoolteachers mete out to their pupils, or that masters mete out to their slaves or their dogs: it is punishment such as one inflicts on "an animal, slave, child, employee or subordinate."[17] For Aristotle and many other Greek authors, such chastisement was one of the two prime purposes of punishment, standing alongside vengeance or retribution (*timoria*). What distinguished these two faces of punishment, to Greek sensibilities, was particularly their emotional tenor. *Vengeance* or *retribution* typically involved some sense of rancor or grievance. In administering *chastisement*, by contrast, well-bred superiors remained serene, being careful not to lose their temper.

Such chastisement, calmly dealt out by superiors to inferiors, seemed to many ancient authors a very good thing indeed. Plato arguably picked up on this tradition in his account of the educative function of punishment: for Plato, too, punishment was an exercise in the serene correction of those who had erred.[18] The idea appealed to the early Christians as well. The Gospel of Matthew described God's punishment as *kolasis*, chastisement.[19] The third-century church father Clement of Alexandria embraced this concept, asserting that God was not a vengeful God, but a chastising God, a God who "put people in their place."[20] And Saint Augustine adopted the same traditional distinction in his own account of Christian justice. Christian judges, Augustine wrote, should chastise, in the unruffled way that good fathers chastised their sons; they should not seek vengeance.[21] All these writers assumed that there was a certain fine style of punishment by which superiors properly smacked their inferiors down, all the while avoiding the heat of vengeful feelings. This was an assumption that made particular sense in an ancient world of highly articulated social hierarchy, of course—a world in which moralists tried to convince masters that they should discipline their household slaves without losing their temper.[22] Nevertheless, it is an assumption that has always remained important in the Christian tradition, which has often praised the virtues of fatherly chastisement,[23] and it is an assumption continues to carry conviction even today. We are all still capable of sharing the intuition that punishment is an activity that at least partly involves firmly *putting people in their place.*

Punishment, indeed, puts people in their place. This is simply obvious. But if it is obvious that punishment partly works by putting people in their place, it is too easy to forget how badly awry such treatment can go. In particular, American policymakers and philosophers have found it too easy to close their eyes to the petty drama described by Nietzsche: the drama of the ways in which punishers can lose themselves in the intoxication of the sense of their own superiority. Putting people in their place can bring out the worst in us. Sometimes this may involve the proverbial sadism of some prison and concentration-camp guards—but only sometimes. Even with the best will in the world, we may lose control of our fellow-feeling when we deal out punishment. This loss of control may have ugly effects on the person punished; but it may go beyond that, having ugly effects on the person doing the punishing as well. This is what Thomas Jefferson meant, for example, when he observed that administering punishments to slaves inevitably depraved their master: "The man must be a prodigy who can retain his manners and morals undepraved by such circumstances";[24] and it is part of what later abolitionists meant too, when they insisted that owning slaves brutalized masters.[25] It is perhaps also part of what Shakespeare meant in the portrayal of the Angelo of his *Measure for Measure*, the "angry ape . . . dressed in a brief authority."[26] These writers all address the same more or less inevitable phenomenon: the phenomenon of the occasional intoxication that can come from lording it over those we punish. It is very hard to control ourselves when we act the part of a superior chastising an inferior, especially to the extent that we tend to think of criminals (as Douglas suggests) as somehow polluted. The serene attitude that the Greek moralists and the church fathers admired is not easy to come by. Chastisement often degenerates into *degradation*.

Here lies, I suggest, the core problem of degradation: in the intoxication that comes with treating people as inferiors. This is a phenomenon may seem to belong more to the world of literature than to the world of hardheaded criminal law philosophy, but we neglect it at great cost. The occasional intoxication of status degradation has everything to do with the way punishment functions in society. Policymakers generally permit themselves to speak of punishment simply as something that furthers the pursuit of soberly set policy goals—as serving the familiar "purposes" of deterrence, retribution, rehabilitation, incapacitation, or expressive condemnation, in ways that have nothing to do with the prospect of degradation. This is not necessarily wrong if our only goal is to acquire a narrow understanding of the policy purposes that motivate most criminal legislation. As a policy matter, penal laws may well aim principally at deterrence, incapacitation, retribution or condemnation of some tame kind; and our calculated policies may have little or nothing to do with any express or even conscious tendency to yield to our urge to degrade others. Nevertheless, whatever our sober policy goals may be, we always invite degrading behavior whenever we authorize punishment. Bentham knew this. As he put it, "Legislators and men in general are naturally inclined" to excessive harshness, since "antipathy, or a want of compassion for individuals who are represented as dangerous and vile, pushes them onward to an undue severity."[27] Bentham's American successors, though, have found this truth easy to forget. However our legislation may generally characterize the aims of punishment, we do indeed tend to regard offenders as "vile," and a certain urge to degrade may indeed take over every time an individual punisher—a prison guard or a police officer—punishes an individual offender. Nor is the issue only about the attitude of the personnel who actually inflict punishment. The general public too may treat the fact of punishment as an invitation to view criminal offenders as status-inferiors. It is an unavoidable fact that an air of *interpersonal degradation* typically clings to punishment, and this fact has important repercussions for the social dynamic of criminal legislation.

Our contemporary philosophers have, for the most part, little to say about this dynamic; and that means that they have far too little to say about the current state of affairs in the United States. This is noticeably true of the most important Anglo-American movement of the last forty years or so: the great philosophical revival of retributivism, led by figures such as Andrew von Hirsch, Jeffrie Murphy, and Hampton. The philosophers who created this movement aimed to reintroduce ideas of moral agency and moral responsibility into the criminal law, abandoning the brute therapeutic psychologism of the mid-twentieth century. [28] Punishment, they thought, should be about what offenders *deserve*. They are all humane philosophers, every one of them, and every one of them has forthrightly declared the importance of avoiding degradation in punishment.[29] Yet none of them finds much to say about *how* degradation happens, and consequently none of them can give any account of how particular societies manage to avoid degrading offenders. Certainly none of them can give an account of how contemporary America acquired its spectacularly harsh and degrading brand of retributivism—a system of sentences measured in multiple decades, served in an atmosphere of humiliation and despair. As I am going to try to show in this book, that American system escapes all philosophical accounting if we cannot grapple with the dynamic of degradation. Like the ancient Greeks, we must remember that retribution is only one face of punishment. The other face is chastisement, which often degenerates into degradation, and punishment always shows this other face as well. This means that the analysis of punishment cannot limit itself to what offenders deserve; the way we punish can have momentous social and interpersonal consequences that have nothing to do with the deserts of the person punished.[30] Most especially, it is wrong to analyze punishment solely by considering its effect on the person punished; acts of punishment can also profoundly affect the person, or the society, doing the punishing. In figuring the equations of punishment, as it were, we cannot hold the punisher constant.

The same objection can be laid at the door of the most recent leading movement in punishment philosophy—the movement in favor of shaming. The major advocates of public shaming, John Braithwaite and Dan Kahan, have different aims. For Braithwaite, shaming can work if it serves the end of reintegration of the offender: persons who have been publicly shamed are persons who, under the right circumstances, can be ceremoniously brought back into the fold of the community.[31] For Kahan, shaming is expressive: it permits the public display of our judgment that the offender has done something wrong.[32] These are again both humane authors; but they both take an overly prettified view of the dynamic of public shame sanctions. Public shaming is much more socially risky than either acknowledges. Practices like televising the names of the busted clients of prostitutes, or making drunk drivers parade around wearing placards describing their offenses, or leading Wall Street brokers out of their offices in shackles, do not just affect the offenders. They affect the public too, encouraging a kind of glee and viciousness. Most important, they lend themselves to an unsettling politicization of criminal justice, with prosecutors and even judges bidding for public support by broadcasting the names and faces of morals offenders and targets of white-collar prosecution. These are authentically troubling phenomena, and they have to do with the dynamic of degradation: shame degrades, and there is always a risk that practices of degradation will have an impact, not only on the person punished, but on the surrounding society.[33]

America is inexplicable if we forget these things, and the same is true of continental Europe. If we neglect the dynamic of degradation, we will miss all the significance of the continental commitment to respectful and dignified treatment for offenders. What, after all, is the significance of treating the offender respectfully—of addressing him as "sir"; or according him an expectation of some kind of privacy; or (to give a gruesome but important example) refraining from gibbeting his corpse? The answer is that this form of mildness involves precisely the attempt to dispel the air of interpersonal degradation—the attempt to insure that offenders are not made to feel like status inferiors. A system that emphasizes the mildness of respectful treatment is a system that aims to guarantee that the punished person will not experience a sense of inferiority. Conversely, it is a system that aims to guarantee that the person inflicting punishment will not indulge whatever urges to degrade that he may feel. European efforts to guarantee respectful treatment are thus inevitably exercises in a kind of psychological engineering, directed, in prison law for example, at both inmates and guards. In a larger sense, they are exercises in psychological engineering directed at the general public—efforts to discourage ordinary folk from treating offenders as status inferiors. These efforts are fundamental to the color and atmosphere of continental punishment, and they are efforts whose significance we will never see if we permit ourselves to ignore the dynamic of degradation in punishment.

Degradation in Sociohistorical Perspective

Part of what we need to cultivate in order understand degradation is thus a sense of the interpersonal dynamic of acts of punishment. We need more than that, though: we also need to understand some history. Degradation in punishment is a complex social act, and the history of degradation in punishment is linked to some complex patterns in human social development. If we want to grasp how particular societies have come to maintain respect for offenders, we need to understand how different social traditions of respect and disrespect have emerged.

That degradation is partly an act rooted in social traditions is obvious enough. How, after all, do we know that a particular act is a "degrading" one? We learn it from our social interactions. We spank a person, or cane a person, because we have learned that spanking or caning are ways to punish. The forms of degradation are not the inventions of any individual psychology; they are forms of social interaction, with all the complexities that implies. But how do specifically degrading acts work as forms of social interaction? The answer manifestly varies from society to society. Not all societies spank, not all cane, not all whip. So what *do* they do, and why?

Adequately answering that question turns out to require a sweeping picture of punishment in human societies—more sweeping than I will try to give here. Nevertheless, it is important to paint on as large a canvas as possible. Even relatively familiar societies like those of France, Germany, and the United States have to be seen against the background of the wide range of degrading punishments to be found in historical human societies, and the long human history of status-based punishment.

Indeed, it is the central contention of this book that degradation in punishment is, and always has been, closely related to traditions and practices of social status. Punishment does indeed involve treating people as inferiors; and the role of the "inferior" is largely defined by the structure and traditions of social status in a given society. The best way to understand this is to begin with the simplest kinds of "degrading" punishments. These are found in societies with *grades*: in hierarchically ordered societies—ones with higher and lower castes, or with higher and lower ranks, or with degrees of free and unfree status. In such societies, a "degrading" punishment is, in the simplest case, a *reduction in rank*, a punishment that reduces the offender from a higher status to a lower status. Such punishments are very common. The most familiar example, to contemporary Western readers, comes from the last well-articulated hierarchical order that still exists in our world, the military. Ranks in the military are carefully defined and signaled through badges and uniforms. They are also marked through rituals of interpersonal deference—in particular through the salute and through respectful forms of address like "sir" and its cognates. Punishment in the military historically included reduction in rank, traditionally symbolized through the ceremonious ripping off of the badge of higher rank.[34] It is important to emphasize that such reduction in rank is no small or "merely symbolic" matter. It is a punishment with real psychological bite, carrying the bitterness of having been of being treated as an inferior. Loss of rank means loss of social esteem, and loss of social esteem, in the hierarchically ordered little world of the military, inevitably means a hard loss of self-esteem for most persons.

This simplest kind of "degrading" punishment—literal reduction in rank within a rank-ordered society—has appeared in many human orders outside the contemporary military, some with literal badges, some with metaphorical ones. In both the Byzantine Empire and Qing China, for example, social rank was indicated through badges and like symbols—in Qing China through wonderful florid embroidered images of different birds and beasts, one for each rank, which are now the subject of a flourishing antiques trade.[35]Complex rituals of deference also marked both societies—again, in particular, by differential forms of address and respectful gestures. In both societies, unsurprisingly, we find degradation in rank as a punishment, symbolized through deprivation of the badge of rank; and in both, loss of rank meant loss of the right to expect rituals of deference.[36] In other societies, without literal badges, status differences have been marked through visible signs of one kind or another. Members of the higher orders, in many human societies, have been entitled to wear special dress, as an insignium of rank, or to bear arms, or to appear in public with retinues of followers—as American revolutionary James Wilson contemptuously summarized it, in 1792, to go "addressed by the proudest titles, attended by the most magnificent retinues, and decorated with the most splendid regalia."[37] "Degrading" punishments—such as what, in Europe, used to be called "degradation from nobility"—in these societies have naturally involved depriving the high-status offender of these public marks of status, and of the pleasure of the everyday receipt of ceremonies of deference.

Deprivation of the insignia of rank, whether literal or metaphorical, is an unpleasant form of punishment, but it is of course also a relatively physically painless one. Related to it, though, are other more painful punishments—punishments that involve publicly displaying the debased rank of the offender while also hurting him. Mutilation punishments are a particularly common example. Mutilation punishments were universal in human societies until the mid-nineteenth century; and they are still in use in many parts of the world. They take a wide variety of forms, from dismemberment (such as cutting off a hand, an ear or a nose; or even cutting the hair or beard); to marking (such as branding or burning the face or the hands; partially cropping the ear; slitting the nostrils; or flogging in such a way as to leave "stripes" or visible weals or scars); to mutilation of the offender's corpse.[38] Mutilation punishments obviously always have an element of public display, serving as a kind of badge of convict status. Importantly, moreover, in many societies, mutilation serves as a badge of low status more broadly. Thus in ancient Near Eastern society, for example, the partial cropping of the ear sometimes identified a person as a slave. (It is for that reason that the Covenant Code begins with ear-cropping: "If your slave says to you, 'I do not want to leave you,' because he loves you and your family and is well off with you, then take an awl and push through his ear lobe into the door, and he will become your slave for life." [Deut. 15:16–17].) Slaves were frequently branded, shaved, or otherwise mutilated in the ancient world; and a mutilated person was a person of low social status.[39] *Stripes*—flogging scars—make another fine example of how mutilation can work a depression of status. In most human societies, only persons of the very lowest social status are flogged or caned. A person carrying flogging scars is thus a person who has been marked out as a member of a low-status group, and indeed, people make great and pained efforts in many parts of the world to hide flogging scars.

Public display is thus a very common aspect of rank-oriented punishments. Nevertheless, it is important to observe that not all rank-oriented punishments involve it. Some rank-oriented punishments simply involve treating the offender in the way that low-status persons are treated, without any necessary element of public display. Thus flogging is a rank-oriented punishment regardless of whether it is done publicly, and regardless of whether it leaves scars. In almost all societies, the persons who are prototypically flogged are slaves and other very low-status workers, and by extension, a criminal offender who is flogged is an offender who has been treated as a low-status person. This can carry a very sharp psychological sting. In other ways too, punishments often operate by lumping offenders together with other low-status persons. Early-modern workhouses, for example, simply commingled criminal offenders with the destitute. In the status-mind of seventeenth- or eighteenth-century Europeans, criminals, poor people, and other members of what would later be called "the dangerous classes" belonged together and could expect the same treatment. Like the badge of mutilation, imprisonment in a workhouse was a treatment that signaled the inferiority of the offender in highly rank-conscious societies.[40]

These are familiar patterns to all historians of traditional societies. What historians do not commonly address, though, is the process of *change* that status-oriented punishment may undergo. We tend to describe traditional societies in static terms. Yet of course they are subject to change, and far-reaching change. As status-hierarchy becomes less stable, punishment practices sometimes begin to shift too, in revealing ways. In particular, such shifts may bring what I would like to call "status abuses."

When rank-conscious social orders are relatively stable, they typically distinguish carefully between the punishments appropriate for high-status persons and the punishment suitable for their inferiors. Such indeed is the nature of *kolasis*, to use once again the ancient Greek term—of punishment as chastisement, punishment that aims to punish hubris, to put people in their place. In particular, humiliating forms of public display, torture, and the infliction of pain are generally scrupulously reserved to persons who are of low status—as at Athens, where, in typical fashion, tradition restricted corporal and mutilating punishments to persons of the lowest social status.[41] Nevertheless, even in relatively stable orders, high-status persons are sometimes subjected to such punishments, such "status abuse."

Status abuses are not universal. They are not part of the usual range of military punishments, for example: we do not punish colonels by compelling them to do kitchen duty. Nevertheless, status abuses do sometimes appear. Sometimes they are inflicted in ways that leave no permanent mark. High-status persons can be flogged or caned in such a way as not to leave scars, and that therefore only temporarily mistreat them. Ordinarily, though, status abuses are inflicted in ways that do leave a mark, representing permanent, and unavoidably degrading, treatment for their high-status victims. Many examples can be offered, especially from societies in the midst of some political upheaval. To take Athens as an example once again, some of the oligarchic plotters of 411 B.C. were subjected to such deliberate humiliation as having their bones scattered after execution, while their assassins were publicly honored.[42] Such aggressive dishonoring has immense symbolic power in societies attached to norms of hierarchical honor. Indeed, precisely because its symbolic power is so great, traditional societies tend to surround status abuse with ritual solemnities. In traditional European society in particular, high-status persons were not subjected to low-status punishment unless they are first ceremoniously reduced in rank, "degraded" from noble or clerical status.[43]

In most stable hierarchically ordered societies, though, such status abuses remain rare. It is a fundamentally important fact, though, that they sometimes appear in *changing* hierarchical orders and can indeed have great symbolic significance. The depth of this symbolic significance is of course familiar to all of us, in the shape of one resonant symbol that has survived from classical antiquity: the cross. Crucifixion was the most degrading low-status punishment inflicted by the Romans, and the crucifixion of Christ, like the wearing of the cross by individual Christians, was long remembered as a fundamental symbol of a Christian uneasiness about status.[44] It drew its power precisely from the revulsion created by low-status punishment. Embracing low-status punishment was a shocking act.

Such status abuses do occur—and not only to Christ—and they occur in ways that can seem to signal momentous change in a society. There are two particularly famous examples, both of which date to antiquity; and one famous example from the early modern period. The first ancient example comes from the later centuries of the Roman Empire. Over the course of the third, fourth, and fifth centuries A.D., high-status persons in the Mediterranean world were increasingly subjected to low-status punishments: "A town councilor might be strung up for torture and only when he had been broken would he be asked the routine question, 'What is your status?'"[45] This shift took place in the midst of much broader tendency toward growing severity. It has been taken by social historians as prime evidence for a dramatic decay in traditional Mediterranean status orders.[46] Nor is the Roman Mediterranean the only world visited by this striking kind of change. Something similar happened in the so-called "legalist" programs of the Qin dynasty, the first historic dynasty to unify China. The Qin, who managed to reunify imperial China in 221 B.C., did so on the basis of a program that aimed to shake the standing of high-status persons. This so-called legalist program, like the Roman law of a couple of centuries later, proclaimed its willingness precisely to inflict low-status punishments on high-status persons: beatings, mutilations, and more.[47] The result was a watershed in Chinese legal history: Chinese law has alternatively denounced and flirted with "legalism" ever since. It was perhaps a watershed in Chinese social history too: the old Chinese aristocracy declined strikingly during the centuries leading up to the legalist onslaught, and it is natural to link legalism with the breakdown of early Chinese status hierarchy.[48]

It is not only Chinese or Roman antiquity that offers such examples of the shock of status abuse. Alongside these ancient examples, it is particularly worth mentioning one from a more recent period—one to which I will return in chapter 5. This is the case of seventeenth-century England, where the periods leading up both to the English Civil War and to the Glorious Revolution were marked by notorious cases of status abuse. The Court of Star Chamber, in the decades before the Civil War, made itself hated partly by applying low-status punishments to high-status persons—in particular, by mutilating members of the gentry. And in the last years before the Glorious Revolution of 1688, the Stuart monarchy inflicted public shame on high-status political dissenters—most notably Titus Oates, who was ordered to be displayed repeatedly in the pillory, another classically low-status punishment. The case of Titus Oates is especially well known to American scholars, since it was out of that example of status abuse that the jurisprudence of "cruel and unusual punishment" grew. The origins of our constitutional punishment jurisprudence can thus be said to lie in a seventeenth-century case of status abuse. In chapter 2, moreover, I am going to suggest that something similar is going on in the United States today. The history of these modern status abuses is significant for the same reason that our ancient Roman and Chinese examples are significant. All of these cases suggest an important generalization in the history of punishment: *status abuse is commonly a symptom of changing and troubled social orders.*

This is not a claim that should seem surprising. Sociologists have often argued that social change is associated with one or another form of harsh treatment, or perceived "inappropriate" treatment, inflicted on people of high status. For T. H. Marshall, for example, the social revolution of the postwar world expressed itself in the fact that rich as well as poor would be compelled to stand on line to register with the government: rich people could no longer send their servants to submit to the everyday humiliation of dealing with the state bureaucracy.[49] A similar thought lay behind Gerhard Lenski's well-known concept of "status crystallization." "Status crystallization," introduced into the sociological literature by Lenski in 1954, is the measure of whether persons with a disproportionate share of economic resources are also persons with a comparable share of social prestige.[50] Lenski offered this concept partly as a way of accounting for events like the French Revolution. People like the wealthy bourgeois of pre-Revolutionary France (as Lenski imagined them) were drawn to revolt precisely because their measure of prestige did not match their measure of wealth.[51] Lenski's idea depended on some outdated Marxian concepts of revolution, but it had its brilliance nevertheless: a mismatch between resources and status can indeed cause resentment, and perhaps revolutionary resentment. Mismatches between status and punishment can be, in much the same way, a sign that a society is in the grip of dramatic change: humans tend to think there ought to be a proper correspondence between status, wealth, and respectful treatment. When there is not such a proper fit, it is commonly fair to conclude that the society in question is in some way a troubled one.

The concept of "status abuse" is thus of central importance for understanding changing social orders—and in particular, as I will try to show, the current American situation. It may finally be important for another, grander, reason as well. Some scholars have gone so far as to claim that *all* punishment, seen from the historical point of view, consists of status abuse. The great philosopher of criminal law Gustav Radbruch offered the most famous version of this claim in the mid-1930s. Radbruch was an eminent liberal jurist at work in the midst of the nazification of Germany. Writing in 1935, at the height of Nazi revolutionary fervor, he took a dark view of the history of punishment.[52] All punishments in Germanic law, Radbruch held, had begun in household discipline—in the punishments masters meted out to their children, wives, and their slaves—most especially to their slaves. Punishments were indeed at their origin nothing other than marks of servitude and forms of discipline applied to slaves, which had gradually crept up the social scale. And such was the character of punishment still in the Germany around him as he wrote in 1935, with its shave-headed convicts and its harsh Nazi punishment practices. "To this day," as Radbruch summarized his views three years later, "the criminal law bears the traits of its origin in slave punishments. . . . To be punished means to be treated like a slave. That was symbolically underscored in olden times when to flogging was joined the shearing of the head, because the shorn head was the mark of the slave." Punishment in Germany, as Radbruch saw it, thus partly grew out of household labor discipline—out of the mechanisms used to keep unfree laborers degraded, and in line. But it also had a moral history, and a distinctly Nietzschean one. As Nietzsche famously claimed in his *Genealogy of Morals*, concepts of the "bad" and the "evil" were, at their origin, concepts of low social status. This too helped explain the roots of punishment: "Slavish treatment meant . . . not just a social but also a moral degradation. 'Baseness' is thus simultaneously and inseparably a social, moral and even an aesthetic judgment. The lowly born is also a 'mean fellow.' . . . In both French and English the unfree peasant the scoundrel are called villains. . . . In the illustrations in the *Sachsenspiegel* the faces of the common people are pictured as ugly and coarse. Not least, the diminution of honor, which ineradicably inheres in punishment to this day, derives from slave punishments."[53] The history of criminal "punishment" in Germany was thus a history in which the state had gradually come to treat more and more of the population on a par with household slaves. As Nietzsche had put it, "Punishment first acquired its insulting and derisive character because certain penalties were associated with the sort of people (slaves, for example) whom one treated with contempt. They were the sort of people one punished most often, and in the end being punished had something to do with being treated with derision."[54] Radbruch's important, but oddly little-discussed, argument was picked up forty years later by Thorsten Sellin, whose book *Slavery and the Penal System* tried to show that the treatment of offenders everywhere in the West, and not only in Germany, had been derived from the treatment of slaves.[55] Punishment, for these authors, thus *is* status abuse.

Now, in important respects, I am going to differ from Radbruch and Sellin in this book. It is true that criminal offenders are often treated as slaves: this is something we discover not only in Radbruch's Germany, but in the furthest-flung parts of the world, from China to ancient Greece to the Thirteenth Amendment of the American Constitution. Nevertheless, as we shall see, it is wrong to suppose that all punishments represent *low*-status treatment. On the contrary, we cannot understand the current European scene if we do not recognize that there are distinctly high-status forms of punishment. The overall pattern of the last couple of centuries in Europe has, in fact, been exactly the reverse of the pattern that Radbruch and Sellin propose: rather than being a history in which low-status treatment has been dealt out to persons of high status, it is a history in which high-status treatment has been afforded to the low. It is a history of reverse status abuse. Nevertheless, to say that recent history shows a pattern exactly the reverse of what they identify is by no means to say that they are wholly wrong. On the contrary, when Radbruch and Sellin argue that the history of punishment is a history of status treatments, and status mistreatments, they sing precisely the song that I want to sing here. But they sing it in minor only; while in fact, as I will try to show, it has been sung, over the last several continental generations, in a different mode altogether.

I beg my reader's forgiveness for the breathless rapidity of this survey. But we need to keep a great deal of history in mind if we are to appreciate the significance of degradation in punishment, even as it exists today in the United States and continental Europe.

Indeed, we need to keep this history in mind if we are to have any kind of rounded understanding of degradation. The history of punishment is, in some large measure, a history of social status; and this is a history that we must read alongside the discussions of interpersonal degradation that we find in Hampton and Nietzsche and others. Degradation is a social act, and it is a social act that can take place in the midst of shifting and unstable status relations. Conversely, social acts of degradation in all periods and places themselves are manifestly filled with the degrading individual affect that Hampton and Nietzsche describe. Individual and social experiences are unintelligible without each other; to borrow Plato's famous terminology, degradation in punishment is something that takes in both psyche and polis.

Harshness and Mercy

Let me now turn to an unexpectedly difficult problem: the problem of defining "harshness."

I began by saying that American criminal punishment is "harsher" than continental European punishment; and many others have said the same thing. Yet this is a claim that must be made with real care. It is much too easy to feel sure that we know harshness when we see it.

This is partly because the "harshness" or "mildness" of a given form of punishment can be perceived very differently from culture to culture, and from era to era. The perception of "harshness" routinely shifts and varies, in ways that complicate any effort to describe alien systems of punishment. Imprisonment, for example, which was once regarded as a mild punishment in the Western world, is now regarded as a harsh one; while public shaming, once regarded as harsh, is now regarded, at least in the United States, as mild. Even the perception of something like the death penalty can vary from culture to culture;[56] indeed, as we shall see, there are some circumstances in which even the mutilation of offenders has been regarded as a mild punishment. What counts as "harsh" depends on the sensibilities and structures of a given society. This means that there are moments when we have to suppress our reflexive horror at what we see if we want to understand the system before our eyes on its own terms.

But cultural differences in the perception of the "harshness" of particular acts of punishment are only the beginning. Deeper difficulties grow out of the fact that criminal justice systems are *systems*. Criminal justice is a complex machinery that begins with investigation and arrest; continues with trial, conviction, and sentencing; and ends only with the reintegration, or as the case may be, with the death, of the offender. Indeed, even the death of the offender may not end the punishment, if the offender's corpse is mistreated or if the offender's family continues to suffer a taint. This machinery can operate in ways that are quite harsh in one respect, but quite mild in another. Unless we bear that fact in mind, we will not have a secure sense of the ways in which American punishment is (as it indeed is) significantly more harsh that continental European punishment.

Nor will we have a secure sense of the ways in which the values of mercy can make themselves felt. Philosophers tend to speak of "mercy" in very general terms, without asking how it is afforded in concrete legal practices. Yet the concrete legal practices matter immensely—perhaps especially for the study of comparative law. Different forms of mercy speak to different forms of harshness; and we must take real care in distinguishing among those forms.

In particular, this book will maintain a careful distinction between no fewer than ten different senses in which we can describe the workings of a given criminal justice system as relatively "mild" or "harsh": five forms of harshness in *criminalization*, three forms of harshness in *punishment*, and finally two important forms of mildness. These various forms of harshness correlate with some distinct and peculiar forms of mercy.

I begin with five different forms of criminalization, of which the last three correlate with peculiar forms of mercy. The term *criminalization* is typically used to describe just one possible measure of harshness: It is used to describe the *range and types of conduct* that are treated as criminal offenses. This is the way that Durkheim used the concept in his pioneering discussion of the turn of the last century.[57] This measure of harshness is undeniably important, and I list it as the first of the forms of "criminalization" that I will discuss in this book:

1. Harshness in *criminalizing conduct*. Many examples can be offered. For example, a system that criminalizes relatively many "morals" offenses can reasonably be called "harsher" than one that criminalizes relatively few "morals" offenses.

If American punishment were harsher than continental punishment by this measure, it would be because American law forbade a wider variety of conduct than continental law. As we shall see, though, this is only true to a very limited extent.

In fact, if we want to describe American harshness correctly, we must look to other forms of harshness in criminalization. First and foremost, we must think not only about *classes of conduct*, but also about *classes of persons*. Criminalization is not just about the number of the penal laws or even the range of conduct forbidden.[58] Systems may also differ in the range and variety of *persons* they treat as potentially subject to criminal liability. To put it in the ordinary terms of criminal law scholarship, systems may criminalize not only different ranges of *offenses*, but also different ranges of *offenders*. Some systems, for example, regard minors as essentially immune from criminal liability, while others do not. Similarly, some systems regard political officeholders as immune from criminal liability, while others do not; and some regard clerics as immune from criminal punishment, while others do not. This is the second type of harshness in criminalization that I will discuss:

2. Harshness in *subjecting numerous classes of persons to potential criminal liability*. For example, a system that prosecutes minors "as adults" can be called "harsher" than a system that treats them "as juveniles." Similarly, a system that prosecutes clerics is, ceteris paribus, harsher than a system that does not.

For some purposes, this measure of criminalization overlaps with the first measure: for example, the prosecution of white-collar crime can be viewed either as criminalization of white-collar *offenses* or as criminalization of white-collar *offenders*.[59] Nevertheless, there are deep and important differences between these two measures; and they are differences that matter. As we shall see, American harshness is much better measured by this standard of criminalization than by the standard of criminalization of conduct. We have been criminalizing a wider range of persons over the last twenty-five years, in ways that are not unconnected to the prevalence of degradation in our system. Status abuse is rife in the current American system.

Other standards are also of great importance for capturing the American state of affairs. A third sense in which we can speak of harshness in criminalization involves the *classification* or *grading* of offenses. Criminal systems not only *forbid* acts; they also *grade* them, typically according to degrees of severity and stigmatization—making distinctions such as those between felonies, misdemeanors, and violations. The choice to grade an offense high typically reflects the conviction that that offense is *malum in se*, intrinsically evil; conversely, the choice to grade an offense low typically reflects the conviction that it is *malum prohibitum*, merely forbidden by the exercise of state power. Systems that display relative harshness in classification are ones that tend to grade offenses high—to classify them as relatively more severe or stigmatizing, and by implication as more evil. This represents yet another measure of harshness in criminalization:

3. Harshness in *grading*. For example, if two systems both treat possession of narcotics as an offense, but one system grades that offense as a felony while the other grades the same offense as disorderly conduct, the first system can be called "harsher" than the second.

This measure is once again quite important for the contrast between America and continental Europe: America shows a comparatively strong tendency to grade offenses high. We should note something else about this measure of harshness too. This is the first of our measures of harshness that correlates with a peculiar form of mercy: A decisionmaker may have the authority to *downgrade* the offense he is punishing, treating it, mercifully, as less serious.

The fourth measure of harshness in criminalization is also one that permits its own peculiar form of mercy. This fourth measure has to do with the rigidity of the doctrines of the law. Some systems have relatively flexible doctrines of liability, permitting defendants to plead excuse or justification—extenuating circumstances, broadly, however defined. A system that recognizes relatively few of such defenses can be called relatively harsh:

4. Harshess in *inflexible doctrines of criminal liability*. For example, a system that does not treat ignorance of the law as an excuse can be called harsher than a system that does.

If a decisionmaker has discretion in the application of flexible doctrines of liability, he has, once again, a form of authority to exercise mercy.

Finally, the degree of effective criminalization in a system depends on the degree to which its criminal law is actually enforced on the ground. This represents a fifth measure of harshness in criminalization, and one that provides its own obvious opportunities for the exercise of mercy:

5. Harshness in *enforcement*. Systems that display harshness in enforcement are systems that let few offenses go unpunished. Thus a society in which the police, or the fisc, routinely ignore violations of the law shows mildness in enforcement.

As for mercy, a society in which the police, or the fisc, sporadically ignore individual offenses is a society that shows sporadic mercy.

Alongside these five measures of harshness in *criminalization*, we should recognize three different measures of harshness in *punishment*. Here I would like to distinguish between three measures in particular:

6. Harshness in *the law of punishment*. This is the harshness of systems that, in their statutes or customs, provide for relatively severe punishments, such as long sentences of imprisonment; or beatings with a heavy club rather than a light stick; or egregious forms of mutilation.
7. Harshness in *the application of punishment*. This is harshness in the way officials actually administer punishment—for example, in maintaining tough prison conditions, or in administering rough beatings.[60]
8. Harshness in *the inflexibility of punishment*. This is the harshness of applying unvarying punishments regardless of any sense of the individual deserts of offenders. Thus a system that forswears measures of "individualization" such as parole or probation can be called relatively harsh. So can a system that beats all offenders equally severely.

The latter two of these, (7) and (8), are forms of harshness that correlate, once again, with peculiar forms of mercy. An official who has the discretion to apply punishments lightly has the discretion to show a species of mercy. Similarly, officials who have the discretion to grant parole or probation have a discretion to show a different species of mercy. We do not ordinarily speak of parole or pardon as "merciful" measures, of course. Modern penological theories treat these measures as devices of rehabilitation, to be used by professionals trained in the techniques of social work and psychology. Yet they are measures that grow historically out of the pardoning power; their use remains deeply colored by the psychology of mercy; and, as I am going to argue in this book, they must be viewed, in sociohistorical perspective, as measures of mercy.

Finally, there are two forms of mildness that are especially important for my purposes in this book:

9. The mildness of *respectful treatment*. This is the mildness involved in treating offenders as persons entitled to dignified treatment—for example, by addressing them respectfully (as "sir" or "madam"), avoiding such measures as compelling them to use toilets exposed to the view of all, permitting them their own choice of clothing; giving their corpses a decent burial; and the like. If two offenders are sentenced to prison terms of the same length, but only the first is addressed and clothed respectfully, the first is enjoying the benefit of a very important kind of mildness; and the same is true of two executed offenders, the first of whom is quietly and ceremoniously interred while the second is gibbeted. Indeed, this mildness of *respectful treatment* is, I am going to argue, of great significance, and I will discuss it in more detail in the following chapter, and throughout the subsequent chapters of this book.

Discretion to treat offenders respectfully is, once again, discretion to treat them mercifully. Finally, the second form of mildness:

10. The mildness of *pardons*. This is mildness by act of sovereign grace, notably through the issuance of pardons, amnesties, and commutations. Thus, to take a famous example, the facial harshness of the eighteenth-century English Bloody Code, which prescribed death for hundreds of offenses, was mitigated by an extensive pardoning practice. While many were condemned to death, many of those were pardoned and transported.

The issuance of pardons is usually regarded as the definitional exercise of mercy. Nevertheless, even with regard to this form of mildness, it is worth distinguishing between more and less merciful forms. A system that issues pardons automatically, without regard to individual deserts, is not best described as a system that is exercising mercy. Pardons are merciful, in the narrow sense, only if they are granted through the exercise of discretion.

These forms of harshness and mildness are not all equally present in all criminal justice systems; and it is wrong to judge the harshness of a given criminal justice system by only one of these measures. We must consider all of them.

This is especially true because these various forms of harshness and mildness often stand in a systematic interrelationship. Systems that are harsh in one way will often *systematically mitigate* by showing mildness in another. For example, a criminal justice system may have no flexibility in its doctrines of liability, opting instead to convict every offender who commits a given act. But that same system may mitigate the inflexibility of its doctrines of liability by providing flexibility in punishment instead, sentencing deserving offenders to probation or eventual parole. (Such, as we shall see, is the broad thrust of the reforms of the French Criminal Code of 1994, for example.) Similarly, systems that impose the same sentence of incarceration on all offenders may nevertheless treat some offenders more mildly by placing them in relatively comfortable prisons. In fact, it is very commonly the case that criminal justice systems threaten much fiercer punishment than they actually mete out. Any description of the "harshness" of a given criminal justice system must take this fact into account. We must always ask whether the system before us engages in *systematic mitigation*.

These complexities in the forms of harshness and mildness, and their systemic interrelationships, are of fundamental importance for any comparison of the United States with continental Europe. To say without further ado that punishment in the United States has grown harsher, while punishment in France and Germany has not, would be false. In some ways, France and Germany (like most countries of the world) have also moved toward harsher punishment in the last twenty-five years. What sets France and Germany apart from the United States is not that those countries show no harshness, but rather that they simultaneously indulge in manifold forms of mildness. Unlike our move toward harshness, which has been a move toward harshness in almost every respect, their move toward harsher punishment has been a move toward harshness in a few respects, mitigated by dramatic moves toward milder punishment in others.

Thus in the United States, criminalization has intensified by at least four of the five measures I have listed. There has been some increased criminalization of conduct; there has been a marked intensification of criminalization of persons; some offenses have been regraded upward; and there have been some striking examples of intensified enforcement. In punishment, sentences have gotten longer; humane programs of rehabilitation and parole have been under severe assault; the movement for prison reform has largely collapsed; the death penalty has been reinstated; and public shame sanctions have been introduced. Respectful treatment has been refused to offenders, in ways that I will describe; and exercises of the pardoning power have been relatively few. Finally, there has been a dramatic campaign against any kind of systematic mitigation. Against all of these movements toward harshness, it is very difficult to point to any mitigating move toward mildness. In Europe, too, criminalization of conduct has been intensified in some ways. But weighed against that intensified criminalization of conduct are a variety of growing tendencies toward mildness in European punishment practice. Thus many offenses have been regraded downward; imprisonment has become a less and less frequent sanction in Europe; the movement for prison reform has constantly gathered momentum; the death penalty has been abolished; ancien régime traditions of pardoning have continued strong in the form of regular amnesties; and humane programs of rehabilitation and parole have continued as well. Indeed, as we shall see, in practice the new harshness of European punishment practice has been limited to longer sentences for a small, and shrinking, class of offenders. For most French and German offenders, and for all prison inmates, the drive has been toward growing mildness.

The right way to describe the contrast between the United States, on the one hand, and France and Germany on the other, is thus to not to say that American punishment is "harsh" whereas European punishment is "mild." That understates the complexity of the problem. The right way to describe the contrast is to say that, over the last quarter century, America has shown a systemic drive toward increased harshness by most measures, while continental Europe has not. And the right way to frame the mystery that is the topic of this book is to ask why some systems choose some forms of harshness, and others do not.

It deserves emphasis that this is a mystery that our standard repertoire of philosophical approaches is not well equipped to resolve. All law students are trained to think of punishment as aiming at one of five goals: deterrence, retribution, rehabilitation, incapacitation, or the expression of society's condemnation. Yet the theories that philosophers offer to justify the pursuit of these various goals generally tell us little about how and why forms of harshness and mildness can vary. To be sure, any policymaker pursuing any one of these standard goals might conclude that it was important to indulge in *some* form of mildness or to inflict *some* form of harshness. Thus a believer in deterrence might suppose that a punishment system ought to be harsh. But his theory would tell him nothing about *how* to be harsh—about what form of harshness to choose. For example, many eighteenth-century deterrence theorists favored forced public labor as the ideal form of harsh punishment; few of their late twentieth-century successors agreed. Yet both eighteenth- and twentieth-century theorists were firmly committed to the theory of deterrence; they simply operated with different, socially conditioned assumptions about the how one person goes about treating another harshly. In much the same way, retributivism is a theory that has proven to be consistent with many possible forms of harshness. There have been retributivists who believed in talionic, eye-for-an-eye punishment, as well as retributivists who believed in prison sentences of differently calibrated lengths, as well as retributivists who believed in public humiliation. All of these beliefs make some kind of sense within a retributivist framework. Nor does the theory of retributivism lend itself to any systematic account of forms of mildness. Similarly, a theorist of rehabilitation might subscribe to *some* practice of mildness. But then again he might not: both European believers in probation and American believers in boot camps are theorists of rehabilitation. Moreover, even if a theorist of rehabilitation believed in mild treatment, it is not clear what form of mildness he would favor. As for the theory of incapacitation, it implies nothing whatsoever about the mildness or harshness of incapacitating punishment. The expressive theory of punishment, too, tells us little about how one form of harshness might express condemnation better than another, and less about the degree to which systematic mitigation is acceptable. The question of how forms of harshness and mildness arise and interact is simply not directly addressed by any of our familiar theories of punishment, and it is inevitable that they give no direct answer.

Let us then leave our most familiar theories of punishment behind and turn to the current state of affairs in America.

2

Contemporary American Harshness

Rejecting Respect for Persons

What is going in contemporary American punishment? Odd though it may seem, I would like to begin approaching this question in this chapter by turning back to the eighteenth century, and to the first classic of modern common law, the *Commentaries* of Blackstone. In particular, I would like to focus on Blackstone's account of the place, in the law, of the value of *respect for persons*.

In 1769, when Blackstone set out to catalogue the punishments inflicted by the common law in his *Commentaries*, he listed some chilling practices. The punishments in use at that date still included some classic forms of low-status mutilation: disemboweling and quartering in some cases, public dissection of the offender's corpse, and various other practices. Blackstone described all of these; but he insisted that they had become rare in his time. Indeed, he felt that the common law of his time was in general much to be praised—especially by contrast with the criminal law of continental Europe. This was not only because the common law was less bloody. It was also because the common law, unlike continental systems, rejected "respect of persons":

> Disgusting as this catalogue [of punishments] may seem, it will afford pleasure to an English reader, and do honour to the English law, to compare it with the shocking apparatus of death and torment, to be met with in the criminal codes of almost every other nation in Europe. And it is moreover one of the glories of

> our English law, that the nature, though not always the quantity or degree, of punishment is *ascertained* for every offence; and that it is not left in the breast of any judge, nor even of a jury, to alter that judgment, which the law has beforehand ordained, for every subject alike, without respect of persons.[1]

This was a high form of praise in the Christian Europe of the Enlightenment. In the first place, to say that the common law rejected "respect of persons" was to call it nothing less than more truly Christian than the law of the continent. "Respect of persons"—or, as we would put it today, respect *for* persons—is a concept used in the New Testament to describe Christ's refusal to respect differences of social station.[2] Christ showed no *respect for persons*, no concern for their rank in this world; and in its unique majesty, Blackstone implied, the common law did the same. To say that the common law showed no "respect of persons" was not only to call it more Christian; it was also to call it more enlightened. Applying the law to all equally, without regard to social station, was dear to the program of every leading Enlightenment philosopher from Cesare Beccaria to Immanuel Kant.

As we shall see in chapter 5, Blackstone, the enlightened Christian Englishman, was exaggerating. "Respect of persons" had by no means entirely vanished in England in the mid-eighteenth century. Nevertheless the contrast he drew between common law and continental law was perfectly justified. In Blackstone's time there was indeed, not only less mutilation, but also far less "respect of persons" in the criminal law of England than there was in France or Germany. And in this chapter, which is devoted to contemporary American harshness, I will argue that the same contrast still holds true in our own time. We still show less *respect for persons* than the continental systems do; and, while there are many currents in American harshness, in hunting for ways to capture the spirit of current American harshness, we could do worse than to return to this claim of Blackstone's.

All Western systems have rejected respect for persons in one way or another. As we have emerged from the old world of low-status mutilation and high-status respectability, we have all moved in the direction of treating all persons alike. But American law has rejected respect for persons in a peculiar way. Indeed, the most evocative way to describe the harshness of the last twenty-five years is to say that we have embarked on a rejection of the value of respect for persons in two quite different senses.

On the one hand, our criminal law consistently aims to treat all persons precisely alike, regardless of personal characteristics—more so than the continental systems. This is something that shows up both in our doctrines of liability and in our sentencing practices. To put it in the technical terms of legal philosophy, we have a comparatively strong commitment to formal equality in the law. We show a real dedication to the kind of ideal preached by Beccaria, Kant, and Blackstone in their Enlightenment day. This amounts to a sort of heroic egalitarianism in American law, which also shows up in American popular culture—for example, in a television series like Colombo, in which, every week, a high-status person was taken down a peg.

At the same time, though, American law shows a lack of respect for persons in a second, and quite different sense. It tends not to treat offenders with respect. On the contrary, American law shows a much stronger tendency than continental law to surrender to the degrading aspects of punishment. We tend to take *all* offenders down a peg, not just high-status ones. We do not mutilate anybody any longer; but we do tend to treat all offenders as relatively low-status persons—something, as we shall see, that was already beginning to be true in Blackstone's time. This second kind of refusal to show respect for persons is, of course, analytically distinct from the first. A thoughtful and humane lawyer—or indeed an enlightened and Christian lawyer—could easily embrace the one form of respect for persons without embracing the other. We could decide to promote formal equality without committing ourselves to treating offenders in a degrading way.

Nevertheless, American punishment culture has generally rejected respect for persons in both of these senses. While the commitment to formal equality is indeed analytically distinct from the refusal to accord respectful treatment, both forms of the rejection of respect for persons belong to a single cultural constellation in America. In American criminal law, *persons* just do not matter as much as *persons* do in Germany and France: all persons receive equal punishment, and all persons receive little respect.

While there are many forces at work in American harshness, it is this more than anything else that distinguishes us from continental Europe. The "shocking apparatus of death and torment" is no more in continental Europe; indeed, today it is mostly Europeans who express shock at what *we* do. But it remains the case that we show far less respect for persons than do our French or German peers; and from that fact follows much—though certainly not all—of what sets our attitude toward criminal punishment apart from theirs.

The Triumph of Formal Equality

Let me begin by contrasting the first of my two measures of harshness—harshness in the criminalization of conduct, and harshness in the criminalization of classes of persons.

Harshness in Criminalizing Conduct

Has there been an intensified criminalization of conduct over the last twenty-five years? Europeans often speak of American "puritanism" in a way that would suggest as much—that we have launched a crackdown on underage drinking, on smoking, on relations between the sexes, and so on. And it is certainly the case that the United States has seen the criminalization of some new kinds of conduct over the last quarter century. The trend, though, is by no means clear.

Some intensified criminalization of conduct is certainly noticeable in two realms of life: commerce and sex. Thus new economic offenses have swollen the roster of acts penalized as "criminal" in the United States. These include the effectively new crime of insider trading, which has been progressively criminalized since the early 1960s, and which has been the basis of some spectacular prosecutions since the early 1970s—most memorably of Ivan Boesky and Michael Milken.[3] They also include some newly criminalized banking practices, and a variety of other forms of white-collar crime. Especially with the Comprehensive Crime Control Act of 1984, a new range of white-collar offenses was brought within the purview of federal prosecutors.[4] Any handbook of white-collar crime can attest to the change in the climate of the last two decades: "The consistent trend in the federal law of bribery and extortion has been to greatly expand liability"; "prosecutors' use of RICO . . . [in] white-collar cases has increased dramatically in the last decade"; "over the past two decades, as corporate exposure to . . . criminal claims has increased, corporate counsel have frequently responded by instituting educational and compliance programs for corporate employees. These programs have been particularly popular in the antitrust area."[5] Corporate counsel now must learn to warn high-level personnel of corporations that they may be indicted—a telling change in American legal culture since the 1960s. (This is true not only on the federal level, but in the states too, where securities fraud enforcement has begun to bring what was once an unheard-of severity in punishment.)[6] Corporate criminal liability has also grown dramatically over the last twenty years or so.[7]

During roughly the same period, some morals offenses have also been effectively newly criminalized in the United States. It is here that we see some of the "puritanism" of which Europeans speak at work. Thus the law, both criminal and civil, has increasingly started to penetrate in new ways into relations between the sexes. In the rise of the criminalization of stalking, for example, we see symptoms of a broader tendency to expand the reach of the criminal justice system in America.[8] The same is true of prosecutions for marital rape—an offense progressively, if only partially, criminalized throughout the United States over the last twenty-five years[9]—and the crackdown on domestic violence, which dates to the same period.[10] Criminalization of the use of drugs is also very noticeable.[11] These are not developments that we always list alongside the criminalization of activities like insider trading, but they are not unrelated. In both commerce and morals, we see American legislatures that have become more willing to see "crime" in new corners of society. It has been a quarter-century of the discovery of new criminal evils.

This intensified criminalization of commercial conduct and of morals offenses is certainly noteworthy. It has something of the look of criminalization in the classic Durkheimian sense. To Durkheim, the most important form of criminalization was the criminalization of conduct, and especially of morals offenses. As he saw it, the function of criminalization was partly to create social solidarity, by rallying the public around the punishment of offenders. Punishing morals offenses had, in his view, a peculiar capacity to mobilize popular solidarity: such practices as the charivari or the stoning of adulteresses tended to cement communal ties, as people joined in the collective merriment and savagery.[12] Durkheim did not have much to say about commerce as such, but his argument might well apply to commerce as much as it does to sex. If punishing adulteresses excites public solidarity, so does punishing Wall Street brokers. All of this makes it tempting to describe the United States as being in the grip of some kind of Durkheimian moment in the criminalization of conduct.

Any such description would be dubious, though. It is patently wrong to claim that the United States has seen some unambiguous move toward the intensified criminalization of either commerce or morality. On the contrary, the story is exceedingly complex. Some sexual activities, such as homosexuality and adultery, have seen a distinct decriminalization in the United States over the same period; it is hardly the case that the last twenty-five years have been a period of unambiguous crackdown on sex.[13] The same is true of commerce. The last twenty-five years have been extraordinarily fertile in the invention of new commercial techniques, and especially of new forms of financing. In other times and other societies, such commercial innovations have always run a real risk of being criminalized. It is remarkable testimony to the liberal spirit of American law that nothing of the kind has happened.

Harshness in Subjecting Classes of Persons to Potential Criminal Liability

The more revealing measure of growing relative harshness in America is the criminalization of new classes of persons; and it is by this measure that we can begin see, in the America of the last quarter century, a deepening refusal to show respect for persons—and indeed a drive toward status abuse of the kind I described in chapter 1.

The category of persons who have reason to fear criminal punishment in America has been growing noticeably. Statuses that once conferred immunity do so no longer. Most notoriously, this is the case with minors. After many decades during which minors were regarded as ordinarily immune from normal criminal prosecution, the powerful movement in American criminal law of late has been to try them "as adults."[14] This American willingness to try minors as adults contrasts strongly with both German[15] and French[16] practice, and the European press has seized on the shift in American criminal justice with a mix of horror and journalistic fascination. The new climate in American justice was exemplified, for European observers, by the arrest of the eleven-year-old Swiss-American boy Raoul Wuthrich, reported to the police by a neighbor for touching the genitals of his younger sister. To the evident astonishment of Europeans, Raoul was not only arrested, but brought into court in shackles and a prison uniform.[17] Other examples, too, have populated the European press for the last several years.[18] And in fact you do not have to be European to feel a little queasy over recent developments. One senses that American justice inched back from an abyss when a Michigan prosecutor decided, in March 2000, not to try a six-year-old as an adult, despite the "public clamor" that he do so.[19]

Perhaps the most striking measure of the shift in American attitudes is the imposition of the death penalty on minors. The United States is one of only six polities worldwide that acknowledge executing persons for acts committed when they were juveniles. (The others almost all belong to the world of the Islamic revival: Congo, Iran, Nigeria, Saudi Arabia, and [until recently] Pakistan and Yemen.)[20] To be sure, American authorities do not have unbounded authority to execute minors. The Supreme Court, in what was perhaps a bygone era of reformism, effectively limited executions to offenders over the age of sixteen.[21] This has not prevented legislators from proposing the death penalty for offenders as young as eleven, though;[22] and there is certainly no doubt that something dramatic is happening.

But why is it happening? There are many commentators who blame racism. African-American minors have been especially hard hit;[23] and one certainly does sense that the image of a dangerous youth in the minds of many Americans is the image of a black youth. Nevertheless, racism cannot be the sole cause of our new turn in juvenile justice. This is not just because some notorious cases, like that of Raoul Wuthrich, do not involve African-Americans. It is also because American racism long predates the shifts of the last twenty-five years. Most important, for my purposes here, it is because racism is not something peculiar to Americans. Continental Europeans are surely quite racist too.[24] Yet continental justice has not abandoned special status for juveniles, despite some American-style agitation demanding that they do so. Something else is going on—some peculiarly American drive toward a peculiarly American way of pursuing crime.

To understand what that drive is, we must lift our eyes beyond the issue of racism in juvenile justice, and acknowledge that American law of the last quarter-century has been dropping *many* sorts of status-immunities to prosecution. In fact, painful though it is, we must acknowledge that the extension of criminal liability to minors is, in its way, an expression of an authentic American ideal. Minors are not the only persons who have become newly liable to prosecution over the last twenty-five years—just as they are not the only ones to have become liable to the death penalty. The universe of criminal responsibility has also spread to cover other persons as well: in particular, increasing numbers of white-collar criminals and political leaders, persons whose high social status would once have largely immunized them, too, from the threat of prosecution. The much-reported case of the Texas soccer mom, jailed for driving without a seatbelt, is one example;[25] so, for that matter, are fathers who now face jail for delinquency on child-support payments.[26] All sorts of persons have come to have reason to fear the machinery of criminal justice over the last couple of decades. And in the rise of this wide-ranging hostility to status-immunity we can catch a glimpse of something different from racism—something that does indeed qualify as an *ideal*, and an Enlightenment ideal, paradoxical though that may sound. Indeed, it is an ideal reminiscent of the attitude of Kant, whose passage I quote once more: "The law of punishment is a categorical imperative, and woe to him who creeps along the serpent paths of the theory of social welfare hoping to turn up some argument that makes it seem like good policy to release him from his punishment, or diminish it." While racism is certainly part of what is going on, it is also the case that we are pursuing evil wherever it may be found; and that, like Kant, we are not allowing considerations of the personal characteristics of "the criminal" to stop us. Thus even the family of a fourteen-year-old sentenced to twenty-eight years without possibility of parole can be heard describing his punishment as "just."[27] Thus even the liberal literature speaks the American language of abstract egalitarianism, treating minors as formal equals, not as children. Minors, it is said, even by deeply humane authors like Martha Minow, must be specially protected *because they cannot vote*.[28] In short, we are not to have regard for their particular characteristics; rather, using the complex techniques of American abstract egalitarian legal reasoning, we are to identify the obstacles to their ability to protect themselves through political participation.[29]

It is through this same lens that the revolution in white-collar crime takes its most striking shape. Suspicion of businesspeople has a long history in America, of course.[30] Nevertheless, the last couple of decades have seen a major shift. It is hardly the case that all commercial conduct has been criminalized, but it *is* the case that prosecution has begun to reach new classes of persons. To quote the classic definition of white-collar criminality by Edwin Sutherland, criminal law has begun to attack an enlarged class of "respectable or at least respected business and professional men."[31] Indeed, it has reached further than Sutherland himself envisaged. When Sutherland first conceived of "white-collar crime" in 1939, he used the term to capture a fairly gross distinction between high- and low-status persons. To him, any crime committed by anyone of high-status qualified as "white-collar." He was quite vague about just *how* high the status was that he was talking about, and early scholars pursuing his ideas tended to focus on such relatively low-status persons as retail pharmacists and meat inspectors.[32] With the shifts of the 1970s, though, attention began to turn to more high-level offenders: insider trading, complex bank frauds, and the like became the preoccupation.[33] This was accompanied by a parallel shift in enforcement: "In recent years," as a 1991 banking text crisply puts it, "the United States Department of Justice has shifted the focus of its bank criminal prosecutions to the bank's own directors, officers, employees and customers."[34] This does not mean that only high-status persons have been prosecuted. Really elite offenders are few and far between, and most of the offenders caught in the widening net remain far from the highest strata of the elite.[35] Nor does it mean that white-collar offenders receive sentences that are in any straightforward way "equal" to the sentences received by others.[36] What it means is something about American cultural perceptions: Americans began to *see* unequal punishment for high-status offenders as a problem.[37]

Nor has this shift in perceptions involved only minors and businesspeople. It has also touched politicians, in a development reaching back to the Watergate era. Political scandals have been around in America for a very long time, of course. Nevertheless, there is surely something to the widespread perception that politicians are more vulnerable to prosecution since Watergate—or perhaps since the Abscam scandals of the late 1970s. The change in atmosphere is one that every American can sense, and that has a kinship that we can all perceive with the prosecution of high-level businesspeople. The impeachment and other travails of President Clinton—something that, once again, astounded Europeans—offers a telling comparative example, since Clinton was pursued for something that did not clearly involve anything like the classic forms of abuse of power. We track evil even into the boudoir of the President.

Of course, to say it again, distrust of highly placed persons has a long history in the United States. Nevertheless, these are palpable changes in sensibility, measurable in real changes in American law. The rise of these forms of high-status criminal liability, like the rise of criminal liability for minors, is evidence of a shift in the currents of American punishment, and one that deserves to be seen in the largest historical and comparative perspective. We do not commonly imagine our society against the background of the "premodern" world—of ancient Rome or ancient China or seventeenth-century Europe—but we should. Something is happening in the United States that does not happen often in human society. It is a commonplace that the category of the "criminal" in most societies more or less coincides with the category of the "marginal"—the category of those who stand farthest away from the ranks of the socially respectable. Thus persons who belong to the unprivileged, "dangerous" classes—persons such as beggars, gypsies, often Jews—are frequently regarded as being potentially and even presumptively criminal.[38] Conversely, persons who stand near the centers of social prestige are typically regarded as more or less immune from prosecution. In most historical societies, correspondingly, the persons perceived as members of the "criminal" class have belonged to the low-status orders of society. It is thus no surprise if, as we saw in the last chapter, criminal punishment and low-status treatment have generally coincided. Nor is it any surprise if societies in which high-status persons are subject to criminal prosecution, and especially to severe criminal punishment, have been relative rarities.

The United States is coming to look more like one of those rare societies. If you will, our recent developments resemble, at a distant remove, the legalism of the Qin in the third century B.C., or the severity of the Romans of later antiquity. Our drive has been to declare that *any* person who commits a criminal act is a criminal, in the fullest sense of the term. Where a criminal *act* has been committed, we see crime; and we are increasingly disinclined to ask whether the *persons* involved are "really" criminals. We wish to pursue all offenses, without any regard for differentiation among offenders. This is true of juvenile justice[39] just as it is true of white-collar sentencing.[40] It will be obvious that this refusal to take account of personal characteristics represents the first of the forms of the rejection of *respect for persons* that I described at the beginning of the chapter: it represents a move toward formal equality.

Now, the United States is not wholly alone in this. Politicians and, to a certain extent, businesspeople have been targets in Europe too, and indeed almost everywhere in the world.[41] Nevertheless, in the next chapter we will see that the fire to prosecute persons of high status is burning far more fiercely in the United States; and this reflects the fact that it falls on drier cultural tinder here. Ours, to put it in the language of Chinese legal philosophy, is revealing itself as the most "legalist" of Western countries.

Harshness in the Inflexibility of Punishment

The same issues present themselves in much the same way when we measure American harshness by another standard: the measure of inflexibility in punishment. Here the United States has seen a dramatic change, with the large-scale turn to *determinate sentencing*.

Over the last twenty-five years, Americans have progressively abandoned the mild philosophy of punishment that reigned everywhere in the Western world as of the mid-1970s and that still reigns in Europe, the philosophy of *individualization*. In its stead, they have tended to turn back to a philosophy of punishment associated with another Enlightenment ideal. This is the ideal of *formal equality in punishment*—of dealing out exactly the same punishment to every person who has committed the same offense. Just as we have been drawn to the proposition that all persons, even minors and businesspeople, should be equally subject to exactly the same criminal liability, so we have been drawn to the proposition that all persons, once convicted, should be subjected to exactly the same penalty. Here again, our current law has the look of a revival of the values of the age of Blackstone and Kant, and there is no better way to understand our contemporary attitude toward sentencing than to turn back once again to the eighteenth century.

Let us then begin by trying to understand Enlightenment ideals in punishment. When Blackstone praised the common law punishment as "ascertained," when he declared that it was "not left in the breast of any judge, nor even of a jury, to alter that judgment, which the law has beforehand ordained, for every subject alike, without respect of persons," he was speaking as a wholly typical Enlightenment reformer. Inflexible, ascertained punishment was the watchword of the reformers of the later eighteenth century.

This Enlightenment punishment theory developed in reaction to the world of criminal law that dominated on the continent up until the French Revolution. In the continental law of the eighteenth century, there was indeed relatively little "certainty." Criminal law was drawn from immensely heterogeneous sources and was applied by judges who enjoyed a large measure of what the eighteenth-century called "arbitrary" power. Crimes and punishments were defined in part by learned legal traditions of baroque complexity, based on Roman and canon law, and in part by criminal statutes that often took confusing and contradictory forms. Penalties were sometimes specified in advance. But frequently judges had the "arbitrary" power to vary the penalty attached to any particular offense. This was a power that judges used in particular to guarantee differing treatment for persons of different social standing. As we shall see in chapter 4, low-status persons could expect spectacularly harsher punishment than high-status ones, and for a much wider range of offenses. They could also expect a different form of death: high-status persons were generally beheaded, while low-status persons were generally hanged. The uncertainty of punishment was moreover magnified by the power of princes to issue pardons. The pardoning power was actively used everywhere in Europe, so that statutory provisions often proved to be a dead letter.

The philosophy that grew up in reaction against all this was largely the creation of the boy genius of Enlightenment criminal law thought, Cesare Beccaria of Milan, whose *Essay on Crimes and Punishments* first appeared in 1764, when he was twenty-six. Beccaria, whose little book collected innumerable enlightened admirers, was an eloquent advocate of the proposition that punishment tariffs should be clearly specified and unvarying. A proper criminal code, in the eyes of the Beccarian school, should consist of a list of forbidden acts, and a tariff of punishments to be inflicted for the commission of each of them.[42] Most of all, no individual variations in punishment were to be permitted: exactly the same sentence was to be imposed on every person guilty of any given criminal act, without exception and without regard for extenuating circumstances or social station.

This was, moreover, a program that was indeed intended to leave nothing to "the breast of the judge." Punishment, for Beccaria and his Enlightenment followers, was to be, in the classic terms of Montesquieu, *legislative*. Criminal sanctions were to be specified in laws of general application, laws that applied in exactly the same way to all persons without individual distinctions, and judges were simply to be the "mouths of the law," "inanimate beings who cannot moderate the force or vigor" of what the legislative power had declared.[43] Judges, that is to say, were not to possess any "arbitrary" power whatsoever to vary the penalties laid down by the law. This meant that punishment was *never* to regard the particular personhood of any offender. Indeed, Beccarian philosophy strongly disfavored all measures of systematic mitigation. In particular, Beccaria was a firm opponent of pardoning.[44] This does not mean, we should hasten to note, that he and his followers were in favor of *harshness*. On the contrary, Beccaria believed that punishment, while it should be unbending, should generally be mild, with relatively brief terms of incarceration and relatively light punishments of other kinds. "Every punishment which does not arise by absolute necessity . . . is tyrannical," wrote Beccaria, following Montesquieu;[45] above all senseless cruelty was to be avoided.[46] It was this attitude that underlay one of Beccaria's most famous campaigns, his campaign against the death penalty.[47] Tenderness was Beccaria's aim, in death as in all things.

Tender but unbending—embraced by Voltaire, Blackstone, Kant, and many other Enlightenment figures, this became the dominant *bien pensant* punishment philosophy within a few years after Beccaria's book appeared. What was it that made such a philosophy so appealing in the Enlightenment? Most discussions of Beccarian philosophy present him as a proponent of deterrence; and it certainly is the case that deterrence played a large role in Beccarian thought.[48] Laws that are uncertain of application are laws that do not deter well. This intuition did indeed lie behind Beccarian objections to pardoning and other forms of systematic mitigation.

But there was more to Beccarianism than deterrence, and if we are benefit from holding our own contemporary American law up against the mirror of the Enlightenment, it is important that we recognize that there was more to it than deterrence. Beccaria's ideas also embodied a belief in a kind of *social equality* that was quite radical in its day. When reading Beccaria, we must bear in mind the image of the society in which he lived. Beccaria wrote for a highly stratified premodern continental society, in which criminal liability and penalties depended on social status. (Indeed, Beccaria devoted a fine, and much-neglected, chapter of his book to this topic.)[49] When Beccaria argued that doctrines of criminal liability should focus not on *offenders*, but on *offenses*, not on *persons* but on *acts*, he was accordingly arguing for a species of egalitarianism—a species in which the law refused to pay attention to the social status of any individual. What Beccaria favored was what we might call *act*-egalitarianism—equal treatment for all persons who had committed the same act. In favoring this, he was campaigning for a radical kind of social equality. Even his opposition to the death penalty can be seen in this light: eliminating the death penalty, in eighteenth-century Europe, by discarding the distinction between beheading and hanging, would have eliminated one of the most important status markers of the day.

This act-egalitarianism had nothing to do with deterrence as such. (Indeed, the goals of deterrence might well be best achieved by tailoring different punishments to persons of different social status.) *Formal equality*, in Beccaria's philosophy, ultimately served the end, not of deterrence, but of *social equality*—it served the end of eliminating respect for persons. Consequences in this life, it proclaimed, should depend entirely on what one does, and not who one is.

This egalitarian sentencing philosophy proved profoundly influential on the makers of both the American and the French revolutions, as we shall see, and its influence remained strong on both sides of the Atlantic well into the nineteenth century. In punishment, the Enlightenment lasted, in many ways, into the 1870s. But at the end of the nineteenth century, during a period of general intellectual rebellion against the heritage of the Enlightenment, Beccarian philosophy began to give way to the new philosophy of *individualization*—a purportedly more "modern" and "scientific" approach that took hold everywhere in the Western world.

In the United States, individualization was especially associated with Zebulon Brockway, who proposed a system of indeterminate sentencing in 1870;[50] in continental Europe, it was especially associated with the avowedly "scientific" reformers Raymond Saleilles and Franz von Liszt.[51] On both sides of the Atlantic, the theory developed along similar lines in numerous international congresses from the late nineteenth century onward. Advocates of individualization viewed crime as a problem of social management; and they held, contrary to Beccaria, that punishment should be tailored to the individual offender. A properly conceived criminal law should allow judges, prison officials, and others to form an assessment of each criminal person, asking how best to suit punishment to the individual offender in light of the degree and nature of his dangerousness. The goal of punishment, moreover, should be to resocialize the offender—to do whatever might be necessary to make him a functioning member of society if possible. The theory of individualization thus held that the target of criminal justice should be not *offenses*, but *offenders*, not *acts* but *persons*. These "individualizing" reformers thus rejected Beccaria's brand of *act*-egalitarianism—of the egalitarianism of equal treatment for the same act. This meant that their theory reintroduced considerable uncertainty into punishment. But it is important to recognize that "individualizing" reformers were nevertheless still quite capable of supporting a version of egalitarianism. The egalitarianism they favored, though, was what we might call *depravity*-egalitarianism: not equal treatment for persons who had committed the same *act*, but equal treatment for persons of *equal depravity*.

Now, individualization is not a theory that always made for mildness or mercy in punishment. On the contrary, the theory of individualization gave birth, in effect, to two different strains in the earlier twentieth century: one a systematically merciful strain, but the other a very harsh one indeed. Adherents of the second, harsher strain viewed certain offenders as incorrigible, and even congenitally incorrigible. These incorrigibilists, whose voices were particularly strong among the fascists, advocated punishments that would permanently incapacitate or eliminate "genetically inferior" criminals and habitual offenders, through both life and death sentences.[52] Nevertheless, if some advocates of individualization had fearsome solutions to propound, there were always others who took a milder view. Adherents of the milder strain of individualization saw their problem differently: for them the issue was to differentiate among different degrees of amenability to rehabilitation. Offenders, in this mild view, could generally be resocialized—but only on different, individualized schedules. Individualization in punishment accordingly meant open-ended sentencing, with corrections officials empowered to judge how far each individual convict had progressed toward rehabilitation. The mildness of this mild strain of individualization was thus the mildness of demonstrative concern for the individual offender.

This mild strain was always present in the twentieth century. (Indeed, as we shall see, even in the fascist world there was not inconsiderable support for mild individualization.) By the 1960s, the mild strain of individualization came to dominate in the United States as well as in Western Europe, as prison reformers managed to institute programs that aimed to release offenders into the general population as soon as they were able to lead useful and law-abiding lives; and as philosophers and sociologists broadly rejected the ideals of retributivism.[53] In particular, reformers instituted supervised release in the classic "individualized" forms of parole, suspended sentence, and probation, with a commitment to equal treatment for persons of equal depravity.

But since the watershed years of the mid-1970s, the spirit of individualization is no longer dominant in America. Quite the contrary: a very great part of what has happened in the United States, since the early 1970s, is the abandonment of this merciful version of individualization.

In part, this has involved a return to the harsh version. In mandatory life sentences, and in the return of the death penalty, we see a program of permanent incapacitation—something that the advocates of harsh individualization have preached since the late nineteenth century, and something that in Europe is closely associated with fascism.

But the shift of the last twenty-five years is not just about a shift to harsh individualization. It has also involved a campaign to eliminate *all* forms of individualization, in favor of a revival of formal equality in sentencing.

Indeed, perhaps the most striking of all the development in current American punishment practice is the return to Enlightenment approaches, in the form of determinate sentencing, as embodied, in particular, in federal[54] and some state[55] sentencing guidelines. Like "three-strikes-and-you're-out" laws, to which I will return in the next section, sentencing guidelines aim to eliminate most discretion to individualize punishment. Under the new regime of determinate sentencing, neither judges, nor any other officials, are supposed to have any but the most limited authority to tailor punishment according to their sense of the deserts of the particular offender.[56] As little as possible, to quote Blackstone again, is to be left "to the breast of the judge." All measures of individualization are laid out in relatively rigid sentencing tables, which are to be consulted in a spirit of maximally mechanical application. (The new schemes also cut back on the possibility of early release.)[57] To be sure, determinate sentencing, as it exists in America today, is a complex brew. It does not by any means abandon *all* efforts to individualize punishment; and it certainly has not produced codes of anything resembling Beccarian simplicity. Judges operating under the sentencing guidelines must manipulate an extremely complex calculus of factors to arrive at the punishment for a given offense. Nevertheless, it is clear that the pendulum has swung back, in America, toward the eighteenth century. Like Beccaria, we are retreating from individualizing mitigation, toward a system of formal equality in punishment—toward a system of *act*-egalitarianism rather than *depravity*-egalitarianism.

Why is such formal equality proving appealing in contemporary America? The answer, at least in part, is no different from what it was in the Enlightenment: the appeal of formal equality in America is once again largely the appeal of social equality, just as it was in Beccaria's day. Social equality was indeed the express goal of one group of supporters of determinate sentencing: liberals. The movement for determinate sentencing can partly be traced back to a widespread sense among liberals, expressed in an influential American Friends' Service Committee report of 1971, that rich, white defendants did better under the system of indeterminate sentencing than poor, dark-skinned ones.[58] Similar concerns were expressed in an important book by Judge Marvin Frankel; and in another influential committee report, *Doing Justice*, published in 1976 on the basis of work by Andrew von Hirsch and a panel of eminences.[59] What attracted these liberals to determinate sentencing was precisely its egalitarian philosophy. Just as Beccaria thought that every eighteenth-century European, whether peasant or marquis, should suffer the same punishment for the same crime, so liberals like Judge Frankel thought that every American who committed the same crime, whether black or white, ought to suffer the same punishment.[60] The same early 1970s return to the ideals of act-egalitarianism also informed the Supreme Court's short-lived invalidation of the death penalty.[61] Studies have shown that this effort has not succeeded, at least to date: disparities in sentencing remain.[62] Nevertheless, the sentencing guidelines testify to the immense power of a liberal ideal of formal egalitarianism in the culture of American criminal justice.

The liberals were not alone in pushing for guidelines, though. The guidelines movement bridged the American political divide, with liberals joined by law-and-order conservatives. Conservative supporters of guidelines raised a variety of their own objections to individualization. One of the most familiar, and most politically potent, was that practices of individualization showed too much concern for offenders, and not enough for victims. "Victims' rights" became a powerful slogan in the 1970s—leading, among other phenomena, to victim impact statements and the striking practices of naming statutes, like Megan's Law, after victims.[63] Law-and-order conservatives also brought a distrust of the courts to the campaign against individualization. Not least, they brought an unembarrassed demand for tough retributivism.[64]

Despite these deep differences, liberals and conservatives were able to unite in supporting the principle of sentencing guidelines. They did, however, differ in the results they expected. Liberal supporters in the 1970s thought that mildness would prevail in a scheme of determinate sentencing. Like Beccaria, they thought that formal equality in sentencing properly implied eschewing harsh punishment. Thus Alan Dershowitz wrote in 1974 that "it is clear that no matter what other factors govern sentence length, the inevitable result of the indeterminate sentence is that sentences of over five years will predominate, and in definite sentencing state sentences of under five years will predominate."[65] Law-and-order conservatives presumably did not particularly share this goal.

As it turns out, the world of the sentencing guidelines has taken on what certainly looks like a law-and-order cast. Indeed, our new regime of formal equality has turned out to be a regime of iron harshness: our punishment has become relatively unbending, but it has by no means become tender. This has been profoundly disheartening for liberals, and a large liberal literature of lament and analysis has appeared, in the last decade, that seeks to explain why the world of the guidelines is so harsh.

This is not a question that is entirely easy to answer.[66] The guidelines are supposed to be composed by "bureaucratic" commissioners, insulated from political pressure.[67] Even to the extent that this insulation is unsuccessful, the harshness of the guidelines cannot be in any simple way the result of law-and-order capture of the federal guidelines drafting process. They impose a determinate sentencing calculus on the sentences provided by other statutes.

The critically important factor thus has to be that those other statutes, as we shall see in the next section, have greatly lengthened sentences during the same period[68]—though the decline of early release under determinate sentencing statutes has magnified their effect. On one level, then, we have to say that the harshness of the guidelines is not a product of the guidelines movement itself. It is merely a consequence of the fact that the movement coincided with the rise to electoral success of law-and-order conservatives who succeeded in shaping other statutes. Many writers have thus concluded that our current harshness is simply not the fault of the guidelines.

But on a deeper level, we should see that this harshness, if it is not directly created by the guidelines, *does* have something to do with their underlying philosophy: it has to do with the consequences of formal equality itself—and especially of formal equality as instituted in a democratic society.[69]

The guidelines movement aims to take the authority to make sentencing decisions out of the hands of the punishment professionals such as judges and prison officials, and make it the subject of Montesquieuian "legislative" decision-making instead.[70] Punishment, under the guidelines, is supposed to be a matter for laws of general application, with nothing left to "the breast of the judge." The guidelines are thus composed in a spirit of "fear of judging," as José Cabranes and Kate Stith have written. This is a spirit that can be very tough on offenders. The sentencing guidelines embody, and encourage, a shift in the culture of judging—a shift away from mercy, which is always an individualizing process. As Montesquieu himself put it, mercy is something you *feel*;[71] it is not something that can be laid out in advance in general rules. This means that the merciful judge must see the individual offender before his eyes. Judges who operate in a guidelines-dominated world are judges who have soaked in a philosophy that has little mercy to it.

But the issue is not only about the attitude of judges. It is also about the attitude of voters. The guidelines are symptomatic of a larger shift away from the judicial and toward the legislative in American criminal law. The guidelines belong to a culture that aims to take criminal justice out of the hands of judges, and return it to "the people"—which means that the guidelines inevitably lend themselves to the worst excesses of American democracy. Harshness and democratization go hand in hand, and for a simple reason: voters never have individual offenders before their eyes; they are never in a position to *feel* the Montesquieuian impulse toward mercy. Ordinary voters are never capable of the kind of routinized, sober, and merciful approach to punishment that is the stuff of the daily work of punishment professionals. The average voter simply sees too few actual offenders before his eyes to develop either an attitude that is either empathetic or blasé. In this sense, what voters lack is precisely the judicial frame of mind. Behind the harshness of the sentencing guidelines thus lies a painful American irony—painful, at least, to liberals who think of themselves as subscribing to Enlightenment values. When formal equality in sentencing is married to the electoral equality of mass politics, the consequences are explosive.[72] It is simply too easy for politicians to mobilize support by advocating harsh punishment for abstractly conceived "criminals." (I am going to argue below, indeed, that the use of law-and-order politics as a way of mobilizing popular support is something we share, disturbingly enough, with the Nazis.) A culture of formal equality will thus always invite law-and-order politics, will always invite the sort "politicization," deplored by David Garland and others.[73]

The New Law of Punishment

Harshness in the Law of Punishment

The measure of the explosive power of mass politics in America can indeed be taken from the law of punishment, where the push for a tough retributivism has had an extraordinary effect. Numerous statutes have lengthened prison sentences. Most especially, certain morals offenses have been the target of particularly increased—sometimes drastically increased—legislated sentencing. Drug offenses especially fall into this category, for example in the much-debated Rockefeller laws of New York State that date to the mid-1970s, the beginning of our era of crackdown.[74] Federal drug laws, too, requiring sentences of sometimes awesome length, have had a tremendous (though somewhat difficult to analyze) impact on the federal prison population.[75] Indeed, it is a striking fact about the growth of the American prison population—particularly striking by contrast with Europe, as we shall see—that most of that growth has involved the incarceration of *nonviolent* criminals. Historically, violent crime is what has lain at the core of what Western legal cultures regard as "criminal." Yet in the United States, a vast disproportion of the immense growth of the prison population between 1980 and 1992 was for drug offenses, nonviolent property crimes, and (occasionally) minor offenses of kinds that Europeans regard as forms of disorderly conduct.[76] The same tendency can be detected in the intensification of criminal liability for American minors: the growth in classification of juveniles as "adults" since 1992 has apparently involved mostly nonviolent offenses.[77]

Other statutes have also brought dramatically longer terms. There are, first and foremost, "three-strikes-and-you're-out" laws, which require fixed long terms, often life terms, for three-time offenders. Legislation of this type actually has a long history in the United States, running as far back as 1797 in New York; and by the late 1960s, twenty-three states had repeat offender statutes that permitted life imprisonment.[78] The American tradition of this kind of harshness runs deep. Nevertheless, the newest generation of these laws, dating to the mid-1990s, in twenty-four states as well as on the federal level, differs in a telling way: old life-imprisonment statutes were directed only at certain serious crimes. The new "three-strikes-and-you're-out" laws,[79] by contrast, frequently apply even to those who have committed what were once regarded as minor offenses. Most notably, these include drug and nonviolent property offenses. This is particularly true where these laws interact with enhancement statutes, which regrade prior misdemeanors as more serious felonies. (I will return to these enhancement statutes shortly.) The interaction between these two statutory schemes has resulted in some much-reported scandals—one notorious sentence of twenty-five years to life, in particular, imposed in California for the theft of a slice of pizza.[80] That sentence, at least, was revisited.[81] Nevertheless, "three-strikes-and-you're-out" laws are particularly dramatic evidence of a new style of American toughness.

These statutes have had an impact on American law that would be strictly impossible under prevailing doctrine in continental Europe. The European systems all subscribe to some version of the principle of proportionality. This principle holds that sentences, though indeterminate, cannot be disproportionate to the gravity of the offense; the legal profession takes it very seriously; and it means that sentences of American severity are effectively impossible.[82] That principle is, by contrast, generally absent from American sentencing practices, and long has been. Indeed, long before the rise of determinate sentencing, the absence of a proportionality principle produced what seemed to many egregious injustices under older indeterminate sentencing statutes. In the California case of *In re Lynch*, to take a well-known example, the petitioner was a prisoner serving an indeterminate sentence after being caught masturbating in his car in 1967, with a prior conviction for indecent exposure from 1958. A substantial part of this sentence had been served in the tough conditions of the maximum security prison in Folsom, and there was no way of being certain when Lynch would ever be released. The California Supreme Court responded to his situation by creating, in 1972, a constitutionalized proportionality doctrine.[83] This doctrine has not effectively survived in the later jurisprudence of the California court, though;[84] and its absence is palpable in the world of determinate sentencing that has sprung up since 1972. Proportionality suffered, indeed, a grievous blow in the Supreme Court's 1991 decision of *Harmelin v. Michigan*, in which the court saw no unconstitutional disproportion in a life sentence imposed for possession of 672 grams of cocaine.[85]

With proportionality setting no clear limit,[86] the promulgation of the new penal statutes of the last twenty-five years has had, it is generally agreed, a tremendous impact on American incarceration rates. Longer sentences mean larger prison populations; and sentences have been getting steadily longer in America. Indeed, we have now reached the point where American convicts, as we shall see, serve sentences roughly *five to ten times* as long as similarly situated French ones; and almost certainly even longer by comparison with German convicts.[87] The results tell in our prisons and jails. The growth in the American incarcerated population over the last twenty-five years has been extraordinary, roughly tripling from the early 1970s until the mid-1990s, and continuing to grow apace since, reaching 2 million in 2000—up from a (then unprecedented) 1 million in 1990.[88] This has a consequence of immense significance for punishment culture in America: massive overcrowding. On both sides of the Atlantic, prison overcrowding is a problem. But the crowd of American prisoners has come to be vastly larger. Depending on how you reckon it, the American incarceration rate now stands at somewhere between 450 and 700 per 100,000 of the general population—on a rough par with Russia;[89] and in certain parts of the United States, like Louisiana and the District of Columbia, the rate stands as high as 760 or 1,700 per 100,000. The typical European incarceration rate, by contrast, stands somewhere between 65 and 100 per 100,000.[90]

Incarceration is by far the most important part of the story of the changing American law of punishment, but it is not the only part. Indeed, it is not the only place where we see a new willingness to treat offenders with a kind of unbridled lack of respect. There is also what we might call a new inventiveness in punishment. In particular, American criminal justice has seen the revival of two styles of punishment that had almost entirely vanished from the Western world: public shaming and public forced labor of an ostentatiously degrading kind.[91] These are developments that date, like most of what I have discussed, to the late 1970s, when they reappeared on the American scene in a completely unexpected way. Since that time, publicly inflicted shaming in particular has been imposed in a new-old class of penalties, which have been crafted by low-level American judges in all parts of the country. The new shame sanctions, imposed for the most part as probation conditions, are often fashioned in ways that deliberately echo the scarlet letter and pillory of the premodern past. Defendants have thus been obliged to parade themselves wearing signs, shirts, or bumper stickers describing their offenses. Accused offenders have been displayed to the press and the public in humiliating ways.[92] Alongside these punishments come chain gangs, for example, the most striking form of public forced labor. Also worthy of note, though not involving public labor, is the reintroduction of forced labor at the rock pile, reintroduced as part of chain gang practice in Alabama, Arizona, and Florida. This practice too is of course rich in associations with a preliberal past in American punishment.[93]

All of these new/old punishments reflect one revealing, if hard-to-interpret, feature of the new American punishment law: a kind of inventiveness in punishment—and of a species of inventiveness that has not been seen in Europe since the fascist era. For Europeans, the notion that judges might try to think up new punishments, or even revive forgotten ones, has something offensive and even bizarre about it. Indeed, as long ago as the eighteenth century, continental Europeans were expressing discomfort with the notion of inventive punishing: "It is not permitted," wrote one 1767 authority flatly, "for judges to invent punishments."[94] Punishment, on the continent, is expected to be surrounded with a kind of sad solemnity and a sobriety that exclude judicial and legislative creativity. That attitude of solemnity and sobriety is noticeably less present in the United States than it was thirty years ago. In the common law world too, "invention" of punishments was once considered unacceptable. Indeed, the Supreme Court has observed that the very prohibition on "cruel and unusual" punishment began its life largely as a prohibition on the invention of novel punishments.[95] Yet novelty in punishment has reappeared in America. Let us call this a shift, in

America, away from the bureaucratic mentality. Punishment, in Europe, is for weary professionals, who do not imagine that it is their job to devise ingenious new practices. In America we have come, at least at times, to view things differently.

Harshness in the Application of Punishment

If the law of punishment in the United States shows a fairly unadulterated picture of growing harshness, the *application* of punishment presents a somewhat more mixed story—though it is still a story of deepening harshness.

Here the most important questions involve prison conditions.

Readers of American novels and viewers of American movies may acquire a thoroughly Dantesque idea of the hellishness of American prisons. Indeed, much of what most strikingly colors current American legal culture is a horror of prisons, and a sense that conditions behind bars are unspeakably barbaric. It is impossible to describe the culture of punishment in America without making some reference to the popular image of prisons. Movies and popular literature convey a fascination with the degradation and violence of prison life; the sense that imprisonment is spectacularly horrific lies near the heart of what makes punishment harsh in the American mind. Here the fear of homosexual rape, which in many societies causes irreversible status degradation, features prominently, and suggestively.[96] In the Roman Empire, according to the books of dream interpretation, people used to have nightmares about being crucified. As classicists observe, this tells us something peculiarly intimate and revealing about how omnipresent harsh punishment was in ancient lives.[97] People in the United States watch movies and read novels about beatings, stabbings, and violent homosexual rape in prison. This also seems to tell us something intimate and revealing about an American culture of harsh punishment.

It is all the more important to observe, then, that conditions in American prisons are a lot better than they used to be, and in some ways even better than conditions in France (though not in Germany). American prisons went through a period of court-ordered reform, some of it massive, that began relatively abruptly in the mid-1960s.[98] During the 1970s, courts actively tested prison practices against a developing Eighth Amendment jurisprudence,[99] abandoning the traditional harsh view that inmates were simply "slaves of the state."[100] Those reforms—which paralleled contemporary reforms in Europe, as we shall see—eliminated some spectacularly frightening and dangerous conditions, especially in prisons in the American South.[101] The impulse toward reform reached its high-water mark in 1980, when Congress passed the Constitutional Rights of Incarcerated Persons Act. This era of reform undoubtedly achieved much of importance. As summarized by Chief Justice Rehnquist, American prisons today, unlike their predecessors of fifty years ago, must provide a certain minimum: "When the State by the affirmative exercise of its power so restrains an individual's liberty that it renders him unable to care for himself, and at the same time fails to provide for his basic human needs—e.g., food, clothing, shelter, medical care and reasonable safety—it transgresses the substantive limits on state action set by the Eighth Amendment ."[102] This, at least according to its letter, is by no means nothing—though as we shall see, its letter provides for significantly less than the letter of European law. The spirit of reform behind it has not entirely died even today: there are still courts actively engaged in improving American prison conditions.[103]

There is, moreover, a further important factor that has improved prison conditions in America. The boom in incarceration over the last quarter century has also been a boom in prison building.[104] Newly built prisons offer relatively good living conditions. This is a particularly important point for contrasting the United States with France. As we shall see, French prisons are by and large very old and poorly maintained, and much of what makes life harsh for French prison inmates has to do with the long-standing neglect of the prison physical plant.

Prison conditions are thus in some ways not as bad in the United States as one might think. Nevertheless, they certainly *are* bad, especially by contrast with Germany. And most important, the trend, as in so much of the punishment of the last twenty-five years, is toward a growing harshness.

The era of reform proved brief in the United States, and this aspect of American punishment practice too has settled into a mood of harshness typical of the last several decades. By the late 1970s, the flush of prison reform had already begun to recede.[105] To be sure, in 1994, the United States ratified the Convention against Torture and Other Cruel, Inhuman or Degrading Treatments—the document that is a principal font of punishment reform in continental Europe. However, the United States made its ratification subject to the express reservation that the dictates of the convention would be interpreted to conform to the American constitutional limitations found especially in the Eighth Amendment.[106] As it turns out, those limitations have proved to be few. The Supreme Court handed down an especially critical decision in *Wilson v. Seiter*, of 1991, which set a high hurdle for court action in cases of alleged inmate abuse, requiring that inmates demonstrate "deliberate indifference" on the part of prison officials.[107] As the court's jurisprudence stands under *Wilson*, complaining inmates must prove in effect that prison officials had a subjective intent to subject an inmate to the "cruel and unusual" punishment condemned by the Eighth Amendment,[108] no matter how objectively bad their prison conditions may be.[109] This is very tough on prisoners, representing a real bar to litigation over objectively bad prison conditions and putting an almost impossible burden of proof on the complainant. In other respects, too, the court has established a deferential standard, denying federal courts that power to intervene to end any practice for which prison officials can claim a reasonable relationship to the management of their institutions.[110] Inmates do retain some protection against "malicious"[111] excessive force by guards,[112] held by the court to violate "contemporary standards of decency." In this as in other things, American law has a special sensitivity to violence. Inmates have benefited from some other decisions too. In particular, bizarrely, but typically of contemporary American legal culture, the Supreme Court has held that inmates may also have a right to protection against secondhand smoke.[113] On the whole, though, conditions have not improved for prisoners in the 1990s. Congressional legislation of the mid-1990s did away with much of the courts' authority to intervene, and more broadly the period of general growing harshness in American punishment has thus also been one in which judicial prison reform "has suffered a succession of heavy blows from the Supreme Court, the Administration, and Congress."[114]

As things stand, courts are being progressively obliged to withdraw from prison management, and matters in American prisons, correspondingly, are moving toward increased harshness. As we shall see, this trend toward harshness stands in sharp contrast to the trend on the continent, where courts have been increasingly intervening to improve conditions. Conditions are undoubtedly worse in American state prisons than in federal ones. Private prisons, which have established themselves throughout the United States, may have relatively good conditions.[115] But it is clear that conditions are frightening in all high-security American carceral institutions, all of which suffer from drastic overcrowding, inmate-on-inmate violence, and guard-on-inmate violence as well.[116] (It is, however, strictly impossible to determine just how much violence there is in American prisons, or any others.)[117] Homosexual rape is, in particular, a constantly bruited fact of American prison life—though one whose real prevalence is again essentially impossible to determine.[118] If technically corporal punishment has been abolished in American prisons, the fact is that American jurisprudence is still comparatively reluctant to pursue violence that is not intended "maliciously and sadistically to cause harm."[119] Guards, moreover, frequently have little special training—certainly less than their European counterparts.[120] Nevertheless, they qualify as "peace officers" under American law and may carry weapons.[121] They may also use force to compel inmates to comply with their orders.[122] Harsh treatment by prison officials, substandard medical care,[123] and the like are widely regarded as common[124]—though here it again it deserves to be emphasized that medical care in particular has improved as a result of the judicial interventions of the 1960s and after.[125] All of the problems of American prison conditions are, moreover, inevitably greatly magnified by overcrowding—a dire problem indeed, intensified by the spectacularly expanding prison population. Unlike their European counterparts, American inmates have very limited power to object to transfers to another prison—a particularly important disability in a country in which the rise of privatized prisons has meant that many are transferred to very distant institutions indeed, where they have little hope of receiving visits.[126] Meanwhile, unlike European courts and legislatures, our Supreme Court has taken a distinctly hands-off attitude toward overcrowding, observing simply that "restrictive and even harsh" prison conditions, if they comport with very minimal standards of existence, "are part of the penalty that criminal offenders pay for their offenses against society."[127] If this is not quite as nasty in tone as the words of the Phoenix sheriff who runs "a very bad jail,"[128] it nevertheless has a sharp edge to it that is not to be heard from any legal official in Europe.

If prison conditions are not unambiguously harsh, it is certainly the case that the law has veered in the direction of harshness in the last twenty-five years. It is important to notice that there are other trends at work, though, too. In particular, there are alternative sanctions—fines, community service, and some of the new shaming penalties I described in the last section. These too have a new prominence, to some extent—and a prominence that reflects, paradoxically, a certain impulse toward mildness in the application of punishment. People who are fined or shamed are people who are not jailed; and this counts as a benefit in the world of American punishment.[129]

The extension of this benefit has to be seen in context, though. The use of alternative sanctions is in part a product of the new harshness in American criminal justice more broadly. Alternative sanctions are applied in areas in which the American drive toward criminalization of conduct and of persons has created new forms of liability, notably in the cases of white-collar offenders, drunk drivers, and some sex offenders. As our drive toward growing criminalization of new persons and some new conduct has created new forms of liability, the system has responded by introducing what are (in the eyes of American culture) relatively mild punishments. The net effect is of course still a harsh one: there is criminal liability where there was not before. Yet it is liability whose actual impact on offenders has been cabined by the application of what, in our culture, are regarded as mild punishments.[130]

There is, finally, one other aspect of harshness in the application of American punishment: the absence of the rules guaranteeing that inmates will be treated respectfully. I leave discussion of this aspect to the last section of this chapter.

Grading, Enforcement, and Doctrinal Flexibility

Let me turn now to my three final measures of harshness: harshness in grading and enforcement; and harshness in inflexible doctrines of liability. These present varying pictures of the state of American criminal punishment.

Harshness in Grading and Enforcement

Harshness in grading and harshness in enforcement can profitably be viewed together. While neither measure is entirely easy to assess, both suggest once again the same relatively strong tendency. It is the quasi-Kantian tendency I described above: the tendency to seek out evil wherever it may be found.

American law clearly shows a trend toward harshness in grading, especially by contrast with continental Europe. As I suggested in the last chapter this is a measure that can reveal a great deal about a given punishment culture. When criminal justice systems grade offenses high—as felonies, in common-law terms—it is typically because they regard those offenses as *mala in se*, as evils in themselves. The attitude toward grading in a given system thus has something to do with its attitude toward the problem of evil.

Now, it is hardly the case that American criminal justice displays no wisdom on the topic of grading. On the contrary, the Model Penal Code in particular, promulgated in 1962, is indeed a model effort to use grading wisely, especially in its treatment of "violations," its lowest grade of offense.[131] It is not that American criminal justice does not see the importance of grading; it is rather that American justice has shown, over the last twenty-five years, a tendency to grade offenses comparatively high. This is a tendency that has taken several forms. Some acts have been graded upward. California, for example, in its epochal crackdown, has been classifying more and more offenses as "felonies," with the total at more than five hundred as of 1998.[132] The same strategy has appealed to other Americans as well during the same period: The U.S. Advisory Board on Child Abuse and Neglect has demanded, for example, that states reclassify child abuse misdemeanors as felonies.[133] Here again, we see typically American strategies appearing both on the right and on the left. Most important, so-called "enhancements" show a similar tendency to grade offenses more severely. Under enhancement doctrine, low-grade offenses can be graded up for sentencing purposes if the offender commits a subsequent offense; and subsequent offenses can themselves be graded up if there is a prior history of convictions.[134] Thus it is that in California, as widely reported in Europe, minor prior thefts can lead to longer sentences, and even life sentences. This, if you like, represents right-wing enhancement doctrine. There is also left-wing enhancement doctrine: it is also a variety of enhancement that is used to penalize bias crimes more severely.[135]

American criminal law is thus in a variety of ways engaged in grading offenses up. Something similar is arguably at work in American enforcement. The question of whether American enforcement has grown harsher is too empirically difficult to resolve: an adequate answer would require too much close study of too many prosecutorial and police practices. Nevertheless, there are some examples of intensified enforcement that deserve to be mentioned because they seem so manifestly symptomatic of the broader changes that have come to American law. One example is renewed efforts to crack down on prostitution.[136] We can also see it in many scattered exercises of prosecutorial discretion, such as the recent decision by a Colorado prosecutor to treat a skiing accident as a case of felony reckless manslaughter.[137] The pursuit of drunk driving is also a matter of changing enforcement rather than changing grading: on the books, drunk driving has long been treated as quite grave. But it is since the early seventies, in this as in so many other aspects of American criminal justice, that the systematic prosecution has come.[138] Perhaps most interestingly, we can see intensifying enforcement in the slow growth of concern about date rape.[139]

These shifts in enforcement are difficult to assess, because they are the product of numerous discretionary decisions by officials all over the country. Nevertheless, where officials decide, in their discretion, to pursue offenses that they did not pursue before, they are making a decision much like the decision to grade offenses up: they are choosing to treat the offense in question as evil, and therefore as meriting prosecution.

Why Americans show this growing comparative tendency to view acts as evil is a question to which I will return. It part, I am going to suggest, it reflects the fact that state power is different, and lesser, in the United States than in continental Europe. In part, it has a spiritual kinship with the American Christian revival. For the moment, though, I want simply to observe that it belongs to the same spirit of Kantian severity that appears in so many other aspects of contemporary American justice.

Harshness in Inflexible Doctrines of Criminal Liability

Here, at last, is one measure by which there does not seem to have been much change in American criminal justice. Our doctrinal flexibility remains more or less what it was twenty-five years ago, whether we are speaking of doctrines of justification, doctrines of excuse, or doctrines of diminished capacity.[140] This absence of change is worth highlighting and suggests how difficult generalizations can be in law. If American law were shifting unambiguously in the direction of a Beccarian rejection of respect for persons, it might be abandoning these doctrines as well. It is not, by and large.

The Mildness of Respect and Pardons

Let me now turn, finally, to the two forms of mildness I listed in chapter 1: the mildness of respectful treatment and the mildness of mercy.

The Mildness of Respectful Treatment

This species of mildness is dramatically absent in American punishment, by contrast with continental European punishment. Prison life and public shaming make the best examples.

American high-security prisons are characterized by a number of practices that have waned or entirely vanished in Europe. Among these are a variety of aspects of prison life that go mostly unquestioned, and even unnoticed, in the United States, but that have been wholly or largely eliminated across the Atlantic. First is the practice of keeping inmates in cells with barred doors and the like[141] through which they are not just *observed* (as they would be through peepholes) but thoroughly *exposed*—inmates having, as the Supreme Court has held, "no reasonable expectation of privacy."[142] Second is the common obligation to wear prison uniforms, a practice with especially interesting psychological consequences.[143] Along with uniforms go prison regulations on personal grooming, regulating hair length, facial hair, and the like.[144] Transvestites in particular (unlike their European counterparts) have been denied the right to wear female clothing and cosmetics.[145] These are all measures through which American inmates are essentially denied all control over their "presentation of self," to borrow a famous phrase of Erving Goffman.[146] Also important are a range of restrictions on visitation, including in some cases the practice of separating inmates from their visitors behind a glass partition;[147] and a spirit of regimentation represented notably by the practice of common dining in a common mess hall,[148] where prisoners may have no choice of foods[149] and may be hustled out after as short a time as twelve minutes.[150]

All of these are practices that Europeans have, in one measure or another, condemned as incompatible with inmate "dignity." They are all practices that show our lack of concern for respect for persons in the second of the two senses with which I began: they all diminish the respect with which inmates are treated. These are, as it were, the outward dramatizations of the "hatred, fear [and] contempt for the convict" that characterize our attitude toward these offenders.[151] There are others, too.[152] One of the most frequently discussed is the deprivation of the right to vote and like civic rights, still widespread in various forms and having a striking impact on the African-American population.[153] Odd reports of prison life, some of them wholly bizarre, further testify to a new spirit of indignity in the American prisons—such as the organization by guards in one California state prison of "gladiator days," during which fights were arranged between inmate members of rival gangs, complete with audiences—fights that often ended in shootings.[154]

More generally—and of particular importance for the contrast with Europe, as we shall see—the expectation of privacy for American convicts is effectively nil. The Supreme Court has held that "it would be literally impossible to accomplish the prison objectives of preventing the introduction of weapons, drugs, and other contraband into the premises if inmates retained a right of privacy in their cells."[155] As one recent reform-minded author describes the resulting situation in American prisons: "Prison and privacy often appear to be antithetical entities. For nonprisoners, privacy is an umbrella concept, protecting a variety of disparate activities. For prisoners, lack of privacy may seem equally wide-ranging. Surveillance in prison can be unremitting and escape to the privacy of one's cell is often impossible. Cell and strip searches occur with no notice. Visits are monitored and private letters are intercepted and read. Personal possessions are strictly limited."[156] The Fourth Amendment guarantee against searches and seizures, principal font of privacy rights in the United States, is at best problematically applicable to prisoners.[157] Non-Fourth-Amendment-based privacy rights are essentially denied to them.[158] No warrants are required for cell searches,[159] which may be conducted without notice, or for searches of personal property.[160] Much of Fourth Amendment jurisprudence revolves around the question of whether items are in "plain view"; and as American prisoners are often placed in cells with barred doors, their belongings are of course often in "plain view."[161] But even items not in plain view enjoy no protection.[162] As Gresham Sykes observed thirty years ago, this deprivation of control over basic possessions is difficult to bear: "In modern Western culture, material possessions are so large a part of the individual's conception of himself that to be stripped of them is to be attacked at the deepest layers of personality."[163] Inmates may be obliged to use toilets within the view of guards of the opposite sex.[164] With regard to privacy, overcrowding is of course again a major factor. Overcrowding has led to multiple occupancy of tiny prison cells, which, as one court observed, "rips away the sense of privacy—of dignity which can make bearable many things which could not otherwise be endured."[165]

There is of course more: body cavity searches, for example,[166] and seizure of inmates' property.[167] Taken together, it amounts to a jurisprudence that, as we shall see, is far less sensitive to dignitary issues—one is tempted to say infinitely less sensitive—than the jurisprudence of continental Europe.

The same can be said of public shaming. The new shame sanctions take a variety of forms. In most cases, they are inflicted on persons who have actually been convicted of an offense.[168] In other cases, though, these sanctions have been visited on persons who have been arrested but not yet convicted. Especially important here is the Supreme Court's decision in *Paul v. Davis*, a case decided in the 1976, early on in the recent American secular shift toward greater harshness in punishment. *Paul v. Davis* involved a local sheriff who circulated photographs of "known shop-lifters" to be posted at cash registers in Iowa markets. This practice was challenged by one "known shop-lifter" against whom all charges had been dropped, and who understandably wanted to avoid the ugly publicity created by the posting of his photograph. The Supreme Court rejected his claim, strikingly holding that there is no constitutional right to protection of reputation.[169] That decision opened the door to a whole variety of politically popular practices. Most widespread of these, probably, is the practice of televising the names of johns arrested for soliciting prostitutes. One enterprising sheriff broadcasts scenes from his jail 24 hours a day on the internet.[170]

There are other classes of cases too. One class in particular runs strongly at odds with the policies of rehabilitation and resocialization that were the bread and butter of individualization in an earlier era: public exposure visited on persons who have completed their prison terms. An example of this is the class of so-called "Megan's Laws" involving sex offenders whose names and whereabouts are disclosed to the public after their release. Perhaps more revealing, though, is a different class. States have been moving to change what had been a deeply rooted practice in American justice: the practice of sealing juvenile criminal records, so that persons could leave youthful transgressions behind. Between 1992 and 1995, forty states enacted legislation making juvenile criminal records more easily accessible.[171]

It is important not to exaggerate the role of most of these new sanctions in American criminal justice. Most forms of public shaming probably remain relatively rare. Nevertheless, they are indicative of an attitude that sharply distinguishes Americans from continental Europeans. It is an attitude that reflects, once again, our relative lack of concern for shows of respect. Shameful public exposure is antithetical to the display of respect. Persons who are exposed to the derision of those around them have been deprived a basic measure of self-respect. To be sure, Americans have never been as sensitive to public exposure as continental Europeans are. The contrast is one that we can see most notably in the comparative law of privacy. Continental concepts of the protection of privacy revolve around shielding people from public exposure in ways that are quite alien to the American sensibility.[172] Nevertheless, Americans too have their dread of being publicly shamed; and even in the American context it is fair to describe the return of public shame sanctions as symptomatic of a reduced commitment to respect for criminal offenders. The decline of respect for persons can thus be detected in the rise of shame sanctions, just as it can be detected in the rise of formal equality in American criminal law.

The Mildness of Pardons

The application of the power of pardoning is so relatively rare in the United States that one would hardly mention it at all, if one were not laying the groundwork for a comparison with continental Europe.

All executives—state governors and the president of the United States—possess a pardoning power; and it is certainly in use. But it is used overwhelmingly for one purpose: to remove the civil and political disabilities that generally attach to a felony conviction in the United States.[173] There are occasional cases in which pardons are issued to mitigate the harshness of some of the new sentencing statutes.[174] There are also occasional commutations of the death penalty; and of course, there remains an appeal for mercy as of right for all persons condemned to die. There are some famous cases of political pardons—the pardon of Richard Nixon; and of the Vietnam-era draft dodgers.

For the most part, though, the pardoning power is little in evidence. The most highly publicized use of it in recent years is testimony, in fact, to its relative weakness. The presidential pardoning power is at the heart of the scandal over outgoing President Clinton's pardon of fugitive Marc Rich, along with other favored recipients. These Clinton pardons have stirred strong American suspicions that the pardoning power is used to benefit the rich and well connected. The Clinton pardons thus touched an egalitarian nerve. As we shall see, this was not unprecedented: such scandals over the pardoning power have a long history in the United States.

3

Continental Dignity and Mildness

America is not entirely alone. The chill of the last quarter century has struck worldwide—most notably perhaps in the Islamic revival. Certainly some of the winds that have blown through the United States have also reached continental Europe. Europeans too have been moved to hit criminals hard over the last couple of decades. As in the United States, there have been some demands to purge individualization and resocialization from the practice of punishment, substituting retribution, incapacitation, and determinate sentencing. Europe too has had a victims' rights movement.[1] As in the United States, some politicians have run on get-tough-on-crime platforms. Thus, after the triumph of the right in the elections of 1978, France saw agitation comparable to the sentencing guidelines movement in the United States.[2] This agitation has had an important impact on French sentencing for certain offenses,[3] and the French prison population has been growing, despite regular amnesties and collective pardons.[4] There have been French voices calling for a crackdown on juveniles too.[5] During the same period, Germany has shown something of the same pattern, if not quite so markedly. Some German scholars have mounted a campaign in favor of retributivist policies.[6] Certain harsh measures have been passed in Germany—especially, as in France, as a consequence of the terrorist crises of the 1970s. As in France, there have been movements to tighten punishment practice.[7] As in France, average German terms have lengthened somewhat; and the prison population has been growing, after reaching a low-point in 1975.[8] Even the

Social Democratic party in Germany tries to portray itself as tough on crime.[9] To some extent, white-collar crime has been a target in both countries; and both countries have seen some drive toward the criminalization of morals offenses. Politicians have been attacked in both countries too. The last quarter of the twentieth century was a time when an impulse toward harshness touched every part of the Western world, to some extent.

But only to some extent. In fact, it would be a very great error to conclude that the European state of affairs is no different from the American. If some of the same bitter late twentieth-century winds that have blown through American have blown through Europe, they have left Europe much less battered; the structures of reform in both Germany and France remain essentially intact. As of the year 2000, mildness is still, at heart, the watchword of punishment practice in both countries. Indeed, the same quarter-century that has been marked by growing harshness in the United States has been a period of growing *mildness* in continental Europe. Victims' rights is perhaps the most striking example. In Germany, despite some political thundering, the victims' rights movement has resulted in alternative, *milder* sanctions. Safeguarding victims, for the German criminal code, means encouraging mediation between offender and victim as a way of avoiding criminal prosecution.[10] This is only one example of many. The large tendencies that have been shaping American punishment practice—the rejection of individualization in favor of a harsh version of Beccarian egalitarianism; the criminalization of new classes of persons; the reintroduction of public shaming; the retreat of the prison reform movement—have all remained fundamentally absent in both European countries. Where a generally unmitigated harshness is the tone that sounded through the last decades in the United States, Europe has actually seen, taken all in all, a growing mildness, which is my topic in this chapter.

Punishment

Any notion that "modernity" somehow dictates convergence in punishment practices cannot survive a survey of the differences between American and continental law—differences that have, all told, been growing markedly over the last twenty-five years. Far from converging, the two sides of the Atlantic are diverging.

Mildness in the Law of Punishment

Sentencing statistics tell the beginning of the tale. In 1999, after more than two decades of get-tough-on-crime politics, the average time served in France was 8 months, up from 4.3 months in 1975.[11] Such is French harshness. American statistics are not directly comparable, since nonviolent offenders who serve no time at all in France are routinely imprisoned in the United States. Nevertheless, we can observe that the average time served for violent offenses in American state prisons was 53 months in 1996, and the average time for all offenses 28 months;[12] while the comparable figures in American federal prison were 91 and 67 months respectively.[13] American violent offenders are thus likely to spend something on the order of five to ten times as long behind bars as French ones. German sentencing statistics are, unfortunately, not directly comparable.[14] Nevertheless, since 1970, German law has mandated that courts avoid sentences under six months, subjecting offenders instead to fines.[15] It is thus normal German practice, at least in theory,[16] to sentence as many offenders as possible to zero prison time; and there can hardly be any doubt that prison sentences are on average far shorter in Germany than in the United States. Reform efforts, moreover, continue in both countries. A new statute that went into effect in 2001 aims to cut back yet further on incarceration in France; and a 2001 draft German legislative reform shows some of the same spirit.[17] Whether in Germany or in France, the same rule holds: even when Europeans decide to ball their fists and strike, they do not strike with the ferocity of Americans.

Mildness in the Flexibility of Punishment

More important, when Europeans ball their fists and strike, they strike at a much smaller class of persons than Americans do. For France and Germany have experienced nothing like the American drive toward harsher punishment for all classes of offenders. Quite the contrary. While French and German legal cultures have in some respects grown harsher, they have grown harsher *only with regard to a shrinking class of mostly violent offenders*. If the map of American society has been recolored to show many more potentially "criminal" zones, the maps of German and French society have been recolored in exactly the opposite way, to show ever fewer "criminal" zones.

To begin with, European imprisonment practice, by contrast with American, has generally restricted itself to targeting violent offenders, and indeed only a proportion of those. In place of the broad-gauged harshness of the American kind, these northern European societies have seen a narrowly crafted harshness aimed at a relatively restricted class:[18] violent offenders, terrorists, certain sex offenders, drug dealers.[19] Indeed, the new French statute deviates strikingly from French traditions of prosecutorial power, putting sharp limits on the incarceration of persons accused of property offenses.[20] What American politicians often claim they are doing—targeting violent crime—is what continental criminal justice systems are in fact doing. If you do not belong to the limited class of targeted criminals in Europe, you have in fact become less and less likely to suffer imprisonment over the last few decades. Much of the apparent new harshness in European *criminalization of conduct* has thus been mitigated by a growing mildness in *flexibility of punishment*. Indeed, the overwhelming majority of nonviolent offenders, and even many first time violent offenders, are no longer incarcerated at all in the European countries. Imprisonment is simply no longer the ordinary sanction. Instead, the alternative sanctions of fines and probation have, by sharp contrast with the United States,[21] increasingly become the order of the day.[22]

The so-called "day fine" system, which has spread throughout northern Europe in the last decades, is the best known of these alternative sanctions.[23] Fines as an alternative to imprisonment have a long history in both Germany and France. In Germany in particular, they have had a steadily growing place in punishment practice since the late nineteenth century.[24] Day fines are thus nothing fundamentally new. Nevertheless, along with probation, they have assumed an increasingly prominent emphasis in the thinking of European criminal justice specialists—an emphasis that is indicative of a continuing assumption that thinking about criminal justice means thinking primarily about milder ways to punish. The day fine system, which originated in Scandinavia, allows judges to commute time servable into fines, which are tailored both to the defendant's ability to pay, and (at least in principle) to the defendant's degree of integration into the society around him. If he is deemed suitable, for each day the defendant would have spent in prison, he is instead obliged to pay a fine calculated according to his earning power. Failure to pay that fine sends him behind bars.

To one degree or another, every northern European country has turned the day fine, or probation in some other form, for all but the most serious, and especially violent, offenses.[25] Indeed, even very high-profile violent offenders often do no time. When Günter Parche stabbed tennis star Monica Seles, Americans expected that he would receive a long prison sentence, as would surely have been the case in the United States. Following normal German practice, though, he received a sentence of probation.[26] Similar examples can be easily multiplied in both France and Germany. Even offenders who have dominated the headlines in Europe often do very little, or no time. But it is important to emphasize that fines are not the only sanction European offenders receive. Probation is also extremely common, especially in France.[27] So is community service, mostly involving maintenance and other "environmental" work,[28] first introduced in 1983 as an alternative sanction in France.[29] Orders of community service have become the sanction of choice for property-offenders in particular, whom French law has come more and more to shield from imprisonment.[30] Under the new draft German statute too, orders of community service should become more and more common.[31]

This is markedly different from the United States. (In American state prisons, property offenders, far from facing sentences of community service, make up roughly half of the total population. As of 1994, 75 percent of burglars were sentenced to either prison or jail in American state courts, and 68 percent of nonviolent property offenders overall.)[32] Indeed, the picture of American prisons—a picture in which disproportionate numbers of inmates serve long sentences for drug possession[33] or for theft—is worlds apart from the picture of either French or German prisons. Drug users (as opposed to drug dealers) simply do not find themselves in prison in Europe, except in the most exceptional circumstances;[34] nor do many thieves, if they do not do violence. Prison in Europe is truly an exceptional sanction. This is reflected in a striking fact about the French prison population: while the total population has sharply risen, the *number of admissions* in French prisons has sharply declined since 1980.[35] Those who are in are staying much longer, but many fewer are going in. The same holds for juveniles: despite the campaign to crack down on juvenile offenders, French efforts have been directed much more toward education than toward more severe punishment.[36]

More generally, individualization, and its associated value of resocialization, have perdured in Europe, despite all political winds that have blown from the right, and despite a loss of faith in rehabilitation not all that different from the American loss of faith. Like their American counterparts, European penologists make only diffident claims about the success of rehabilitation programs. Nevertheless, European bureaucrats keep those programs alive. So do European politicians, who remain receptive to professional advice. Indeed, the same French Criminal Code of 1994 that set nominally longer sentences also set a new benchmark in its commitment to the practices of individualization for almost all convicts.[37] While nominal sentences in the code are sometimes long, they are compensated for by an elaborate system of individualization, supervised by a special class of judges. This system presupposes that inmates will typically be released early. In Germany, too, individualization, oriented toward treatment and resocialization, remains unchallenged orthodox doctrine in the practice of punishment, even if academics occasionally raise doubts about it.[38]

Moreover, in both countries, even among those who have raised doubts about resocialization, there has not been anything like the dramatic American turn to Beccarian act-egalitarianism. On the contrary, the ideas of Beccaria remain, in the thinking of continental punishment theory specialists, an obvious dead end.[39]

The inhospitability to Beccarian act-egalitarianism in Germany and France is indeed of capital interest for my story; and it is well worth summarizing the standard European wisdom on Beccaria, which opens vistas of differences between continental and American cultural traditions. It has been a standard critique of Beccaria for a very long time in Europe that his tariff of punishments really constitutes a list of *prices* and not a list of *fines*—an invitation to commit crimes offered to all who are willing to pay.[40] Beccarianism, for Europeans, has long represented a kind of market-orientation in punishment—and it goes almost without saying that Europeans are less hospitable to a market-orientation than Americans are.

But the European distaste for Beccaria goes beyond that. Europeans often observe that Beccaria's focus on criminal acts rather than on criminal depravity does not really comport with sound ideas of justice. Nineteenth-century criminal law scholars and judges, they observe, began to drift away from Beccarian ideals from an early date—and for a reason: they were quickly faced with cases in which it seemed unjust to subject different offenders to the same penalty.[41] Indeed, the century-long retreat from Beccarianism after the initial phase of the French Revolution is, Europeans argue, telling evidence of the weakness of Beccaria's concepts. True egalitarianism in punishment, the European standard literature argues, involves, is not an egalitarianism of the equal treatment for all persons who have committed the same act; rather it is the egalitarianism of equal treatment for all persons who have shown the same degree of moral depravity.[42] Indeed, punishment must always be tempered by some sort of regard for the person. This necessary respect for persons can be accomplished, in the standard European view, as it was accomplished in the nineteenth century: by easing the punishment of some individuals whose acts have been accompanied by "extenuating circumstances." Or it can be achieved as Europeans achieve it today: through individualization. But it must be achieved in some way. Some sort of systematic mitigation, founded in regard for the individual offender, must be introduced. (The same orientation toward depravity, informed by an understanding of the individual personality of the offender, governs European conceptions of proportionality in punishment.)[43]

This skeptical view of Beccaria could once be heard in America as well. Today it is dying out among Americans, while it hangs on in Europe. Thereby hangs a tale of very deep cultural difference.

Mildness in the Application of Punishment

What about life in prison for those who do receive prison sentences in Europe? The answer is that here too the United States and Europe have embarked on different paths. Indeed, differences in the law of prison conditions offer some of the most dramatic and revealing evidence of the widening divide in Western punishment.

It was not always so. The law of prison conditions is an area in which, for a long while, American and European developments seemed to run parallel. As we have seen, the brief high era of American prison reform began in the early 1960s and reached its high point in the early to mid-1970s, culminating with the Constitutional Rights of Incarcerated Persons Act in 1980. During the same period, European history was not terribly different. Thus in Germany, modern reforms effectively began in 1961.[44] The impact of a number of scandals led to a gradual change, though throughout the 1960s many German law still generally held (as the Nazis had held) that the purpose of prison was to inflict painful retribution, not to resocialize.[45] A massive criminal law reform of 1969, which decriminalized many morals offenses, signaled a change in attitude, which was encouraged by a 1972 decision of the Constitutional Court.[46] Reform agitation multiplied,[47] and in 1976 a new, reformist Code of Punishment (*Strafvollzugsgesetz*) was passed, which is still in effect. The reform impulse has waxed and waned since, especially under the impact of terrorism, but overall the drive toward reform has clearly continued.[48] In France, reform began earlier, with an epoch-making reform measure of 1945. Agitation during the 1960s, especially during the crises of the Algerian war and of 1968, met with some governmental resistance against further prison reform. By the 1970s and 1980s, though, French reform seeming to moving in tandem with German and American, with major pieces of reform legislation passed in 1975 and 1981.[49]

As of about 1980, indeed, one would have said that the law of prison conditions was developing in the same reformist direction on both sides of the Atlantic, and on more or less the same timetable. Since that time, though, everything has changed. The American attitude has shifted profoundly, as we have seen; while Europeans have continued on the reformist course.

That is not to say that French and German prison conditions have become unambiguously good. Especially in France, and especially in French investigative custody, prison conditions are scandalous at times.[50] Indeed in both countries, there are horrors associated with investigative custody, to which I will return shortly. Moreover the French, unlike the Americans, have not been engaged in a large-scale prison-building program; and the French physical plant is in a state of terrible decay, despite some systematic efforts at improvement over the last ten years.[51] But the question is not so much what prison conditions are currently like, as whether the desire to reform conditions is still alive; and the desire to reform conditions is very much alive in both France and Germany—while American law has embraced views that range from a Pilatelike washing of the hands to pure vindictiveness.

The result is undoubtedly that the situation in the prisons of Europe has gotten much better than the situation in the prisons of America. It should be admitted at once that it is no easy matter to discover what prison conditions are really like, either at home or abroad. The black-letter source of information is the book of prison regulations; but it is hard to believe that the prison regulations of any country are scrupulously followed in practice. The fact that the rules say that a prisoner should be treated in such and such a way is small assurance that prisoners are in fact so treated. The prisoners themselves are untrustworthy sources, and so are prison officials.[52] One can visit the prisons—and indeed one should, if one wants to write a comparative study. Nevertheless, a visit to a prison in any country undoubtedly leaves a cheerier impression than insider's knowledge of that prison would warrant; what one sees is always a façade.

Still, it has to be said that European façades are handsomer. And indeed, there are good reasons for accepting the common wisdom that European prison conditions are far better than American prison conditions. To be sure, France in particular has been the scene of regular scandals, with two official government inquests publishing a severe indictment of conditions in July 2000. Violence is unquestionably a part of the French prison experience. Some of this violence takes the form of beatings and sexual abuse by prison personnel.[53] Some of it—undoubtedly most of it—takes the form of inmate-on-inmate violence.[54] As for German prisons, they undoubtedly still have their hierarchical order, and prisoners are undoubtedly still exposed to abuse both from guards and from other prisoners (though a standard German treatment makes this point by citing *American* sociology).[55] Most especially, German imprisonment remains a miserable experience for nonnative Germans.[56]

Still, Europe is not America. First and foremost, Europeans remain committed to improving conditions. Even the French scandal of 2000 is evidence of that. The scandal of 2000 was kindled by an exposé, published by a doctor who had worked in La Santé, a large investigative custody institution in Paris. This exposé was not entirely fair;[57] but it had a powerful impact on French politics. A major inquest began; and French politicians of all major tendencies, and in every branch of French government, vied with each other over the issue of prison reform, with both houses of the legislature producing reformist reports that ran into the hundreds of pages.[58] What was stunning about all this, from the American point of view, is that these French politicians entered into a contest to show who had the deeper commitment to making punishment more *humane*. I was, as it happens, present in France during the summer of 2000, and I can report that French politics, during the weeks of scandal, involved denouncing your opponents for failing to care enough about the rights and dignity of convicts. This is so wildly different from the pattern of American politics that I fear that my readers may simply not believe it; and yet it is so. As the Paris newspapers summed the situation up, whatever conflict there may be in French politics, there is a "republican consensus"[59] that the values of republicanism in France require that offenders be treated with dignity. (The report of the Sénat was tellingly entitled "Prisons: A Humiliation for the Republic.") *Everybody* claims to be for reform, in a society in which the republican tradition evidently means something other than what it means in the United States. (Indeed, for some commentators, the 2000 prison scandal was the occasion for pointedly distancing French democracy from American.)[60]

The politics of punishment in France—and in Germany as well[61]—is indeed profoundly different from the politics of punishment in the United States, which in turn suggests that French and German cultures are profoundly different. It is not that Germany and France lack for the sorts of scandals, egregious crimes, and horror-stories that fuel the politics of crackdown. German and French newspapers and television shows are full of frightening crime stories, just like American papers and shows.[62] The difference, rather, is that public fear and outrage do not have the impact on continental politics that they do in the United States.[63]

The same differences show in the continuing involvement of European courts in the reform of prison conditions. As we have seen, American courts have lost much of what authority they had to intervene in prison conditions after *Wilson v. Seiter*. During the same period, European courts have entered a new age of interventionism. This interventionism comes partly from the domestic German and French courts themselves, which have not ceased to engage in reform—though to be sure, they have never had the authority to issue structural injunctions of the American kind. But European interventionism also comes from a different quarter: from the European Union, and the European Court of Human Rights in Strasbourg, whose pronouncements are doing immense work in reshaping punishment practices in both France and Germany.[64] Both domestic and European Community courts have been able to invoke conventions on human rights that have gone unsigned, unratified, or ratified only with crippling reservations in the United States, and they are increasingly doing so. The twilight age of withdrawal from prison reform for American courts has thus been the age of dawning engagement on the other side of the globe. This is one area where America's common-law courts are growing weaker while continental courts are growing stronger.

Moreover, bad as things undoubtedly can still be in European prisons, there are a number of reasons for believing that the problem of both official and unofficial violence is less on the European Continent—especially in Germany—than it is in the United States. While there are undoubtedly some ferocious guards in European prisons, one important thing sets them apart from their American counterparts: European prison guards are ordinary civil service appointees, who receive training in programs that typically last about eighteen months in Germany, and six to eight months in France.[65] Indeed, the French have just invested in the construction of a handsome multimillion-dollar campus for training prison personnel at Agen in the Southwest. To chat with a German or French prison guard is to encounter a person who has been very carefully indoctrinated in professional norms of individualization and respect. This means something in a world in which there is a spirit of professionalism that one often (though not always) misses in the United States. The fact that European prison guards absorb a professionalized attitude is simply typical of a world in which bakers and hairdressers too are proud of displaying professional knowledge and training. Because norms of professionalization are so strong, one guesses that, while prison regulations may sometimes be flouted in Europe, they are nevertheless flouted less often than they are in the United States. Guards, moreover, in both countries, do not ever ordinarily carry weapons. (This is in theory also the case in the United States; but there is room here for doubt.)

As for violence between inmates, it too can hardly have been eradicated in either Germany or France. Still, the problem of overcrowding, while it is present, is far less severe than it is in American prisons, and this must have some effect on inmate-on-inmate violence. We will never know how much violence there is in any prison; but we can hazard the guess that where violence remains a raging plague in American prisons, it may have become something more like a chronic illness in European ones. This is reflected in the literature of denunciation that has grown up around European prisons as it has around American. One recent description of life in a French prison makes out the experience of the overcrowded investigative custody jail in which the inmate is first placed in to be fearsome; but describes life in Fresnes, the large institution for prisoners serving longer sentences, to be quite humane.[66] Certainly persons who have seen prisons both in America and Europe are likely to prefer European ones, and especially German ones—as is witnessed, for example, by the efforts of fugitive financier Martin Frankel to remain imprisoned in Hamburg rather than being extradited to the United States.[67] The problem of violence is thus almost surely less urgent in European prisons than in American ones.

To be sure, it would be a mistake to paint too simple a picture. One form of European incarceration is the locus of pronounced problems: investigative custody, in heavy use in both France and Germany. Continental investigative custody is an institution that, at first glance, seems to confirm inveterate American suspicions about the unfairness and harshness of European justice. Continental, and especially French, law-enforcement officials have long had powers that seem nearly tyrannical to Americans. Investigating magistrates have historically had the power to hold suspects with few of the procedural checks that Americans take for granted. Richard Frase has offered some powerful arguments to show that French investigators do not in fact have more unbridled power than American ones,[68] but it is certainly true that continental justice has a long history of granting fearsome leeway to investigating authorities. Thus it may seem entirely unsurprising to American readers that investigative custody facilities are routinely the worst in continental Europe. Bad prison conditions, long terms of incarceration, and overcrowding have dogged investigative custody facilities in both Germany and France.[69] In this, Americans may see the dark side of continental justice—a world of the relatively raw exercise of state power.

And there is some truth in the notion that investigative custody reveals the continental dark side—but only some. First and foremost, while the powers of investigating officers, and the conditions of investigative detention, can be disquieting in Europe, the critical fact is that Europeans are trying to *reform* them. This is especially true of France, where a new "law on the presumption of innocence" went into effect in 2001. This massive reform created a host of procedural protections for accused persons, and even a new class of judges charged with the task of safeguarding the rights of accused persons.[70] This reform had some shortcomings: in particular, the French government did not provide enough funding to support it—with the result that there was considerable resistance from criminal justice professionals.[71] Nevertheless, the point remains: even with regard to procedural protections, historically better maintained in the United States than in continental Europe, the Europeans are pressing to make punishment *milder*, during the very era of the American crackdown. (As for German protections against the exercise of state power, they are certainly lacking in ways that would shock Americans.[72] Nevertheless, limitations on such things as investigative custody are quite serious,[73] and the last couple of decades have seen many reforms—though in the wake of the attacks of September 11, 2001, German police powers were expanded.)[74]

There may be a dark history of deference to state power on the continent, but nowadays Europeans are generally groping toward the light. Moreover, it is important to understand why conditions are (again: relatively) bad in continental investigative custody institutions. In part, conditions are undoubtedly bad because these facilities are indeed used for a kind of raw exercise of prosecutorial power. Investigating magistrates have an interest in maintaining bad conditions in detention facilities: it gives them a strategic advantage if they can threaten offenders with a stay in bad conditions. At least one French magistrate acknowledged to me that this was the case. There is a prosecutorial constituency for maintaining tough conditions in investigative custody. On the other hand, there is an entirely different reason for those same bad conditions—a reason emphasized to me by prison administrators in both France and Germany. Investigative custody facilities are very difficult to control from the bureaucratic point of view. Administrators have no means of predicting how many prisoners will be delivered to them, at what hour of the day or night, and for what offense. A soccer match in Munich or Paris can result in the sudden appearance of dozens of detainees for whom administrators have no dossier, and about whom they have too little information to arrange safe housing. The administrative problem in these facilities is not just that there is too much state power; it is also that there is too little: Investigative custody facilities escape bureaucratic control, and for that reason it is hard to maintain civilized conditions in them.

At any rate, there certainly are bad conditions in continental prisons, and they are most especially to be found in investigative custody. Moreover, violent criminals and recidivists are not quite the only persons imprisoned in Europe. Certain crimes—some thefts, military infractions, immigration offenses—continue to carry prison sentences.[75] Most important, there is another class of persons who are not an avowed target, but who are nevertheless clearly singled out: ethnic and national minorities. Foreigners represent about a quarter of the incarcerated population in France—down from about 30 percent in 1993.[76] In Germany in 1994, more than 20 percent of inmates were classified as "non-German," and in certain types of institutions their representation was considerably higher—as much as 45 percent of those being held in investigative custody in the German state of Nordrhein-Westfalen,[77] and roughly two-thirds in the Munich investigative custody facility Stadlheim.[78]

Clearly, there is racism in European justice. Moreover, the problem is magnified by the practice of keeping aliens pending deportation in investigative custody—by contrast with the United States, where deportable aliens are kept in special camps.[79] (Such special camps would be difficult to introduce in Europe: They would carry too many associations with the concentration camps of the fascist period.) There can be no doubt of the existence of real, and entrenched, racism in continental criminal justice. This is a significant fact—but a fact whose significance deserves some careful explication. There *is* racism in continental Europe, just as there is in the United States. Nevertheless, punishment in continental Europe remains far milder, and far more respectful, than it is in our own country. Persons of dark skin are far more likely to get entangled with the criminal justice system in France or Germany, just as they are in the United States. Yet the French and German systems continue to take a very different approach from the American. As we observed in the last chapter, this is a strong indication that racism *as such* is not what "causes" harshness in American punishment: the cultural constellation is much more complex than that.

In any event, "foreigners" do belong to the universe of imprisonable persons in continental legal culture. Nevertheless, the fact remains that, taken all in all, that universe is far more restricted than its American counterpart. Where the overall American tendency has been to land more and more persons, of more and more varied description, in prison, the overall European tendency has been exactly the opposite.

Criminalization

Harshness in the Criminalization of Conduct

This is a category in which the differences between continental Europe and the United States is not all that stark.

Certainly, governments throughout Europe have engaged, since the late 1960s, in large-scale decriminalization of morals offenses. Various kinds of sex and intoxication offenses that would once have carried a prison term have been stricken entirely from the books. Prostitution makes for a particularly striking contrast with the United States. American prostitutes, and their clients, have been the subjects of a growing crackdown in many parts of the United States; clients in particular have been the favorite targets of shame sanctions; and police departments have expended considerable manpower on suppressing prostitution. In northern Europe, by contrast, prostitution has been legalized everywhere, although procuring remains an offense.[80] Indeed, prostitution may now be moving toward the sort of normalization that includes extending the ordinary benefits of the social welfare state to prostitutes; and that may end with the legalization of procurement and of brothels. The treatment of drug users shows a similar pattern.[81] This sort of decriminalization has had an impact on the changing incidence of punishment in Europe. Decriminalization of morals offenses is something that is not directly reflected in the statistical figures on European sentencing; those figures reckon only sentencing for what are defined as crimes. Yet decriminalizing "immoral" acts is the equivalent of reducing the sentence for those acts to zero.

Still, there has been much that directly parallels American developments, and that has sometimes been directly inspired by American developments. White-collar crime has been attacked in both countries—indeed, both have adopted the American term "white-collar" to describe it. This attack has not gone as far in Europe as it has in the United States, though. In France, a 1975 law against "economic and financial infractions" represented an important attack on white-collar offenses. By the mid-1980s, however, French law began to move in the direction of decriminalization.[82] In part, this involved decriminalizing something that has never been criminalized to the same degree in the United States: bankruptcy. As we shall see, one of the critical factors distinguishing European from American development has been the greater European willingness to prosecute bankruptcy as a crime.[83] Moreover, imprisonment for debt in one form or another remains theoretically possible, and carefully regulated, not only in France but also in Germany—though actual imprisonment for debt is anything but common.[84] But the "dépénalisation" that began in the mid-1980s goes beyond bankruptcy; and at least one prominent book has argued that all economic offenses should be treated as civil and not criminal matters.[85] Moreover, the punishment of economic crime is limited in a very important way. Uncomfortable with the idea of inflicting ordinary criminal punishments, the French system has developed a whole class of special mild punishments. These are called "criminal administrative sanctions"; and they are regarded as so fundamentally different from ordinary criminal punishment that they have raised serious constitutional questions in France.[86] Ordinary criminal sanctions are still available; but they are limited effectively to fines, with imprisonment almost never inflicted on white-collar offenders.[87] Even where there has been criminalization of white-collar offenses over the last twenty-five years, in short, the French system has shown a drive toward systematic mitigation in the law of punishment.

In Germany too, punishment is systematically mild. To be sure, on paper the German treatment of white-collar crime looks rather like the American treatment. Offenses like insider trading have found their way into German law as well as American law, for example. But it is misleading to look at the statute book alone. In practice, in Germany (as indeed elsewhere in Europe), prosecutions are rare and convictions even rarer. As the *Wall Street Journal* informed its readers in a recent study, "Europe's Police Are Out of Luck on Insider Cases."[88] European businessfolk still have far less to fear than their American counterparts. In Germany in particular, this is also partly true because of traditions of mildness in *grading*. German law has a long tradition of treating economic offenses as mere *Ordnungswidrigkeiten*, violations of good order. This concept was indeed first introduced in the 1950s as a way of effectively decriminalizing the many economic and monetary offenses that had been penalized under Nazi and occupation law. Criminalization of white-collar crime in Germany has partly meant grading offenses upward, so that they are no longer treated as such *Ordnungswidrigkeiten*. But the Germans, like the French, show some real discomfort about this. Some white-collar offenses, after much debate, are still graded simply as *Ordnungswidrigkeiten*.[89] Like the French, the Germans show some hesitation to pursue all economic offenses as clear evils in the fullest sense.[90]

In important ways, moreover, both German and French approaches to white-collar crime do not reflect the new spirit of harshness of the last quarter-century at all. White-collar criminalization in both countries is not innovative as it is in the United States; rather it is rooted in older concepts of liability. Bankruptcy is an example. In both countries, the old criminal law of bankruptcy remains important: debtors who conceal assets are subject to imprisonment, and indeed, even in Germany ordinary insolvents may theoretically be imprisoned for short periods.[91] There are certainly criminal frauds that show up in American bankruptcy courts; but the traditional notion of criminal bankruptcy has long since vanished.[92] Beyond bankruptcy, though, it is striking that white-collar offenses are frequently conceived, in both Germany and France, in wholly traditional ways: as violations of *trust*—as crimes of "disloyalty"—or as variants on traditional forms of fraud.[93] These are venerable and familiar ways of thinking about white-collar crime. Europeans thus display much less of the spirit of inventiveness in detecting new forms of crime than we do;[94] and such white-collar criminalization as there has been on the continent makes for less of a dramatic departure from the traditions of the law than is the case in the United States.

Mildness in the Criminalization of Classes of Persons

Nevertheless, it would be wrong to deny that we can see some degree of criminalization of new classes of persons in the continental pursuit of white-collar crime. Milder though continental law is, it does show some of the same tendency as American law to allow criminal liability to creep up the status scale. This is, once again, a worldwide phenomenon—though it is one that has found a particularly congenial home in American culture.

The same is true of the pursuit of politicians. Like the United States, both Germany and France have had high-profile political scandals in the last few years. Yet even those scandals suggest that the fire that is burning everywhere is burning more fiercely in the United States. The most notable of the scandals in Germany is the funding scandal surrounding former chancellor Helmut Kohl. Kohl was vigorously attacked in 2000 for collection of unaccounted-for slush funds—and more particularly for offenses his opponents sought to characterize, in typical continental fashion, as "Untreue," disloyalty.[95] This is surely a sign of real change in German culture. At the same time, Kohl defended himself with at least some political success by invoking his "Ehrenwort," his "word of honor." Refusing to disclose the sources of the funds in question, he asserted that he had given his "word of honor" to his donors—a defense that would only occasion incredulity in America, but one that apparently still carries political weight with much of the German public.[96] Men of "honor" remain, in important ways, more immune from liability in Germany than in the United States.

In France too, there have been quite a number of scandals—such, for example, as the Elf-Aquitaine prosecution, which resulted in the conviction and imprisonment of Roland Dumas. Something like American developments is clearly going on in France as well. Nevertheless, there remain revealing differences of degree, as, for example, in the so-called "Tainted Blood Scandal." Three leading officials, including former prime minister Laurent Fabius, were prosecuted before a special tribunal for knowingly allowing the distribution of HIV-tainted blood. In 1999, Fabius and former social affairs minister Georgina Dufoix were acquitted. Former health minister Edmond Hervé was convicted, but not sentenced.[97] Their prosecution was no small thing. But they came off easy by comparison with many American officials since the time of Watergate; and their very prosecution made some French jurists quite uncomfortable. To Olivier Beaud, for example, a leading specialist in public law, it seemed a fundamental violation of norms of good government to subject officials to any criminal liability for official acts.[98] There are other examples too, though—both of successful pursuit of politicians, and of failures.[99]

There has been, in short, more liability for more classes of persons, but by no means as much so as in the United States. And, of course, juveniles in Europe remain juveniles.[100]

Mildness in Grading

Grading is an especially important measure for understanding continental mildness. European jurists have been struggling for generations to develop concepts that will redefine a variety of offenses as something other than "crimes." Mildness in grading has a deep, complex, and old juristic tradition behind it in Europe. As early as the Napoleonic criminal code of 1810, European lawyers began to distinguish among different grades of offense. The 1810 code established what are still three grades in French criminal law, subject to three different kinds of punishment: "contravention," "délit," and "crime."[101] Neither of the first two was understood to rise fully to the level of crime. Germany too has seen, over the last half-century, a considerable effort to expand the range of offenses understood to be, not crimes, but mere *Ordnungswidrigkeiten*, "violations of good order."[102] More and more offenses have come to fall under this rubric, and the pressure to expand the category of *Ordnungswidrigkeiten* continues. The contrast with the United States is striking indeed. While the drive in American law has been to reclassify more and more matters of "disorderly conduct" or "violations" as crimes, the tendency in continental Europe has been exactly the opposite.

These are not just matters of terminology. First of all, this kind of terminological decriminalization is of real dignitary importance: a person convicted of something that is not "really" a crime is a person who has not been stigmatized as "really" a criminal. Thus it is significant that French law tends to regard white-collar offenses as *délits* or *contraventions* rather than as *crimes*; just as German law has long regarded them as *Ordnungswidrigkeiten*. The treatment of drug offenses is similarly significant: drug-*dealers* on the continent are generally treated as criminals, and they belong to the shrinking class of persons who find themselves in prison. Drug consumption, by contrast, is generally graded low if it is penalized at all.[103]

Moreover, there is an ongoing European drive to downgrade offenses, which is an essential doctrinal predicate for the growing leniency of continental punishment. To apply a phrase coined by Daniel Moynihan, continental law shows a continued strong drive to "define deviancy down,"[104] in a way that contrasts sharply with the current American drive toward "zero tolerance."[105] Thus the French reform of 1975 gave courts the option of substituting "complementary punishments" for imprisonment is cases of délit; indeed, it is precisely these "minor" offenses that have generally ceased to carry any prison term since 1975.[106] Redubbing "complementary punishments" as "alternatives," the 1994 Criminal Code allowed judges and prosecutors to use them to replace the fines ordinarily assessed in cases of contraventions as well.[107] French judges thus now have considerable authority to craft lesser penalties that will keep those offenders who are not defined as "criminals" out of prison. And, it deserves emphasis, they have this authority partly *because* the code has found ways to define offenders as something other than "criminals." The shrinking universe of the criminal and the growing mildness of punishment are two sides of the same coin.

Harshness in Inflexible Doctrines of Liability

This is an area in which European criminal law has come, at first glance, to look somewhat harsher. Doctrines of extenuating circumstances have been abandoned, in the new French Code, in favor of individualization in punishment.[108] In similar ways, the German Criminal Code aims to guarantee that offenders will not benefit from double-counting, receiving milder treatment both at the sentencing phase and in the course of the individualization of their punishment.[109] These do not reflect any drive toward increased harshness, though. Rather, in both countries, flexibility in doctrines of liability is gradually being replaced by flexibility in the application of punishment.

Harshness in Enforcement

It is too empirically difficult to form any firm sense of how continental law should be measured by this category.

Respect and Mercy

Let me come, finally, to my last two measures of mildness.

The Mildness of Respectful Treatment

We have seen that prison life is probably less violent on the continent than it is in the United States. Focusing exclusively on the question of violence would however be a mistake. For a large part of what most strikingly characterizes the law of European prisons is its concern with something that is almost entirely missing in the law of American ones: a concern with the *dignity* of prisoners. With this indeed we come to the matter of central importance for my argument. Dignitary concerns are pursued in Europe with an intensity unlike anything to be found in the United States, and it is to those concerns I now turn.

The intense interest that surrounds dignitary questions in European prison law can be disconcerting to Americans; reading the European literature is, from time to time, a strange experience. What can Americans think, when they discover that one of the most lively controversies in the German prison law of the late 1990s turned on the question of whether guards should be required to *knock* in all cases before entering prisoners' cells?[110] What can they think when they discover that the very first of complaints about prison conditions raised by Mme. Baste-Morand, a prominent French reformer in 1982, was the absence of—a "right to respect"? "The Right to Respect.

Guards are forbidden to address a prisoner as 'Monsieur.' Exactly the opposite should be the rule."[111]

Other reformers have certainly detected worse scandals in French prisons. Nevertheless, the very fact that anyone could give first priority to the proposition that prisoners need to be addressed as "Monsieur" shows that matters are different in France from what they are in the United States—and in a way that we need the resources of a cultural anthropology to explain. Even harsher denunciations of French prisons can fall oddly on American ears. Thus a 1999 exposé in *Le Monde*, during the initial run-up to the current round of prison reform, deplored behavior by guards that included "racist insults, sexual harassment, and regular beatings."[112] How striking that, in a summary that is meant to express outrage, two varieties of disrespectful insult should precede any mention of violence! What denunciatory account of an American high-security facility would ever begin by complaining of insults? Violence is, in fact, only a part of what European reformers care about. As the German debate over knocking, and Mme. Baste-Morand's list of complaints suggest, the right to "respect" and the right to "dignity" also play a large role in the humanitarian law of European prisons—and it is dignity of a deeply different kind from the kind pursued by American reformers.

That "dignity" matters in European prisons is, of course, not news. European thinking has produced a number of much-admired declarations and recommendations on safeguarding "human dignity" in prison conditions.[113] It is easy to cite regulations according to the letter of which, at least, to be a convict in continental Europe is to enjoy safeguards for one's "dignity" that few would claim for American prisoners. But what exactly does this "dignity" consist in? The important answer is that dignity in European imprisonment is much like the "dignity" that prevails in other corners of European legal culture: it is a dignity that blends concepts of entitlement in the modern social state with much older ideas of personal honor. Moreover, it is "dignity" that pursues one extremely revealing goal: it aims to avoid the sort of *status-degradation* that is a prime feature of American criminal justice culture.

Indeed, by contrast with American punishment law, the punishment law of both France and Germany is expressly designed to avoid any sort of punishment practice that would create any sense of status differentiation between prisoners and the general population. On the contrary, practices in both countries are supposed to dramatize the fact that inmates are *just like everybody else*. In part this has involved one reform in the technical legal consequences of conviction: Europeans have fully abolished "civil death," the old erasure of civil personality and political rights that used to be a consequence of many criminal convictions. (Full-scale "civil death" is gone in the United States too; but loss of political rights remains common.) The contrast is striking. Very few European offenders suffer the expulsion from political and public life that can come with a felony conviction and its attendant disabilities in the United States. European judges still deprive some offenders of their civic rights for some period of time. But this is never done automatically, and it is always imposed as a temporary measure. There is none of the American notion that every felon should instantly be classed as something less than a full citizen. (Quite the contrary: in both France and Germany, efforts are made to encourage convicts to exercise political rights as a way of reintegrating them into normal society.)[114] European offenders do not lose membership in the political community.

But it is perhaps even more important that they do not lose membership in what we might call the *social* community. The effort to keep offenders symbolically integrated into society involves what sometimes are some very striking measures. Most notable of all, perhaps, is one measure that has much preoccupied both French and German law, and that shows that there are ideas coursing under the surface of the continental idea of dignity that are alien to any we can find in America. Under modern reforms, the obligation of wearing prison uniforms has been generally eliminated, on the grounds that this practice diminishes the dignity of prisoners. Though practices differ somewhat under the letter of French and German law, and according to the rules in different continental prisons, the general tendency is the same everywhere. Where uniforms are required at all, they are required only in the prison workplace; and where they are required, efforts are made to guarantee that they resemble ordinary clothing in the outside world. This is, from the point of view of cultural anthropology, a revealing reform: changes in dress are a classic means of signaling a change in status.[115]

The question of uniforms has played a particularly prominent role in French reform discussions; there is in fact a kind of horror of uniforms that runs through the French law.[116] Moreover, French punishment professionals also see the same sorts of dignitary issues at play in other questions too—such as whether visitors may be kept behind a glass partition.[117] (In both Germany and France, the use of glass partitions is restricted, and the partitions themselves are frequently low panes of glass that divide an otherwise open table.) This hostility both to the wearing of uniforms and to isolation behind glass partitions are central to the atmosphere of French reforms, and both suggest something important. There is a deep disinclination, in French law, to accept an idea that has a powerful grip on American punishment culture: the idea that conviction works a deprivation of the offender's humanity, as measured by isolation from other human beings and loss of control over the presentation of self. Prison uniforms and isolation in various forms, like routine searches and other lack of privacy protections, are part of what makes American convicts feel that they have been branded as lesser human beings.

Now, it should be emphasized that these ambitions do not make French prisons humane places. Life in French prisons is very rough. Nevertheless, the ambitions certainly make some difference, and they are revealing about the reigning spirit in French criminal justice. French convicts, at least in theory, are indeed not supposed to feel *branded*. On the contrary, it is the drive of French dignitary legislation to insist that convicts are just like everybody else. The same drive is to be found in Germany—strikingly captured, in the German Code of Punishment Practice, by what is called the *Angleichungs-*

grundsatz, the principle of approximation, or, as I will call it, the "principle of normalcy." This principle, enshrined in the third paragraph of the Code of Punishment and worked out with typical juristic care by the German legal profession, holds that prison life must resemble as closely as possible life in the outside world.[118] In some respects, the principle of normalcy has left German inmates a shade less well off than French ones, at least in theory.[119] Thus the letter of German regulations says that they, unlike French prisoners, must ordinarily wear prison uniforms.[120] (Prison officials do have discretion to lift this requirement, though, and in the maximum security prison that I visited in Berlin, inmates did not in fact wear uniforms. Only in the investigative custody facility that I visited in Munich were uniforms in use, and there only in the workplace.) The story does not end there, though. Even where they are obliged to wear uniforms, dignitary concerns set German practices apart from American: German uniforms must resemble the clothing worn in the outside world.[121] American-style day-glo uniforms are carefully avoided on dignitary grounds, as are stripes or anything else that might make convicts feel branded. German rules also carefully specify that inmates, at their initial admission, are to be dressed in their uniforms outside the presence of third parties.[122] Explicitly sensitive to the idea that special dress works a status degradation, German reformers have tried to eliminate whatever is most humiliating about uniforms.[123] Many other provisions reflect a far-reaching concern, in German law, that prisoners should not feel that they have been cast out from ordinary society.[124] Any regulation that could be understood as in any way symbolically branding prisoners is out. Such an approach is unimaginable in the world of American jurisprudence—a world in which the Supreme Court takes it for granted that prisoners could not conceivably expect to live in the way persons in the outside world do.[125] The German code does not "mandate comfortable prisons"[126] any more than the United States Constitution does; but it does mandate circumstances that will minimize the degree to which inmates feel themselves assigned to a subclass of human beings, different from those on the outside.

This idea of "normalcy" for convicts, shared by both French and German systems, this ambition to guarantee that inmates will not undergo symbolic status-degradation, may seem a minor thing to my American readers, who will think of problems in prison conditions primarily as problems of *violence*. Who cares, they may ask, if prisoners do or do not wear uniforms? Yet if my American readers find these dignitary issues to be minor matters, that only shows that they are American readers. If American readers find these issues to be minor ones, that fact only effectively poses the question of this book all the more sharply. Why are American perceptions different, and with what consequences?

At any rate, the continental commitment to normalcy, to the proposition that prisoners should be just like everybody else, also expresses itself in some further revealing dignitary measures. Deserving special emphasis are two programmatic efforts in both France and Germany: an effort to guarantee convicts the privileges of the social welfare state; and an effort to guarantee them the privileges of ordinary legal protections for their dignity and honor.

Thus "resocialization," in prisons both French and German, involves, first of all, a complex effort to integrate inmates into the same system of state socialism that everybody else is integrated into. In France the 1981 law that is the main basis of the current regime of prison regulations established a large variety of new rights that were conceived by the government as "social" rights in the fullest sense of the term—including, for example, not only a "right to information" but also a "right to leisure and culture."[127] The avowed ambition behind this grant of rights was to avoid any kind of fundamental status differentiation between "criminals" and "noncriminals"—to guarantee that "the rights that prisoners enjoy by virtue of their status as citizens (right to work, right to culture) are not, in the absence of particular circumstances, suppressed or suspended solely on account of incarceration."[128] As the "right to leisure and culture" in particular was described in 1982:

> Our society must furnish the means (both in terms of finances and of time) for the collectivity of individuals to cultivate and amuse themselves. This obligation to society in general cannot exclude the prisons. It is true that, for a long time, many believed that there was an irreducible incompatibility between prison and leisure. Notions of austerity had primacy in policies of incarceration, which made any serious cultural development impossible. . . .
>
> It is in this spirit that we are trying to develop those manual activities that will be maximally accessible to the great number of prisoners. A series of projects is being worked out at this time that aim to allow prisoners in numerous institutions to exercise a meaningful choice between artisanal and artistic activities such that they can explore a mode of expression through basket-weaving, pottery, drawing, painting etc.[129]

It is easy to laugh at this, with its earnest Marxist humanism—this sounds very much like what French politicians today deride as "gauchisme laxiste," "leftism gone soft." Nevertheless, this passage represents something significant about French penal ambitions. When the French socialist government set about to reaffirm the national commitment to a socialized state that would raise the cultural status of all, it did not hesitate to include prison inmates. (It also reflects an important fact about French theories of the personality: their intimate connection with ideals of artistic self-expression.)

In Germany, too, prison reform is thoroughly entangled with the "social state" and its constitutionalized values of human dignity.[130] The statutory requirement of fostering a "socially responsible way of life" for convicts is understood to derive directly from the constitutional sanctifications of human dignity and of the social state principle that protects everybody. Integration of inmates into the German social welfare state has some important corollaries. Notably, when German inmates work—and they are, at least in principle, all entitled (and indeed required)[131] to work—they receive unemployment insurance contributions at the going rate for the outside world.[132] This means that they can expect to draw unemployment benefits on their release. (They receive health coverage too—indeed, one recent newspaper article complained that inmates were better covered than civilians.)[133] Even more strikingly, they are subject to a slightly modified version of ordinary labor law. Among other consequences, this means that, while at work, they are supervised by outside entrepreneurs rather than guards. They receive a version of ordinary protections against discharge. (In conversation with employers at two German prisons, I was told that it can be difficult indeed to fire prisoners.) They even receive paid vacation, just like Germans in the outside world.[134] Until recently this totaled only three weeks—half of the six that are customary for most Germans. But efforts to improve the working conditions of inmates have continued. New legislation raised their wages as of January 1, 2001,[135] and they have also now received six further vacation days, which they may either use as vacation time or bank toward eventual early release.[136]

The normalcy of French and German dignity in the prisons does not end with membership in the social welfare state, moreover. Just as they are supposed to be participants in the social welfare state, convicts are supposed to be participants in the general culture of dignity. In particular, it is repeatedly said that they enjoy the same sorts of "personality" and "privacy" rights that reign in the honor culture of the outside world. As a French passage puts it:

> The "freedom of personal choice" characterizes the ensemble of rights that aim to guarantee respect for privacy and intellectual freedom. A number of recent prison reforms can be classified as belonging to this model. The generalization of visiting rooms without glass partitions, the improvement of everyday life in the prisons, the extension of contacts with the outside world, and especially with the family, are all illustrations. There are also measures that belong to the same tendency but that are more symbolic or expressive: notably the end, in 1983, of the obligation to wear a prison uniform, as well as the right to correspond with any person, or, finally, as of the 15th of December 1985, the authorization given to prisoners to have a television in their cell.[137]

In all of this, the problems of dignity within prison are not understood as fundamentally different from those outside. French prison regulations include, for example, provisions on insult. (Here American readers may need some background. Continental European legal systems include a category of law that is essentially absent in America: the law of *insult*. This body of law criminalizes insulting or disrespectful speech.)[138] A version of the law of insult is to be found in the French prisons too. Under regulations promulgated in 1996, inmates may be disciplined not only for insulting prison personnel but also for insulting other inmates.[139]

As for Germany, there, too, and there especially, the value of human dignity has been taken to guarantee inmates the same sorts of dignitary rights that Germans in the outside world enjoy.[140] Thus inmates' right to furnish their cells with their own belongings has been held to be dictated by their right to a "private sphere."[141] (In American prisons, by contrast, to repeat, inmate's possessions may effectively be summarily seized by prison officials.) The same is true of German inmates' right to visits—including regular visits with family that are permitted to unmarried as well as married convicts.[142]

(German jurists also view the Basic Law as guaranteeing, not only contact with family members, but also the possibility of striking up new romantic relationships with denizens of the outside world.)[143] This commitment to privacy can have some consequences that are quite remarkable from the American point of view. In the maximum-security prison that I visited in Berlin, for example, inmates—almost all housed one to a cell, despite the current overcrowding crisis—had doors without peepholes, behind which they could enjoy a kind of privacy to which maximum-security American prisoners can hardly think of aspiring. During the day, moreover, their cell doors stood unlocked.

Like American prisons, German ones come in more and less harsh varieties: German law distinguishes between "open" and "closed" facilities, with open facilities something like American halfway houses. The letter of the German statute declares that inmates are presumptively to be housed in "open" facilities, with "closed" punishment the exception.[144] This is a dead letter: in a system in which only very serious offenses result in imprisonment, the notion that offenders should routinely be placed in halfway houses never had any hope of success.[145] Nevertheless, the very aspiration to make halfway houses the norm speaks volumes about the statute's attitude toward prisoners.

Not least, as in France, one sees the penetration of the general culture of interpersonal respect into German prisons. A particularly odd example, from the American point of view, is one with which I began: a German requirement that guards *knock* before entering cells. A standard introductory text explains the thinking behind this rule:

> Before entering a place of confinement, prison personnel are obliged to *knock*. This does not present a question of mere politeness. . . . Rather, it is the right of the prisoner to protection and respect for his human dignity (Art. 1 GG) as well as his intimate sphere (Art 2 GG), which, taking into account the principle of normalcy, make it appropriate for the managers of the institution to work to create suitable forms of polite interaction between guards and inmates. . . . For entering a place of confinement without first knocking means imposing limits on prisoners which are not necessary as an indispensable consequence of the deprivation of liberty.[146]

This rule, which was endorsed by a number of appellate courts, was a bit too much for the Constitutional Court, which held in 1997 that it lay within the discretion of prison personnel whether or not to knock.[147] Nevertheless, here as so often, the very fact that an absolute bar on entering without knocking had a few years of life testifies to the strength of an idea of dignity that rests to a remarkable degree on inherited ideas of politeness.[148] So too does the prominence of matter from the law of insult in the prisons. The regulations require German prison guards, to address prisoners as "Sie," the respectful formal form of address.[149] Germans inmates have not infrequently brought successful actions against guards who addressed them disrespectfully; what could be further from the world of American prisons? The application of the law of insult in German prisons is however a more one-sided matter than the application of rules of insult in French prisons. Where it is clear that French convicts may not insult their guards, the vigorous free-speech jurisprudence of the German Constitutional Court has left German guards less well protected. Convicts have protections for their honor, but also for their freedom of speech[150]—with some comical consequences.[151] In one important case, an inmate who had been handed an unfavorable decision of the Constitutional Court burst out at his guard, "Don't be so snotty [vorlaut], you uppity jerk." Subjected to disciplinary measures for this insult, the inmate carried the case to the Constitutional Court once again, which carefully ruled that, while criminal insults were naturally punishable, prison officials had a special obligation to weigh that interest against the inmate's interest in free expression.[152] Strangely enough, German convicts may thus actually be *more* free to hand out insults than ordinary Germans are. Whatever the oddities of insult jurisprudence, the main point remains that the culture of dignity and respect that prevails generally in German society also sets the terms of discussion for "dignity" in imprisonment.

The greater continental concern with dignity in prison is paralleled by a greater continental dislike of *public exposure.*

Both German and French law display a resistance, if only a limited resistance, to public exposure for offenders—a resistance that sets these systems sharply apart from the American criminal justice. This resistance is something we can see, not only in the absence of shame sanctions in Europe, but also in a horror of barred celled doors that characterizes French and German prisons much more than American ones. It is also something we can see in other aspects of French and German criminal law. French and German jurists continue to think of public exposure as a frightening and barbaric thing.

Of course, there are always limits to the extent to which criminal justice systems can avoid subjecting offenders to public exposure. The identity, and the dangerousness, of some offenders has to be publicized, and no system could completely do without public exposure. Abolishing public shame sanctions is one thing; keeping the public in ignorance of the identity of offenders is something else entirely. Nevertheless, in France, and especially in Germany, the law is much more chary of exposing defendants and convicts to publicity than the American system is. The most striking expression of this chariness was the famous *Lebach* decision of the German Constitutional Court, handed down in 1973—roughly contemporaneously with the United States Supreme Court's decision in *Paul v. Davis. Paul v. Davis,* readers will recall, permitted the circulation of the photo of a "known" shoplifter against whom charges had been dismissed. The *Lebach* decision took a very different attitude. The case concerned a 1960s radical who been convicted of the terrorist murder of soldiers stationed in the town of Lebach. This convict had been involved in a homosexual relationship with one of his accomplices. The story was too good for journalists to keep away from, and German television sought to broadcast a film about him. In the *Lebach* case, the convict objected, successfully, on the grounds that broadcasting his story in such a way would both violate his constitutional right of personality and impede the re-socialization that was his entitlement as a German prisoner. German constitutional jurisprudence has since retreated a bit from the specific holding in *Lebach,* but the case is still regarded as the font of both dignitary law in German prisons[153] and of modern German privacy law. It reflects, clearly enough, the fact that Germans feel far greater discomfort with public exposure than Americans do.[154] There are other rules and practices that reflect the same discomfort. A German inmate's privacy is now protected, for example, through a rule permitting him to demand the destruction of the file describing his personal characteristics, fingerprints, and the like, after his release from prison.[155] Perhaps most noticeably, for an American experiencing day-to-day life in Germany, newspapers there still frequently avoid naming defendants.[156]

France has a less developed jurisprudence of this kind, but it still shows a much more lively sensibility with regard to public exposure than America does. Most striking here is the law surrounding the codified right to privacy, added to the Code Civil in 1970—again about the same time as the *Lebach* decision.[157] This right, framed in general terms, embodied aspirations that were perhaps not practically achievable with regard to convicts. Nevertheless, the right to privacy of defendants and convicts became a vibrant issue of discussion, and in 1993 the code was modified expressly to protect defendants against adverse publicity. Article 9-1 of the code declares "every person has a right to respect of the presumption of innocence." This provision allows judges to order the publication of a retraction, without prejudice to any other suit for damages. Under the resulting jurisprudence, still developing, newspapers have been successfully sued for coverage that did not carefully make it clear that accused persons had not been found guilty.[158]

In all of these rules, we see the same deep-seated continental sensibility at work—a sensibility that associates any kind of public exposure with a loss of dignity. We also see, once again, the strength of the drive to generalize ordinary social dignity to criminals. Even criminals, these rules hold in effect, should not be subjected to the intense shame and loss of social standing that public exposure carries with it.

The Mildness of Mercy

Alongside all of these aspects of European punishment practice, finally, it is important to mention one last practice that will seem to Americans exceedingly strange: the granting of amnesties. This is, in fact, one of the most telling and characteristic expressions of the broad European urge toward mildness. General amnesties for convicts serving shorter sentences are a regular business in European justice. Mildness in European law is pursued partly through something almost wholly missing in the United States: systematic mercy.

The practice is most noticeable, and most frequently discussed, in France.[159] There, the granting of amnesties has an old historical pedigree.

The royal prerogative of granting large-scale celebratory amnesties[160] extends far back into the ancien régime. It was an important aspect of the sacral practices of the prerevolutionary monarchy to grant amnesties, and kings regularly did so, on such events as their coronations or their birthdays. The granting of amnesties was, indeed, closely associated with the king's claim to hold a sovereign power of grace that stood outside the law, and accordingly many Enlightenment reformers, including Beccaria and Kant, objected to it.[161] Nevertheless, despite some strong objections during the revolution, it never died. Indeed, the practice has played a regular role in France ever since. Frequent amnesties have played an important role in limiting the prison population since the World War II.[162] Notably, these amnesties often celebrate the accession to power of a new government, a French republican tradition that continues a distinctly regal ancien régime tradition.[163] (This has some comical results. In 2001, for example, as French citizens expected the election of a new president in a year's time, one kind of lawlessness increased in anticipation of a general amnesty: illegal parking was rampant.) Convicts are also beneficiaries of this tradition: Bastille-day amnesties result in the annual release of some inmates as well.

In Germany, amnesties have had a more complex history, to which I will return later. To focus for the moment only on their place in current punishment practice, while they are less publicized, amnesties are as regular a practice in Germany as they are in France—though illegal parkers and the like do not benefit in Germany.[164] In particular, every German state grants regular Christmas amnesties, which free all inmates serving short sentences. German lawyers, indeed, can try to plan around these amnesties, in the effort to guarantee their clients the shortest possible stay in prison. It is known, in the various states, that inmates must serve a certain minimum time—typically a month—before they may benefit from any amnesty. Savvy offenders can try to delay their admission to prison until one month before the effective date of the annual Christmas amnesty, effectively shortening their sentences to one month.[165] The fact that the German justice system tolerates these tactics reflects a systematic toleration for relative mildness.

Amnesties, a general reluctance to incarcerate, a strong commitment to individualization and resocialization, a drive to define offenses as mere "contraventions" or *Ordnungswidrigkeiten*, "dignity" of a variety of types for prisoners, a concerted effort to guarantee that convicts will not be regarded as having a different status from anybody else, a resistance to public exposure: these are all measures of an instinct toward mildness that sets Europe sharply apart from the United States. As the United States has entered its late-twentieth-century ice age of harshness, the climate has become somewhat colder in Europe, too, as we have seen. Nevertheless, there is a warm countercurrent in Europe as well, a tendency toward compensating mildness in the criminal justice systems of France and Germany—a tendency that shows especially in French and German commitment to relatively dignified, and relatively easy, sentences of punishment.

This attachment to dignity, moreover, reveals something about the fabric of social relations in modern northern Europe; for the attachment to dignity in punishment partakes of social assumptions that also reign outside the world of the criminal law. Here the law of prison conditions is especially revealing. As the resemblance between dignitary regulations in prison and dignitary law in the outside world suggests, European punishment practices, with their (at least aspirational) orientation toward the dignity of the offender, are typical of much more far-reaching patterns. *Dignity* and *honor* matter throughout the law and legal culture of Germany and France: they matter in the law and legal culture of insult, both inside prison and out; they matter in the law and legal culture of privacy, both inside prison and out; they matter in the law and legal culture of sexual harassment, both inside prison and out; and more.

That they matter so much tells us, indeed, something important about prisons. Prisons may be "total institutions," as Goffman said, in which every aspect of life is regulated.[166] But the ways in which prisons in different societies regulate life reflect far-reaching differences in social attitudes—differences that can make for significant disparities in the dignitary well-being of prisoners. The law of prisons, and more broadly of punishment, in both Germany and France, rests on a set of instinctive assumptions about how society is organized—instinctive assumptions that instruct Europeans that one is to have *respect for persons*. The fact that those assumptions have had a shaping impact on prison life tells us something about the ultimate inadequacy of Goffman's discussion, and of Foucauldian and Foucault-derived discussions as well. What Foucault famously claimed is surely true: prisons everywhere are characterized by a drive toward "discipline" and control. Yet the norms that that "discipline" embodies differ from society to society in ways that matter immensely for the lives of the inmates of modern institutions, and that cry out for careful comparative analysis.

The deep-seated assumption that social relations are founded on respect for persons has, moreover, affected aspects of European punishment that go beyond prison conditions. In particular, the same assumption has served, in Europe, as a barrier to the kinds of changes that have swept through the American law of sentencing. There are Europeans who have preached act-egalitarianism of the American neo-Beccarian kind, but, at least as yet, their arguments have mostly fallen on deaf ears. At least as yet, Europeans are not ready for a world in which *acts* matter so much more than *persons*—for a world in which the consequences that befall you depend so much on *what you do* rather than *who you are*—and as a result sentencing guidelines of the American type, though they have been vigorously advocated, have not established themselves. Not least, the assumption that social relations are founded in respect for persons shows in the remarkable ensemble of regulations designed to guarantee "normalcy" for European convicts—to guarantee that they will not undergo a status degradation that sets them apart from everybody else.

Europeans simply perceive the legal world differently from Americans. They tend to perceive it as a world in which it is always right and proper to judge *persons*, and not only *acts*; and as a world in which it is imperative to maintain the dignity of persons, even when they have been convicted of criminal offenses.

This is nothing new. It is nothing new in continental Europe; and it is nothing new in the United States. As my opening quote from Blackstone at the head of the last chapter suggests, these are very old differences. In the following pages, I would like to trace these cultural differences far back in history on both sides of the Atlantic. The United States on the one hand, and France and Germany on the other, have emerged differently from the old world of mutilations, of hangings and beheadings, of low and high status; and it is in that old world that we must begin.

4

The Continental Abolition of Degradation

In a 1718 drawing by the comte de Caylus, we see Voltaire, confined to the Bastille, as he sits at his writing desk before the fire, laboring at the first version of his epic poem on toleration, the *Henriade*. Heroic images of the imprisoned Voltaire composing the *Henriade* would continue to appear into the nineteenth century.[1] In a sketch by Fragonard of 1788, a few months before the outbreak of the French Revolution, we see the courtyard of the Bastille, where elegantly dressed members of the Paris beau monde have come to visit their friends and relatives. Turning to Germany, more than a century later, we see Adolf Hitler, in photographs taken surreptitiously in 1924 and later republished in a Nazi-era hagiographical book. Confined in the Fortress Landsberg after the unsuccessful Beer Hall Putsch of 1923, Hitler strikes a pensive pose before his cell window and meets with Nazi followers in a garden and a common room, dressed in traditional Bavarian *Tracht*. It is during his months of confinement in Landsberg that he will compose *Mein Kampf*.

We do not often think of Voltaire and Hitler together; but in fact they both suffered the same traditional form of imprisonment. These are all images from the lives of high-status continental prisoners, whose dignity was protected through measures that remained much the same on the continent from the time of Louis XV through the Weimar Republic. They are images we should hold in the back of our minds as we try to understand continental justice even today. As I shall show in this chapter, the norms of dignity that reign in French and German punishment today are echoes of norms of dignity that date back to the eras of the confinement of Voltaire and Hitler. What are at work today are traditions that grew up in an era when the "dignity" and "honor" that the law primarily took cognizance of was the "dignity" and "honor" of *high-status* persons, in a world of well-articulated and well-defended social hierarchy. As for the traditions of mercy, in them, we can see the lingering ghost of the powerful princely states of the early modern world. Those are the two themes of this chapter: in the first part, the long-term conflict between historically low-status and historically high-status punishments on the continent; in the second part, the history of pardoning, from the eighteenth century into the Nazi period.

Imprisonment and Dignity in Punishment

To capture the conflict between high and low status in continental punishment—the first of my two themes—I am going to be painting an unfamiliar picture of the history of two topics: imprisonment and dignity in punishment. It is well to begin by acknowledging how odd my history of these topics is likely to seem.

My account of the history of imprisonment may seem especially strange. Readers who know anything at all about the history of imprisonment in Europe are likely to know the story that Foucault tells: the story of the decline of the bloody corporal violence of the early modern world and its eventual replacement, in the early nineteenth century, by cellular imprisonment on the American model. This is indeed one of best-known stories of modern history. Even people with only a smattering of legal historical knowledge know that the old violent punishments were replaced by imprisonment. They also know that European reformers of the 1830s frequently traveled to America to examine two competing cellular systems of imprisonment: the Auburn, or "silent" system, in which inmates slept in solitary cells but worked together in silence; and the Pennsylvania or "separate" system, in which inmates were subjected to unrelenting solitary confinement. Not least among the French reformers who came to examine these systems was the celebrated Tocqueville, who, along with his coauthor Gustave de Beaumont, tried to convince the French to institute cellular imprisonment in 1833. German reformers came as well; and both Germany and France had large-scale Americanizing penitentiary movements in the mid-nineteenth century.

This is all true, but I will have little to say about it in this chapter. The old violent punishments will certainly play a role; but I am not going to talk much about their violence. Instead, I am going to focus on their *status* meaning. Violent punishments like mutilation and flogging are not just ways to inflict pain on people; they are also ways to degrade them. And for my purposes, the history of the disappearance of such punishments will be a history, not so much of a declining toleration for *inflicting pain*, as of a declining tolerance for *degradation*. The tolerance for inflicting pain surely did decline, as Pieter Spierenburg has brilliantly demonstrated;[2] but the tolerance for degradation declined too. The decline in the tolerance for degradation was indeed once a commonplace of continental historiography: to nineteenth-century authors, it went without saying that progress in punishment had been progress in the abolition of degrading, low-status treatment.[3] This aspect of the "progress" of the continental nineteenth century has however often been neglected since, especially since the publication of Foucault's *Discipline and Punish*.[4] My goal is to bring it back to the center of our discussions. As for cellular imprisonment, I will mention it only briefly. This is not because it did not matter in the nineteenth century: it surely did, for the overwhelming majority of low-status prisoners. But my interest here is not in the lives of this great majority; it is in the lives of a tiny minority of *high-status* prisoners, especially political dissidents and debtors. These high-status prisoners were never subjected to standard forms of cellular imprisonment. And what I want to show is precisely that the treatment of this vanishingly tiny minority carried the seeds of the development of what has become normal treatment for all by the beginning of the twenty-first century.

As for dignity in punishment, the story I tell will be different here too. When contemporary European lawyers try to explain the place of dignity in their systems of punishment, they do not spend much time on the eighteenth century. Instead, they speak of the last hundred years, and especially of the last fifty years. Thus in part they think of their dignitary values as the product of the great social scientific reforms of the late nineteenth-century. French lawyers tend to think of modern dignity, in particular, as beginning with the so-called *loi Bérenger* of 1891.[5] This famous law, dating to the beginnings of the individualization movement, introduced *sursis*, suspended sentence, into French practice. With suspended sentences, the French literature commonly observes, French law entered a new era of growing humaneness, one in which it was possible for the judge to look down upon the offender and see a person who deserved to be released.[6] The German literature, for its part, notes the rise of the fine and conditional pardons as a substitute for imprisonment in the late nineteenth century,[7] and then goes on to emphasize a variety of reform measures of the Weimar era, which introduced resocialization and education as the principal goals of punishment in Germany—without, however, yet introducing probation.[8]

But Europeans do not focus exclusively on late-nineteenth-century reform. They also see dignity in their punishment systems as the product of a more recent, and uglier, history—as the product of a reaction against fascism. Standard authors in both France and Germany emphasize that the fascist era marked a major, and ultimately formative, setback in the rise of humane punishment in Europe. Nazi criminal law in particular, they note, ostentatiously rejected the humanizing reforms of the Weimar era.[9] Indeed, almost from the first moment they came to power, the Nazis campaigned against the "liberal" excesses of Weimar punishment philosophy, rejecting the values of rehabilitation and insisting (uncomfortably enough, rather like current American politicians and scholars) that the proper goals of imprisonment were retribution and deterrence. Imprisonment in particular, the Nazis held, should be an *empfindliches Übel*—"something nasty that makes them hurt"; only in that way would punishment deter; only in that way would it achieve retribution. As the principal 1934 Nazi policy statement put it: "Through serving their prison time, convicts are to atone for the wrong they have done. Imprisonment is to be designed in such a way that it is an *empfindliches Übel*, which will produce lasting inhibitions against any temptation to commit further punishable offenses, even among inmates whom it is impossible to educate."[10] In the European literature, this Nazi statement stands as a prime example of inhuman fascist harshness in punishment.[11] There are of course other examples too. In particular, though technically standing outside the ordinary regime of prisons, there were the Nazi concentration camps, which at first housed political prisoners in "protective custody," and later came to include Jews and other social undesirables.[12] Conditions in the camps were, of course, proverbially inhumane. Vichy law, for its part, standard authors observe, rejected the measures of individualization that had been the hallmark of French liberalism since the 1890s. Suspended sentences in particular, after a nearly half-century-long history, were abandoned after France was overrun in 1940. Vichy law, orienting itself toward a Nazilike harshness, limited the power of judges both to grant suspended sentences and to consider extenuating circumstances.[13] The fascist era in both Germany and France thus meant a sharp turn in the direction of harshness.

As most of the standard continental literature tells the tale, the making of the humane conditions of today began in earnest only after World War II, when that fascist-era harshness was forthrightly rejected. Reform efforts with the fascist experience firmly in mind came immediately at the end of the war,[14] and the postwar period saw a near flood of international conventions forbidding torture and other "cruel, inhuman, or degrading" practices.[15] Throughout, the guiding image of a truly reprehensible prison was the Nazi concentration camp. With these horrifying examples before their eyes, Europeans returned to the tradition of rehabilitation with renewed energy as the continent recovered during the 1950s. In laws of 1951, 1954, and 1958 the old liberal measures of "individualization" were fully restored in the French courts.[16] These now included the introduction of probation—*sursis avec mise à l'épreuve*—alongside suspended sentence. As for Germany, the standard literature tells us that probation—in Germany called *Strafaussetzung zur Bewährung*—was finally instituted there for the first time in 1953.[17] Full-scale probation of the Anglo-American kind was thus a creation of the early 1950s in both countries. By the mid-1950s, as European reconstruction went into full swing, the drive toward fundamental reform, of a fundamentally antifascist coloration, was set. That drive has continued in the evolving jurisprudence of the European Union. It has expressed itself, not least, in the universal abolition, in Europe, of the death penalty.

All this makes for what seems, at first glance, a coherent and persuasive explanation of the humane values that prevail in France and Germany today. And indeed, European law today is unintelligible if we do not understand how forcefully European elites have reacted against fascism. Nevertheless, this frequently repeated account of the making of dignity in European punishment, while it contains much that is correct, lays many accents falsely and passes over some important truths. During the last several years, a few scholars have raised doubts about this standard account, and I am going to raise some doubts about it too.[18] The history of the rise of dignity in European punishment has to be seen in a light different from that offered by the standard juristic literature.

This is especially true if we want the kind of wisdom that only a deeper sociological perspective can offer. The standard literature portrays most doctrinal developments correctly enough, but it misses the large sociohistorical drama behind the rise of dignity in European law. Seen in large sociological perspective, European offenders are the beneficiaries of a history that reaches well back into the eighteenth century—a very long history of the gradual extension of a claim to dignity down through all the ranks of society. Seen in the large, dignity is a much older value in European law than 1945—and older than 1891 as well. "Respect" and "dignity" became fundamental values in European law at a time when showing respect meant primarily guaranteeing norms of dignity and deference for persons of high status. As for the death penalty, the history of its abolition is not the only thing that matters. On the contrary, if we want to grasp continental values of "respect" and "dignity," we must remember that debates over the death penalty were for a very long time largely debates about different *modes* of death: the traditionally dignified way to die, in the premodern Western tradition, was through beheading. Correspondingly, the first stage in the making of a European jurisprudence of dignity was not the abolition of the death penalty but the extension of the privilege of being beheaded to all.

The World of the Ancien Régime

Let us begin with the hierarchical continental world that predated the French Revolution. There was well-articulated social hierarchy everywhere in the continental Europe of the sixteenth, seventeenth, and eighteenth centuries. These were all societies that included Tocqueville's "aristocratic element." We should be wary, though, of thinking of these societies as simply "aristocratic" in any simple or uniform way. These were societies of "orders"—societies with elaborate pyramids of honor, in which many persons on many levels of society enjoyed some degree of honor. France, famous for its highly developed system of precedent and rank, undoubtedly had the most nationalized status culture of the continent by the late seventeenth century, and it probably had the strongest association between social honor and noble status.[19] German social organization showed great regional diversity in this as in all things. More important, social honor in the German-speaking world was probably less closely connected with noble status than it was in France: Germans tended to mark out a couple of very low, almost untouchable, statuses while insisting that all respectable people who did not stand at the very bottom of the ladder had a protectable right to honor.[20] These hierarchical social orders were not fixed and unchanging. On the contrary, the continental law of hierarchy, especially in France, was largely a creation of the sixteenth century. It would be foolish to treat these societies and these centuries as identical in any but the broadest sense.

Nevertheless, speaking in the broadest sense, we can say that articulated social hierarchies existed in both the French and German-speaking worlds before the French Revolution—just as they existed in contemporary hierarchical orders in places like Ottoman Turkey or Qing China or Mughal India. All these complex societies of the Eurasian land mass were divided between, on the one hand, high status persons, elegantly dressed and deferentially treated, and, on the other hand, their inferiors.

In all of these places, it was regarded as morally imperative to maintain clear distinctions between high and low. Indeed, continental Europe in particular was a world in which lawyers saw nothing strange in describing low-status people as "disgusting": a French lawyer writing as late as 1789, for example, could describe peasants who did not know their place as simply "revolting."[21] Clearly enough, this world had a sensibility about status that is very difficult for us to grasp with any sympathy. To be sure, the idea that there is something "revolting" about inferiors has hardly completely vanished. Americans with strongly racist feelings undoubtedly regard African-Americans as "revolting" in something like the way that high-status seventeenth-century French could regard peasants as "revolting." Mary Douglas is surely right that we continue to react to down-and-out people and criminal offenders as "dirty." Nevertheless, it seems fair to say that disgust at low-status people is no longer as widely shared, and certainly no longer as socially acceptable, as it was in the seventeenth and eighteenth centuries, and we must struggle a little to try to understand it. The eminent French historian Emmanuel Le Roy Ladurie has recently tried to capture this vanished premodern sensibility by comparing the court society of late-seventeenth-century France to caste society in India, in ways inspired by the anthropologist Louis Dumont. Dumont, in his book *Homo Hierarchicus*, analyzes Indian status as a phenomenon associated with perceptions of purity and pollution. High-status people are regarded as clean people; low-status people as dirty. This analysis of Indian society inspires Le Roy Ladurie's account of the world of the seventeenth century. Le Roy Ladurie sees precisely the vocabulary of caste ideas at work in the France of Louis XIV, which displayed an obsession with "purity"—purity of descent, purity of the body, and so on.[22] Of course there were many differences between Indian caste and premodern status, and we should not make too much of the comparison. Nevertheless, it is a useful comparison indeed for bringing out the highly charged importance of status distinctions in this world.

In particular, it is a useful comparison for trying to understand the hierarchical sensibility that lay behind the law of punishment: As Spierenburg has emphasized, early modern punishment belonged to a much larger culture of "honor" and "dishonor" that always involved feelings of disgust and perceptions of untouchability.[23] Persons of high social standing expected, and received, different punishments from their inferiors, and the harshest forms of punishment were thought of as inflicting, not merely pain, but dishonor as well.[24] Things were not as harsh as they once had been. The sixteenth century marked the high point of painful punishment, and by the mid-eighteenth century, much of the savagery of sixteenth-century punishment had waned.[25] Nevertheless, continental sensibility still required that punishments display status differences that were regarded as essential to the maintenance of a healthy social order.

In particular, low-status offenders throughout these centuries could expect humiliation, whether in death or in life. Let us begin with death. Modes of execution are of peculiar symbolic importance in every society; and status differences in premodern continental Europe were marked by two traditionally charged symbolic modes of death: hanging, "the most shameful death," was traditionally the normal form for low-status persons, while beheading, "which has always been regarded as the most honorable and mildest,"[26] was viewed as "specially established for nobles."[27] This distinction was very old, extending back to ancient Greece and Rome.[28] It was obeyed much more scrupulously in French law than in German: by the late seventeenth century, beheading was in use for all social ranks in the German-speaking world, notably for infanticides and murderers with a defense of provocation.[29] In this as in other things, "honor" was more widely diffused in the German-speaking world than in France. Nevertheless, even in Germany, the association of beheading with nobility remained.

This represented in some ways a strange choice of symbols: beheading is after all a form of mutilation, and one would expect it to be the *low*-status way to die. Indeed, in the Chinese tradition, the standard European symbolism was reversed, with beheading serving as the normal punishment for low-status persons, and strangling the normal punishment for the high.[30] Nevertheless, in the Western tradition, beheading was by tradition for high-status and honorable persons. Low-status folk, for their part, were traditionally dispatched through hanging, along with a variety of other dishonoring modes of execution such as breaking on the wheel or burning alive.[31]

The distinctions went beyond death, moreover. Low-status persons who were not condemned to die could expect one of two kinds of punishment: painful public humiliation, or imprisonment at forced labor. Jurists regarded the first of these as the normal form. Technical juristic theory of the seventeenth and eighteenth centuries declared that ordinary low-status criminals in the ancien régime should not receive imprisonment as a punishment at all.[32] If low-status persons were sometimes kept in jails, standard doctrine held that they were simply being detained there, while awaiting their true and more suitable punishment. That true and more suitable punishment normally involved the infliction of some kind of pain in some emphatically public place. Flogging and branding were common practices. Mutilations—severed hands, severed ears, severed noses, brandings—were also common; as were punishments of public display like the pillory or being hung from the gallows by the armpits.[33] These punishments were also typically inflicted on the scaffold, the place of public display, and the place associated with hanging. If these were deemed the normal low-status punishments, though, the reality is that in the seventeenth and eighteenth centuries they were joined by another type of punishment: imprisonment at forced labor—with the accent on forced labor. Being compelled to labor under the whip of another was a major marker of low social status in the premodern world; and it lent itself naturally to a status-oriented scheme of punishment. During the seventeenth and eighteenth centuries, two major species of forced labor institutions developed on the European continent: galleys (and later shipyards), typical especially of France and the Mediterranean world; and workhouses, typical especially of England, the Netherlands, Scandinavia, and the urban German-speaking world.[34]

Both forced labor and public humiliation had something in common: they were *dishonorable* kinds of punishments, and indeed carried a kind of ritual taint. Their dishonorable character deserves some emphasis. To Foucault, the garish punishments of the early modern period had the primary purpose of displaying state power: they were intended to "reconstitute" a "wounded" sovereignty through a gaudy public show of authority.[35] This interpretation has become common in France,[36] and of course it is by no means wholly false. Nevertheless, it is important to see that low-status punishments did not just dramatize the power of the state. They dramatized the hierarchical ordering of society as well,[37] and that fact matters immensely for the development of continental law. Much law revolved around the status meaning of punishment. As early-modern Europeans generally understood it, being publicly punished was "infaming" and so was being subjected to forced labor. "Infamy," in the eyes of European jurists, took two forms: there was infamy *in law*, which basically involved loss of civic rights; and then there was infamy *in fact*, the loss of honor and status in the eyes of the general public. Being subjected to a low-status punishment carried, it was almost universally agreed by lawyers, the second of these, infamy in fact.[38] A person who had been publicly flogged or the like was, as a matter of social fact, a person of diminished status, and indeed of profoundly diminished status. The early modern sense of the status-degradation that resulted from being subjected to low-status punishment was so strong, in fact, that being subjected to a low-status punishment permanently diminished even an innocent person. As standard legal authorities of the early modern period explained, "It is not so much the crime, as the type of punishment inflicted that causes people to become dishonored."[39] Despite the fact that ancient Roman jurists saw things differently,[40] this was the view that prevailed in the early modern world, and it was a revealing view. In the early modern world, punishment was in many ways less about guilt than about taint. It was less about what you had done than about whether you had been defiled by being subjected to a low-status punishment. This meant that a person who had been subjected to a flogging or the like could effectively never be rehabilitated: such a person was indelibly dishonored. It also meant, significantly, that even the family of a person

I. Scenes from the Lives of Continental Political Prisoners

Comte de Caylus, *Voltaire in the Bastille* (1718). © Bibliothèque nationale de France.

Jean-Honoré Fragonard, *The Courtyard of the Bastille* (1788). © Bibliothèque nationale de France.

Honoré Daumier, *Souvenir de Sainte-Pélagie* (1834). Daumier appears on the far left. © Photothèque des Musées de la ville de Paris.

Victor Jean Adam, *The Room of the Imprisoned Philosopher* (n.d.). © Photothèque des Musées de la ville de Paris.

Anonymous, *The Poet Enters Prison* (n.d.). © Photothèque des Musées de la ville de Paris.

Anonymous, *The Courtyard of Sainte-Pélagie* (n.d.). © Photothèque des Musées de la ville de Paris.

Benard, *The Salon of Sainte-Pélagie* (n.d.). © Photothèque des Musées de la ville de Paris.

Adolf Hitler in his cell in the Fortress Landsberg, 1924.

Adolf Hitler, Rudolf Hess (fourth from left), and others in the Common Room of the Fortress Landsberg, 1924.

Adolf Hitler (left) in the garden of the Fortress Landsberg, 1924.

II. Modes of Execution in the French Revolution

Anonymous, *Machine Proposed to the National Assembly by Monsieur Guillotin* (1789). © Photothèque des Musées de la ville de Paris.

J. F. Janinet, *The Corpses of the Agasse Brothers, Returned to Their Families* (1790). Print Collection, Miriam and Ira D. Wallach Division of Art, Prints and Photographs, The New York Public Library, Astor, Lenox and Tilden Foundations.

III. English High-Status Offenders Degraded

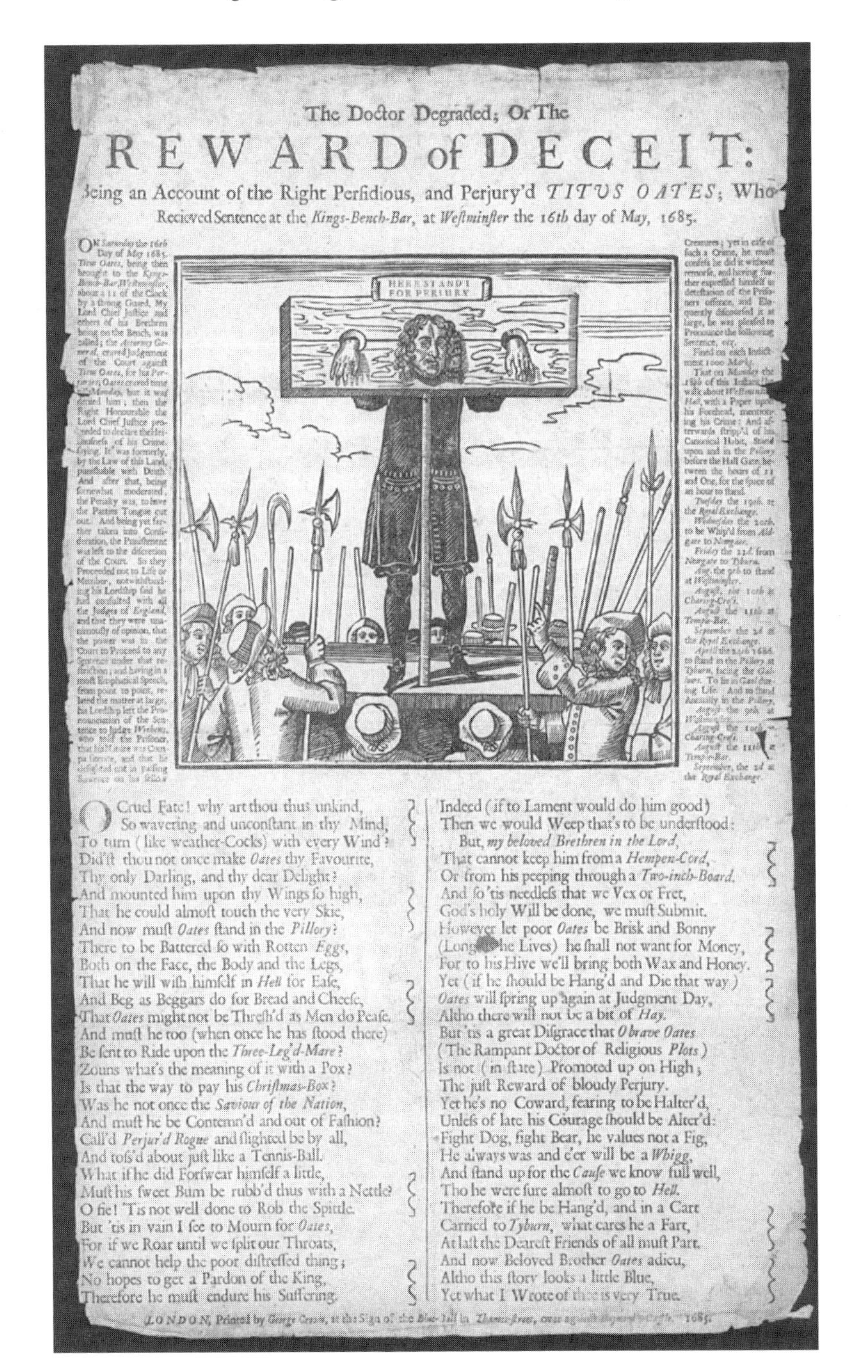

The Doctor Degraded; Or The

REWARD of DECEIT:

Being an Account of the Right Perfidious, and Perjury'd *TITUS OATES*; Who Recieved Sentence at the *Kings-Bench-Bar*, at *Weſtminſter* the *16th* day of *May*, 1685.

ON *Saturday* the 16th Day of *May* 1685. *Titus Oates*, being then brought to the *Kings-Bench-Bar, Westminster*, about 11 of the Clock by a strong Guard, My Lord Chief Justice and others of his Brethren being on the Bench, was called; the *Attorney General*, craved Judgment of the Court against *Titus Oates*, for his *Perjury*; *Oates* craved time till *Monday*, but it was denied him; then the Right Honourable the Lord Chief Justice proceeded to declare the Heinousness of his Crime, saying, It was formerly, by the Law of this Land, punishable with Death. And after that, being somewhat moderated, the Penalty was, to have the Parties Tongue cut out. And being yet farther taken into Consideration, the Punishment was left to the discretion of the Court. So they Proceeded not to Life or Member, notwithstanding his Lordship said he had consulted with all the Judges of *England*, and that they were unanimously of opinion, that the power was in the Court to Proceed to any Sentence under that restriction; and having in a most Emphatical Speech, from point to point, related the matter at large, his Lordship left the Pronunciation of the Sentence to Judge *Withens*, who told the Prisoner, that his Nature was Contra [illegible], and that he delighted not in passing Sentence on his fellow Creatures; yet in case of such a Crime, he must confess he did it without remorse, and having further expressed himself in detestation of the Prisoners offence, and Eloquently discoursed it at large, he was pleased to Pronounce the following Sentence, etc.

Fined on each Indictment 1000 *Marks*.

That on *Monday* the 18th of this Instant he walk about *Westminster Hall*, with a Paper upon his Forehead, mentioning his Crime: And afterwards stripp'd of his Canonical Habit, Stand upon and in the *Pillory* before the Hall Gate, between the hours of 11 and One, for the space of an hour to stand.

Tuesday the 19th. at the *Royal Exchange*.

Wednesday the 20th. to be Whip'd from *Aldgate* to *Newgate*.

Friday the 22d. from *Newgate* to *Tyburn*.

Aug. the 9th to stand at *Westminster*.

August, the 10th at *Charing-Cross*.

August the 11th at *Temple-Bar*.

September the 2d at the *Royal Exchange*.

April the 24th 1686. to stand in the *Pillory* at *Tyburn*, facing the *Gallows*. To lie in *Goal* during Life. And to stand Annually in the *Pillory*.

August the 9th at *Westminster*.

August the 10th at *Charing-Cross*.

August the 11th at *Temple-Bar*.

September, the 2d at the *Royal Exchange*.

O Cruel Fate! why art thou thus unkind,
So wavering and unconſtant in thy Mind,
To turn (like weather-Cocks) with every Wind?
Did'ſt thou not once make *Oates* thy Favourite,
Thy only Darling, and thy dear Delight?
And mounted him upon thy Wings ſo high,
That he could almoſt touch the very Skie,
And now muſt *Oates* ſtand in the *Pillory*?
There to be Battered ſo with Rotten *Eggs*,
Both on the Face, the Body and the Legs,
That he will wiſh himſelf in *Hell* for Eaſe,
And Beg as Beggars do for Bread and Cheeſe,
That *Oates* might not be Threſh'd as Men do Peaſe.
And muſt he too (when once he has ſtood there)
Be ſent to Ride upon the *Three-Leg'd-Mare*?
Zouns what's the meaning of it with a Pox?
Is that the way to pay his *Chriſtmas-Box*?
Was he not once the *Saviour of the Nation*,
And muſt he be Contemn'd and out of Faſhion?
Call'd *Perjur'd Rogue* and ſlighted be by all,
And toſs'd about juſt like a Tennis-Ball.
What if he did Forſwear himſelf a little,
Muſt his ſweet Bum be rubb'd thus with a Nettle?
O fie! 'Tis not well done to Rob the Spittle.
But 'tis in vain I ſee to Mourn for *Oates*,
For if we Roar until we ſplit our Throats,
We cannot help the poor diſtreſſed thing;
No hopes to get a Pardon of the King,
Therefore he muſt endure his Suffering.

Indeed (if to Lament would do him good)
Then we would Weep that's to be underſtood:
But, *my beloved Brethren in the Lord*,
That cannot keep him from a *Hempen-Cord*,
Or from his peeping through a *Two-inch-Board*.
And ſo 'tis needleſs that we Vex or Fret,
God's holy Will be done, we muſt Submit.
However let poor *Oates* be Briſk and Bonny
(Long [illegible] he Lives) he ſhall not want for Money,
For to his Hive we'll bring both Wax and Honey.
Yet (if he ſhould be Hang'd and Die that way)
Oates will ſpring up again at Judgment Day,
Altho there will not be a bit of *Hay*.
But 'tis a great Diſgrace that *O brave Oates*
(The Rampant Doctor of Religious *Plots*)
Is not (in ſtate) Promoted up on High;
The juſt Reward of bloody Perjury.
Yet he's no Coward, fearing to be Halter'd,
Unleſs of late his Courage ſhould be Alter'd:
Fight Dog, fight Bear, he values not a Fig,
He always was and e'er will be a *Whigg*,
And ſtand up for the *Cauſe* we know full well,
Tho he were ſure almoſt to go to *Hell*.
Therefore if he be Hang'd, and in a Cart
Carried to *Tyburn*, what cares he a Fart,
At laſt the Deareſt Friends of all muſt Part.
And now Beloved Brother *Oates* adieu,
Altho this ſtory looks a little Blue,
Yet what I Wrote of thee is very True.

LONDON, Printed by *George Croom*, at the Sign of the *Blue-Ball* in *Thames-street*, over against [illegible] 1685.

Anonymous, *The Doctor Degraded* (1685). By permission of the Houghton Library, Harvard University.

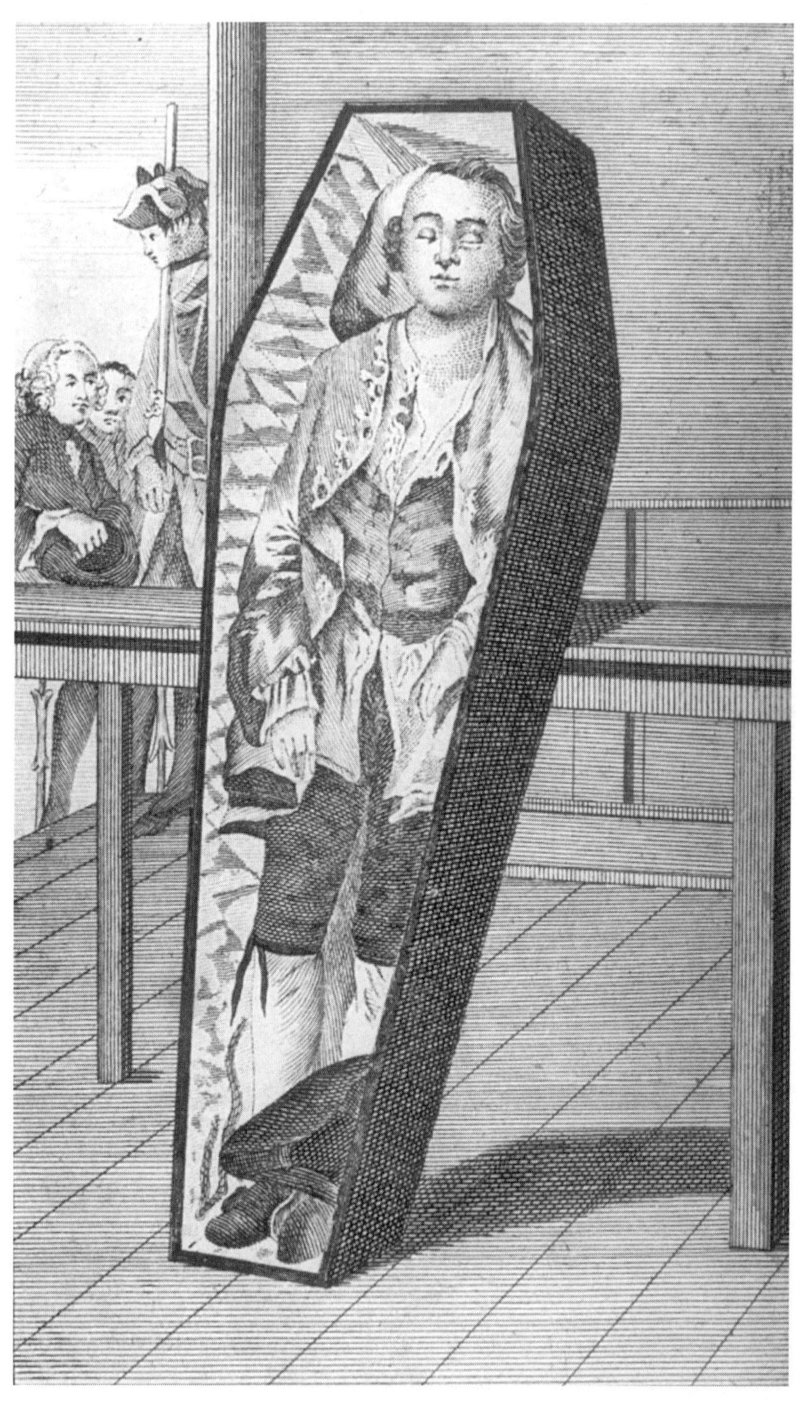

Anonymous, *The Corpse of Lord Ferrers, Awaiting Dissection* (1760). General Research Division, The New York Public Library, Astor, Lenox and Tilden Foundations.

subjected to low-status punishment was subjected to a permanent taint of dishonor.[41]

It was natural, in this world, for high-status persons to avoid treatment that would "taint" them. Indeed, continental systems, like those of other premodern hierarchical societies, showed a strong tendency to avoid inflicting "infaming" punishments on persons who belonged to the higher social orders.[42] In particular, high-status Europeans who were not condemned to die tended to seek, and frequently succeeded in receiving, a special form of punishment: imprisonment, out of the public eye.[43] This high-status imprisonment, which has been the subject of illuminating studies by Pieter Spierenburg and Jean-Claude Vimont, deserves some close attention; for it set the terms for progressive amelioration of punishment in Europe down to the present day.

Imprisonment for high-status people already had a long history in the eighteenth century. There were many forms of imprisonment in the Western world before the early modern period. The Romans, for example, used disciplinary cells for their slaves, and creditors sometimes held their debtors as captives. In trying to understand the character of high-status imprisonment in Europe, though, it is especially useful to focus on two medieval sources. The first was clerical imprisonment. The church was forbidden to administer punishments that shed blood; at the same time, clergy were regarded as persons who were by right of status too good to be subjected to ordinary punishment. Instead, from a very early date, monks and other clergy were punished by imprisonment, in cells where they were obliged to do penance.[44] This practice of clerical imprisonment continued into the early modern period and served as the model for some important experiments, particularly in the Catholic world. By the seventeenth century Catholic reformers had begun to extend the practice of clerical imprisonment to nonclergy—most importantly at San Michele, a Roman prison for minors that was much admired and much imitated in the Catholic world.[45] Late-eighteenth-century, Anglo-American experiments with the "penitentiary" also deserve to be seen against the background of this very old tradition of Christian imprisonment. Indeed, the importance of clerical imprisonment deserves real emphasis in any description of the *longue durée* of the development of occidental punishment practices. Like other kinds of "penitential" practices, the spread of imprisonment reflects a kind of migration of monastic norms into society in general. The first Europeans to be required to do "time" and other forms of penance to expunge their guilt were monks; over many centuries, all offenders have come to be treated in the same way. This represents a kind of secularization of the discipline of the monastery, reminiscent of the ethical secularization famously identified by Weber in his *Protestant Ethic*.[46]

These monastic roots of imprisonment have attracted a great deal of attention, and for good reason. But there is arguably another historical model for high-status imprisonment, too, whose role is more difficult to trace but also of real importance. This is a model that came from medieval aristocratic society. In particular, it was normal, in the course of medieval warfare, to take defeated opponents captive and hold them for ransom. Holding captives for ransom was indeed a major source of war booty in the later Middle Ages. Such captives were expected to be held, ordinarily, in appropriately well-appointed circumstances, in fortresses. More broadly, high-status persons held captive in the Middle Ages, tended to be held in one or another form of fortress.[47] This was a practice that would survive. As we shall see, through the nineteenth century, high-status prisoners would continue to be held in what would be called "fortress confinement," a term with resonant romantic associations with the Middle Ages.

Both the penitential tradition and the tradition of "fortress confinement" colored the treatment of high-status offenders in the continental world that predated the French Revolution. Instead of being subjected to mutilation, humiliation, or forced labor, high-status offenders typically found themselves in what Central Europeans often called *custodia honesta*, "honorable custody."[48] They were confined for a variety of reasons. Some were convicted of crimes through the ordinary process of law and were assigned to imprisonment through the power of their judge to alter punishment according to "the quality of the person."[49] This is what was technically called the "arbitrary" power of the judge—the power to choose a punishment at his discretion. This arbitrary power was also exercised in the case of another class of relatively high-status persons: debtors. European law had a long history of holding defaulting debtors prisoner, and a long history of subjecting them to garish shame sanctions as well. In France, by the mid eighteenth century, imprisonment, subject to the arbitrary authority of the judge, had become normal for these offenders too—for defaulters were indeed regarded as criminal offenders: for a very long time, failure to pay one's debts was understood to be a species of theft.[50]

Not all high-status prisoners, however, had been convicted of crimes. Others, especially but not exclusively in France, were imprisoned through the infamous "lettres de cachet," ex parte arrest warrants issued by state officials. In France, some of these lettre de cachet prisoners were political opponents of the crown, or at least persons regarded as dangerous by the crown. Others—the overwhelming majority, in fact—belonged to a different class: they were persons imprisoned at the request of their own families—dissolute and recalcitrant children and the like.[51] Foucault and Arlette Farge interpret this practice as demonstrating the entanglement of the French sacral monarchy with the enforcement of family authority. But as Spierenburg has shown, the business of permitting families to imprison some of their members on ex parte petition, often for life, was quite common in early modern continental Europe—including the Netherlands, which certainly did not have any kind of sacral monarchy of the French sort.[52] (The practice has also, we may note, reappeared in contemporary American juvenile justice.)[53] Indeed, more broadly, as Spierenburg has shown, high-status Dutch and German offenders were confined in "honorable" circumstances, shielding them from public exposure, just as French ones were.[54]

Lettre de cachet prisoners were of course generally persons of high social standing, and they were accordingly generally supposed to be well treated once imprisoned: housed in relative comfort, sometimes dining quite well, often at the table of the prison warden, entitled to regular visits from family and partisans. In the Netherlands and other parts of urban Germanic Europe, they were sometimes held in inns, treated more as guests than as prisoners. In France and other parts of the German-speaking world, they were commonly held either in religious establishments, or in fortresses or castles.[55] The most prominent of the fortresses, though not the only one, was the Bastille in Paris, which housed many such "guests" in relative comfort (along with low-status prisoners who received the usual sort of harsh treatment).[56] Indeed, political prisoners like Marmontel and Morellet could treat the Bastille as "a certificate of social honorability"—a wholly tolerable, and even pleasant experience—not to mention an experience that paved the way to literary fame.[57] Like Voltaire, visited by the angel of inspiration in Caylus's 1718 drawing—or, for that matter, like Hitler—they regarded prison as a place for the liberation of creative literary-political energies.

The rules of privileged treatment that these confinees expected were undoubtedly sometimes flouted. Indeed, personages like Mirabeau, Linguet, and the marquis de Latude became famous all over Europe for their claims of mistreatment while in confinement.[58] Nevertheless, the underlying assumption behind the books and pamphlets of Mirabeau and Latude was that high-status confinees did not *deserve* mistreatment, and there is no doubt that norms of high-status treatment were taken extremely seriously. Norms of imprisonment were established during the eighteenth century—the right to buy and prepare one's own meals, the right to unencumbered visitation, most broadly the right to respectful treatment—whose subsequent history can be traced right up into the present, both in France in Germany.

Indeed, the status history of contemporary European punishment is largely the history of the generalization of high-status norms of "honorable" imprisonment. No European prisoner today is treated in the way that Voltaire was treated, or in the way that Hitler was treated. But hovering in the background of contemporary prison reform is the image of the treatment that these high-status persons once received. For that matter, no European prisoner today faces execution. But it matters immensely that prisoners who *did* face execution, by the latter part of the nineteenth century, faced *beheading*. After the mid eighteenth century, the classic high-status forms of punishment slowly but steadily came to replace the classic low-status forms, and by the late twentieth, a form of honorable detention vaguely modeled on the privileges of the past came to seem the appropriate ideal for all offenders, if they were to be imprisoned at all.

A Revolution of Status

It was a commonplace of the nineteenth- and early-twentieth-century literature that much of continental reform of the period after the French Revolution had to do with the elimination of "infamy." Any standard treatment of the history of punishment written before the 1930s or so had something to say about this topic. Beheading in particular has always been understood as an old form of "noble" punishment that was generalized to the whole population during the French Revolution.[59] Nevertheless it seems to fair to say that the influence of Foucault—especially in France—has driven discussion of this secular decline in "infamy" to the far margins of our historiography, with the ever-important exception of Pieter Spierenburg, whose *Prison Experience* focuses squarely on the question of infamy.

Yet the question of infamy does indeed belong at the center of our discussion of the history of continental punishment—and not only in Spierenburg's early modern period, but right up through the twentieth century. It is a critical fact that, in continental Europe, low-status treatment has been abolished—and that, conversely, high-status treatment has slowly been generalized to the whole population. This has transpired somewhat differently in France and Germany. Beheading was generalized in both countries. But whereas this happened in France within the first years of the revolution, in Germany the process took longer. The decline in the classically "infaming" punishments also happened far more slowly in Germany. With regard to imprisonment, too, the histories differ somewhat. In France, the tale is one in which privileged forms of imprisonment that were once the preserve of aristocrats and other high-status persons were first generalized to two particular classes of internees: so-called "political prisoners" and debtors. Indeed, for most of the nineteenth and twentieth centuries, the only French offenders who enjoyed privileged forms of imprisonment were political dissenters and debtors, the classes of persons were not considered in French legal culture to be *really* criminals. It is only during the last twenty-five or thirty years that high-status imprisonment has been generalized to all in France. The French pattern of leveling up in status thus runs from *aristocrats and the like; to political dissenters and debtors; to everybody.*

The German tale of imprisonment is somewhat different. In Germany, privileged imprisonment began with a high-status class of persons that included aristocrats, duelists, military officers, and a few other "honorable" groups. When German forms of privileged imprisonment were first generalized, in the nineteenth century, they were principally generalized to persons of "high moral standing." Only since the early 1970s have privileged forms of imprisonment been definitively generalized to all prisoners in Germany. The German pattern thus runs from *aristocrats and the like; to persons of good morals and debtors; to everybody*. Despite these differences, the broad pattern is the same in both countries. In both, the low-status punishments of the eighteenth century were slowly abolished, and the relatively dignified terms of the privileged imprisonment of the mid-eighteenth century slowly became the norm.

The critical shifts in continental justice began with the first years of French Revolution, and it is with those are years that we must begin.

They are years whose history we must read carefully. In particular, we must begin by lifting our eyes up from our Foucault. For Foucauldian historians, the first years of the French Revolution marked a seismic shift from corporal punishment to imprisonment as the normal mode—a shift from disciplining the body to disciplining the soul. This is not entirely false. In a tentative and confused way, imprisonment did begin to establish itself during the revolution. Nevertheless, the large drama of those years involved something else—something that Foucault's familiar sociology obscures. It involved the beginnings of a difficult and slow process by which the old norms of status-differentiation began to break down and take new forms.

Commentators often observe that the first three or four years of the French Revolution were marked by a drive toward egalitarianism in punishment.[60] This is certainly true. But in the context of the stark hierarchical traditions of French society, "égalité" was of course ambiguous: was equality to be achieved by inflicting the old high-status punishments on all offenders, or the old low-status ones? In the early years of the revolution, there were some leaders who clearly aimed to generalize high-status punishment. These reformers, who included most especially Guillotin, enjoyed one especially great success: as we all know, they managed to generalize beheading as the standard mode of execution, in the form of the guillotine. The history of the generalization of beheading is, however, more ambiguous than it looks at first glance; and in other respects—in particular with regard to imprisonment—there is no doubt that status-differentiation survived the revolution.

Let us begin with the history of beheading, and in particular with Maximilien Robespierre. Well before the revolution, in 1783, Robespierre had already argued for generalized beheading. In a prize essay of that year, the future architect of the Terror pleaded for the extension of beheading to all condemned offenders. But he did so for unexpected reasons. The young Robespierre did not of course yet wish to establish a system of terror. But neither did he quite yet wish to safeguard the dignity of executed offenders themselves. Instead, what concerned him, in 1783, was the dignity of offenders' *families.* As we have seen, in the honor-obsessed eyes of the ancien régime, low-status execution stained the entire family of the dead man, which was subjected to a permanent loss of social honor. Robespierre regarded this as a piece of barbarism, and in particular a piece of *inegalitarian* barbarism. Noble families, he observed, were protected in a way that commoner families were not. Even though nobles were subject to the corporal punishment of beheading, "the family of an illustrious offender escapes dishonor: While hanging in the gibbet disgraces the relatives of a commoner forever, the iron that hacks off the head of a grandee does not stain his posterity."[61] Would it not be more enlightened, he asked, to avoid dishonor for family-members by extending beheading to all classes of citizens?[62] Robespierre's aim in this essay was by no means anything so radical as to claim that all offenders should be treated as persons of honor. His aim was to accord commoner *families* the same privileges as noble ones.

The idea that offenders themselves should be treated as persons of honor was apparently too much for Robespierre in 1783, and it remained too extreme an idea once the revolution began. There had been some famous scandals involving "barbaric" punishments in the years before the revolution, and in particular campaigns to abolish judicial torture and the death penalty.[63] Reform was certainly on the table. But with regard to questions of *dignity* in punishment, in the early years of the revolution, the accent almost always remained, not on individual offenders, but on their families. To be sure, there were occasional declarations, in the early months of the revolution, in favor of honor for individual offenders. Most famously, the aristocratic revolutionary Adrien Duport, in a committee report of late December 1789, demanded a system of punishment that would not "insult" the offender: "When the condemned man undergoes his punishment, he loses all or part of his rights as a citizen; but he always retains his rights as a human being. To insult him or mistreat him is a piece of cowardice, and a punishable offense."[64] This statement is often quoted.[65] But we should realize that sentiments like this were rarities in the early years of the revolution—and no surprise. It is important to recognize how profoundly radical Duport's superficially innocuous declaration was. For almost all criminals, prerevolutionary punishment had been *intended* to be insulting. Even in our own American society today, it is difficult to think of offenders as people to be treated in any but a degrading way. A man like Duport was arguing for an authentically radical revaluation of values in punishment in 1789—just as he argued for similar revaluations in other contexts as well.[66]

This was not a program that many others were ready to espouse in the early years of the revolution: ancien régime assumptions remained much too strong. This hesitation to plead for the honor of individual offenders is evident in the history of the generalization of beheading. The great champion of generalized beheading was Joseph Ignace Guillotin, the unfortunate physician whose name will always be associated with the guillotine. Throughout the autumn of 1789, Dr. Guillotin, joined by a couple of others,[67] pressed for legislation eliminating mutilation punishments and guaranteeing that beheading would be the fate of all condemned offenders, regardless of social rank. It was as part of this campaign that he first proposed his "simple machine" in early December 1789. The idea of a beheading machine was not new. Scholars have discovered numerous versions of the guillotine that preceded the French Revolution, dating back at least to the late fifteenth century. There had been many artistic representations of beheading machines, from a Lucas Cranach print to a chillingly merry little 1782 drawing by Henry Fuseli. Such machines had been in use too. Indeed, being beheaded by machine had at least occasionally been a high aristocratic privilege before the revolution. Thus in a famous case in France, Marshall Henri II de Montmorency was beheaded by an early version of the guillotine in 1632, which spared him the shame of being so much as touched by the executioner. And in Bologna, as a French traveler reported in 1730, "When it is a question of executing a gentleman or someone having a privilege of nobility, the executioner uses the *mannaya*," as Bolognese dialect called a device known elsewhere in Italy as the *mandara*. (Only in Scotland, in the very different world of the British Isles, was guillotining generalized to all offenders.)[68] Guillotin's guillotine was thus clearly meant to confer on all Frenchmen the most honorable form of execution possible. The color of Guillotin's aspirations for the guillotine can be read from a print published in 1789, which shows the machine as he conceived it. His beheading machine was to be erected outside the city, far from urban crowds. Those who did come to watch the execution were to be kept at bay by walls. Even the executioner was to avert his eyes, leaving the beheading to be witnessed only by the offender's confessor. A death, in short, with repentance, but without shame.

But who exactly was this "honorable" death to benefit? It is possible that Guillotin, like Duport, wanted his machine to benefit the individual offender—to avoid "insulting" the executed man. In making his public arguments, though, he, like the young Robespierre, spoke of the offender's family. As a contemporary newspaper reported, Guillotin first proposed his machine, on December 1, 1789, "with a touching & pathetic discourse . . . on the barbarism of the punishments concocted by our ancestors, and the bizarre character of a prejudice that covered an honest man with infamy simply because of the misfortune of having, for a relative, a scoundrel who had died by the executioner's hand."[69] This appeal did not succeed, at least partly because of Guillotin's famous ineptitude as an orator. His gory and overheated description of the workings of his beheading machine simply made the Constituent Assembly laugh.[70] Guillotin did achieve an important victory, though, persuading the assembly to pass a law decreeing that "similar offenses shall be sanctioned by similar punishments, without regard to the rank and station of the offender."[71] There was, at least in theory, to be equality in the modes of punishment. But it was not yet to be *high-status* equality.

More success came for Guillotin a few weeks later, but it was still limited success of the same kind. The details deserve some attention, for they show how politically charged the transition to high-status beheading was—how much the French Revolution was a revolution of status. The months of January and February 1790 were marked by two much-discussed hangings, one of an aristocrat, one of a pair of commoners. The aristocrat in question was the marquis de Favras, who had mounted an inept plot to crush the revolution. The marquis was condemned in January and duly hanged in February—shocking treatment for a nobleman, which stirred much comment at the time and which was still being lamented years later.[72] The hanging of an aristocrat "for what the aristocrats call heroism," as Camille Desmoulins sneered, was in effect a revolutionary argument in favor of generalized hanging as the normal mode of death.[73] But there was another celebrated hanging, too, of two commoner brothers, A.-J. and A.-J.-B. Agasse; and this commoner hanging helped Guillotin in his push for a measure of reform intended to benefit commoner families. The Agasse brothers were merchants who, in 1787, had passed some false bills of exchange in London. Bills of exchange were the lifeblood of commerce and forging them was a grave offense.[74] Back in France, the Agasse brothers were tried and convicted in the early months of the revolution. Technically, their offense was counterfeiting—a form of treason that was traditionally treated with horrific harshness. The brothers were condemned to death in December of 1789, and on January 21, they were sentenced to be first publicly displayed, then hanged, before the crowds of the Place de Grève. As was customary, their surviving families were to suffer "infamy" along with them and to be denied possession of their corpses, which were to suffer a shameful burial.[75]

If the hanging of the aristocratic marquis de Favras was something to cheer revolutionary hearts, the hanging of the commoner Agasse brothers seemed scandalous. Indeed, it prompted a classic revolutionary event: a coordinated mobilization in the legislature and the streets. In January 1790, the district of Saint Honoré elected an uncle of the brothers Agasse as its president, thus declaring its solidarity with the infamed family. This was greeted by at least one other district as a courageous and enlightened act.[76] The district of Saint Honoré then marched on the Assembly to demand reform. Meanwhile, on January 21, 1790, the day on which the Agasse brothers were sentenced, Guillotin succeeded in persuading the Assembly to pass three new articles to be added to the law requiring equality in punishment. These articles were effectively to abolish the attachment of infamy to the offender's family:

> Art. 2. Offenses and crimes are personal. The punishment imposed on the offender, and whatever infaming judgments are visited upon the offender, do not impose any stigma on his family. The honor of those who are near to him is not stained in any way, and they shall continue to be admissible to any profession, employment, or dignity.
>
> Art. 3. Confiscation of the offenders' goods shall not be ordered in any case [thus avoiding impoverishing the offenders' surviving family].
>
> Art. 4. The body of the punished person shall be returned to his family if they wish. In any case, it will be buried in the ordinary manner, and no mention of the form of death shall be made in the register.[77]

This was a triumph in its way, but it was still not all that Guillotin wanted: his proposal to make beheading the ordinary punishment was rejected once again.[78] Still, the principle was established that offenders' families were no longer to suffer the taint of dishonor. As for the Agasse brothers, they were hanged on February 8, but the honor of their families was declared intact, and their corpses were returned. This was regarded as a great revolutionary event. Three days after the new law was passed, the District of Saint Honoré held a ceremony honoring Uncle Agasse and received a flowery communication from the president of the assembly, congratulating them in the name of the assembly for having saved "a family from the menace of an unjust prejudice."[79] And the brothers' hanging was celebrated too, in a leading contemporary print series, along with such great events of the revolution as the Tennis Court Oath and the march on Versailles. Janinet's *Principal Events Since the Opening of the Estates General in 1789* included a moving depiction of the brothers' limp bodies being handed over to their families at the foot of gallows.[80]

The revolutionary assembly thus declared the honor of commoner families to be intact in 1790. Nevertheless, this declaration evidently did not eliminate the problem, for the honor of families was still very much at the center of discussion when universalized beheading was finally introduced sixteen months later, in the summer of 1791. In late May, the Assembly was presented with the text of a new criminal code, the Code Pénal of 1791, one of the major achievements of the early years of the revolution. The draft code included at last what Guillotin had sought. Its Article III made a declaration that would appear in continental codes for generations thereafter: "Tout condamné aura la tête tranchée" ("Every person condemned to death shall be beheaded"). This was the article that would stand behind the use of the great republican device, the guillotine, for the next two centuries. But once again, its adoption had to do at least in large part with the honor of families. As the rapporteur of the drafting committee explained, there were two reasons for generalizing beheading. First, the committee regarded it (as others did too) as a gentler way to die than hanging. The committee was thus partly moved by a desire to inflict less pain—a desire of the kind that Pieter Spierenburg has traced in his histories of punishment. But the committee had a second reason as well: "Since opinion attaches no infamy to being beheaded, one is assured of destroying the ancient prejudice that stained an entire family on account of a crime committed by one of its members." One legislator, perhaps thinking of the law of January 1790, objected that that prejudice no longer existed. Nevertheless, the new article passed.[81] A few months later, in March 1792, the guillotine was adopted as a simple and sanitary means of generalized beheading,[82] to be remembered as a symbol of the Terror—but also as a symbol of the republican extension of high-status punishment. It would survive as a republican symbol in France until the abolition of the death penalty in 1981.

How should we interpret these events? What must be emphasized is that they have little to do with anything in the sociology of Foucault. The fundamental conflicts in all this were about status, about honor—and most especially about an idea of punishment that was connected with deeply sensed fears of pollution. In 1789 and 1791, the prevailing sensibility—"l'opinion" as the rapporteur of the Code Pénal put it—still held, as it had held in the ancien régime, that infamous punishment infamed everybody touched by it, regardless of questions of individual guilt. It was for this reason that families seemed endangered. The first generalization of beheading on the continent was thus not precisely about individual *dignity*. It aimed, rather, at establishing a system of individual *guilt*, to replace an older system of collective *pollution*.

Foucauldian sociology explains this history poorly. And the truth is that it explains the early history of imprisonment poorly as well.

Imprisonment too began to establish itself in the early years of the revolution—though it too established itself in tentative and ambiguous ways that were rich in status associations. The Code Pénal of 1791 was once again the critical law. The 1791 code is often treated, in the wake of Foucault's work, as the law that marked the first epochal turn toward imprisonment and away from corporal punishment.[83] This is fair enough, up to a point. The code did eliminate the old mutilation penalties, which is no small thing, and there is no doubt that its principal author, Le Peletier de Saint-Fargeau, set out to place the deprivation of liberty at the center of French punishment.[84] The new code did indeed introduce a variety of types of imprisonment for some offenses, alongside a few other punishments. Nevertheless, the reforms of the Code Pénal of 1791 cannot be understood if we regard them only through the lens of Foucault's sociology. The new system of punishments was not just about a straightforward shift to imprisonment. It was about wrestling with the old system of status-differentiation in punishment—and about a push in the direction of a new kind of status-differentiation.

The great criminal law reform of 1791 was founded on egalitarian principles broadly drawn from the philosophy of Cesare Beccaria. As we have seen, Beccaria had preached, in his influential *Essay on Crimes and Punishments* of 1764, a philosophy of formal equality that condemned the use of mitigations in punishment. Criminal law, according to Beccaria, was to impose exactly the same punishment on every person who committed the same act, and it was not to employ any kind of mitigating devices that might undercut the impact of that punishment. These ideas had proven very attractive in the decades before the revolution, and in 1791 they worked their way into the new code.[85] The reform of 1791 established strict tariffs of punishments to be inflicted every time a given act was committed. It also showed a pronounced hostility to mitigation: the new criminal code made, in general, no provision for extenuating circumstances.[86] At the same time, as we shall see, the practice of pardoning was formally abolished.

This did not mean that the code offered no way of distinguishing among offenses, though. On the contrary, the code introduced an important range of distinctions. But following ancien régime status-traditions, those distinctions were distinctions in the *mode of punishment*. Article I of the code, as it eventually emerged from the legislative process, established no fewer than eight different modes of punishment, which included no fewer than four different varieties of imprisonment: "The penalties that shall be pronounced against persons found guilty after a trial by jury are the death penalty, irons (*fers*), indoor imprisonment (*réclusion dans la maison de force*), the *gêne*, detention, deportation, civic degradation, and the *carcan*."[87] To Foucault, the code of 1791 belonged to a large family of "modern" codes that were pushing toward a new age of imprisonment.[88] There is certainly some truth in this. Yet the punishments specified in this Article I did not by any means represent a simple break with the practices of ancien régime. On the contrary, what they represented was a recasting and revaluation of those practices.

Up to a point, 1791 marked the first step in the abolition of "infamy" in France.[89] But it was in many respects a small step. Certainly beheading, as we already seen, was a triumph for the elimination of at least family infamy. But "civic degradation," loss of rights of citizenship, was an updating of the "infamy in law" of the ancien régime.[90] Certainly the old mutilation punishments were gone, as was branding. But the *carcan*, a heavy wooden collar that resembled shaming devices in other traditional societies, survived. Other forms of prerevolutionary shaming survived too. Everyone subjected to *any* of these penalties was to be publicly shamed, and lose all civic rights.[91] At the same time, showing a characteristic sensitivity to traditional status questions, the code carefully specified procedures by which offenders could, after some years, be rehabilitated as citizens with full honor.[92] Even if they were to be "insulted" for a period, offenders were not to forego all place in the world of honorable Frenchmen.

As for imprisonment, it is wildly underdescriptive to characterize the 1791 code as a code that introduced imprisonment in place of corporal punishment. What it introduced was a *variety of modes* of imprisonment, all of them with roots in the ancien régime. The punishment of "irons" was a recasting of the forced labor in the galleys and shipyards that predated the revolution—a standard form of low-status imprisonment, to be served with ball and chain, though now limited by a provision forbidding life sentences.[93] "Indoor imprisonment" was the punishment for women and girls who would otherwise be subjected to "irons": they were now to be enclosed in workhouses like those of the ancien régime.[94] The *gêne* and detention, finally, were especially interesting forms, for they were two versions of the old modes of high-status imprisonment. The *gêne* was an isolation cell, which was to be well-lit, and in which the offender was to sit unshackled, but alone.[95] Offenders condemned to the *gêne* were to be permitted to work, and to use a third of their earnings to provide better food for themselves.[96] This was not imprisonment à la Voltaire, but it did spare offenders the shame of shackles; and the right to have food from outside the prison was an important marker of high status. As for those condemned to detention, they were to be segregated from other offenders, and they too were to be allowed to apply their earnings to food.[97] Prisoners were also to be allowed to apply their personal wealth to maintaining themselves while in detention, unmistakably "perpetuating the inequalities in the treatment of prisoners" of the ancien régime.[98]

And who was to receive these more privileged forms of imprisonment? It can hardly be surprising that they were destined principally for political offenders.[99] Prerevolutionary political prisoners, as we have seen, were lettre de cachet prisoners, typically held in relatively comfortable circumstances. The traditional notion that political offenders were entitled to special treatment had not died with the revolution. Widespread liberal agitation against the imprisonment of political dissenters through lettres de cachet had been, of course, a leading theme of 1789, and famously, the revolution itself commenced with the storming of the Bastille, which contained lettre de cachet prisoners. In March 1790, the assembly had abolished lettres de cachet, with the intention of freeing high-status prisoners.[100] Nevertheless, it is not news that political dissidents continued to be arrested during all phases of the revolution. Under the 1791 Code, though, they were, like their lettre de cachet forbears, to be entitled to better forms of imprisonment. The new code specified a wide range of offenses "against the Constitution." A few were punishable by death or civic degradation, but for the overwhelming majority the punishment was a number of years in the *gêne*.[101] Detention was also a punishment destined for a type of political offender: for those private citizens who disobeyed the orders of the authorities without using arms;[102] and for recalcitrant government officers and jurors as well.[103] This was rougher treatment than political dissidents had received before the revolution—but it was at least special treatment, which spared them "irons," the normal fate of common criminals. A few other minor offenses were also to be punished with detention,[104] but the basic thrust of the code was to preserve relatively milder forms of imprisonment for those who resisted the state, a well-established French tradition.

The Code Pénal of 1791, in short, was not just about imprisonment. Like the law of the ancien régime that preceded it, it was about different forms of imprisonment for different persons. So is it correct to say that 1791 marked a stage in the rise of imprisonment, as Foucault would suggest? Yes, seen from a certain distance, it is perfectly correct: if we abstract from the detailed provisions of the code, we can see in it the beginnings of a regime of imprisonment that would last into the late nineteenth century. Nevertheless, abstracting from the details makes for risky history writing, and in this case in particular, it clouds our perception of a crucial fact. Imprisonment in the early years of the revolution preserved critical dimensions of status differentiation—dimensions that would be of immense importance for the development of styles of continental justice deeply different from American styles by the end of the twentieth century.

The tradition of special treatment did not die in subsequent years. Political prisoners were, of course, taken in large numbers as the revolution swung toward the Terror.[105] One commissioner reported in 1793, unsurprisingly, that they were suffering from overcrowding. He recommended that one prison be devoted exclusively to holding them.[106] Overcrowding was the least of the problems that political prisoners faced during the Terror. Nevertheless, the tradition of special treatment was not forgotten: a few weeks after the fall of Robespierre, the new government commissioned a study of the prisons, which declared that political prisoners were once again being treated with appropriate respect, held in "spacious, healthy and commodious" places of detention, in which the screams of horror that had accompanied the Terror were no longer heard.[107] Nor were political prisoners the only high-status persons to remain in confinement. Debtors too remained imprisoned. There were moves afoot in both 1791 and 1793 to abolish imprisonment for debt.[108] Nothing came of these, though, and in the year VI (1798), a law was passed which ratified imprisonment for debt—this time leaving judges with no arbitrary power to liberate debtors.[109]

Both classes of high-status prisoners, dissidents and debtors, thus remained in confinement during the early years of the revolution, and both would remain in confinement in France for a long time to come. In fact, with the Napoleonic legislation, debtors were effectively subjected to *life* imprisonment—sentenced, as it was said, "to be released from the custody of prison into the custody of the grave."[110] As for political prisoners, the Napoleonic period continued to accord them special regard. The critical moment for the survival of the old distinctions in punishment was the year 1810, a year at which the Napoleonic Empire stood near the peak of its glory. In that year, the government of Napoleon undertook a variety of reform measures.[111] The most lasting of these was the Criminal Code of 1810, which was to form the framework of French justice—and much of continental justice more broadly—for generations. That code was especially important, for my purposes here, because it reinstituted certain low-status punishments, notably branding.[112] But there was more to the seminal program of 1810 than that. For if the Napoleonic reformers reestablished these classically *low-status* punishments, they also reestablished some classically *high-status* ones. Indeed, the Napoleonic reforms of 1810 represented a watershed: it was in that year that ancien régime traditions of status-differentiation in punishment decisively reasserted themselves, and did so in forms that would continue to shape European law down into the present day.[113]

The reforms of 1810 require indeed some close attention, for they took complex forms, and set the tone for the entire nineteenth century. First of all, the Napoleonic Criminal Code of 1810 used the old tradition of special high-status treatment in a way that established a pattern whose importance for continental Europe I have already described. This is the pattern of distinguishing between full-throttle "crimes" on the one hand, and mere "délits" and "contraventions" on the other.[114] As I suggested above, these distinctions are of central importance for a European law that has avoided expanding the universe of the "criminal" as American law has done. They are also of central importance for a European law that finds ways to convict offenders without stigmatizing them as "criminals." European mildness and dignity in punishment is predicated on the practice of grading some offenses as less than fully "criminal." The rise of this practice is thus of great interest.

And when we look to the rise of this practice, as it was first formulated in 1810, we discover that it drew precisely on the ancien régime tradition of distinguishing high-status and low-status punishment. The very opening phrase of the code, indeed, established differences in modes of punishments as nothing less than the code's fundamental ordering principle:

> Art. 1 An infraction that the laws punish by police punishments [peines de police] is a *contravention*.
>
> An infraction that the laws punish by correctional punishments [peines correctionelles] is a *délit*.
>
> An infraction that the laws punish by an afflictive or infaming punishment [peine afflictive ou infamante], is a *crime*.

6. Criminal punishments are either afflictive and infaming, or simply infaming.
7. The afflictive and infaming punishments are:
    1. Death;
    2. Life imprisonment at forced labor;

3. Deportation;
4. Term imprisonment at forced labor;
5. Imprisonment without forced labor [réclusion].

Branding and general confiscation of goods can be imposed concurrently with an afflictive punishment in cases specified by law.

8. The infaming punishments are,
   1. The carcan;
   2. Banishment;
   3. Civil degradation
9. The correctional punishments are,
   1. Term imprisonment in a place of correction;
   2. Loss of civic, civil, or family rights for a certain period;
   3. Fines.
12. Every person condemned to death shall be beheaded.
13. Any offender condemned to death for the crime of parricide shall be led to the place of execution in a simple shirt [en chemise], barefoot, with his head covered by a black veil.

    He will be displayed on the scaffold while the sergeant at arms reads the order of condemnation to the people; subsequently his right hand shall be severed, and he shall be immediately executed.
15. Men condemned to forced labor shall be set to tasks of the hardest and most servile kind [aux travaux les plus pénibles]; they shall wear a ball and chain, or shall be shackled together two by two, providing that the work to which they have been set allows it.
16. Women and girls condemned to forced labor shall not be compelled to labor except in the interior of a prison.

The punishments specified in this code were intended to be somewhat harsher versions of the punishments of 1791;[115] and that is what they are. In these punishments, we can indeed see, as in 1791, an updating of the old repertoire of low-status, shameful punishments, and of some of the old high-status punishments as well. Branding is back. (Already in 1801, Target, the Napoleonic era draftsman, was arguing that the old low-status punishment of branding had to be reintroduced, and a law of 1802 had done so.)[116] The concern for offenders' families has faded: confiscation of offenders' goods, appearing here in the code, inevitably impoverished the offenders' children, as the drafters readily admitted.[117] We can see more too. We can see how the drafters of the code aimed to define offenses that merited honorable, high-status punishment as mere "contraventions" or "délits." This is particularly true of one classically high-status activity: the dueling insult, carefully defined as a "contravention."[118] We can see that some forms of honorable punishment—the "correctional punishments," the *peines correctionelles*—were precisely the forms that would eventually be generalized to all French prisoners at the end of the twentieth century: imprisonment without forced labor, fines, and deprivation of certain rights. And in all of this, we can see the dawning initial stages of a rebirth of the old hierarchical world—of a world in which honorable persons who were not *really* "criminals" committed honorable offenses that were not *really* "crimes."

The new Criminal Code of 1810 was, moreover, only one of the fateful major reforms of that year. In 1810 also came the revival of old-style special terms of imprisonment for high-status persons, and especially for one particular kind of offender, the political dissident.

Here too, the critical practice was established by the reforms of the glorious Napoleonic year of 1810; and it was a practice that revived one of the traditional cultural markers of high status in punishment: imprisonment in a fortress. The new criminal code abolished the *gêne*, the isolation cell once destined for political prisoners. This punishment, the Napoleonic government explained, was so horrible that it could never practically be inflicted.[119] This did not mean that political offenders were simply to be treated as common criminals, though. The government rapporteur explained that dissidents were now to be banished: "In suppressing [the *gêne*], we have reestablished the punishment of relegation or banishment; this punishment has seemed to us appropriate for certain political crimes . . . which must not be punished by penalties reserved for deeply corrupt persons."[120] Only certain political offenses were to bring banishment, though.[121] Others were to meet with death, confiscation of goods, or a whole range of penalties, including *réclusion*, the mildest form of imprisonment.[122] But where was that *réclusion* to be suffered? A decree of March 3, a month after the promulgation of the code, regularized a prison system that gave special treatment to high-status prisoners in a form that would survive for generations in Europe: so-called "fortress confinement." March 3, also a day when Napoleon issued a decree permitting the Napoleonic nobility to reestablish their specially marked "palaces" and "hôtels" in Paris,[123] brought special housing for high-status convicts as well. Fortresses had always been the places where high-status prisoners, whether convicts or hostages, had been held, and they were to resume that function. Royalists, nobles, and persons of wealth, as well as other high-status political dissidents, were channeled to several *châteaux*, among them Vincennes (where Mirabeau among others had once been held) and the Château d'If, off the coast of Marseilles (familiar to all readers of *The Count of Monte Cristo*).[124] By the end of the Napoleonic period, something close to the ancien régime system of comparatively honorable confinement for aristocrats and political prisoners had thus returned.

The Revolution of 1830

The collapse of the Napoleonic empire saw the temporary end of such special terms of imprisonment, at least for dissidents. The Restoration did not generally indulge in favored treatment for political activists. On the contrary, the large-scale political persecutions of the so-called "White Terror" of 1814–16 resulted in the imprisonment of some leading liberals. Shockingly, to the consciousness of persons with a sense of social hierarchy, these prisoners were frequently treated as "common criminals." Complaints were bitter, and they showed a strong, and deeply stung, status-sensibility: it seemed wrong, and indeed offensive, that persons who were not "really" criminals should be mixed with persons who were. As one affronted dissident wrote in 1817, "Instead of being considered a prisoner of state, or at least simply as a man condemned to an indefinite term of imprisonment, I was placed in Bicêtre [a leading prison of the day] in an insalubrious place, on a mat of straw, between two convicts who doubtless should have had only convicts for companions."[125] One liberal dissident, subjected to the humiliation of being publicly shamed, became a popular martyr, with flowers strewn on the spot where he had been displayed.[126] In 1823, there was a flood of angry literature about the treatment of a dissident attorney, who had been chained to "common criminals" in the "convoy," the humiliating public forced march of convicts. It was, said the victim, a shocking way of treating an "homme de bien."[127] Stirred by these sorts of scandals, French liberals of 1820s began to agitate once again for special treatment for "political prisoners"; as de Broglie, a leading political figure, wrote in 1829, at the very least politicals should be confined with such honorable persons as those who had committed homicides under provocation—not with ordinary convicts.[128]

Opposition to the death penalty—which lies, of course, at the core of modern European humanitarianism—was associated with the treatment of political dissenters as well. Largely under the influence of Beccaria and others, the eighteenth century had seen considerable agitation against the death penalty.[129] Nevertheless it survived the revolution, and was in heavy use throughout the nineteenth century. Nineteenth-century opposition followed the nineteenth-century pattern I have been tracing. The leading text of the early part of the century was another product of the strained politics of the 1820s: this was Guizot's *The Death Penalty in Political Cases*, published in 1822. Guizot, the great liberal leader operating in a climate of reaction, was careful to limit his claims. The death penalty, he confined himself to saying, should not be inflicted on political offenders.[130] This was not because he did not wish for a more complete abolition some day,[131] but because sparing political dissidents was, for the moment, all that one could hope for.

Political dissidents were not the only respectable persons whom liberal thinkers of the 1820s deemed mistreated. There were two other classes, too: debtors and duelists. Under the Napoleonic legislation, as we have seen, debtors were subject to life imprisonment. Efforts of 1817 and 1818 to shorten their sentences were rejected by the Chambre de Pairs, the newly established French equivalent of the House of Lords. In 1820, though, the government did improve debtors' conditions of imprisonment by decree, guaranteeing them at least better food.[132] Finally, as the Revolution of 1830 approached, a draft bill of 1828 proposed to shorten their sentences and to allow judges to grant *sursis*, suspended sentence. This would become the basis of a major reform in 1832.[133] As for duelists, their lot too began to seem unduly harsh. Dueling was the classic offense of "honorable" criminals—an offense that many French authors for centuries had declared to be wholly pardonable in a man of honor. Nevertheless, the French monarchy had engaged in a dogged effort to suppress it, and it had been subject to the death penalty since the sixteenth century.[134] The new criminal legislation of the Napoleonic period no longer specifically forbade dueling, but it treated it as murder or (as the case might be) attempted murder. And in its Beccarian simplicity, the Napoleonic criminal code made no provision for excusing, justifying, or extenuating murder in a duel. Murder, in the code, was murder. This would perhaps have seemed hard under any circumstances, but it may have seemed particularly hard in Restoration France, where the practice of dueling had begun to spread from the aristocratic and military classes to the high bourgeoisie.[135] Dueling was yet another "criminal" activity in which "hommes de bien" engaged. Correspondingly, the 1820s saw considerable efforts to ease the treatment of duelists. The great shifts came, though, with the Revolution of 1830.

With 1830, my story deviates once again from our familiar historiography of nineteenth-century punishment. Our standard histories of imprisonment focus heavily on the years after the Revolution of 1830. These were the years when Tocqueville and Beaumont (alongside other reformers) brought back the cellular system from America to France, and this has seemed to most historians the tale to be told.[136] Yet the Revolution of 1830 can be seen otherwise too. As Tocqueville, Beaumont, and their contemporaries who lived through the revolution recognized, it can be seen as a revolution against infamy in punishment. The revolution was both preceded and followed by literature raising much doubt about the propriety of infamy in punishment.[137] Indeed, Tocqueville and Beaumont themselves proudly noted that the Revolution of 1830 had succeeded in eliminating such practices as branding, the *carcan*, and the amputation of the right hand of the parricide.[138] To be sure, many aspects of low-status treatment remained until 1848 and after. Frenchmen were not ready to eliminate dishonor from punishment entirely.[139] Nevertheless, contemporaries perceived the Revolution of 1830 as partly a revolution against low status in punishment, and it was.

Moreover, the revolution can be seen as a revolution in favor of *high* status. For it was in many ways a revolution that benefited "respectable or at least respected business and professional men,"[140] to borrow Sutherland's famous characterization of white-collar offenders. Cellular imprisonment did arrive on the scene. But the years after 1830 were also the watershed era for special treatment for high-status offenders—political dissidents and debtors in particular.

With regard to political dissenters, the Revolution of 1830 resumed the work of 1810, this time firmly securing to them non-"common criminal" status. An initial law of April 28, 1832, subjected political prisoners to five years of a kind of confinement called "detention," to be served, not in prison, but, once again, in a "fortress."[141] To one liberal deputy, this seemed complete proof of the advanced character of France: "The new punishment of detention," he declared, "is intended above all for the suppression of political offenses. It will demonstrate to future ages the high degree of civilization that our Fatherland has attained."[142] Nevertheless, further protests followed from those imprisoned, and the government of Adolphe Thiers responded with further reforms. In particular an *arrêté* of July 7, 1834, set the terms for what would be considered "humane" prison conditions in France down to the end of the twentieth century. This edict accorded political prisoners the following rights: (1) They were dispensed from forced labor; (2) they were given the right to wear clothing of their own choice, rather than being subjected to the humiliation of special prison uniforms; (3) they were guaranteed a superior dietary regime; (4) they were given the choice of their own doctor; (5) they were given the right to receive books from outside; and (6) they were given the right to a "parloir particulier," a visiting room in which they could entertain without interference from guards.[143] Well down into the mid-1840s, French authors were celebrating the majestic humanity of the new special treatment instituted in 1832–34.[144] "Fortress confinement" seemed of capital importance in the world of politics after the Revolution of 1830.

It mattered in art and literature, too; high-status imprisonment was a theme of the revolutionary day. The most famous of nineteenth-century prison memoirs, *My Prisons*, by Silvio Pellico, reached Europe in the early months of 1832. Pellico, the author of the high romantic play *Francesca da Rimini* and a prisoner of Metternich's Austrian reaction for ten years in the Fortress Spielberg, became the prime example everywhere of a maltreated political detainee.[145] And in 1839 Stendhal, a *littérateur* always quick to sense the interests of the public, published his *Charterhouse of Parma*, whose hero spent many romantic chapters imprisoned in his own Austrian fortress.[146] Meanwhile artists initiated a whole minor tradition of representations of the lives of political prisoners. The most famous example is Daumier's unusually haunting "Memory of Sainte-Pélagie," published in 1834 after the young artist had served some time as a prisoner in Sainte-Pélagie, the standard place of confinement for politicals.[147] (Sainte-Pélagie, Daumier reported in a letter from the prison, would not leave any "terrible memory—quite the contrary.")[148] But there were many others as well, with such titles as "The Poet Enters Prison."

All this had nothing to do with cellular imprisonment, or indeed with the lives of the overwhelming majority of French offenders. The fate of political prisoners may indeed seem properly the stuff of Stendhal novels, of little importance to the main currents of prison reform. Nevertheless, as French scholar Jean-Claude Vimont has argued, it was with the creation of this special regime of imprisonment, harking directly back to the old world of lettre de cachet prisoners, that what would be the twentieth-century history of French prison conditions began to unfold. Every one of the reforms of 1832–34 was to reemerge in the great modern French prison reform of the early 1980s; indeed, more broadly, the story of French prison reform since the 1830s has largely been the story of the extension of these rights. For nonpolitical prisoners, public punishment survived into the mid nineteenth century in France. Ordinary French convicts were still obliged to submit to being publicly displayed; and despite the reforms of the revolution, infamy was still attached to many of their punishments, as Tocqueville and Beaumont felt compelled to note.[149] As for their humiliating obligation to submit to forced labor: that would survive deep into the twentieth century.

But for political prisoners, the story was different after the revolution of 1830. The rights decreed by the government of Thiers became the basis of a so-called "special regime," instituted in particular in a special prison section famous throughout the nineteenth century: the "Pavillon des Princes" or "Red Corridor" in Sainte-Pélagie, a prison since demolished, but then situated in the Quartier Latin in Paris. Sainte-Pélagie, founded in 1792, housed journalists and other political undesirables for generations. Its privileged population was made up primarily of debtors in the early decades of the nineteenth century, but after the reforms of 1834 they were joined by political dissidents.[150] Especially in the latter part of nineteenth century, governed by the liberal rules of the "special regime," it was to become well known for its vibrant social life, its fine meals (catered daily by a local restaurant with the charmingly belligerent Parisian name "Mieux Ici Qu'en Face," "Better Here Than Across the Street"),[151] and its heavy use of prostitutes.[152]

The debtor inmates of Sainte-Pélagie also benefited from the Revolution of 1830. The draft bill of 1828 became law in 1832, with drastically abbreviated sentences and provision for specially housing detained debtors.[153] (In other ways too, French law after the revolution found methods to favor debtors: at least one court, the Tribunal de la Seine, newly empowered to vary the sentence meted out to debtors, regularly treated nonpayment of debt as a *contravention*, sending debtors into detention for the period served by persons convicted of public drunkenness.[154] Grading offenses low in this way is, as I have suggested above, an important form of mildness, which goes far to diminish the stigma of conviction.)

As for duelists, they arguably benefited from one of the most dramatic legal reforms of the early 1830s. The Criminal Code of 1810 had retained the Beccarian cast of early revolutionary criminal legislation, avoiding all forms of mitigation. An 1824 law introduced the doctrine of extenuating circumstances for some offenses; and in 1832, the doctrine was extended to cover all. This reform, which represented the most important theoretical departure in forty years, entrusted the criminal jury with the authority to acquit offenders for whom extenuating circumstances could be shown. Which offenders were those? They were especially offenders who had committed "honorable" offenses—most particularly violence that had been "justifiably" provoked by one insult or another. Such offenses, in the mentality of the day, did not really deserve to suffer the full brunt of the law. Duelists fit easily within the category entitled to this mild treatment. So juries at least apparently saw it. In 1836, the government of Louis Philippe, following centuries of royal tradition, declared that it would treat this "honorable" activity under the law of attempted murder.[155] In the event, though, juries simply acquitted the duelists who were brought before them. As French practice developed in the 1830s, duelists who had been obedient to the rules of the leading French version of the Code Duello were routinely acquitted by juries—a practice that would continue right up until World War I.[156]

Political prisoners, debtors, duelists: these are not the persons we usually talk about when we discuss French punishment after 1830. On the contrary, the story that is usually told is the story of cellular imprisonment as advocated by Tocqueville and Beaumont. Does that story fit in at all?

In fact it does. Tocqueville and Beaumont were hardly unaware of the traditions of honor in French law. Indeed, they explicitly acknowledged that those traditions posed problems for the introduction of cellular imprisonment in their country. As we shall see in the next chapter, the continental drive to eliminate the old low-status punishments was hardly to be found in the United States. Indeed, Tocqueville and Beaumont's 1833 report on cellular imprisonment had to acknowledge the fact that the United States seemed attached to "barbaric" punishments that the French were in the course of abandoning. The American states, the two aristocratic authors had to report, imposed the death penalty for what seemed a shocking range of offenses.[157] Moreover, American criminal law still included "the most infaming punishments, such as the pillory; and others, of a revolting cruelty, such as branding and mutilation." There were also fines at a level indistinguishable from the confiscation of goods, long associated with familial dishonor in France.[158] Within the prisons, too, they found practices that were difficult for a French observer to accept. Flogging was in widespread use, as we shall see in the next chapter.[159] This disturbed Beaumont and Tocqueville. Such punishment was "ignominious," as they noted; was not its effect then contrary to the great goal, which was to "raise the morality of a man who viewed himself as fallen in his own eyes?"[160] To this they could only answer that American society conceived things differently from French: sailors too were flogged, to which "no idea of infamy is attached."[161] Americans had not yet learned the importance of suppressing "infamy." This endangered the whole American penitentiary project, Tocqueville and Beaumont thought: "How could one hope to raise the morality" of offenders who had been "degraded" and indeed indelibly marked with a brand?[162] They admitted that there was a real danger that "l'opinion publique" in France would not accept prison discipline involving such "infamy."[163] Americans were going to have to learn to outgrow degradation, and introducing the penitentiary system into France would require eliminating its infaming practices.[164] (They noted other disturbing features of American imprisonment too. Americans did not permit prisoners to use their earnings to provide better food for themselves, as had long been standard for higher-status prisoners in France. This Beaumont and Tocqueville regarded as too severe.)[165] Tocqueville and Beaumont did indeed see America through the eyes of Frenchmen, accustomed to two generations of efforts to eliminate "infamy" from punishment. Their admiration for America was predicated on a pious hope—the hope that the American attachment to infamy would fade with time.

As for the two contrasting cellular systems: these too they interpreted through French eyes. Total isolation on the Pennsylvania model risked destroying men's health and minds, they famously concluded. But they also made the interesting observation that persons "with souls endowed with a certain elevation, and polished by education" could tolerate isolation better.[166] This was something that other Frenchmen thought, too—including Bérenger, the great late-nineteenth-century reformer.[167] Solitary confinement, for these Frenchmen, was something like the *gêne*, the isolation cell destined by the early revolution for political dissidents. When Tocqueville thought about the Philadelphia system, which attracted him very much,[168] he was thinking about traditions connected to high-status punishment in France.

Still, their system was certainly not meant for the "more cultivated" class. It could not have been, given the strength of French status sensibilities. (Tocqueville indeed presumably did not think that political dissenters should be prosecuted at all: when he described the "benign" character of American criminal justice seven years later in his *Democracy in America*, the prime piece of evidence that he offered was that America had no political prisoners.)[169] In fact, the idea of subjecting the tiny minority of honorable prisoners to the sort of cellular confinement seen in either the Auburn system or the Pennsylvania system was unacceptable and indeed almost unimaginable. As one writer put it in 1840, as the cellular reforms were being debated, it was inconceivable that anyone could want the "pain and humiliation" of imprisonment to strike "the elevated class of society."[170] Indeed, one of the reactions that greeted Beaumont and Tocqueville in 1840 was an indignant refusal to subject persons of honor to the treatment they were proposing.[171] Beaumont was in fact forced to include a special provision preserving the privileges of political prisoners, and they were saved from the menace of cellular imprisonment.[172] This perhaps mattered little to Tocqueville and Beaumont, who were indeed primarily concerned with the vast majority of inmates convicted of ordinary crimes. For the history of French punishment practice, though, it mattered immensely: the treatment of the tiny minority of high-status prisoners was the germ from which much of twentieth-century punishment practices would eventually spring.

1848 and After

The basic pattern of development was set by the events that followed the Revolution of 1830. There were some further reforms after 1848—though reform was certainly slow. The last of the old low-status punishments of public exposure and corporal violence were eliminated after 1848, but forced labor survived.[173] Intellectual assaults on "infamy" gathered momentum.[174] Another attempt to abolish imprisonment for debt failed.[175] These were simply continuations of the basic trends of the previous twenty years or so. Meanwhile, in the 1850s, after Napoleon III's seizure of power, France began to take what was an important tack in the direction of strange kind of quasi-reform. While continuing the progress of abolition in metropolitan France, the French began to export harsh punishment to penal colonies in Algeria and the new world.[176] Serious political offenders too were to serve their "fortress detention" on Devil's Island after 1854—a place where the privileges of the political offender, if technically maintained by the law, would hardly amount to a pleasant life;[177] and subsequently other like places would be established in Guyana.[178] If the old punishments were no longer tolerable within France itself, they could nevertheless be maintained abroad.

Still, within the charmed hexagon of "civilized" metropolitan France, almost all of the historic low-status punishments had been eliminated by the late nineteenth century, at least in theory;[179] and political dissidents and debtors sat in relatively comfortable "detention." Indeed, for journalists toward the end of the century, a stay in the riotous environment of Sainte-Pélagie as a political prisoner had become part of the normal course of a career. There they hardly lived badly. Nor did debtors—which led inevitably to occasional indignant reports, like this one from 1850:

> We note the scandal of the famous capitalist who, possessing a fortune of ten million, preferred to spend five years in Sainte-Pélagie rather than to pay the two and a half million that he owed. . . . The debtor, finding himself too confined in the handsome apartments that the director had assigned to him, paid the debts of the poor devils who were his neighbors, and who were in his way. Then, having demolished the walls, he transformed his prison in a garden of delights worthy of a satrap. There, he lived the life of a grand seigneur, hosting Parisian celebrities at his table every day, and giving parties frequented by the most stylish ladies.[180]

This may be balderdash—but then again it may not be. Certainly there is plenty of evidence that political confinees lived high in Sainte-Pélagie.[181] The class of imprisonable debtors was limited effectively to those whose obligations arose from criminal matters and debts to the state in legislation of 1867 and 1871.[182] Imprisonments for debt nevertheless remained a common occurrence, debtors remained a presence in the prisons, and jurists continued to write carefully about their treatment.[183] As for political prisoners. all of the old ideas about special treatment for them survived the fall of Napoleon III and the establishment of the Third Republic.[184] Political prisoners like the socialist agitator Louise Michel could still talk much as their eighteenth-century forbears had done: "In prison," wrote Michel in 1885, "I have found a happiness that I never knew when I was free. I have the leisure to devote myself to my studies."[185] This was the old idea of cultured confinement that extended back to Voltaire and that would extend up to Hitler.

Fine conditions for political prisoners were naturally not entirely welcome to French governments, and the "special regime" suffered ups and downs over the nineteenth century. Efforts to eliminate the "special regime" later in the century did have an interesting sort of mixed success. A late-nineteenth-century plan by the minister of the interior, Constans, to forbid inmates to receive visits from anyone but family members stirred outraged opposition. Constans was forced to issue a decree formalizing the "special regime" on January 4, 1890.[186] The journalists and politicians who occupied Sainte-Pélagie were not to be deprived of their privileges.[187] But agitation against the special regime for "anarchists" had more success: *they* were refused special treatment through legislation of 1893-94.[188] Like terrorists in current European law, anarchists were people whom French criminal justice had no difficulty hitting hard. *They* at least were criminals, not merely opponents of the state. Yet despite the legislation of 1893–94, and the elimination of Sainte-Pélagie,[189] the "special regime" did not die in France. A circular of 1923 reaffirmed and reregulated it;[190] and it remained in force right up through the late 1930s.

Nor did it perish with World War II and its aftermath. On the contrary, the great postwar reforms that set the terms for modern prison law were undertaken very much under the star of this old tradition of special treatment for political prisoners. Indeed, the making of humanitarian prison law in France since 1945 has always been bound up with the problem of political prisoners and indeed has tended to take the form of generalizing the old "special regime" to everybody—of taking the model of the political prisoner in creating a world in which no convict ever quite acquires the low status of "criminal" as it once existed.

To understand the crucial last half-century of development, we must begin in the spring of 1945, and we must bear in mind the sheer chaos of the immediate postwar situation. Today, one tends to think of 1945 as a time when the principal task facing the Allies was the elimination of fascism. But the problems of the day were much more complex than that. First of all, the record of Vichy on prisons was more ambiguous than one might suppose. As Pedron has shown, Vichy, while it certainly displayed some harshness, was also a period of some important reform movements—movements that paralleled developments in Germany to which I will return.[191] Second, the problems that faced administrators in the wake of the war were not all problems created by the fascists. In 1945, France was faced with a staggering number of prisoners, living in miserable prison conditions, very many of whom had been collaborators.[192] Indeed, the postwar situation was horrific not just on account of what the Nazis had done. The treatment of collaborators, real and suspected, was terrible as well. As one recent author describes it: "At the same time that the first prisoners started returning to France after having been deported, incarcerated and tortured for having participated in the Resistance, the liberation offered the spectacle of massive internments of collaborators. These sinister forms of 'on-the-job learning' ['travaux pratiques'] testified to the end of an epoch, in which respect for man had been totally unknown."[193] This is a situation that we must not forget in trying to understand the making of postwar reforms. Undoubtedly knowledge of Nazi atrocities played a very great role in the thinking of French administrators. But the immediate problem they faced was not Dachau; the immediate problem they faced was the chaos of vengeance-taking, summary trials, and summary executions—a chaos of lynch justice largely directed *against* former fascists.

Faced with these problems, the newly installed government followed a hallowed French pattern, trying to guarantee standards of humane treatment that largely redounded to the benefit of the newest class of "political" prisoners. To be sure, it proved impossible to accord ex-fascists and collaborators the special status of "political prisoners" in 1945. A petition to that effect was apparently rejected.[194] Indeed, unlike the honorable political prisoners of the past, collaborators were widely sentenced to "national degradation," a "perpetual dishonoring penalty." (In the event, "perpetual" lasted only until the early 1950s, when these offenders generally benefited from amnesty legislation.)[195] But if the losers of the war were not treated as "politicals," they nevertheless benefited from a program that spared them the worst of the treatment that they had been receiving, in the form of the government's fourteen principles, promulgated in May 1945, which established the norms of resocialization that continue to rule in French punishment practice to this day. The 1945 regulations established a generally applicable regime of resocialization, including the reform, critical at the time, of requiring professional training for guards:

1. The essential goal of imprisonment is the improvement and social reintegration [*reclassement social*] of the offender.
3. The treatment inflicted upon prisoners, who are to be shielded from all corrupting promiscuity [i.e. from the mixing of different classes of offenders together], must be humane, without petty torments, and it must tend principally toward his general and professional instruction and amelioration.
4. Every common criminal is obliged to work, and benefits from legal protection against accidents. . . .
8. A progressive regime is in force in each establishment, which aims to adapt the treatment of the prisoner to his attitude and his degree of improvement. This regime ranges from confinement in a cell to semi-liberty.
10. In every penitentiary establishment there is a social service and a medical-psychological service.
11. All punishments for a term have the benefit of conditional parole.
12. [Prisoners to receive assistance to aid in social reintegration.]
13. Every agent of the penitentiary service is do a course of study at a special technical school.

This was, on its face, a regime for all. Yet it simply must be the case that these "humane" provisions aimed largely to protect collaborators and accused collaborators, who were the victims of the most shocking treatment of those troubled months. In this there is perhaps an irony: the "dignity" protected by French (and German) law is often, at its origin, the dignity of real or accused fascists.[196] But that irony is not of any great moment. What matters is that French justice was treading familiar ground, giving itself over to humane instincts where the interests of the political losers were at stake after a change in regime.

At any rate, the prison reforms that followed were real enough to provoke denunciations, during the ensuing years, of "four-star prisons."[197] There was still plenty of resentment at the idea that convicts should be treated as anything but lesser human beings. The postwar reforms were, however, only the beginning of a process that would gather steam all through the second half of the twentieth century, carrying the process of the generalization of the old special regime ever further. For as we trace the history of recent prison reform, we can see, as Vimont has shown, that at every stage it was bound up closely with the problem of political prisoners. Raising the status of prisoners in France has consistently meant identifying them with "politicals," with persons who are perceived as opponents of the state rather than, more darkly, as criminals.

Political conflict, and especially arrests of political dissidents, thus made for reform at every stage in recent French history. The first critical moment in recent history came with the upheavals of the Algerian war. The social conflict that accompanied the Algerian war in France led to what were, by the standards of the day, mass imprisonments, especially in the prison of Fresnes, outside Paris. Those imprisoned regarded themselves, perhaps understandably, as "politicals"; and following very old French tradition, they demanded better conditions than were afforded other prisoners.[198] The government of de Gaulle, caught up in a socially destructive conflict, resisted the demand to treat those imprisoned as politicals for a very long time.[199] Eventually, though, faced with massive protests, the government gave in. One consequence was a reinscription of the special regime in the Code of Criminal Procedure in 1958, with further regulation in 1960.[200] Another was a particularly important reform, ending one of the most deeply rooted of low-status punishments: the definitive abolition of forced labor came at last, with an ordinance of June 4, 1960.[201]

More collapsed though, in 1960, than official resistance to the idea that Algerian war protesters were political. The very idea that there should be some categorical difference between "politicals" and others began to crumble as well. Out of this period sprang a reform literature that gathered momentum throughout the 1960s. (Indeed, it is this literature of prison reform agitation that eventually produced Michel Foucault's activities of the early 1970s.)[202] The reform movement gathered momentum as the troubles of the late 1960s recapitulated the troubles of the Algerian war. Left-wing militants demanded treatment as political prisoners, and eventually received it. The result was yet another modification of the "special regime" in 1971, and the creation of a committee to reconsider the whole body of law. That committee produced yet further changes in the "special regime," which are embodied in enactments of 1975 and 1983.[203] The pressures of the time thus partly meant renewed attention to, and renewed ratification of, the "special regime."

But something far more important than the reforms of the "special regime" itself came as a consequence of these crises: in the legislation of 1975 and

1981, the basis of the dignitary regime that governs French prisons today, the very idea of a "special regime" declined into effective collapse. For the old privileges of the "political prisoners" were at last extended to the "ordinary" confinees of the "droit commun."[204] In effect, one of the most radical demands of the 1960s was successfully realized in France: all prisoners came to be treated as politicals, as rebels against the established order.

This pivotal development came under pressures that were felt everywhere in the West. Just as there were prison riots in the United States and Germany in the early 1970s, so it was a series of highly publicized prison riots that led to a first major French humanization reform in 1975.[205] This reform was preceded by some wonderful Republican pomp: Valéry Giscard d'Estaing, newly elected president and fresh from a newly voted prison amnesty, visited the prison of Saint-Paul in Lyon. There he shook hands with some inmates and declared that while French prisoners might of necessity be denied Liberty, they would never be deprived of Equality and Fraternity.[206] Prisoners were to be beneficiaries of the revolution just like everybody else in France. To be sure, some of the language of the following year's reform sounded a shade Orwellian: it abolished the terms *punishment* and *reward*, substituting "disciplinary sanctions" and "measures intended to encourage the inmates."[207] But there were real changes. Largely concerned, in the traditional way, with "promiscuity" between "real" criminals and others, the reform of 1975 set out to separate inmates guilty of less serious from those guilty of more serious offenses. [208] As we have already seen, the reform of 1975 also established a range of new penalties that for many convicts dispensed with the short sentences they previously would have served; receiving suspended sentence, they now served no prison time at all.[209] Both of these measures had roots deep in French reform tradition.

It was with the arrival of the Socialist government in power in 1981, though, that the definitive shift came. In the name of dignity, a 1982 decree eliminated maximum security prisons entirely in France.[210] The idea that prisoners should be held in anything that resembled cages was too much for French reformers. From now on there were simply to be *maisons d'arrêt*—jails, limited in principle those in investigative custody and serving sentences under a year[211]—and *maisons centrales*—prisons. Most important for my tale, over the next several years, reforms were instituted by means of which the old special regime was at last definitively extended to all. As one recent text puts it, "The liberalization of the conditions of imprisonment has emptied the 'special regime' of its special content, notably with regard to wearing one's own clothing, the right to receive daily visits without a glass partition, and the absence of an obligation to work."[212] We can, indeed, list the "dignitary" reforms of the last twenty years in France one by one. Almost all of them draw on the old tradition of special treatment for political prisoners, from visitation rights to the right to buy food, to the end of forced labor, to (most strikingly of all) the end of the prison uniform. The "special regime" still theoretically exists: the new criminal code prescribes a special form of "criminal *detention*," rather than imprisonment, for those guilty of political offenses.[213] (And occasionally prisoners—for example Corsican nationalists—can still be heard demanding the old "special" treatment.) On the international level too, French advocates of human rights still imagine that "political" prisoners should be specially treated.[214] Nevertheless, treatment for "politicals" has become in practice, less special. "Special" treatment is now something that every French prisoner is entitled to. Like the political prisoners of past eras, they are no longer to be treated as persons different from anyone else.

The German Path

The history of status in German punishment has taken a somewhat different course. Beheading did not play the central symbolic role that it did in France. It was used more broadly in the early modern period, and the Terror of the French Revolution and the ugly associations of the guillotine complicated its nineteenth-century history.[215] While eventually the continental pattern of symbolically universalized beheading did come in, considerable regional differences remained.[216] If beheading did not matter as much in Germany, though, "infamy" certainly did. Indeed, it is a fact of critical comparative importance that the rejection of "infamy" came in more slowly in Germany than in France. Well into the 1850s and 1860s, Germans were showing much less sensitivity to the imposition of "infamy" than their French contemporaries showed.[217] To be sure, by 1871, as the new German Empire established itself, German lawyers were ready to declare that the most "humiliating and shaming" punishments "are now rejected as a matter of criminal justice."[218] Nevertheless, as we shall see, infamy survived strong even after 1871, in the form of a particularly degrading type of imprisonment known as *Zuchthaus*. If over the long run Germany has shown the same continental pattern of abolishing low-status punishments as France, the social conservatism of Germany has clearly been stronger.

Moreover, the handling of political prisoners has not played quite the role in German development that it has in French; political conflict in Germany has simply been too brutal for the French tradition of high-status treatment to prevail. By the Weimar period, and certainly by the Nazi period, most German political prisoners could expect worse treatment, not better; and correspondingly, it is not out of the tradition of political imprisonment that modern German practices grew.

Nevertheless, the German pattern is in important ways closely parallel to the French; and it is fair to speak of a common continental tradition that embraces both countries. Beheading *was* generalized, just as it was in France. In Germany as in France, current prison conditions have roots that can be traced back to the "fortress confinement" of the ancien régime. Indeed, in Germany as in France, the 1970s saw a reform movement that finally abolished humiliating terms of imprisonment, substituting something like "fortress confinement" for all. In all of this, we can see exactly the same drive toward generalization of high status that we see in France.

But something else happened too, in Germany, of distinctive importance. In the process of hashing out differences in terms of imprisonment, German lawyers began to make a revealing shift from a preoccupation with *honor* to a preoccupation with *morality*. While the terms of fortress confinement were in some measure extended to political prisoners in the German nineteenth century, the main beneficiaries were defined differently by German jurisprudence: if in France, the persons who were regarded as not "really" criminal were the political opponents of the state, in Germany, the persons who were regarded as not "really" criminal were much more often persons who, as judged by their intentions, could be deemed morally good at heart. At first, the categories "high-status" and "good" were simply mixed in German punishment practice, in a way that neatly recalls Nietzsche's famous claim in *The Genealogy of Morals* that concepts of the good always grow out of concepts of high social status.[219] Easy terms of imprisonment, in the German nineteenth century mind, were thus at first regarded as appropriate *both* for persons of high social standing, *and* for persons of "good character." Gradually, though, the second category, the category of "good character," came to occupy the field alone. This provision of fortress confinement for persons of good character was a fateful development, for it lay some of the foundation for individualization in punishment as it exists down to this day in German practice. What the history of fortress confinement in Germany shows, indeed, is how what began as individualization *on the basis of social status* gradually became individualization *on the basis of moral goodness*—a formative transition from status to morality that does indeed recall Nietzsche's famous book.

Early modern German states were no different from early modern France in housing their high status offenders in "fortresses"—though high-status prisoners were perhaps not as studiously well-treated in the German world as they were in the French.[220] Here again, noble status did not matter quite as much in Germany as it did in France. The tradition continued in the nineteenth century too. Germany had a history of turning to cellular imprisonment much like France's.[221] There were significant and distinctive features to German development, though. With varying terminology, almost every German state provided for three kinds of prisons in the nineteenth century. Unlike modern American prisons, though, which are differentiated by their degree of security, nineteenth-century German prisons were, strikingly enough, differentiated according to their degree of dishonorability: *Zuchthaus*, the most dishonorable and harsh type; *Gefängnis*, a medium-dishonoring prison; and, *Festungshaft*, fortress confinement, regarded as not dishonorable at all. (These distinctions in honorability would survive, in German prison law, until the reforms of the late 1960s and early 1970s.) Within the fortresses, the honorable places of imprisonment, persons benefited from something close to the "special regime" that prevailed in France—they had the important privilege of wearing their own clothing and were sometimes permitted to provide their own food and other comforts.[222]

But who were these "honorable" fortress detainees in Germany? Candidates for the fortress at the beginning of the century were in some part political prisoners; harsh as the political intolerance of the German world could be in the age of Metternich, there were political prisoners even in the 1830s who enjoyed certain relative freedoms for short periods.[223] But the general rule said nothing about politics as such. Rather, early nineteenth-century fortress confinement was understood to be appropriate for other classes of persons. Most of all, it was regarded as appropriate for what Germans generally called "die gebildeten Stände"—"the cultured status-groups."[224] Speaking of status-groups according to their "Bildung," their degree of culture, was a classic nineteenth-century German practice, much discussed by historians, which permitted the assimilation of the higher ranks of the bourgeoisie to the aristocracy. To speak of the "cultured" classes was to speak of a mixed high stratum of society that was no longer exclusively aristocratic. The sensibility behind the idea that "cultured" persons should receive special terms of imprisonment was a familiar one: "the cultured offender, whose deed is not the product of a lowly character [*einer niedrigen Gesinnung*], suffers too severe a punishment if he is locked together with uncultured and rough convicts, and treated like them."[225] Cultivated persons were regarded as superior in status—without the ritual taint that attached to "real" criminals. Germans had, indeed, a sheer inability to imagine that high-status persons could be subjected to low-status treatment, which lasted well into the later nineteenth century.[226] As one 1872 author could almost touchingly observe, regular imprisonment was incommensurably hard on "cultured" persons, for even if they were not compelled to labor like others, they were obliged to perform such tasks as *household chores*, and to take orders from prison personnel who were their social inferiors:

> [One cannot fail to see] that with the mere condemnation to such normal penalties the entire social position of a cultured person is shaken much more deeply than is the case with an uncultured person. Moreover there are certain common and unalterable practices in penal institutions, such as complete dependence on officers of the lowest social class, the obligation to clean one's cell and its furnishings, and much more of the same kind, which cultured men find it much harder to take than uncultured ones. . . .
>
> . . . indeed, it seems in some circumstances not just a piece of pointless torture, but a kind of coarse barbarism utterly out of place in our age.[227]

One is tempted to laugh at this, and maybe one should laugh. And yet—this passage, with its delicate horror at the idea of even minimally degrading prison conditions, belongs to a cultural pattern of delicacy in discussing imprisonment that has come very much to benefit German inmates today.

At any rate, fortress confinement was thought of as appropriate for privileged persons in the German nineteenth century—and also, significantly, for privileged acts. In particular, it was regarded as appropriate for certain "nondishonorable" offenses: seduction, manslaughter, *Mißhandlung* [abuse of a kind which in these circumstances would include brutal treatment of underlings], "insults" to the sovereign and to persons in high office, and especially dueling.[228] The list is a revealing one, which manifestly recalls some of the honorable offenses deemed mere "contraventions" in the Napoleonic Penal Code of 1810 or shielded from liability in France through the doctrine of extenuating circumstances after the Revolution of 1830. On the one hand it shows, once again, the prominence of crimes of honor—not just dueling, but also seduction, manslaughter, and *Mißhandlung*, all offenses into which persons of high social standing could easily be tempted. On the other hand, it shows how political crimes, in the Germany of the romantic era, had some of the dash of dueling. Adversary politics was thought of as "insulting" the state, and accordingly as something not all that far removed from the culture of dueling. The same romantic air that clung to dueling could indeed cling to a variety of political offenses for German jurists of the 1820s: "People seemed to start from the correct assumption that there are certain crimes which can be committed, not only by decadent and dissolute persons, but also by persons of moral nobility, who let themselves by carried away into committing forbidden acts through class prejudices [*Standesvorurtheile*] or excessive emotion. One must also ask oneself if there are not also other offenses that similarly merit fortress confinement, such as many forms of insulting the sovereign, resistance to the state, or attempts to free a prisoner."[229] Dueling itself, of course, could be thought of as "political," in the sense that duelists obstinately denied the authority of the state to forbid their activities. Indeed, for one jurist writing in 1871, the *only* crimes for which fortress confinement was appropriate were the twin forms of romantic self-assertion against the state: political offenses and dueling.[230] Even where Germans thought of political offenders as candidates for the fortress, it was because they associated them with patterns of high-status behavior.

Among many jurists, right up into the 1870s, the tendency was thus to reserve fortress confinement for crimes of honor, and for political offenses that were themselves thought of as a species of crime of honor. The tale did not end there, though. Other ideas also began to waft through German law and German literature in the nineteenth century. From a relatively early date, other German jurists began trying to reconceive the basis for assignment of convicts to the fortress, driving the law (in typical German fashion) in a more abstract moral-philosophical direction.

There had long been Germans who expressed discomfort with the idea that there should be special punishments for persons of privilege.[231] Rather than reserving fortress confinement to those of high social status, some draftsmen and text-writers began to argue, from an early date in nineteenth century, that courts should consider "not just the social status [*die bürgerlichen Verhältnisse*] of the offender, but also the quality of the circumstances, namely those that condition the attitude [*Gesinnung*] of the malefactor."[232] This interest in *Gesinnung*, in attitude or character, became characteristic of a powerful German tendency: the thoroughly Nietzschean tendency to reconceive status privileges as moral ones. The focus on *Gesinnung* was itself, to be sure, by no means without status-overtones. To Austrians, for example, the formula read "ehrlose oder nicht ehrlose Gesinnung," "dishonorable or nondishonorable *Gesinnung*."[233] Nevertheless, it was through its focus on

Gesinnung that German justice began to develop both of the classic alternatives to Beccarian act-egalitarianism: the doctrine of extenuating circumstances, and the philosophy of individualization.

The doctrine of extenuating circumstances developed first—and developed directly out of the traditions of status differentiation in punishment. By mid-century, "honorability" and "extenuating circumstances" coexisted as grounds for ordering fortress confinement. As a typical 1849 statute put it: "Courts are to commute penalties of *Zuchthaus* or workhouse into fortress confinement, whenever it seems justified in light of careful consideration of the particular circumstances of the crime, and the previous honorability of the offender."[234] Unsurprisingly this form of punishment was thought of, in the first instance, as suitable for duelists, the most "honorable" of criminals.[235] But other conduct was not by any means excluded. A draft Prussian code of 1847 proposed that assignment to fortress confinement should depend exclusively on "the quality of the circumstances"—and it was careful also to insist that fortress confinement itself should be free of any "beschimpfender Charakter," any insulting character.[236] By the 1850s and after it was easy to discover jurists who believed that all concerns about social status should yield in favor of analysis of the *Gesinnung* of the offender. In 1862, the Juristentag, the conference of German jurists, stated a new orthodoxy, which agreed that the critical question was whether the offender had shown a "dishonorable" *Gesinnung*.[237] All of this had an effect on the making of the great Criminal Code of 1871, which did indeed permit honorable fortress confinement to be ordered where extenuating circumstances called for it.[238] Jurists would continue to regard the "dishonorable" *Gesinnung* as the critical factor in determining who would receive fortress confinement.[239] Just as in France, the rise of the doctrine of extenuating circumstances remained closely connected with the problem of the "honorable" offender.

Moreover, not only a doctrine of extenuating circumstances, but also a kind of quasi-modern individualization began to establish itself in German law.[240] Like the individualization that emerged at the end of the nineteenth century, the aborning idea of individualization focused on character, on the capacity of the offender to be integrated into "society." But rather than prescribing individualization in sentencing, it prescribed individualization in terms of imprisonment. And the sort of "society" into which the first offenders offered this individualization were reintegrated was, in the first instance, *high* society. Thus did morality begin to exercise its grip on modern German individualization, springing up out of old forms of status differentiation.

All of this was fateful for the making of German law. By the time of the drafting of the Criminal Code of 1871, new concepts like "human dignity" and "humane" had made their way into a discourse about fortress confinement which revolved around the "indignity" and "inhumanity" of locking political offenders and moral and honorable persons up with "scum [*Hefe*]."[241] The Code of 1871 accordingly included an open-ended provision permitting fortress confinement.[242] It was to be the exclusive punishment in cases of dueling (§§201ff.), hostile acts against friendly nations (§ 102), and in cases of political crimes accompanied by a variety of extenuating circumstances (§§81ff). Significantly, it was also to be the exclusive punishment in other cases involving certain extenuating circumstances. (§§83ff). The classic sorts of honorable political crimes also came in. Fortress confinement was available as an alternative punishment in various cases of insult and obstruction aimed against government officials.[243] The whole mix was thus there: honor, both social honor and the honor of opposition to government, blended with slowly developing concepts of the morally good.

By the late nineteenth century, there were thus, in practice, two leading tendencies in the German law of fortress confinement. On the one hand, as in France, the practice of subjecting political offenders to this milder form of imprisonment had established itself in Germany too. On the other hand, fortress confinement also became the norm for persons whose crimes had proceeded from an "honorable" *Gesinnung*, a concept in which questions of honor and questions of morality coexisted uneasily. Of these two tendencies, only the latter would survive intact in the twentieth century; but it would survive strong.

The death of special treatment for politicals in Germany makes a dramatic story—and one that shows us how hard it is to walk the French route toward relatively high status for convicts. The French, as we have seen, made the transition to characterizing some offenders as not "really" criminals by first characterizing political offenders that way. The capacity to characterize political prisoners as mere "opponents of the state" rather than "criminals" assumed a political stability that German would lack in the twentieth century. To be sure, German political prisoners at first were treated much as their French counterparts were treated—perhaps even better. In later-nineteenth-century Germany as in France, even political prisoners of the left wing demanded and received gracious treatment. One turn-of-the-century imprisoned labor leader, for example, wrote that he was in favor of better provisioning in the prisons, as long as it benefited "above all political prisoners" and not common criminals.[244] He himself received special treatment.[245] Specially privileged fortress confinement remained a norm, if one that was not always obeyed, throughout the period before World War I;[246] in Germany indeed there were privileged conditions even for dangerous radicals like the anarchist Erich Mühsam, regarded as a "better" prisoner; given a larger, lighter cell; and permitted to provide his own food and to smoke cigars.[247] Anarchists thus had it easier in Germany than in France.

Yet the old tradition of special treatment for "politicals" collapsed much more suddenly and completely in twentieth-century Germany than in twentieth-century France. With defeat in World War I came a transformation. Political prisoners—at least, left-wing political prisoners—discovered that fortress confinement was no longer a privileged, and certain not a pleasant, state.[248] Ernst Toller wrote of Bavaria in a 1920 letter from prison: "The government of the Free State of Bavaria has robbed fortress confinement of the character that it possessed when it was still intended for officers and students, whose honorable affairs called for honorable confinement. Revolutionary socialists are sentenced to fortress confinement. But they are locked into what used to be ordinary prisons, and subjected to torments and martyrdoms under which their souls grow brittle and crack."[249] For right-wing prisoners the tale was different, as the famous case of Adolf Hitler, also a political prisoner in Weimar Bavaria, testifies. Right-wingers could expect old-style fortress confinement still.[250] And like political prisoners of the previous century, Nazi prisoners during Weimar could be heard insisting that they were not to be confused with "common criminals."[251] (As we shall see in the next section, though, even for left-wing prisoners, not everything turned sour in Weimar; they benefited from political amnesties.)

Special treatment for political prisoners was beginning to die during the Weimar Republic, and it died at last in the Nazi period: As Georg Dahm, a leading Nazi legal thinker, said, there was no room for honorable "fortress confinement" for the political opponents of the new regime.[252] The change was partly a question of law, with the Nazis redrafting the regulations.[253] And of course, it was also partly a matter of the lived practice of the concentration camps. As a matter of lived practice, we can say, indeed, that special treatment for politicals ended in the middle of a single night in March 1933, in Dachau, the first of the concentration camps. For the first few days of its operation, the prisoners of Dachau were still treated, in effect, as politicals. At first, the local police managed the camp. These men evidently regarded their ill-fated prisoners more or less as status equals. Together, prisoners and guards built facilities. They sat down together and shared the same meals, as political prisoners and their jailers had done in Europe for centuries. But after a few days, units of the S.S. arrived. Roused in the middle of the night, prisoners whose confusion and terror is hard to imagine were made to hear the following speech: "Comrades of the S.S.! You all know what the Führer has called upon us to carry out. We have not come to this place in order to greet the swine inside as human beings. We do not regard them as human beings, but as second class human beings. . . . The more of these *Schweinehunde* we shoot, the less feeding we have to do."[254] Where political prisoners had always been treated as superior in status to "common criminals," they were abruptly declared to be nothing less than subhuman. From persons who had been immune from status degradation, German political prisoners were now subjected to a more determined and total program of status degradation than European prisoners had perhaps ever experienced.

After the concentration camps, the ideal of fortress confinement for political prisoners had largely vanished in Germany. To be sure, after the war some prisoners still enjoyed it—most famously the ex-Nazis Rudolf Hess, Albert Speer, and Baldur von Schirach, confined, in the old fashion, in the Fortress Spandau. Nevertheless, despite the postwar fate of these ex-Nazis, the fundamental reality is that political conflict in Germany after 1918 was too brutal and embittered for the "special regime" to play the role that is has played in France. Correspondingly, the tale of German prison conditions as they exist today is not the tale of the generalization of the special status of political prisoner, which effectively died in 1933. The idea that political prisoners get special treatment has not entirely disappeared, as a 1990 handbook for prisoners reports.[255] And the classic French "special regime" is still to be found in one aspect of German prison practice. German law permits civil imprisonment in certain cases. Persons subject to such civil imprisonment—basically a form of imprisonment for debt—benefit from the classic provisions of the "special regime": they may be housed together, they may use their own clothing, they may purchase goods, and they are dispensed from any obligation to work.[256] But other prisoners benefit from only fragments of the special regime. The special regime for political prisoners has thus not been directly generalized in Germany. It is a measure of this fact that the German Code of Punishment still envisions prison uniforms—even if those uniforms have sometimes vanished as a matter of fact. That ordinary German prisoners are still theoretically subject to the obligation to wear uniforms shows that they have not been fully assimilated to the status of political prisoners as their French counterparts have been.

Nevertheless, if the special regime for political prisoners ended in Germany, special treatment for "honorable" persons and persons of good character did not. On the contrary, the nineteenth-century pattern of individualization on the basis of character continued unabated—through the Weimar period, through the Nazi period, and into the present. The Nietzschean transition from status to morality became the dominant German tendency.

Let us pick up the tale again in the later nineteenth century. In the last decades of the nineteenth century, while political prisoners were still being treated well in Germany, other developments were also afoot. Modern individualization, propounded in the 1880s and 1890s as the basis of a new style of social planning by Franz von Liszt and his followers, came a little more slowly to German practice than it did to French.[257] Where suspended sentences entered French punishment practice in 1891, nothing quite of the kind happened at first in German law. Instead, where French practice introduced suspended sentences as a matter of *law*, German practice did something different, and more closely connected to older traditions of honor. Starting in the 1890s, the various German states introduced forms of probation as a matter of *grace*, as a practice of the pardoning power that had always been exercised to excuse honorable offenders, and especially duelists, from punishment.[258] Throughout the first decades of the twentieth century, this extension of honorable grace to the whole population of offenders made slow progress—progress in which we can see how closely the making of "modernist" mildness in punishment rested on old forms of privileged treatment for persons of honor.

The great German leap toward individualizing mildness in punishment really came with the Weimar Republic. In part, Weimar mildness involved an intensification of the practice of "gracious" probation.[259] But it also involved new applications of the old idea of fortress confinement. As the standard literature observes, the Weimar reforms represented in many ways a real departure from criminal justice of the nineteenth century, focusing squarely, for the first time, on education and resocialization.[260] At the same time, it is important to observe that even the new reforms of the Weimar era continued to breathe an old German air. The new practices of "education" that formed the core of humane Weimar-era punishment practice drew directly on a distinctly traditional idea: that the right way to treat prisoners of good character was to give them better terms of imprisonment.

In part this involved an effort to update fortress confinement. The term had some comical associations with the old world of honor, and draft statutes had sometimes proposed replacing it with the word *Haft* ("confinement") without the "fortress."[261] In failed reform proposals of the mid 1920s, Gustav Radbruch, then minister of justice, tried once more to achieve such a change in terminology, by proposing to rebaptize *Festungshaft* as *Einschließung*, another word for "confinement."[262] This terminological reform would have to wait until after World War II. But other reforms did succeed—in particular, the key practice in the Weimar educational approach to punishment: *Strafvollzug in Stufen* ("punishment by progressive stages"). In this interesting system, moral improvement was to be encouraged by admitting inmates to progressively easier terms of imprisonment. As inmates came closer and closer to demonstrating good character, they also came closer and closer to enjoying the old terms of fortress confinement. A prison warden explained the system as follows in 1928:

> Upon admission, every prisoner is placed in Stage 1. There *Zuchthaus* prisoners stay for at least nine months, adult *Gefängnis* prisoners at least six months, minors at least three months. . . . The same time periods apply to Stage 2. The prerequisites for elevation to Stage 2 and 3 is not merely the passage of the minimum time, but—for Stage 2—demonstrated will and capacity to change for the better, shown through serious and upright, good and decent general pattern of behavior; and for Stage 3 a general pattern of behavior that justifies the prognosis of continuing change toward proper behavior after release. . . .
>
> . . . In Stage 1, prisoners receive fundamentally no privileges. The increasing level of privileges in Stages 2 and 3 consist primarily in shortening the waiting period for letters and visits, in increased authorization for the delivery of outside foodstuffs, in increased leisure and reading material, in permission to have one's own books, newpapers and writing and drawing material, in the decoration of the cell and in longer periods of illumination. Moreover, prisoners in the higher Stages are granted freedom of movement, which demonstrates to them that they are being shown greater confidence; they are allowed to work outside the prison, they are given positions of trust, and for prisoners in Stage 3 supervision is limited and they are permitted a measure of self-government, in that they may choose their own representatives who then are responsible for maintaining order.[263]

This was an intriguing approach to punishment[264]—but one that rested on some very old assumptions. For what inmates "progressed" toward in this system, as at least one contemporary observer noted, was the kind of treatment traditionally associated with fortress confinement.[265] In one respect, to be sure, treatment in Stage 3 fell interestingly short of the norms of fortress confinement. Uniforms were still to be worn—though they were now to signal relatively *high* status: "Outwardly, the Stages are distinguished by three narrow light-colored strips on the left lower sleeve."[266] There were other important, and real, innovations, too. In particular, the decision to admit inmates to the higher stages was to be made with all of the modern apparatus of psychology and social work.[267] Nevertheless, seen in historical perspective, the background to this system in the norms of the nineteenth century is evident. Humanization of the prisons in Weimar still meant gradually admitting morally improved inmates to the old, easier, forms of high-status confinement.[268] (Indeed, comically enough, it meant permitting inmates to engage in the classic pursuits of high-status and political prisoners: *writing and painting*! These were precisely the pursuits to which Adolf Hitler gave himself over as a high-status Bavarian political prisoner.)[269] Liberal Weimar reformers like Gustav Radbruch thought of themselves as engaged in a revolutionary enterprise, as being social planners who had broken with all of the old social traditions. Nevertheless it was with the old social traditions that they worked; societies are not so easily revolutionized.

Moreover, even among the Nazis, who were considerably more ruthless social revolutionaries, old ideas of honorable individualization did not die out. Needless to say, almost all of the Nazi brand of "individualization" belonged to the harsh strain. Nazi criminal justice policy turned especially harshly on habitual offenders and the "incorrigible." These were individuals to be eliminated, just as the genetically inferior were to be eliminated. To read Nazi prison-law literature is, accordingly, regularly to stumble across chilling bits of bureaucratic matter—such as a passage laying out for prison officials the correct accounting methods for the costs of sterilizing and castrating their charges.[270] Still, as some recent authors have pointedly observed, harsh or not, the fact is that the Nazi era represented one step in the continuous growth of the tradition of individualization in Germany.

Indeed, Nazi practice showed a very deep connection with the longstanding German patterns I have traced. If we examine Nazi individualization practice closely, we can see how intimately it too embraced the old ideas of honorability. This shows in some of the proclaimed goals of Nazi punishment: the Nazis, as recent historians have noted, did not abandon the goal of education and respect for convicts entirely. Punishment, in the Nazi plan, still belonged to the old German thought-world, for it aimed partly to "awaken, respect and strengthen" the inmate's "sense of honor."[271] (Vichy law showed some very similar tendencies.)[272] This focus on the "sense of honor" drew from the purest sources of German individualizing mildness in punishment. (It also drew on a much larger Nazi tendency, which I have discussed at length elsewhere: the tendency to guarantee a claim to "honor" for all "Germans." As I have tried to demonstrate, this extension of "honor" belonged to seminal pattern of Nazi leveling up, which has continued to shape German dignitary law down to this day.)[273] Moreover, in encouraging inmates' "sense of honor," the Nazis did not abandon the principal innovation of Weimar individualization: punishment in progressive stages. On the contrary, Nazi theory retained this "progressive" practice almost wholesale, while slightly rewording its terms to emphasize the aspect of honor involved in the punishment program. If inmates in Nazi prisons wished to move up to a new, easier stage of confinement, what they had to show was not only their susceptibility to punishment [*Strafempfänglichkeit*] but also their worthiness for promotion to a new stage.[274] This was to justify their readmission to what the Nazis always declared to be the most "honorable" state of all: membership in the *Volk* community.[275] The connection to Weimar practice here was close, and Nazi theorists knew it. As they explained, in deciding whether prisoners had made the necessary showing, "complete individualization" was to reign.[276] To be sure, the Nazi period brought change, but it was change that must be seen in light of what came before. For generations, German justice had been experiencing a shift from norms of honor to norms of morality. Nazi punishment aimed to turn the clock back, focusing exclusively upon "honor" once again. In practice, the resulting practices may have been very brutal—but in their core concepts, they were not so different from what had come before. "Gracious" probation continued, too, under the Nazis, and indeed became for the first time a fully routinized practice, as I will discuss in the last section of this chapter.

Still and all, even if there were continuities with the practices that predated 1933, and even if there were some tendencies toward mildness in punishment among the Nazis, it would be arrant lunacy to imagine that their criminal justice policies were either nothing new or nothing terrible. Their policies were unprecedentedly bestial. Real mildness has indeed come only after the war, just as the standard literature claims. Still, it is important to emphasize something not said in the standard literature. The rise of postwar mildness continues, from the large sociological point of view, to display exactly the same tendency we find in Nazi prison policies: a tendency to extend high-status, "honorable" treatment to all.

In particular, this same tendency made its power felt in the great German prison reform of the late 1960s and early 1970s. With the postwar reforms of 1953, *Festungshaft* was finally renamed *Einschließung*, as the Weimar reformers had wanted. It was not abolished, though.[277] Right up through the 1960s, despite Weimar reforms and postwar reforms, German criminal practice maintained the old nineteenth-century distinctions between types of imprisonment. Offenders were still subjected either to *Festungshaft* (now *Einschließung*), *Gefängnis*, or *Zuchthaus*, just as they had been in the 1840s. Moreover, the practice of distinguishing these forms of confinement by their degree of *honorability* still survived. German law still treated confinement in a *Zuchthaus* as *dishonorable*, and organized punishment in the *Zuchthäusern* accordingly.[278] Thus, right up until the end of the 1960s, *Zuchthaus* inmates were subjected to a range of "dishonoring" practices that dated back into the early modern period.[279] Prisoners in *Gefängnis*, by contrast, were spared such "dishonorable" treatment. (Fortress confinement, while it still theoretically existed, was little applied).[280]

The reforms of 1969 and 1976 marked at last the end of this old tradition of distinct honorable and dishonorable treatment; and marked it, again, with a classic move toward leveling up. The "honorable" norms of *Gefängnis* imprisonment were simply extended to all. By ending *Zuchthaus*, the reforms were intended to eliminate the stigma of punishment.[281] As things stand today, there are no longer *Zuchthäuser* and *Gefängnisse* in Germany. German penal law simply distinguishes between "closed" and "open" institutions.[282] "Open" institutions, close in spirit to American halfway houses, have little or minimal security and assume relatively free contact between inmate and outside world. The letter of the German statute declares that "open" confinement should be the ordinary sanction.[283] As we have seen, this has turned out to be largely a dead letter. In a German system in which only violent and repeat offenders are routinely imprisoned, the idea of extending "open" treatment to all never had much hope.[284] Nevertheless, it is revealing that the idea should ever have made its way into the statute at all. For with the declaration that "open" confinement should be the normal form for everyone, German imprisonment has taken, if only rhetorically, a decisive step toward what once would have seemed clearly a kind of ennoblement of everyone held in a German prison.

Dishonorable punishment was thus abolished in Germany in 1969–76, a few years before it was abolished in France. More or less simultaneously came the development that in a sense caps the whole history I have recounted: the *Lebach* decision of 1973. This was the decision of the Constitutional Court that forbade the televising of a movie about the life of a homosexual convicted murderer. It was, clearly enough, a decision that grew out of the same sensibilities about personal honor that I have been tracing: old sensibilities that thought of public exposure as central to the dishonorability of low-status punishments, and that correspondingly imagined safety from public exposure as central to honorability in punishment. *Lebach* was a seminal decision on more than one front. It is from *Lebach* that the law of dignity in punishment is regarded as flowing in Germany.[285] All of the dignitary prison law that I have discussed, in the eyes of German jurists, begins with the centuries-old recognition that honorable persons must be shielded from public exposure. Moreover, it is also from *Lebach* that much of the developing German law of privacy flows. In *Lebach* we can see, indeed, that the traditions of honor in punishment lie at the sources of aspects of dignitary law in Germany that go far beyond the world of punishment itself. Those are aspects that I must leave, however, to be explored elsewhere.

Amnesties, Grace, and the European Tradition of Mercy de Haut en Bas

By the mid-1980s, the old high-status forms of confinement had driven out all other forms in the prisons of both Germany and France—at least in theory. The actual practice of punishment was, to be sure, probably somewhat worse in Germany and, beyond all doubt, much worse in France. Nevertheless, the ideal had established itself, and it was having at least some effect in both countries—though it was an ideal that would be badly tested by the changes of the 1990s—including in particular the flood of immigration that followed the fall of the Berlin Wall, and the difficult consequences of closing East German prisons. Generalizing carefully, we can say that the history of the both countries had shown the same pattern: low-status punishments had all been eliminated; only high-status punishments had survived, to be applied now to all offenders.

Alongside that revealing piece of continental history comes another, without which the story would not be complete: the history of grace and amnesties. This is the history to which I now briefly turn, in this last section.

I have already mentioned the practice of amnesties, which features so strikingly in both French and German criminal justice today. One might think this was a practice whose history spoke for itself. Self-evidently, the annual amnesties of Christmas and Bastille Day in contemporary Germany and France, and the celebratory amnesties on the succession of a new regime in France, are relics of an old era of sacral sovereignty. Self-evidently, what we see, in the survival of large-scale amnesties in both France and Germany, is a tradition of the paternalistic exercise of state sovereignty—a tradition that is noticeably absent in the United States.

Yet there are also aspects to the history of grace in France and Germany that are not self-evident at all—surprising, and unexpectedly important aspects, that we can discover only by digging more deeply into continental history. The history of grace is a more complex history of mildness than one might think, and a history without which we cannot fully understand the shape of the humane dignitary law of France and Germany today. It is also, more particularly, a history of startling developments during the Nazi period.

Let us return once again to the eighteenth century. If it goes without saying that the hierarchical societies of the premodern continent distinguished between high- and low-status punishments, it also goes without saying that they engaged actively in pardoning. Pardoning is one of the classic exercises of monarchical sovereignty, and it was actively engaged in by all premodern states. The English monarchy engaged in it just as the continental ones did; indeed, one of the best-known analyses of pardoning as a display of sovereign power is Douglas Hay's account of eighteenth-century England. Yet Hay's account, to which I will return in the next chapter, needs to be read in some comparative perspective. It is certainly true that English pardoning partly displayed the sovereign authority of the British king—as Blackstone put it, "these repeated acts of goodness . . .contribute more than any thing to root in the hearts [of the king's subjects] that filial affection and personal loyalty which are the sure establishment of a prince."[286] But French pardoning practices displayed the sovereign authority of the *French* king much more unambiguously.

In France, the power of grace was exercised in ways that were both dramatically ceremonialized and carried a strong aura of the individualized exercise of grace—of the personal mercy of the king, exercised in the affirmation of an individual relationship between king and subject. From the late fifteenth century onward, the power of grace was the exclusive prerogative of the king in France, part of his claim to unique sovereignty,[287] and a symbol of the divine character of royal power.[288] Thus on the one hand, grace was exercised through amnesties on the accession of the King and other joyous occasions, or as part of a collective pardon granted to such enemies of the state as religious dissenters. On the other hand, it was exercised through responses to individual petitions.[289] To receive mercy in France was, in theory, to beg it individually from the hand of the king. French law did not neglect the ceremonial trappings: royal statutory law required supplicants for grace to come bareheaded, upon their knees, before the king.[290] Nor did French law forget its status orientation: petitioners were required to declare their social status,[291] and commentary took it for granted that royal mercy, which was after all a favor of king, would be bestowed primarily on persons of high honor.[292] Such, at any rate, was the theory. The practice was inevitably different. High-status supplicants clearly made efforts to evade or minimize the humiliating requirement that they appear bareheaded and on bended knee.[293] As for the king, despite the fiction, he inevitably did not himself decide on the merits of these petitions, and decisions on most routine matters were delegated to special panels attached to the local courts.[294] Moreover, as a statistical matter, French pardoning overwhelmingly benefited low-status offenders, not high-status ones.[295] Low-status offenders were presumably the large majority of all offenders, and the privileges of the high-status took other forms. Nevertheless, the French system of pardons really was designed to convey symbolically the sovereign grace of the monarch. Moreover, French grace did not benefit *every* low-status offender. Receiving a pardon in France required mobilizing considerable support—in particular, petitions from local notables.[296] Those who received mercy in eighteenth-century France were not high-status persons, but they *were* persons with connections. As we shall see, English pardoning showed comparative differences on all these counts. Pardoning was not even in theory an exclusively royal prerogative; the English attachment to the symbolism of sovereignty was weaker; and English mercy was much more generally granted.

Indeed, the continent, not England, was the classic locus for the link between pardoning and the vigorous display of royal sovereignty. Certainly the idea that pardoning was linked to the display of royal sovereignty was widespread among continental thinkers. Continental philosophers routinely analyzed pardoning as "monarchical," and so inconsistent with republican values. To Montesquieu, pardons, while acceptable in a monarchy, violated the principle of popular sovereignty in a republic.[297] Kant's disconcertingly bloody-minded attack on pardoning in his *Metaphysical Elements of Justice* clearly reflected much of Montesquieu's concern that the power of pardoning be kept out of any republic founded on popular sovereignty.[298] The early French revolutionaries took these philosophical critiques with the utmost seriousness, and abolished the practice of pardoning entirely with the revolutionary penal reform of 1791.[299]

Nevertheless, in a fashion typical of continental history, this revolutionary effort failed.[300] Pardoning soon returned to French practice, and it survived everywhere through the nineteenth century.

Indeed, pardoning throughout most of the nineteenth century was the main source of individualization in punishment. It is a familiar fact of legal history that the individualization that would later be accomplished through probation and parole was accomplished through pardoning in the nineteenth century—through the exercise of sovereign grace. Grace, as nineteenth-century lawyers vaguely understood it, was not a technically "legal" power at all. It grew out of the old royal prerogative of mercy. This carried great ideological weight, even in the nineteenth and twentieth centuries. As one 1821 author put it, the royal power of grace was "nearly divine," a piece of magic.[301] Morever, as another French author of 1866 emphasized, monarchical mercy was still the true source of new doctrines of individualization, such as the doctrine of extenuating circumstances: "In all the ages of our history, the severity of the laws has been tempered by the right of grace, liberally exercised by our kings, who frequently preferred mercy to the rigors of the system of justice. Even magistrates . . . took into consideration the poverty, the young age, or the repentance of the suspect, and were already cognizant of extenuating circumstances, even though the term had not yet been introduced into the letter of the law."[302] Authors of the mid nineteenth century would declare that justice without grace was simply unattainable.[303] The authority to exercise grace was to be sure no longer strictly confined to the person of the monarch by the later nineteenth century. In some parts of Europe, the bureaucracies of justice had even constituted themselves as the Ministry of Law *and Grace*—a title still held by the relevant ministry in Italy, for example. In other ways, too, the exercise of grace had become routinized and formalized.Governments in nineteenth-century Europe conducted important parts of their ordinary business through a many-faceted exercise of grace. It was through the power of grace that the governments of Napoleon III or Wilhelm II managed the hierarchical order of their societies: through the exercise of grace, they granted titles of nobility, as well as academic titles. (Indeed, a current German handbook on the law of grace still makes reference to this old title-granting aspect of the power.)[304] All of this was built with the old timbers of sacral monarchy. Among the nineteenth-century attributes of the power of sovereign grace was of course the prerogative to vary the terms of individual punishment. This prerogative was regularly exercised by nineteenth-century states—notably in the commutation of the sentences of duelists.[305] Duelists were, of course, also the beneficiaries of fortress confinement; individualization by grace grew out of exactly the same world of status that privileged terms of confinement grew.

From these nineteenth-century beginnings grew fundamentally important practices in the twentieth century. Indeed, if we are to understand how modern European individualization established itself—and in particular if we are to understand the impact of the fascist experience—we must trace the development of both of these species of individualization in the twentieth century.

This is especially true of the interwar years, when the study of grace and the fascination of grace captured the imaginations of leading legal thinkers on both the left and the right, in both Germany and France. In Germany, the power of grace inspired, in fact, a kind of intellectual passion in the interwar years, which mixed mysticism with Weberian social science in a way typical of the era.

By the end of the nineteenth century, Germans had begun to make more and more generalized use of the "conditional pardon," in a way that paralleled the introduction of probation in contemporary France.[306] Grace was thus in the air for German legal thinkers. And to students of Weber, by the 1920s, it had the look of a *charismatic* power, one that stood outside the gray world of the "law." That kind of charismatic power inevitably appealed to Weimar Weberians and post-Weberians. Moreover, grace could not fail to attract a kind of excited attention within the doctrinal world of Weimar constitutionalism. For the article of the Weimar Constitution that regulated the power of grace was Article 49—which stood next to, and amplified, the famous, or notorious, Article 48.

Article 48 is sometimes identified as the textual culprit for the instability of Weimar democracy.[307] It was Article 48 that vested the president of the Weimar Republic with the supreme ultimate power to rule by emergency decree. This Article 48, in Weberian fashion, aimed to leave room for the popularly elected, presumably more charismatic president to break through the bureaucratized rule of parliamentary parties. Article 48 always carried a special fascination in the Weimar age of high political Weberianism. In particular, it was the article that inspired some of Carl Schmitt's famous antiliberal theories of the sovereignty.[308] Constitutional debate throughout the Weimar era indeed revolved around Article 48, and that meant that the question of grace, regulated in Article 49, was tied to all of the most troubling and fateful questions of Weimar presidential prerogative.

So it was that grace rose to prominence in the 1920s—not only in the theory, but also in the practice of Weimar governance. In Weimar legal theory, a figure of special, indeed shining, importance was Gustav Radbruch, the legal philosopher who served as reforming justice minister in the early 1920s. We have already encountered Radbruch in chapter 1, as the pioneer of the idea that punishment grows out of slave discipline. His activities also involved more prosaic legal work. Radbruch was a man of the progressive party: it was he who, as minister of justice, presided over the introduction of individualization into German criminal justice. After the war, Radbruch, who had been deprived of his teaching post by the Nazis, would become famous in America for his call to a return to traditional principles of natural law.[309] But during the Weimar era, he struck a different note, notably in an influential, and somewhat dreamy, passage on the nature of grace that would continue to be cited all through the Nazi era. Nineteenth-century positivist scholars had engaged in a slightly dreary doctrinal debate over whether grace was a "positive" power—a power to create rights—or a "negative" power—a power simply to refrain from punishing.[310] Radbruch left all of that behind, instead characterizing grace, in recognizably Weberian ways, as a kind of breakthrough of the true "value" into the everyday world of the law: "The legal institution of grace signifies the undisguised acknowledgement of the doubtfulness of all law, of the tense relationships between law and other ideas, such as the ethical and the religious. Precisely for that reason, unproblematic ages, ages that acknowledged the omnipotence and supremacy of reason, like the age of natural law and the Enlightenment, struggle against the law of grace, as Beccaria did first, followed by Kant, who viewed grace as 'the slipperiest of all sovereign rights.'" Grace, to be sure, was something, as Radbruch saw it, that was susceptible to a kind of Weberian routinization. It was this that allowed grace to combat the great danger identified by Beccaria: the danger that pardons would undermine formal and social equality:

> Grace seems to present itself as a legal institution peculiarly suited to arrive at "correct law" ["zu richtigem Rechte"—a reference to the legal philosophy of Stammler], in the sense of the German legal proverbs "justice without mercy is unjust" ['Recht ohne Gnade ist Unrecht'] or "mercy is next to justice" ['Gnade steht beim Rechte']. Doubts may of course be raised about this conception if we include, in our concept of law, the generality of its prescriptions and the equality of those to whom legal norms are addressed. He who possesses the authority to accord mercy, of course makes efforts to administer it, not arbitrarily, but according to legal guidelines. Grace too aims at general application of its fundamental maxims.

Nevertheless, in the last analysis, it represented something that transcended law:

> Grace means the acknowledgement of the fact that this world is not simply a world of law according to the slogan 'Fiat iustitia, pereat mundus' ["let there be justice, though the heavens fall"], that there are other values alongside law, and that it may become necessary to help these values to be realized. When for example joyous patriotic events create the occasion for amnesties, this is not something that can be founded on legal values . . .
>
> . . . Jhering described grace as the "safety valve" of the law. This does not exhaust its function. It is a symbol that there are values in the world that are drawn from deeper sources than the law, and that rise to greater heights.[311]

Other Weimar authors too spoke of grace as a kind of sovereign magic indulged in by the state.[312] Grace was a theme for the time, one that inspired some of the most characteristic writing of a half-mystical age of scholarship. It even penetrated popular culture, in the climax of Brecht and Weill's *Threepenny Opera*. The *Threepenny Opera* was modeled on Rich and Gay's *Beggar's Opera* of 1728, and like its model, it ended with the pardoning of MacHeath. But the pardon of Rich and Gay's MacHeath was a quasi-absurdist business, in which the "Rabble" was abruptly instructed to "call a reprieve" in order to save a happy ending[313]—dramaturgy for a country in which the deeper drama of mercy had mostly vanished. As we shall see, pardoning practice in England was deeply routinized. Brecht and Weill's Weimar pardon was different: it was, in continental fashion, the result of a grand royal amnesty, to celebrate a coronation. And it included a whole closing number that spoke of grace, somewhat as Radbruch did, as something that penetrated unpredictably and inexplicably into everyday life:

> FRAU PEACHUM: So everything ends happily.
> Life would be so easy and peaceful,
> If the mounted messengers of the King always came . . .
>
> PEACHUM: The mounted messengers of the King do not come often.[314]

The idea of sudden, and inexplicable, grace was something that spoke to some real yearning in Weimar: mounted messengers, abruptly descending, were something that many Germans were prepared to wish for in the 1920s.

Nor was grace absent from governmental practice. On the contrary, it lay at the heart of a fundamentally important innovation: the political amnesty. Indeed, the history I recounted in the previous section of this chapter is not complete without this aspect of grace. We have seen that left-wing German political prisoners lost their old privilege of fortress confinement during the Weimar era. That did not mean that all hope was lost for them though. Where the French continued to imprison their political losers under the "special regime" after World War I, the Germans moved in a new direction, beginning to give amnesty to their losers under the sovereign power of grace. Indeed, the period from 1918 to 1933 was punctuated by regular, almost constant, political amnesties.[315] To say that the old tradition of fine conditions for political prisoners died is thus misleading: the correct characterization is to say that the old tradition of mildness migrated from the realm of law to the realm of grace.

And this Weimar migration of mildness from law to grace is of real significance, for it established a pattern that continued in the Nazi period. Indeed, in the realm of grace, the Nazis too, astonishingly, accepted norms of mildness.

Grace, which had fascinated so many jurists in Weimar, could hardly fail to fascinate the Nazis as well, and it did fascinate them, just as other aspects of the sovereignty regulated by the Weimar Constitution did. Nazi practice continued, and even extended, Weimar uses of the power of grace. Indeed, the Nazis engaged in a lively pardoning practice, which has gone almost wholly undiscussed in the secondary literature.

Partly this Nazi pardoning practice involved just what it involved in Weimar: periodic political amnesties. In remarkable fact, a series of Weimar political amnesties was followed by a series of *Nazi* political amnesties. The Nazis, despite their programmatic brutality, repeatedly issued amnesties for their minor political opponents: that is to say, those who had violated Nazi legislation against "insulting" the regime. Those who had been careless enough to express their contempt or dislike for the Nazis where they could be overheard were always convicted; but they were also regularly released, especially under celebratory amnesties such as the Hitler amnesty of 1934 (celebrating, in ancien régime fashion, Hitler's birthday), the amnesty of 1938 (celebrating the *Anschluß* of Austria), and others.[316] These general amnesties are a remarkable and little-discussed feature of Nazi governance. Their importance goes, moreover, beyond the Nazi era itself. For these Nazi amnesties are the immediate ancestors of the Christmas amnesties that are still a feature of the mildness of German justice today. Indeed, it deserves emphasis that the basic text that governs amnesty practice almost everywhere in Germany is still, in the year 2001, based on a Nazi text. This is the *Gnadenordnung*, the Grace Ordinance, of 1935—still cited in the standard literature on the law of grace in Germany, and still providing the framework for amnesty practice in the *Bundesländer*.[317]

The exercise of Nazi grace was not limited to the granting of amnesties. Through the power of grace, the Nazis also introduced what remains the core of modern German mildness: regularized probation. Regularized probation in fact appears for the first time in the same Grace Ordinance of 1935, which confers on courts the power to sentence defendants to probation as a matter of "grace."[318] Despite some discomfort among Nazi-era commentators over the idea that probation should be routinized, routinized it was.[319] This perhaps deserves to be repeated: regularized probation in Germany first appeared as part of the old sacral sovereign tradition of grace, and it appeared *during* the Nazi period. This Nazi introduction of regularized probation is rarely mentioned in the secondary literature.[320] Yet it too set the basic framework for the liberalizing reforms of the postwar period. The *Gnadenordnung* conferred the power of "gracious" orders of probation on judges—which means that the judges who received the power to issue orders of probation, supposedly for the first time, in 1953, were the same judges who had had that power as a matter of grace for a decade under the Nazis. Of course, German lawyers knew this in 1953, and they even commented on it at the time.[321] One slightly puzzled jurist wrote an article in 1953, for example, asking for guidance: was the new "legal" probation the same as the old "gracious" probation, he asked, or not?[322]

Since 1953, though, this fact has been, willfully or carelessly, forgotten. Maybe this is not surprising. Regularized probation is, by every account in the standard literature, the core practice of humane punishment in Europe today, and it may seem nothing short of bizarre to discover that it is a Nazi innovation. Yet what the Nazis did was simply typical of fascist practice: the Italian Fascist Criminal Code also introduced probation.[323] As for Vichy, the pattern seems to have been something like the German pattern. Interwar French legal scholars, like their German counterparts, had waxed eloquent about sovereign "grace," and it seems that in the Vichy period too, they followed the German model, if perhaps only at a distance. The 1943-44 lectures of Joseph Barthélemy, Vichy minister of justice, expended hour upon hour on the topic of grace.[324] As for legal practice, there, too, although "legal" probation was eliminated, the memoirs of the same Barthélemy point proudly to an active practice of grace.[325]

These fascist probation practices, like other fascist practices of grace, go unmentioned in our secondary literature, which continues to describe probation as either an innovation (in Germany) or a renewal (in France) of the early 1950s. From a very narrow doctrinal point of view, this neglect of fascist probation may seem justified: after all, what the fascists exercised was probation founded on *grace*, not probation founded on *law*. Yet as a matter of cultural history, and even of the history of lived legal practice, this distinction is wholly specious. In Germany, in particular, the same judges who began issuing "legal" orders of probation in 1953 had issued "gracious" orders of probation in the Nazi era, as authors of the early 1950s were still well aware. Indeed, it is foolish to take the Nazi characterization of their practice of "grace" at face value. In fact, Nazi "grace" was a distinctly lawlike phenomenon, regulated by a thick book of heavily annotated rules. The Nazi *Gnadenordnung* of 1935 retains its influence in the practice of the German states, indeed, precisely because it is a body of elaborate rules. The idea that Nazi probation represented unrationalized "grace" is wholly improbable and is in fact false. What Nazi probation grew out of, to return to Weber, was routinized grace.

The truth of the matter is that, seen in proper historical perspective, probation did not represent a rejection of fascism, but a continuation of fascist practices. Fascist individualization was no all harsh; some of it was mild.

What can we say about this? It shows what so much of what I have discussed in this book and elsewhere shows: that in the world of European dignity, there is much more continuity with the fascist period than most Europeans have been ready to acknowledge. It shows something else too: it confirms how much the European tradition of mildness grows out of a tradition of strong state power, and especially out of a tradition of state power with a distinctly sacral, and distinctly hierarchical, tinge. For the Nazis, it made political sense to engage in heavy use of grace, because it is an attribute of strong state power to show mildness—to show a kind of indulgence de haut en bas. Grace is the act of the sovereign as *seigneur*, of the sovereign as merciful patron.

Indeed, the Nazi case is simply a particularly powerful example of something that runs throughout European history. As the ongoing practice of amnesties in both France and Germany suggests, mildness and the de haut en bas sovereignty of European state power continue to go together. If the Nazis indulged the gracious mildness of sentences of probation, that shows only how powerful that state tradition is in Europe: even the regime that was most dedicated to harshness in punishment could not withhold mildness in the effort to create public legitimacy for itself.

5

Low Status in the Anglo-American World

In the 1880s, Petr Kropotkin, the feared nineteenth-century anarchist, found himself in Clairvaux, one of the main French prisons. At the time, anarchists still received the privileges of political prisoners in France, so Kropotkin was spared confinement with "common criminals"—a fact that should perhaps make us skeptical of the praise that he had for French prisons.[1] Nevertheless, he did have some praise for them—at least by contrast with English prisons, which he had also experienced from inside and which he found far more degrading. In particular, Kropotkin, like Beaumont and Tocqueville forty years earlier, was struck by the fact that the "ignominious" punishment of flogging had survived in England:

> The fact is, that if in a French central prison the inmates are perhaps more dependent upon the fancies and caprices of the governor and the warders than they seem to be in English prisons, the treatment of the prisoners is far more humane than it is in the corresponding institutions on the other side of the Channel. The medieval revengeful system which still prevails in English prisons has been given up long since in France. The imprisoned man is not compelled to sleep on planks, or to have a mattress on alternate days only; the day he comes to prison he gets a decent bed, and retains it. He is not compelled, either, to degrading work, such as to climb a wheel, or to pick oakum; he is employed, on the contrary in useful work . . . .
>
> . . . Moreover, if the punishment for insubordination is very cruel, there

> is, at least, none of the flogging which goes on still in English prisons. Such a punishment would be absolutely impossible in France.[2]

What Kropotkin says is true: flogging had indeed been long since abolished in French prisons, but in the English-speaking world, it was different. Flogging would survive in England until 1948, in Canada until 1957, and in the state of Delaware until 1973.[3] There are indeed still Americans who propose reintroducing it.[4] Degrading labor had been abolished in France—but not in England—as well.[5] Treadmills and oakum picking—a particularly grueling task—were not the lot of French convicts by the 1880s.

These differences were already old when Kropotkin arrived at Clairvaux.

The English Background

In an important sense, the comparative history of Anglo-American punishment is simply typical of the comparative history of the common law more generally. There are many features of the common law that we best explain by recognizing that things simply happened *sooner* in England than they happened in the continent. The English monarchy succeeded in consolidating its power centuries before the French monarchy did. The paradoxical consequence is that the common law preserves many medieval forms that have vanished in France. The common law keeps the marks of its birth, and its birth came in the twelfth century. Peculiarly Anglo-American punishment traditions are not as old as the twelfth century; but they are old. In particular, the history of the decline of status-differentiation in punishment is old. Status-differentiation in punishment too broke down earlier in England; and it broke down differently.

This was evident by the mid-eighteenth century. The briefest and clearest summary of English punishment as it existed in the mid-eighteenth century is still Blackstone's catalogue of the punishments, and I will begin by quoting in full the passage I excerpted at the beginning of chapter 2. Of punishments, wrote Blackstone:

> some are capital, which extend to the life of the offender, and consist generally in being hanged by the neck till dead; though in very atrocious crimes other circumstances of terror, pain, or disgrace are superadded: as, in treasons of all kinds, being drawn or dragged to the place of execution; in high treason affecting the king's person or government, embowelling alive, beheading, and quartering; and in murder, a public dissection. And, in case of any treason committed by a female, the judgment is to be burned alive. But the humanity of the English nation has authorized, by a tacit consent, an almost general mitigation of such part of these judgment as savour of torture or cruelty: a sledge or hurdle being usually allowed to such traitors as are condemned to be drawn; and there being very few instances (and those accidental or by negligence) of any person's being embowelled or burned, till previously deprived of sensation by strangling. Some punishments consist in exile or banishment, by abjuration of the realm, or transportation to the American colonies: others in loss of liberty,

> by perpetual or temporary imprisonment. Some extend to confiscation, by forfeiture of lands, or moveables, or both, or of the profits of lands for life: others induce a disability, of holding offices of employments, being heirs, executors, and the like. Some, though rarely, occasion a mutilation or a dismembering, by cutting off the hand or ears: others fix a lasting stigma on the offender, by slitting the nostrils, or branding in the hand or face. Some are merely pecuniary, by stated or discretionary fines: and lastly there are others, that consist principally in their ignominy, though most of them are mixed with some degree of corporal pain; and these are inflicted chiefly for crimes, which arise from indigence, or which render even opulence disgraceful. Such as whipping, hard labour in the house of correction, the pillory, the stocks, and the ducking-stool.
>
> Disgusting as this catalogue may seem, it will afford pleasure to an English reader, and do honour to the English law, to compare it with shocking apparatus of death and torment, to be met with in the criminal codes of almost every other nation in Europe. And it is moreover one of the glories of our English law, that the nature, though not always the quantity or degree, of punishment is *ascertained* for every offence; and that it is not left in the breast of any judge, nor even of a jury, to alter that judgment, which the law has beforehand ordained, for every subject alike, without respect of persons.[6]

Indeed it was so. The old low-status punishments had been in retreat for a long time in England—much more so than on the continent. As for "respect of persons," it was by no means absent from English law in the eighteenth century. But it *is* true that "respect of persons" mattered noticeably less in the English world than it did on the continent.

These peculiarities of English development can perhaps be traced, in some respects, very far back into the later Middle Ages. In the high Middle Ages, England had a law of status not entirely unlike the law of status on the continent. There were two especially important legal statuses: villein, at the low end of the social scale, and peer, at the high. English peers were different in one important respect from their French counterparts: only eldest sons generally inherited noble status in England, which kept the very highest order of society small in number. Nevertheless, peers, few though they may have been, did have noble status of a kind much like that of the continent. They were of course entitled to trial by their peers, which came to mean trial before the House of Lords.[7] Respect for their persons was protected through a typical sort of law of deference, the law of *scandalum magnatum*, the law against "scandalizing persons of importance" by showing them disrespect.[8] None of this was all that dramatically different from what was to be found on the contemporary continent.

During the centuries after the high Middle Ages, though, the English law of status began, intermittently, to break down. The law of deference decayed in the later Middle Ages: *scandalum magnatum*, strikingly, became a body of law oriented more toward protecting the state than protecting individuals of high status.[9] On the other end of the spectrum, the legally defined low status of "villein" had essentially collapsed by the end of the sixteenth century. Villeins were effectively treated no differently than other Englishman by mid-century, and at the end of the century their special status formally vanished—though the term hung on as a more or less meaningless survival in the common law.[10] The high status of "peer" survived, of course, and continued to carry some important legal privileges. Nevertheless, it can be argued that, in important ways, the English nobility proved less successful in creating legal privileges for itself than did the continental nobility, though these are matters I will not discuss in detail here.

Certainly a pattern of difference showed up in the law of punishment. In particular, it showed up in one of the most famous aspects of English criminal law: benefit of clergy. All over the Western world, as we have seen, clerics were entitled to specially mild punishment—immune from mutilation and execution, they were typically imprisoned from a very early date.[11] Indeed, seen in the longest historical perspective, the rise of imprisonment as it is practiced on the continent today can be viewed as a kind of generalization of clerical status. In continental punishment, the norms of the monastery have, over the course of many centuries, migrated into secular society. This process has really been achieved, however, only over the last two centuries on the continent.

Something of the pattern can be found in England as well—but at a much earlier date, and in a different form. A kind of generalization of clerical status took place very early in English criminal law, in the form of "benefit of clergy." The test of clerical status in medieval England was literacy: people who could read were presumptively clergy, entitled to benefit from relatively mild punishment. From the late fourteenth century onward, this benefit was broadly generalized. The full history of this practice involves more complexities than deserve discussion here. What matters is that by the early modern period, defendants accused of their first offense (including, by the end of the seventeenth century, women) were permitted to feign literacy and so acquire the technical status of clerics. Indeed, even the reading test was abolished by statute in 1706, so that neither sex nor status had any bearing on the extension of the privilege of clergy.[12] Defendants were classified as "clerics," branded on the brawn of the thumb, and allowed to go free—though occasionally they suffered the traditional punishment of clerics, imprisonment.[13] This did not represent full attribution to them of the status of clerics, of course. Branding on the thumb was a form of mild mutilation. (Indeed, for a period in the early eighteenth century, it was regarded as too mild, and was replaced by statute with branding on the cheek—a requirement apparently evaded by English court officials.)[14] Mutilation, however light, is a kind of punishment, and a distinctly low-status one. Moreover, on a second offense, offenders were subjected (at least in theory) to the full force of the criminal law. Most important, from the late fifteenth century onward, Parliament defined increasing numbers of offenses as "nonclergyable," subjecting first offenders to ordinary forms of punishment.[15] The full benefit of clergy status was thus never extended throughout English society.

Nevertheless, even though Parliament reacted against it, the pressure within the common law to extend benefit of clergy to the general population in England represents a striking kind of early leveling up—a kind of early dissemination of effectively high status. And the history of benefit of clergy does suggest that the status distinctions that mattered so fundamentally on the continent were of lesser importance in England.

In other ways too, there were signs, in the seventeenth century, that status distinctions were less firmly fixed in England than on the continent. Status certainly mattered profoundly in seventeenth-century England. There was plenty of law, in particular, that revolved around questions of status. For example, John Selden, one of the great jurists of the first half of the century, invested the time necessary to produce a substantial treatise on the law of titles and forms of address[16]—a topic that could only seem consequential in a society which set great store by relations of deference. Nevertheless, there are signs that English status hierarchy was on shakier ground than continental status hierarchy. The differential forms of address "you" and "thou" had vanished by the beginning of the century[17]—something that is still not the case on the continent. There was of course a leveler literature, in the middle of the century, that preached, in a limited way, the end of status distinctions.[18] Stuart efforts to introduce a French style of court-centered government famously failed. These are familiar historical facts. They deserve to be repeated only because they bear on the critical question of whether status distinctions in the law were growing weaker over the seventeenth century.

And indeed, there are scattered indications that exactly that is the case. I suggested in chapter 1 that status abuse, the application of low-status punishments to high-status persons, can be taken as a symptom of changing status relations in a society. The two historical examples that I emphasized in chapter 1 are famous ones from antiquity: the example of the Mediterranean during late antiquity, where punishment crept up the status ladder; and the example of China in the Qin dynasty, where the Legalist program called for the application of historically low-status punishments to high-status persons.

Something of the same kind can arguably be detected in the great constitutional conflicts of the seventeenth century. Among the bitterest of complaints against Star Chamber in the years before the English Revolution was that this hated court inflicted low-status punishments on members of the gentry, who suffered such treatment as ear-cropping and public display in the pillory.[19] Similarly, among the striking aspects of the last years of crisis leading up to the Glorious Revolution was the novel prosecution of some high-status dissenters and the subjection of others to low-status punishments. As George Fisher has recently argued, much of the legal drama of the period before 1688 grew out of the treason trials of the high:

> [T]reason trials had peculiar power to spur reform because of the status of those charged. As Stephen said, "What the political trials of the seventeenth century really did was to expose men of high ranks and conspicuous position to the calamities that must have been felt by thousands of obscure criminals without attracting even a passing notice." And indeed, the Parliamentarians who met in 1689 made repeated reference to Algernon Sydney and William Lord Russell—two men of power who had suffered traitors' deaths when James II took revenge on those who orchestrated the trials and executions of several of the

> King's adherents. Little wonder, then, that members of the House of Commons who supported the Treason Act declared "[t]hat their design, in passing this Bill, was, to prevent those abuses in Tryals for Treason . . . for the future; by means of which, during the violence of the late Reigns, they had observed divers had lost their lives."[20]

Some of the same status drama can be detected in the case of perhaps the most famous defendant of the era, Titus Oates, who was convicted of perjury in 1685 for having concocted the story of the "Popish Plot." Oates was sentenced to literal degradation—degraded from the status of clergyman—and ordered to be pilloried repeatedly. The court decreed:

> That he should forever be Degraded, and forthwith stript of all his Priestly Habits.
>
> That he should stand in the *Pillory* before *Westminster-hall-gate* on *Monday,* the *18th,* instant, one hour . . . with a Paper on his Head, writ, *Perjury, Perjury,* twice; and walk round the Hall with the said Paper on his Head.
>
> On *Tuesday* the *19th,* to stand an hour in the *Pillory* . . . with the same Inscription over his Head.
>
> On *Wednesday* the *20th,* to be *whipt* from *Ald-gate* to *Newgate.*
>
> And on *Thursday* the *21st,* to be *whipt* from *Newgate* to *Tybourn.*
>
> On *Friday* the *22nd,* to stand in the *Pillory* at *Tybourn,* with the same Inscription of *Perjury* over his Head, his Face towards *Tybourn.*
>
> And for these Two *Perjuries* to pay a 1000 *Marques* for each *Perjury,* and to abide in Prison.
>
> And when he has performed this Ceremony, he is to stand in the *Pillory* Three time Annually.[21]

Now, Oates's punishment did not technically constitute low-status treatment of a high-status person. Perjury was an "infaming" offense—one that automatically deprived the offender of legal honor.[22] Moreover, Oates was formally degraded before being punished. Nevertheless, the literature of the time shows that part of the drama in this celebrated case involved Oates's status. Numerous broadsides appeared with different versions of the same woodcut, showing Oates in full clerical garb in the pillory. These had such titles as "The Doctor Degraded"[23] or "Oates Exalted Above his Brethren,"[24] and included verses that mocked Oates precisely for the undignified treatment he was receiving: "He stands in state, and well becomes his station / Using a Truckling-Stool for Recreation."[25] "O cruel Fate!" as the doggerelist of "The Doctor Degraded" put it:

> Did'st thou not once make *Oates* they Favourite . . .
> And mounted him upon thy Wings so high,
> That he could almost touch the very Skie,
> And now must *Oates* stand in the *Pillory*?
> There to be battered so with Rotten *Eggs*,
> Both on the Face, the Body and the Legs.[26]

Some of the meaning of Oates's punishment had to do precisely with his fall from high station. Indeed, more broadly, the anxieties of the day were colored by fears of status abuse. As one 1689 pamphleteer put it, whippings "upon Clergymen . . . who can never be deemed Vagabonds and Slaves in a Nation where they have a liberal Education while young, and reverence and maintenance afterwards" raised the threat that "the best Commoner in *England* might fall under the lash as well as a Priest of the Church."[27] These anxieties are well worth remembering when we discuss the most famous aspect of Oates's case. It was because of the way Oates was treated that the Bill of Rights of 1689 included a prohibition on "cruel and unusual" punishment—the same prohibition still to be found in the American Bill of Rights. Our standard historiography of the phrase "cruel and unusual punishment" has nothing to say about the drama of status.[28] Yet part of the "cruelty" in the way Oates was treated clearly had to do with his "station." As in Qin China, some of the revolutionary drive in English law had to do with status abuses: highly placed persons who are subjected to indignities are persons who make revolutions, and this is something we should not forget in trying to understand legal history anywhere in the human world.

There are further hints, too, of a malaise in the status-traditions of punishment in seventeenth-century England. High-status persons were traditionally beheaded rather than hanged in the occidental world. We have seen the great symbolic importance of this in both France and Germany, where nineteenth- and twentieth-century criminal punishment demonstratively guaranteed that all persons executed would be beheaded and not hanged. The status-distinction between hanging and beheading prevailed in English practice too. But seventeenth-century English jurists were strikingly unwilling to concede that this practice was legitimate. Thus Coke, the great early-seventeenth-century jurist, treated beheading as in derogation from the common law—even though he was compelled to admit that it had been applied to some noble offenders:

> True it is that the Lord of Hungerford of Heytesbury was in 32 H. 8. attainted of Buggery, and had judgement to be hanged by the neck untill he was dead; and yet on the twenty eight day of July in the same year was beheaded at the Tower-hill. But as true it is, that Thomas Fines Lord Dacres of the South, in anno 33 H. 8. was attainted of murder, and had judgement to be hanged by the neck untill he was dead and according to the judgement was hanged at Tiborn the twenty eighth of June in the same year. And true it is that Edward Duke of Somerset was attainted of felony in anno 5 E. 6. and had judgement to be hanged by the neck until he was dead, and on the twenty second of February in the same year was beheaded at the Tower-hill. And as true it is, that in 3 & 4 Ph. and Mar. the Lord Stourton was attainted of murder, and had judgement to be hanged by the neck untill he were dead, and according to the judgement. The sixth of March in the same year was hanged.
>
> In the Case of High Treason [beheading is proper]. But if a man being attainted of felony, be beheaded, it is no execution of the judgement, because the judgement is, that he be hanged until he be dead. . . . *Judicandum est legibus, non exemplis*. . . .[29]

Matthew Hale repeated this view at the end of the seventeenth century.[30] These were the leading authorities of the century; and unlike their French contemporaries, they vigorously rejected traditional norms of high-status execution. There were doubts in the seventeenth-century English air about some low-status punishments as well. The introduction of forced labor in workhouses provoked particularly interesting anxieties. Workhouses were on the rise over the century. Moreover the idea that criminals should be put to hard labor, and indeed enslaved, was attracting support. Thomas More in particular had praised penal enslavement in his *Utopia*.[31] Nevertheless, it is striking that authors who defended forced labor felt obliged to insist that introducing such practices was not inconsistent with the tradition of English "liberty."[32] Objections of that kind were at best rare in France. Clearly "respect for persons" was weaker in England. This does not by any means imply that there was a complete breakdown of English status distinctions, but it does suggest that those distinctions did not have the sacrosanct position in England that they did in contemporary France.

By the time of Blackstone, though, it seems clear that something dramatic was afoot. Status-distinctions in the law of punishment took on noticeable fuzziness—a fuzziness that, when contrasted with the contemporary continent, makes a strongly egalitarian impression.

Early eighteenth-century English law certainly often ran broadly parallel to the law of the continent. In early eighteenth-century England as on the eighteenth-century continent, punishments were inflicted along the familiar status-differentiated lines: despite the objections of Coke and Hale, persons of "quality" were commonly beheaded rather than hanged—a privilege granted them by the exercise of royal grace.[33] Thus César de Saussure, reporting on the English scene to his family in the early eighteenth century, described precisely the sort of status-consciousness common on the continent. Executed criminals were ordinarily carted to Tyburn before a hooting public, he wrote. There they were executed in one of two humiliating ways—if they were persons of low status. Spectators watched, he reported, from "a sort of amphitheatre erected . . . near the gibbet":

> There is no other form of execution than hanging; it is thought that the taking of life is sufficient punishment for any crime without worse torture. After hanging murderers are, however, punished in a particular fashion. They are first hung on the common gibbet, their bodies are then covered with tallow and fat substances, over this is placed a tarred shirt fastened down with iron bands, and the bodies are hung with chains to the gibbet, which is erected on the spot, or as near as possible to the place, where the crime was committed, and there it hangs till it falls to dust. This is what is called in this country to 'hang in chains.' The lower classes do not consider it a great disgrace to be simply hanged, but have a great horror of the hanging in chains, and the shame of it is terrible for the relatives of the condemned. Peers of the realm are executed by beheading; their heads are placed on the block and severed with a hatchet.[34]

Peers were to be sure a narrow class of persons, much narrower than in France. Hanging was thus much more general in England than in France. Respectable persons without the technically noble status of "peer" did, though, manage to secure other privileges for themselves: in particular, rather than being carried to the gallows in an open cart, early eighteenth-century felons of respectable status had themselves brought in much more stately and less shameful fashion: in a coach decked out as a hearse.[35] Even though hanging was more widely inflicted in England than in France, then, respectable persons managed to have themselves hanged differently in the early part of the eighteenth century.

Status privileges extended beyond execution, moreover, just as they did on the continent. Duelists in eighteenth-century England, like duelists in post-1830 France, could expect to be acquitted by juries if they had followed the code of honor.[36] Lettres de cachet did not exist in England, but the practice of holding high-status persons in places of high-status detention—notably the Tower of London—certainly did.[37] There was, as far as I have been able to discover, no carefully defined special regime of "fortress confinement" in the Tower. But it is well documented that high-status prisoners—who of course included political prisoners in England just as they did in France—received treatment that closely resembled the treatment that was the lot of their high-status contemporaries in the Bastille.[38] Moreover, English jailers, like Dutch ones, could keep special wings for those prisoners who could afford better treatment, or else house finer prisoners in their own apartments.[39] In eighteenth-century English justice, it remained indeed a natural assumption that high-status persons should be spared contact with the lower sort: witness, for example, the 1782 jury that petitioned the king to show mercy to a gentleman sentenced on conviction to six months in a common jail for dueling. The jury had not intended that a gentleman be subjected "to so grievous a punishment," as their petition declared.[40] Whippings for gentlemen remained unthinkable.[41] All this was little different from the eighteenth- or nineteenth-century continental pattern.

Nevertheless, it is a fact of cardinal importance that by mid-century high-status privileges in punishment were undergoing a real assault in England. Douglas Hay, learned critic of the inequalities of eighteenth-century English society, has traced some examples of a kind of egalitarianism in English punishment that are markedly different from anything to be seen on the continent. He rightly notes that status mattered in English society and punishment, as indeed it did. Nevertheless, he points to examples of an egalitarianism in mid-eighteenth-century punishment that was, by continental standards, noteworthy indeed:

> As executions for forgery became increasingly common throughout the century . . . respectable villains went to the gallows. The crime was punished with unremitting severity even though it was often committed by impecunious lawyers of good family. This rigour was distressing to many middling men: the agitation led by Johnson against the execution of the Reverend Dr. Dodd, a former Royal Chaplain and Lord Chesterfield's old tutor, was enormous. Dodd died at Tyburn in 1777 but he lived in popular culture for a long time, his case persuasive evidence that the law treated rich and poor alike. The occasional sen-

> tence of transportation or death passed on gentlemen with unusual sexual tastes or guilty of homicide, cases widely reported in the *Newgate Calender* and other versions, similarly served to justify the law.[42]

Low-status execution for high-status criminals played, Hay observes, a great role in the popular culture of the law. Lawrence Shirley, Lord Ferrers, having killed his steward, retained the noble privilege of trial before the House of Lords. This did not save him from grotesque execution: "[He] was captured by his tenantry, tried in the House of Lords, sentenced to death, executed at Tyburn, and dissected 'like a common criminal' as the publicists never tired of repeating." This was eighteenth-century England, and all status had not vanished, to be sure:

> He was hanged in his silver brocade wedding-suit, on a scaffold equipped with black silk cushions for the mourners. But hanging is hanging, the defenders of the law repeated enthusiastically. An enormous literature surrounded his execution in 1760, much of it devoted to celebrating the law. Later in the century the event was often recalled as an irrefutable proof of the justice of English society. An anti-Jacobin in the 1790s advised his "brother artificers":
>
> > We have long enjoyed that Liberty and Equality which the French have been struggling for: in England, ALL MEN ARE EQUAL; all who commit the same offenses are liable to the same punishment. If the *very poorest and meanest man* commits murder, he is hanged with a hempen halter, and his body dissected. If the *Richest Nobleman* commits a murder, *he* is hanged with a hempen halter, and his body is dissected—*all are equal here.*
>
> . . . In some counties the story of the wicked aristocrat who met a just end on the scaffold was told at popular festivities until well into the 1800s.[43]

Steven Wilf, too, has discovered important evidence of a breakdown in status-differentiation after about 1760. As he explains, "One of the most notable changes wrought by mid-century reformers was to abolish the customary right of bourgeois felons to ride during the execution procession in a coach, rather than in an exposed cart."[44] Agitation from the late 1760s onward led to a distinct leveling down in England, as high-status felons were deprived of their right to be coached rather than carted.[45] To scholars like Hay, all of this is as much the occasion for ironic comment as anything else—as "irrefutable proof" of the egalitarianism of a society that still was deeply committed to enforcing differences in the distribution of wealth. And indeed, if one regards questions of the distribution of status as of no significance, one will not set much store by measures like the generalization of hanging. But the distribution of status is not a matter of no significance; it is something that human animals care about deeply, and these mid-eighteenth-century developments do indeed seem wholly remarkable. Hanging *is* hanging—or at least, it was in the eighteenth century.[46] (In Ferrers's case it seemed momentous enough that the hangman and his deputy scuffled over who would get to keep the rope.)[47] For the matter, dissection is dissection—as a contemporary print showing Ferrers's corpse ready for the surgeon's table reminds us. (Though as it turned out, Ferrers was at least spared some humiliation: only a small audience witnessed his dissection.)[48] The distribution of status does indeed seem to have been dramatically reshuffled, at least for a while, in the English mid-eighteenth century, and this is something that happens rarely in complex societies.

Status distinction in punishment was clearly breaking down in England. This seems true, not only with regard to the treatment of figures like Lord Ferrers, but also with regard to the perception and application of low-status punishments such as mutilation. In England as on the continent, mutilation had been in decline since the sanguinary sixteenth century, though it was still practiced, as Blackstone indicates.[49] Change was afoot, though. Dissection itself makes an interesting example. The dissection of a noblemen like Lord Ferrers clearly represented a shock to status norms, as the contemporary literature suggests. Yet this was presumably possible partly because dissection was losing some of its old ritual meaning. As J. M. Beattie observes, the Murder Act of 1725 required that murderers "be 'dissected and anatomized' by surgeons, a powerful mark of infamy. Even more terrible punishments were frequently proposed. Breaking on the wheel and similar forms of pain were favored, especially in the first half of the century (prompted perhaps by Continental practices). B[ut b]y the 1750s they were giving way to suggestions more in step with the march of science."[50] Scientizing dissection meant removing it from the thought-world of traditional punishment. And indeed, numerous scraps of evidence suggest that England was shifting away from traditional norms by mid-century.[51] Whipping too was on the decline by the second quarter of the century.[52] As for branding of the thumb, the mild mutilation marking benefit of clergy, by the early eighteenth century, it seems often to have been administered merely symbolically, with a cold iron;[53] and it was abolished in 1779.[54] Whippings and the pillory were certainly did not vanish.[55] But the most striking form of punishment in the English eighteenth century was not drawn from the traditional repertoire at all. This was transportation. Eighteenth-century defendants, who faced the death penalty for an extraordinary number of offenses, were very commonly pardoned and transported to America.[56] It is not easy to say whether this did or did not represent harsh treatment. But it certainly departed in some measure from the continental practice of using punishment as a way of publicly displaying status differences. Transportation was simply not a classic marker of low status, and the French, for example, abandoned it after a brief early-eighteenth-century experiment. [57] In France mutilation and forced labor remained the norm. There was some mutilation in England, as we have seen, in the form of branding. There was some forced labor, too, especially after the American Revolution put a temporary end to the system of transportation. Faced with large numbers of unexportable convicts, the English put them at forced labor on the Thames, in the 1780s, housed in the notorious "hulks." This closely resembled the French shipyards and fit within standard continental patterns of forced labor.[58] Moreover, forced labor would return with a vengeance in the "penal servitude" acts of the nineteenth century.[59] There was the pillory in England too—for perjury until as late a date as 1837.[60]

Nevertheless, in the eighteenth century, the English attitude toward forced labor showed much more discomfort with status-differentiation than did the continental attitude. In the English literature, indeed, discomfort with forced labor had noteworthy symbolic value within the ideology of English liberty. When reformers like Mandeville or Bentham proposed hard labor as a normal punishment, they felt compelled, like their seventeenth-century predecessors, to answer the objection that forced labor was a form of slavery incompatible with the English constitution.[61] Other marks of servitude also troubled English commentators: there was opposition, for example—though unsuccessful opposition, to be sure—to the use of fetters.[62]

Mid-eighteenth-century English punishment practice thus showed clear signs of breaking away from continental status norms. What was true of English practice was also very noticeably true of English theory. Standard continental authors never failed to describe the system of status-differentiation as central to the order of punishment. If we open a text by a continental author like Muyart de Vouglans or Jousse we find a careful presentation of the different punishments meted out to persons of different quality.[63] Not so in England. Status-differentiation in the forms of punishment played only a minor role in English writing.

Blackstone, to be sure, described some status differences. He was too faithful a reporter of the contemporary scene not to do so. In his account of the crimes of petty treason, in particular, he gave a faithful account of the status-hierarchy of his time. "Petty" treason characterized offenses by low-status persons against persons who had authority over them, and there were plenty of such offenses. Blackstone's accounts of petty treason differed little from contemporary French accounts of the corresponding French offenses.[64] When it came to the system of punishment, though, Blackstone parted company with French authorities. Blackstone did pick up on one important bit of general early-modern jurisprudence on punishment. As we have seen, early-modern sensitivities were strongly affected by status-taint of infaming punishments. Blackstone took the same attitude. Moreover, Blackstone certainly did observe in a general way that the "quality" of the offender might serve as an extenuating circumstance. Courts were to consider "the Baseness, Enormity, and dangerous Tendency of [the crime], the malice, Deliberation and Wilfulness, or the Inconsideration, Suddenness and Surprize with which it was committed, the Age, Quality and Degree of the Offender, and all other Circumstances which may any way aggravate or extenuate the Guilt."[65] The formula "Age, Quality and Degree" is Blackstone's distant echo of ancient Roman law, under which all trials began by determining the status of the defendant.[66] But "Age, Quality and Degree" appear low on Blackstone's list, as just a few among many considerations, and Blackstone did not bother to discuss what all his continental contemporaries regarded as the critical question: whether the *form* of punishment should depend on the "quality" of the defendant. Not a word did he let drop about different forms of execution, about mutilation or forced labor. Nor was Blackstone alone in this. Other commentary of the period said quite simply nothing about status.[67] All this was typical of the age: even though a 1413 statute required that all indictments specify the accused's "estate or degree," clerks simply listed all defendants *pro forma* as "labourer"—a fine piece of English indifference to status, at least as compared to the continent.[68]

The contrast between mid-eighteenth-century England and the continent emerges especially clearly in the history of the spread of Beccarianism. Beccaria, with his emphasis on formal equality, had essentially nothing to say about status differences in punishment and to embrace Beccaria was correspondingly to declare oneself, effectively, indifferent to status. It is thus no surprise that, for orthodox continental authors, Beccarianism remained more or less taboo. To be sure, there was a wealth of inventive Beccarian literature in later-eighteenth-century France. But it was distinctly *speculative* literature, and indeed a radical literature. People like Voltaire were eager advocates of Beccarianism.[69] But authoritative French treatise writers like Muyart de Vouglans or Jousse were hostile, and they insisted unswervingly on the maintenance of status-differences in punishment.[70] (Muyart de Vouglans wrote, indeed, a much-cited attack on Beccaria.)[71] Beccaria was universally read on the continent; but he was heterodox. This is, of course, why the embrace of Beccarianism in the early years of the French Revolution was a revolutionary act.

Not so in England. There Beccarianism fell on fertile theoretical soil much earlier (though to be sure English practice remained essentially unaffected).[72] The theoretical appeal of Beccaria was most notable in the dominant authority on the English common law, Blackstone. Unlike Muyart de Vouglans or Jousse, Blackstone was, famously, directly influenced by Beccaria. Indeed, his *Commentaries* were studded with Beccarian observations.[73] What in late-eighteenth-century France was mere speculation thus worked its way directly into the most important doctrinal writing of England. It was possible for practically minded English lawyers to talk about Beccaria—evidence of striking difference in legal culture.[74]

The same Beccarian tone was to be found in the English theoretical attitude toward pardons. The practice of pardoning was attacked everywhere in the mid and late eighteenth century. But on the continent, as we have seen, the assessments of the pardoning power, from Montesquieu to Kant, generally belonged, not so much to the technical reasoning over mitigation and deterrence, as to the world of high political theory. For continental philosophers, pardoning was analyzed as "monarchical," and so inconsistent with republican values.[75] This line of analysis was hardly absent in England; Blackstone himself echoed it.[76] Nevertheless, English attacks were in general distinctly more Beccarian in color than the continental ones. English authors, like Beccaria, were less political theoreticians than penological ones, principally concerned about the impact of pardons and similar mitigations on the deterrent effect of the law. Henry Fielding is a famous example of a mid-eighteenth-century exponent of the view that a criminal law mitigated through pardons was an ineffective one.[77] Bentham too took the same tack, with characteristically vigorous rhetoric: "From pardon power unrestricted, come impunity to delinquency in all shapes: from impunity to delinquency in all shapes, impunity to maleficence in all shapes; from impunity to maleficence in all shapes, dissolution of government: from dissolution of government, dissolution of political society."[78] In general, monarchy as such was not at issue. Pardoning was assessed less as a matter of grand political theory than as a matter of nuts-and-bolts criminal justice policy; and in this respect the English literature was distinctly more Beccarian.

What about the actual practice of pardoning?

Of course, there was an enormous amount of it, as we have already seen. It is one of the most famous facts about eighteenth-century English justice that pardons were granted regularly throughout the century. The machinery of pardoning was in the process of routinization by the end of the seventeenth century,[79] was "fully routinized" by the third quarter of the eighteenth,[80] and continued to soften the impact of the criminal law into the early nineteenth.[81] Hay has famously argued that this symbolized the supremacy of the monarchy and the power of norms of social deference, and to some measure it manifestly did. On the other hand, it is important to see how much less ostentatiously monarchical power was asserted in England than in contemporary France. In France, as we have seen, pardoning unambiguously displayed the quasi-sacred status of the king. French grace, in this way, was what Weimar Weberians would later rhapsodize over: occasional penetrations of sovereign magic into the routine world. French grace also was accorded to persons with social connections, on petition from local notables. In England, connections certainly mattered.[82] Procedures left room for petitions subscribed by local notables, which certainly did sometimes influence both judges and on the royal court.[83] Testimony from witnesses of high social standing influenced pardon decisions.[84] On the other hand, the most recent study shows that, by the later eighteenth century, "respectability or higher social status" was far more rarely mentioned as the reason for granting a pardon than such factors as good character or poverty.[85] To be sure, questions of "character" were undoubtedly poorly differentiated from questions of status;[86] nevertheless, this is striking data. Moreover, English law was not designed to favor the interventions of well-placed persons. The law required execution to be swift, precisely in order to forestall petitions,[87] and in the 1780s in particular there was a concerted effort to put an end to them.[88] Finally, successful interventions did not necessarily come from persons of the highest status. "It is not difficult," writes Peter King, "to find cases in which the middling sort successfully petitioned for mitigation of sentence without the support of high social groups. In 1787, for example, William Glaves was pardoned after nine Southwark traders—three butchers, two chandlers, a druggist, a publican, a grocer, and a ropemaker . . . had petitioned on his behalf. Three years later another convict under sentence of death escaped with a year's imprisonment after thirty Southwark inhabitants, including four parish officers and the prosecutor, supported his petition."[89] This, we should note, may not be entirely different from France, where letters supporting petitions for grace were sometimes similarly subscribed by "entire parishes."[90] Indeed, none of this data is entirely easy to interpret, and all close students of eighteenth-century pardoning are cautious in drawing conclusions.[91] Nevertheless, these scholars raise forceful doubts about any interpretation of eighteenth-century English mercy that identifies it too closely with the sacral character of the monarchy or the importance of highly placed connections, and they seem right to do so.[92] The contrast with France is a relative one, but it is a telling one nevertheless. Hay to the contrary notwithstanding, English grace did not represent anything like the pure display of sacral sovereignty and hierarchical order to be seen in an institution like the French monarchy.

Moreover, the exercise of mercy was less an exclusive exercise of sovereign power in England than it was on the continent. Parliament, too, could issue pardons, and Parliament's pardons carried important procedural advantages over the king's, as Blackstone reported. Not least, English mercy was also dealt out not only by king and Parliament but by judges[93] as well as by juries in the famous form of the "pious perjury."[94] As English statutes were drafted, thefts of goods worth less than 40 shillings did not carry the death penalty. This left room for juries to spare the lives of defendants by undervaluing the goods they had stolen, and it is well-documented that juries did exactly that.[95] In this respect, England was, if not a place of untrammeled liberty, at least in place in which the criminal law was less obviously devoted to dramatizing the power of the monarchy and the leading men of the realm than was the case in France.

The English exercise of mercy, seen in comparative perspective, was a relatively routine business, accorded, from an early date, more freely to all classes of persons who came before the court. Routinization and wide social extension of pardoning would eventually appear on the continent as well, as we have seen—but only at the end of the nineteenth, and to some extent twentieth, centuries. The history of pardoning thus displays a pattern akin to that of the history of benefit of clergy: a pattern of the relatively strong early development of institutions that would only establish themselves on the continent significantly later.

All of this is consistent with a picture of mid-eighteenth-century England as a world in which norms of deference had, by continental standards, severely broken down. It is hardly the picture of an *egalitarian* society of the modern type, of course. It is not even the picture of an egalitarian society of the Dutch seventeenth-century type. But it is certainly the picture of a society that lacked something that was central to contemporary continental ordering: a system of status-differentiation that was both firmly established in practice and doctrinally well-articulated.

Status and Punishment in the Colonial Era

What was true of England in the seventeenth and eighteenth centuries was generally true of its American colonies as well. The American colonies too were part of the Anglo-American world. There too, while relations of status continued to matter greatly through the eighteenth century, they mattered distinctly less than they did in continental Europe—and indeed, even somewhat less than in metropolitan England itself. The American colonies had virtually no aristocrats, and as Lawrence Friedman observes, their criminal justice correspondingly had a more "popular" flavor than metropolitan justice did.[96]

England's American colonies did not, of course, boast egalitarian societies. Familiar occidental sensibilities about low- and high-status punishments were present among the American colonists too. There were regional differences, which David Hackett Fischer has done a wonderful job of tracing in his book *Albion's Seed*. The patterns of English deferential society were much more pronounced in Virginia than elsewhere, and great variations can be found throughout all of the colonies. In the backcountry in particular, norms of hierarchy and deference started breaking down earlier than elsewhere.[97] Nevertheless, in the large, we can say that the overall tendency was much like that of metropolitan England. Status differentiation mattered, but at the same time continental patterns of deference had already been shaken everywhere in the colonies in the later eighteenth century, and they would continue to decay.

And this decay of deferential relations inevitably made itself felt in the development of American punishment, as it did in other aspects of everyday life. The classic ordinary forms of low-status punishment in continental Europe were also the reigning forms in the American colonies—though of course there were again quite significant regional differences. Although colonial codes permitted a wide range of punishments, including public exposure and some forms of mutilation, banishment, and hanging, fines and whipping were the most commonly inflicted.[98] Public exposure certainly took place, though the extent of the application of punishments of public exposure has been exaggerated in the popular memory.[99] Branding took place as well.[100] Whipping followed by expulsion was commonly meted out to outsiders.[101] As for forced labor, there were workhouses, as in metropolitan England,[102] and in them, hard labor was sometimes inflicted as a criminal punishment. Hard labor also appeared in a different, distinctly frontier form: North American offenders (like South American ones)[103] were sometimes sold into private penal servitude.[104]

Classic low-status punishments were thus in use, up to a point. Certainly there was status-differentiation too. It was undoubtedly the case that high-status colonists received better treatment; persons of high status receive better treatment in every legal system. Studies of seventeenth-century New England suggest that high-status offenders were generally fined, while low-status ones were whipped.[105] The same is true of Virginia.[106] Still, the mid eighteenth century may present a different picture in the colonies, just as it does in England. Some of the evidence is mixed. On the one hand, the classically low-status punishment of losing the ears—meted out especially to counterfeiters—seems often not to have been inflicted in North Carolina.[107] On the other hand, it does seem to have been inflicted in New Hampshire.[108] Virginia, a world of high social-status consciousness, had a legal system that aimed to dramatize the supremacy of the planter class.[109] On the other hand, a careful study of North Carolina has shown "no class bias at all. For each of five common offenses (assault, theft, homicide, animal stealing, and trespass), the courts sentenced planters and laborers to an identical proportion of corporal and monetary sanctions . . . sentencing practices were largely status blind."[110] Even whipping was sometimes not carried out.[111] North Carolina thus showed a striking pattern of punishment egalitarianism—for the white population.[112] In eighteenth-century New York, too, "the courts could be very severe in their treatment of the 'very low,' but they often were no less vigorous in trying persons of established standing in the community."[113] Capital criminals in America may have escaped execution, if they were persons of high status. They never escaped hanging, though: the classic European high-status marker, beheading, never established itself in American practice. (Though there are occasional cases of beheading in the colonial period, the practice does not seem to have been used as a high-status marker. On the contrary, beheading took place *after* death, as a form of specially degrading corpse mutilation, inflicted on figures like the New York rebel Jacob Leiser, the pirate Blackbeard, or the rebellious black slave.)[114] Perhaps the most revealing result of our studies of eighteenth-century colonial punishment practices, however, is the frequency of fines as a penalty. Fines had been a distinctly high-status penalty in the seventeenth century. Generalizing the fine can thus perhaps be viewed as a kind of leveling up. Paying a fine apparently carried little social stigma in colonial New York, for example: defendants who did not regard themselves as guilty at all seem to have pleaded guilty because they preferred a fine to the difficulty and (one guesses) shame of a trial.[115]

In all this, the mid-eighteenth-century British American colonies were like metropolitan England—only (perhaps) more so. They were also like metropolitan England in their sheer apparent lack of interest in analyzing the nature and forms of status-differentiation in punishment. This is noticeable, for example, with regard to public shaming. Shaming, to repeat, was probably less common than we today think. These were not societies that relied overwhelming on the scarlet letter. Nevertheless, shaming certainly did go on. What is remarkable is how rarely colonial Americans felt any obligation to talk about the status-meaning of this classically low-status punishment. High-status offenders were surely rarely publicly shamed; American was not wholly different from Europe in that respect. But on some level Americans manifestly cared less about questions of status than continental Europeans did. They were rarely moved to *declare* that public shaming was for low-status persons; their sensibilities were simply not pricked by status questions in the way that contemporary French sensibilities were. No French commentator ever touched on the question of public shame, in the eighteenth or early nineteenth century, without making observations about the structure of social honor in his country. Americans did not perceive punishment in the same way.

This failure to perceive the status-significance of shaming has left traces in the American literature down to the present. American historians, in describing the colonial practice of public exposure, have tended to analyze the system of public exposure as evidence that the British-American colonies were still made up small communities, in which public shame could be expected to act as an effective deterrent. Such, for example, is the tenor of Adam Hirsch's frequently cited study.[116] Now it may be true that the use of public exposure demonstrates that American communities of the eighteenth century were relatively small—though to say so leaves many questions unanswered.[117] Nevertheless, to interpret public shaming only in light of the theory of deterrence is to miss something fundamental about it. Public shaming may or may not *deter,* but in the eyes of all European commentators of the eighteenth century, it certainly *degraded*. Public shame, to every non-American observer of the time, was a mark of low status; and while every continental polity made heavy use of public shaming, lawyers in every one of those polities were at pains to insist that such public shaming was suitable only for low-status persons. Americans did not feel quite the same need to articulate their status differences in the language of legal doctrine. The highly wrought, symbolically elaborated, continental systems of honor and dishonor that characterized the German and French worlds were absent—as Americans of the period would undoubtedly have cheerfully confirmed.

The same can be seen in colonial imprisonment as well. The elaborate status-distinctions that marked continental imprisonment were barely in evidence in the British American colonies. American prisons tended to mix inmates together indiscriminately, in a way that contemporary French observers would have considered scandalous. Incarceration remained an exceptional sanction in the eighteenth century;[118] as in Europe, jails were for holding offenders pending punishment, not for punishing.[119] As in Europe, colonial American workhouses mixed criminal offenders with other low-status persons.[120] What was missing, in these institutions, was separate and better treatment for the highly placed. As we have seen, persons of high status received some form of comfortable detention in continental Europe—even in egalitarian Holland. I have found almost no evidence of this in the British colonies. Fortress detention existed, especially in military law, and perhaps for persons accused of disloyalty in time of war. Indeed, it would continue to exist right down into the time of the Civil War.[121] But, as in England, it did not establish itself as part of an articulated system of status-differentiation in punishment. As in the early-modern Netherlands or northern Germany, colonial jails were regarded as a kind of household, managed by a resident keeper and his family.[122] But in the less status-conscious culture of the British colonies, conditions tended to be the same for all who were confined, from thieves to debtors. Prisoners were indiscriminately housed together, embezzlers with murderers, first offenders with multiple recidivists.[123] In the eyes of American law, there were no distinctions to be made in the terms of imprisonment. Sometimes this may have meant that conditions were good for all. Sometimes they were clearly bad—indeed reports show that in New York they were horrific.[124] Sometimes, inevitably, everything depended, as in England, on how much money prisoners could find: "So long as they did not cost the town money, inmates could make living arrangements as pleasant and homelike as they wished."[125] There is no clear single story to be told about conditions of incarceration, beyond saying that they showed, typically, little of the highly articulated status consciousness that mattered so much in continental Europe.

As for mercy, it was a regular part of eighteenth-century American justice just as it was of metropolitan justice. America too had the pious perjury, by which juries assigned a low value to stolen goods in order to spare the offender.[126] Both judges and juries exercised their discretion to distinguish among deserving and undeserving defendants.[127] Pardons, too, were common.[128] For the years in which figures are available for colonial New York between 1691 and 1776, no fewer than 51.7 percent of accused offenders were pardoned after trial.[129] Colonial officials were, in fact, besieged by pardon petitions.[130] As in continental Europe, the pardoning power seems sometimes to have been integrated into the structure of social status: the persons who were pardoned were inevitably, if not exclusively, persons of honor and reputation in eighteenth-century Pennsylvania, for example: "It was important to have reputable people to vouch for one's character to the court. Without such recommendations, convicts were less likely to receive mercy, except in cases of real doubt about guilt or of youth."[131] Importantly, there were other classes of pardons too: offenders requested pardons at times to "enlist out of jail"—that is, to be released into military service. Masters, too, sometimes asked that their slaves be pardoned, so that they not suffer the property loss occasioned by an execution.[132] Pardoning and clergyability were both used as mitigating devices: a jury might find a defendant accused of murder guilty either of manslaughter (a clergyable offense) or of chance medley (a pardonable one).[133] (As in England, women sometimes "pleaded their belly" as well.)[134]

What about the influence of Beccaria? We find that too—though as the prevalence of pardons suggests, it established itself only very tentatively. Determinate sentencing as such did not come to dominate.[135] Judges in Pennsylvania, for example, were given wide discretion in the 1786 statue establishing forced public labor as the normal sanction to vary punishment depending on the character of the offender.[136] Sentencing in nineteenth-century Pennsylvania codes similarly continued to allow for discretion,[137] as did those of New York[138] and Massachusetts.[139] Practical Beccarianism thus hardly triumphed. Nevertheless, as we might expect, Beccarianism proved to have a real intellectual appeal. Beccarian opposition to pardoning as undermining deterrence could already be heard from figures like Benjamin Franklin in the early eighteenth century;[140] and many late-eighteenth-century Americans took the same view.[141] American critiques were for the most part simply typical of the Atlantic world, focusing on the threats of monarchical government and the imperative of deterrence. Nevertheless, it is important to remark that one characteristically American theme began to appear in these colonial-era critiques: the claim that the power of mercy was exercised in a status-conscious way. Francis Hopkinson, for example, thought that the "prerogative of mercy" would always be used by the powerful and well-connected to benefit their friends. To him, this was simply a form of despotism.[142] As we shall shortly, see, this suspiciousness of the pardon as a tool of the mighty would become a regular American theme by the early nineteenth century.

At any rate, status-differentiation in punishment was relatively absent in eighteenth-century America; and from this we can conclude what abundant other evidence also allows us to conclude: that status-hierarchy mattered less in eighteenth-century America than it did in Europe.

The Revolution in Punishment

That certainly does not mean that ideas of status-hierarchy were wholly absent. The British colonies were still societies with strong norms of deference and status-display.[143] Nevertheless, by continental standards, the American colonies already had the look of an un-status-conscious world in the mid eighteenth century. The contrast only grew in the later eighteenth century and after, and by the late nineteenth century, classic status concerns had become a very faint memory in the United States, as Americans became remarkably less conscious of the traditions of status-differentiation in punishment than their continental European contemporaries.

As Gordon Wood stirringly describes the "radicalism of the American Revolution," it was a radicalism that especially targeted the patterns of hierarchical deference that had always shaped all complex human societies—not, to be sure, a Marxian *economic* radicalism, but a radicalism of *status*:

> By the time the Revolution had run its course in the early nineteenth century, American society had been radically and thoroughly transformed. One [economic] class did not overthrow another; the poor did not supplant the rich. But social relationships—the way people were connected one to another—were changed, and decisively so. . . . In 1760 . . . the less than two million monarchical subjects who lived in [the American] colonies still took for granted that society was and ought to be a hierarchy of ranks and degrees of dependency and that most people were bound together by personal ties of one sort or another. Yet scarcely fifty years later these insignificant borderland provinces had become a giant, almost continent-wide republic of nearly ten million egalitarian-minded bustling citizens who not only had thrust themselves into the vanguard of history but had fundamentally altered their society and their social relationships. Far from remaining monarchical, hierarchy-ridden subjects on the margin of civilization, Americans had become, almost overnight, the most liberal, the most democratic, the most commercially minded, and the most modern people in the world.[144]

In my view, Wood is exactly right, and right in ways that we can often see with fine-grained clarity if we contrast the development of American punishment practices with those of the continent.

We can make out the character of American revolutionary changes particularly clearly if we view them against the contrasting background of the French Revolution. As we have seen, some of the French revolutionaries were in favor of egalitarian punishment practices early on in the history of their revolution. Notably, some of them—Duport and Guillotin in particular—were in favor of extending high-status punishments to all; and in one important symbolic way, high-status punishment was indeed extended, as beheading became the normal form of execution for all French persons up until 1981. Nevertheless, by the Napoleonic period, and especially after the watershed year of 1810, the old two-track system of punishment had reestablished itself in France. Especially after the Revolution of 1830, France was once again a country with two classes of offenders: "common" criminals, who continued to be treated very harshly right through the nineteenth century; and the special high classes of political prisoners and debtors, who were ordinarily subjected to some form of old-style "fortress confinement." The turmoil of the 1830s also introduced innovations in substantive criminal law and in criminal procedure that tended to benefit high-status offenders: the jury acquired the important, and frequently exercised, authority to acquit duelists; and new doctrines of extenuating circumstances were introduced to excuse (or justify?) men of "honor" who committed violent offenses. In these various ways, the 1830s continued the work of 1810, shielding persons of honor from the harshness of the criminal justice system.

These roughly fifty years of revolutionary turmoil in French punishment practices, from 1790 to 1840, were also years of revolutionary turmoil in American punishment practices. The tenor of change in America was quite different, though, from the tenor of change in France.

The revolutionary history of American punishment that bridges the decades of the 1790s and the decades of the 1830s is one of the most famous and much-explored periods in the history of punishment, for it is the seminal period of American experimentation with the penitentiary. It is a history that has been exhaustively described and analyzed elsewhere. All that I want to offer here is some commentary on how different a history it was from the contemporary French history—sometimes obviously different, sometimes only subtly so. Most of all, as I want to show, it is a history that took a different turn in its treatment of status: where the French nineteenth century marks the beginning of a slow, definitive decline of low-status punishment, the American nineteenth century marks the beginning of a slow, definitive decline of high-status punishment.

Status questions in punishment hardly vanished with the revolution. In particular, traditional problems of status growing out of English conflicts of the seventeenth century worked their way into the Bill of Rights. The early-modern history of low- and high-status punishments affected two noteworthy provisions, in ways that would leave a hard-to-digest legacy for American constitutional law. The Fifth Amendment to the Constitution required that indictments for "capital or infamous" crimes be on presentment of a grand jury. This made perfect sense in a world in which the practice of inflicting "infaming" punishments was still alive. Indeed, the original version proposed by

Madison read, "In all crimes punishable with loss of life or member, presentment or indictment by a grand jury shall be an essential preliminary."[145] Madison's concern was thus with mutilation, the definitionally low-status treatment. The same is true of the prohibition on "cruel and unusual punishment" in the Eighth Amendment, which also grew directly out English seventeenth-century conflicts over Oates's status mistreatment.[146]

Such abuses still seemed to call for a response in the America of the early 1790s, and the Bill of Rights put typically American procedural limits on them. Yet the solution was, it deserves to be emphasized, *procedural*: the idea that such punishments should be abolished outright did not carry the day. Thomas Jefferson drafted a "Bill for Proportioning Crimes and Punishments" in 1778 that condemned "cruel and sanguinary laws" but that continued to call for mutilation and flogging.[147] New legislation continued to assume the propriety of historically low-status punishments. The Judiciary Act of 1789 limited the criminal jurisdiction of the district courts to cases "where no other punishment than whipping, not exceeding thirty stripes, a fine not exceeding one hundred dollars, or a term of imprisonment not exceeding six months, is to be inflicted."[148] The first Crimes Act of the United States, promulgated just a year before the French revolutionary reform, imposed both flogging and the pillory as punishments.[149] No real sign here that the American Revolution would bring what Duport hoped at the same hour from the French: an abolition of low-status punishment.

To be sure, there were punishment reformers in the early republic who did want such an abolition, just as French contemporaries did.[150] This is especially true of one of the most important of the markers of low status: corporal punishment. Corporal punishment was a form of low-status treatment everywhere in the Western world, of course, but in the early American republic, its status connotations came to be especially pronounced. For a simple reason: corporal punishment was associated with the definitionally low status in America, the status of black slaves. Thus Benjamin Rush opposed forced public labor in the 1790s because he believed that the association of labor with criminality would poison the public's willingness to work—just as the association between labor and African slavery poisoned whites' willingness to work in the South.[151] People who were flogged in America risked being thought of as slaves. Indeed, in the South there were, as one might expect, movements to eliminate flogging precisely because of its association with black slavery—though unlike the parallel European movements, these southern efforts to put an end to "infamy" failed.[152] Corporal punishment was widely regarded in the antebellum republic as "unrepublican," and by the early nineteenth century there was a striking campaign to end corporal punishment in places like the navy.[153] As in Europe, moreover, there was a noteworthy new revulsion against corporal punishment in the early nineteenth century—a change in sensibility that was symptomatic of a new kind of nineteenth-century "civilization" that was ill-at-ease with pain and violence.[154] A movement to generalize high status in American "republican" punishment might thus be expected to be a movement to abolish corporal punishment. And indeed, in the 1790s and early 1800s, as the prison movement began to dominate the American scene, various reformers opposed corporal punishment in the prisons as inconsistent with republican ideals.[155]

Yet this campaign strikingly failed. Quite the contrary: the story of American punishment as it developed with the rise of the prison movement became, fatefully, a story of the generalization of *low*-status treatment. Corporal punishment became the norm in American prisons. So did forced labor. Indeed, it is the most striking fact of early-nineteenth-century punishment in America that the status of prisoners came, by the time of the Thirteenth Amendment, to be explicitly assimilated to that of slaves.

The Triumph of Low Status

This identification of prisoners with slaves is of central importance for the history of the generalization of low status in American punishment. It is closely bound up with the rise of the penitentiary, and to understand the relationship between prisoners and slaves in American, we must begin by reviewing, if only briefly, the familiar history of the Anglo-American penitentiary movement. The beginnings of the penitentiary movement in England, under the leadership of John Howard, William Blackstone, and William Eden, are well known and much studied.[156] The Christian inspiration of these reformers is also common coin.[157] These leading English figures secured the passage of a bill, never put into effect, which would have created the first "penitentiaries" in the 1780s, the first places designed to make imprisonment the ordinary form of punishment as a way to encourage "penitence."

Similar efforts, with a similarly Christian bent, followed the revolution in the former colonies: imprisonment famously became, during this period, the normal form of punishment in the northern American states. Philadelphia was particularly important. There, after the revolution, began a period of experimentation with forced public labor, following the common Beccarian prescription.[158] The much-admired and much-visited Walnut Street Jail succeeded this experiment with public labor.[159] Around the same time, Boston saw the establishment of the similar Castle Island Jail. Following the lead of English reformers twenty years earlier, American innovators were coming to embrace a distinctly Christian idea of the "penitentiary."[160]

At the beginning, this movement could certainly have taken on some kind of aspiration to treat offenders respectfully, as persons of relative dignity in society. The very "penitentiary" idea can easily be traced back to monastic and clerical imprisonment, and one can imagine a world in which American Christian reformers might have displayed some of the attitude that is common among punishment professionals in Europe today—a world in which they at least aspired to guarantee the dignity of convicts, even if the hard realities of punishment defeated that aspiration. In the event, this was not the attitude that they took.

As the penitentiary movement developed over the following decades, explicit discussion of the status connotations of punishments remained relatively muted in the United States, compared to Europe—just as it had been relatively muted for a long time. Debate revolved around different sorts of questions, principally around the respective merits of the silent and separate systems of confinement.[161] And the sorts of justifications offered for these two alternatives had little or nothing to do with traditional ideas of status treatment. On the contrary, what characterized American debate was a mix of utilitarian and Christian arguments.

Nevertheless, if discussion of status was relatively muted, it was by no means absent. On the contrary, by the 1820s, as the penitentiary movement began to triumph, status reemerged. Imprisonment took on a distinctly *low-status* color, and indeed the status-color of slavery. This was not what all reformers might have wished. The penitentiary movement was certainly motivated partly by a distaste for the kinds of punishments continental Europeans inflicted on low-status persons. As the Pennsylvania reformer Roberts Vaux put it in 1823, for example, the new style of penitentiary promised precisely to substitute "wise and compassionate" reformation for "those cruel and vindictive penalties which are in use in the European countries," such as public display and public beating.[162] There were some ways, moreover, in which the penitentiary movement brought a decline in the historic pattern of treating inmates as persons of low status. One of the markers of the low status of early modern offenders, as we have seen, was the fact that they were mixed in with vagrants and other low-status persons. The penitentiary movement put an end to that. Newgate Prison in Greenwich Village was first to exclude vagrants, witnesses, debtors, and suspects, housing only convicted offenders.[163] To be sure, reformers were not ready to make *no* distinctions among inmates. The early-nineteenth-century prison in Charlestown, Massachusetts, had an elaborate system of prison uniforms, distinguished by different colored stripes and numbers for the number of terms of imprisonment of recidivists.[164] Similar innovations appeared throughout the United States in the 1790s.[165] But with time, a relative absence of distinctions within the inmate population became the norm. Public punishment went into decline too, at the same time that it was in the process of decline in continental Europe.[166]

Yet this hardly implied that the American penitentiary was meant to represent high-status treatment. On the contrary: something took place that troubled Beaumont and Tocqueville deeply, as we saw in the last chapter. What they called "infamy"—low-status treatment that included flogging and even branding[167]—became the norm in American penitentiaries.[168] The penitentiary became a place of forced labor and corporal punishment, the forms of "unrepublican" treatment most strongly associated with slavery in the United States; and by the time of the Thirteenth Amendment the identification of prisoners with slaves effectively became a part of American constitutional law. Indeed, in the age of liberal revolutions, America became the prime example of a country that did not abolish low-status punishment. Tocqueville and Beaumont were not the only ones to note this. For at least one German conservative, writing in the wake of the Revolution of 1848, America was an inspiration, precisely because the Americans (like the English) had not abandoned corporal punishment. To this author, America, with its tradition of liberty, was also the model of a country that had not embarked on the dubious "philanthropical experiment of abolishing corporal punishment" in order to protect the "human dignity [Menschenwürde] . . . of the scum [Hefe] of the people."[169] American was thus a beacon for at least one continental observer who wanted to preserve degrading punishment.

And indeed, the postrevolutionary attacks on "unrepublican" corporal punishment in the prisons waned by the first couple of decades of the nineteenth century. Starting around 1815, harsh and degrading disciplinary practices began to entrench themselves in the American penitentiaries.[170] Corporal punishment came to be universal in the prisons, even as reformers worked to abolish it in the outside world. Flogging inmates was permitted by an 1819 New York statute, which rejected an 1801 attempt by Thomas Eddy to forbid it.[171] Flogging continued in the prisons and attracted the attention of such commentators as the marquis de Lafayette and Francis Lieber.[172] By the 1830s, flogging and other harsh corporal punishments were common all through the new penitentiaries. "The whip was common place in Auburn and Charlestown, in Columbus and in Wethersfield. Pennsylvania had recourse to the iron gag, Maine to the ball and chain, Connecticut to the cold shower."[173] To prison officials, to be sure, the issue was one of discipline; and the imperative of discipline meant that "it would be most unfortunate . . . if the public mind were to settle down into repugnance to the use of such coercive means."[174] Nevertheless, corporal punishment and slavery had gone hand in hand, in American thought, for a very long time.

Forced labor, too, was central to the penitentiary system as it developed. In Philadelphia, convicts were expressly condemned to do "labor of the hardest and most servile kind."[175] The New Jersey statute used the same phrase, and New York put its inmates on a treadmill.[176] This was enforced, by sharp contrast to the continental European norm, with regard to every inmate regardless of status. Officials ended "the colonial practice of having prisoners pay the jailer for their board, . . . deciding that even inmates with property would have to work while serving their sentences."[177] There were certainly American voices that objected to prison labor as degrading both to inmates and to the values of free labor itself.[178] Organized labor objected to competition from inmates as well. Nevertheless, the pressure on prison officials to use inmate labor, or to attempt to use inmate labor, as a means of financing their institutions was strong.[179]

And all of this was inevitably associated with slavery. As we have seen, forced penal labor had been linked with slavery in the English literature since the sixteenth century. Of course, it is also true that requiring inmates to labor had been regarded for centuries as a way to cure idleness, the root cause of crime in the minds of many northern European Christian observers.[180] Nevertheless, the idea that imprisonment at hard labor was to be understood as something like slavery was very old,[181] and historians have demonstrated at length that early American penitentiaries were colored by an association with slavery. Prisons were akin to plantations:[182] "The 'overseer' resided in the penitentiary as well as the plantation, and he supervised the performance of 'hard labor' by inmates as well as slaves. Inmates and slaves were both distinguished from the free community by . . . the color and quality of their garb. And the most resonant symbol of the slave plantation—the clanking of chains—echoed just as loudly from within the prison walls."[183] "Just as masters demanded that slaves address them in submissive tones, 'whenever it is necessary for [a convict] to speak to a Keeper, [he must] do it with a humble sense of his degraded condition.'"[184] Convicts were "to be reduced to a state of humiliation and discipline."[185] Slavery was to be the lot of American convicts. Indeed, early-nineteenth-century America was almost the locus classicus of the tendency Gustav Radbruch thought to be universal: the tendency to fashion criminal punishment out of the degrading discipline inflicted on slaves. "To this day," any American observer could have said by the 1860s, as Radbruch said of Germany in 1938, "the criminal law bears the traits of its origin in slave punishments. . . . To be punished means to be treated like a slave."

There is an abiding puzzle about this. In some sense, there was nothing mysterious about the American treatment of convicts as slaves: most human societies in most times and places have done the same—not only in Radbruch's Germany, but in ancient Greece, too, for example, where the chains of slavery were always the symbol of criminal punishment.[186] Yet slavery for convicts in America does seem strange, simply because many of the leading advocates of the penitentiary system were also leaders of the antislavery movement. These were men for whom the corporal violence and forced labor of slavery smacked of "monarchical or aristocratic regimes."[187] Yet they saw little difficulty in imposing what they themselves understood as a form of slavery on convicts.[188] As Adam Hirsch has observed, this is particularly mysterious in light of English tradition, since English reformers regularly pointed to the slaverylike character of imprisonment at forced labor. Yet, in both America and Britain, advocates of imprisonment at hard labor were often conspicuous opponents of slavery.[189] Beaumont and Tocqueville once again stated the point in a famous observation: "While society in the United States gives the example of the most extensive liberty, the prisons in the same country present the spectacle of the most complete despotism."[190] It is not that reformers did not understand the association between forced labor and corporal punishment on the one hand, and low status on the other. It is not as though they were not against low status in the American republic. It is that they actively embraced low status in punishment—unlike their continental contemporaries, who saw the core values of progress in punishment precisely as requiring the abolition of "infamy."

This even penetrated the Constitution, and at the very moment of the abolition of slavery. Despite some loosening of the early-nineteenth-century practices of degradation,[191] the Thirteenth Amendment expressly permitted prisoners to be reduced to the status of slaves: "Neither slavery nor involuntary servitude, *except as punishment for a crime whereof the party shall have been duly convicted*, shall exist within the United States, or any place subject to their jurisdiction."[192] The result was that prisoners could be effectively enslaved for life—a fate that befell thousands of southern blacks in particular well into the twentieth century. (This is a history that may soon give rise to lawsuits comparable to the litigation over Nazi use of slave labor.)[193] As we have seen, prisoners would continue to be regarded in law as "slaves of the state" into the 1970s.[194] There is no doctrine that more strikingly reflects the deep differences that divide American sensibilities from European ones. In America, nobody was troubled by the symbolic declaration that prisoners should have the status of slaves; they remained untroubled by it for a century; and it can be said that, by the 1980s, they were untroubled by it once again. As Justice Stevens put it in his 1984 dissent to *Hudson v. Palmer*, the leading American case denying dignitary protections to prisoners: the court "declares prisoners to be little more than chattels, a view I thought society had outgrown long ago."[195]

America against Europe

In continental Europe, by contrast, this view *was* being progressively "outgrown." Indeed, as badly as low-status offenders had historically been treated on the continent, the idea that they should be reduced to *slavery* had already begun making continental jurists uneasy as early as the sixteenth century.[196] Certainly by 1865, low-status forms of punishment were in dramatic decline in France. As we have seen, a dramatic leap forward in the elimination of historically low-status punishment was made in 1848. All but one of the "bagnes," the forced-labor shipyards that dated to the eighteenth century, were suppressed by the 1850s,[197] as was civil death.[198] A typical French book of 1864 expected imminently the "definitive abolition" of infaming punishments.[199] After fifty years of revolution, classic low-status treatment had come to be considered unacceptable, indefeasibly unrepublican, at least within the territory of metropolitan France. By contrast, American constitutional law formally embraced the idea that convicts were to be reduced to slaves in 1865—the year of the completion of the second revolution in America, the shining date in the history of American abolitionism. This is a strange and striking fact, which caught the attention of at least one French observer, writing in September 1865, a few months after the Civil War ended. As this author noted, after reading some vague reports of American prison conditions, "torture of a certain sort is still in favor [in American prisons], for sometimes prisoners are subjected to treatments that whites used to inflict on blacks."[200] "Happily," he felt able to add, "there is nothing resembling American punishments in France."[201] This author was probably overestimating the extent of actual improvements in France at that date,[202] but there is no doubt that French ideologies and aspirations had taken a different form from American ones. Nor was America entirely alone. England, too, was not following the French path. "Penal servitude" laws were enacted in England in 1853 and 1864. Passed in response to the decline of transportation as well as to panics over crime, these acts, as their name suggests, subjected offenders to a regime of hard servile labor. This was followed in 1877 by the establishment of the so-called Du Cane system, which rejected religious reform in favor of "hard fare, hard labour and hard bed."[203] Despite occasional reform efforts, flogging too would survive in England until 1948—indeed, Parliament would pass a statute inflicting flogging for robbery as late as 1920.[204] In fact, down to the present day, the jurisprudence of human rights in the European Union would struggle to digest what, on the continent, seemed "barbaric" English punishment practices.[205]

The continental drive to eliminate low-status punishment, and substitute high-status punishment, had simply failed to establish itself in the Anglo-American world.

Why? Why, in the age of Atlantic abolition, was low-status punishment abolished in France and not in England or the United States? The problem of England is one I leave for another time. But of America we can begin by saying this: American society was a society that was in the process of rejecting high status in *many* things. What is more, it was a society with a tradition of rejecting high status in punishment in particular, since at least the mid eighteenth century.

Beyond that, we can point to one fundamental American institutional fact, with roots in a yet deeper institutional reality: *Respectable persons found themselves in prison less frequently in the United States than they did in continental Europe.* Unsurprisingly, inmates in nineteenth-century American penitentiaries were almost exclusively from the lowest-status orders of society, as far as we can judge.[206] Blacks and immigrants made up a disproportion of the inmates in New York in 1870.[207] The situation was much the same everywhere, beginning in the 1850s.[208] Europe was not much different, of course—except for the presence of a tiny minority of respectable persons. Tocqueville was right when he observed that America differed from France because Americans did not have political prisoners.[209] Indeed, French and German prisons housed two important classes of high-status prisoners who were generally not confined in the United States: political prisoners, and debtors. (Duelists, too, were comparatively little in evidence in American justice, at least in the north.)

The deeper institutional reality that lay behind this was the greater weakness of the American state. Our states simply did not systematically imprison high-status persons. There were occasional odd categories of high-status confinees in America, such as witnesses held pending their testimony, and accused persons who could not make bail. Such prisoners were guaranteed treatment essentially indistinguishable from that guaranteed political prisoners in Europe.[210] But the large-scale categories of continental Europe—the categories of political dissenters and insolvents—were little in evidence in America, and consequently the pressure to develop a tradition of high-status treatment was slight. Little developed jurisprudence of high-status treatment appeared.

To be sure, during the intensely polarized duration of the Civil War, the government of the northern states did imprison "dissenters" of a sort, and when Lincoln suspended habeas corpus, he declared that rebels were to be "imprisoned in any fort, camp, arsenal, military prison, or other place of confinement."[211] Perhaps this represented some dim echo of the European tradition. On the whole, though, it is hard to find anything like fortress confinement in the United States. The special class of political offenders simply did not exist in the United States (just as it did not exist in England),[212] and correspondingly, the French pattern did not emerge. Of course high-status persons became entangled with the criminal justice system; and of course they received better treatment, as they always do. But what was missing in the United States was the ideological focus provided by a special category of high-status prisoners, defined as persons who did not really "deserve" punishment. What America lacked was a tradition of defining a class of honorable persons who were imprisoned despite the fact that they were not "really" criminals.

Thus there was no reform movement of the Guizot kind, preaching abolition of the death penalty for political offenders. Thus there was no reform movement of the Thiers kind either, preaching comfortable conditions of imprisonment. Comfortable conditions of imprisonment generally found little voice, partly for the simple reason that few high-status Americans could expect to be imprisoned for their opinions—unlike France, where, as we have seen, journalists continued to be imprisoned regularly in the comparative *luxe* of Sainte-Pélagie down to the end of the nineteenth century.

If high-status Americans were not generally imprisoned for their opinions, neither were they generally imprisoned for their insolvency. One of the perduring themes of American resistance to the machinery of the law is our uniquely far-reaching tradition of protecting debtors against execution by their creditors. This has taken many forms, among them astounding liberal exemptions and reorganization procedures. It also took the form, very early on in American development, of the decline of imprisonment for debt. Debtors were certainly imprisoned in the eighteenth century. Indeed, in Philadelphia, center of experimentation with the penitentiary, debtors complained about being lumped in with "common criminals" just as their European counterparts did.[213] The same is true of New York debtors, though Massachusetts debtors had special privileges.[214] Debtors remained theoretically subject to imprisonment in the United States throughout the century. In the early nineteenth century, moreover, horror stories of imprisonment for debt were common—indeed some reached the ears of Tocqueville and Beaumont.[215] But careful study shows that true imprisonment for debt was in fact rare. After the first couple of decades of the century, almost everywhere in the United States the so-called "bounds" system had established itself.[216] Under this wonderful fiction "imprisoned" debtors were required to remain within the "bounds" of the prison. Those "bounds" were however defined broadly to include a large section of the city in which the prison sat, or everything up to the county line, or even everything up to the state line. In reality, debtors were rarely imprisoned at all: the "bounds" system coexisted with measures of outright abolition in some places. Debtors who owed penal fines were imprisoned into the second half of the century, though this practice too declined.[217] In broad outline, this pattern was in some ways not all that different from the European pattern. In France too, imprisonment for debt was essentially limited to those who owed penal fines after 1867. Nevertheless, debtors remained a common sight in French prisons. The American resistance to imprisoning debtors was stronger from the eighteenth century onward, and the consequence was that, unlike the French or the Germans, we never developed a body of law of the continental type: a body of law carefully specifying the privileged forms of imprisonment to which debtors would be subjected. Thus American legal thought lacked any focus on a second critical class of high-status prisoners, whose treatment defined (and continues to define) norms of decent treatment on the continent of Europe.

In all of this there was an irony of liberty. The value of liberty was strong in America. But the strength of the value of "liberty" sometimes meant freedom from a certain kind of fear, for a certain class of people—freedom from fear of imprisonment for respectable persons. This had the consequence that there was little pressure, of the European kind, to maintain high-status norms of confinement.[218]

Nineteenth-century continental European punishment was marked by a two-track, two-status system for many generations; ours was not. This was a fateful difference. On the continent, the two-track system is essentially gone today, but questions of status, translated in modern legal language into questions of dignity, have survived at the core of European punishment thinking. Dating at least back into the mid eighteenth century, the Anglo-American tradition was different. Anglo-American punishment did not have a clearly symbolically developed de jure two-track system—although, to repeat, high-status persons have presumably always received better treatment de facto in both metropolitan England and in the colonies. And in the nineteenth century, Americans in particular never developed the special high-status forms of imprisonment and execution that appeared on the continent. (Indeed, it is striking that the American Supreme Court in 1878 could casually refer to "beheading" as one of a list of obviously cruel punishments forbidden in the United States.)[219] Nor did Americans show the status sensitivities that pushed Europeans to end the vestiges of low-status punishment. While there was certainly a powerful reform movement in the America, it took a different form from that of the abolition of low-status treatment of prisons. What it took, above all, was a *Christian* form—the Christian form of reform that we see in the penitentiary movement. As Tocqueville and Beaumont observed, "In America, the movement that has shaped reform has been essentially religious."[220] This Christian tendency produced little reflection on the questions of status that moved European reformers, and by the end of the twentieth century, it has left us with only the faintest commitment to defending the dignity of offenders.

This does not mean that Europeans and Americans could not exercise a mutual influence, and sometimes a mutual fascination. The differences I describe are relative and not absolute ones, and there has always been a give-and-take in transatlantic punishment. In particular, it certainly does not mean that early-nineteenth-century American practices could not influence continental Europeans. It is a famous fact that the influence of American practices during the 1830s and 1840s was profound, and they continued after.[221] What matters, though, is that the influence of American practices was an influence on the treatment of *low-status* prisoners in Europe—who were, of course, the overwhelming majority. The idea that anything like the Auburn system should be applied to political dissenters, or to debtors, remained anathema in Europe. Indeed, as we have seen, when Tocqueville and Beaumont returned to preach the beauties of American punishment in the 1830s, they inevitably faced the vehement objection that such treatment was not appropriate for high-status persons. And indeed, everywhere in Europe, despite the influence emanating from America, it remained a matter of course that the tiny minority of high-status prisoners would be treated differently. And they *were* a tiny minority—but they were a minority whose treatment set the pattern for the development of dignity in continental punishment a century and a half later.

The Pardoning Power

Let me now turn to pardoning. As we have seen, the pardoning power has a long and lively history in continental Europe, one that continues strong down into the present. Here too, the long-standing strength of the European states has made itself felt: this is a venerable feature of these "monarchical, hierarchy-ridden," societies, to quote Gordon Wood again.[222] The pardoning power was often exercised to individualize punishment in the nineteenth century and into the fascist period, and it is the power out of which modern measures of individualization grew.

What about America? Nineteenth-century Americans, like their eighteenth-century predecessors and their continental contemporaries, had pardons. In many critical ways, indeed, the American history is little different from the continental history. But it is characteristic of American legal culture that the pardoning power faced bitter opposition—and distinctively *egalitarian* opposition.

As one might expect, the very idea of pardoning raised hackles in the American revolutionary period, just as it did in the early years of the French Revolution. Jefferson, for example, voiced doubts about whether any such monarchical power had a place in an American Republic: "By executive powers we mean no reference to those powers exercised under our former government by the crown as its prerogative. . . . We give him those powers only, which are necessary to execute the laws (and administer the government) and which are not in their nature either legislative or judiciary."[223] This attitude was strong: in the early years of the revolution, eight of the thirteen states took the pardoning power out of the control of the governor, vesting it in various ways in an executive council.[224]

Nevertheless, the pardoning power survived. By 1789 and 1790, the states had begun to return the pardoning power to the governor.[225] On the federal level, too, the Constitution granted the president a pardoning power, as advocated by Alexander Hamilton in particular, who thought the president would be hamstrung without it.[226] Soon thereafter, George Washington made the first historically important use of the power, pardoning the participants in the Whiskey Rebellion.[227] The political pardon continued to be used throughout the next two centuries: participants in Fries' Rebellion were pardoned; Jefferson pardoned those who had deserted from the Continental Army, and Madison and Jackson, too, pardoned deserters. Lincoln, Johnson, and Grant pardoned supporters of the Confederacy.[228] The practice of the political pardon continued, indeed, into the twentieth century. Harding pardoned Debs; Theodore Roosevelt, Coolidge, Franklin Roosevelt, and Truman all pardoned persons imprisoned in wartime; and Theodore Roosevelt issued a pardon for Filipinos whose crimes predated the United States' conquest of their country.[229] This tradition continued, not least, with two famous pardons of the 1970s: Ford's pardon of Nixon, and Carter's pardon of the Vietnam-era draft evaders.

In ordinary punishment, too, pardons continued in heavy use, especially in the early nineteenth century. This is not surprising: it was more or less impossible to manage a nineteenth-century penal system without them. Mass pardons were partly necessary to deal with overcrowding. Thus in early-nineteenth-century Philadelphia, they were used as a means to ease overcrowding in the Walnut Street Jail.[230] In order to relieve pressure on the governor to grant pardons, the New York legislature conferred on prison inspectors the authority to diminish by one quarter the sentences of inmates who displayed good behavior in the early nineteenth century.[231] The resulting frequent use of pardons to deal with problems of overcrowding led to complaints in New York, which were reported by an 1835 English visitor to the United States: "Most commonly, prisoners fulfilled no more than fifty percent of the imposed sentences and felt unduly wronged if no pardon were forthcoming at that point. The problem was heightened by the dubious practice of semiannual clemency sessions which resulted in release of forty to fifty convicts simultaneously, thus increasing anxiety both within the waiting convicts and among the citizens living near the prison."[232] Nevertheless, New York governors continued to use the practice as a measure to deal with overcrowding—though they repeatedly had to defend it against vociferous objections.[233] Prison discipline was also a natural arena for pardoning. Prison inspectors could offer pardons, and they were used, in standard individualizing fashion, as a tool of prison discipline.[234] Elizabeth Farnham, warden of Sing Sing's female wing, advocated leaving the pardoning power with prison officials in order to further discipline.[235] The official association of nineteenth-century prison officials in New York favored pardons as a mechanism for discipline, too.[236] Pardoning remained an important part of sentencing practices at Sing-Sing from 1817 to 1847.[237] In Pennsylvania, pardoning of inmates was already used as a disciplinary mechanism in the Walnut Street Jail,[238] and it continued into the 1870s.[239] In the southern states, governors were overwhelmed with petitions for pardons, sometimes running out of forms.[240]

Pardoning took place on the federal level too. Indeed, pardoning retained great vigor on the federal level throughout the nineteenth century. In the period from 1860 to 1900, 49 percent of federal pardon applications were granted, and in the last five years of the century, 43 percent of federal inmates received some kind of pardon.[241] This statistic should be read with some caution. Federal criminal jurisdiction was limited in the nineteenth century, and the class of federal prisoners was a peculiar population.[242] Nevertheless, the late-nineteenth-century pattern on the federal level is clearly not all that different in the United States from what it was in France or Germany: pardoning in the federal prisons was a part of the ordinary management of the population. This continued in an attenuated way into the twentieth century: in 1936, for example, Franklin Roosevelt pardoned some 390 federal inmates out of a population of 14,000.[243] Overall, from 1900 to 1936, the rate of federal pardons dropped sharply.[244] This reflected exactly the same pattern to be found in France: the pardon was being replaced by new practices of parole, just as advocates of modern methods of penology had long said it should.[245]

Indeed, the practice of pardoning in the United States was not all that different from the practice in Europe. As in Europe, a fairly active pardoning practice in nineteenth-century America simply gave way to parole and probation.[246] By the 1850s and 1860s, now-familiar doubts about incarceration began to be voiced in the United States. Prisons came to be regarded as schools for crime, and various societies agitated for ticket-of-leave programs and the practice of probation.[247] Meanwhile, there were important experiments in Massachusetts with a Christianized version of probation under influence of John Augustus.[248] Sentences of probation and indeterminate sentences remained rare in New York in the 1860s and 1870s,[249] as they did in Pennsylvania,[250] but in Augustus's home state of Massachusetts probation made real headway.[251] Eventually probation established itself everywhere. Moreover, in the early part of the twentieth century, what had been a "pardoning" power passed into the control of parole boards.[252] All this closely resembled the development of practices and institutions in continental Europe.

What was different about American pardoning was not so much the practice, however, as the perception. American officials needed pardoning, and they used it. But doing so touched a raw egalitarian nerve among Americans, as it would continue to do down to the Clinton pardons of 2000. And in that we see some deep-seated cultural differences between American and continental traditions.

Indeed, there have always been doubts and fears surrounding the pardoning power in America. Sometimes these doubts have been expressed in the classic tones of European philosophy, but sometimes they have been expressed in a more American way. The influence of Beccarian ideas opposing pardons remained strong from early on the history of American reforms.[253] As William Bradford put it in 1793: "The prospect of escaping detection and the hope of an acquittal or pardon, blunt [the] operation [of the criminal law] and defeat the expectations of the Legislature. Experience proves that these hopes are wonderfully strong, and they often give birth to the most fatal rashness."[254] This was the classic Beccarian objection. There was also the classic Montesquieuian objection that pardoning was inappropriate in a republic. I have already quoted Jefferson's denunciation of pardoning, which turned on Montesquieuian notions of the separation of powers. Francis Lieber, too, repeated this argument in 1853: "The monarch alone was considered the indisputable dispenser of pardon; and this again is the historical reason why we have always granted the pardoning privilege to the chief executive . . . forgetting that the monarch has the pardoning power, not because he is the chief executive, but because he was considered the sovereign."[255] This was familiar eighteenth-century stuff.

But alongside these familiar objections came characteristically American expressions of a different anxiety: that pardons were being used to benefit persons with good connections. This anxiety appeared early. Pennsylvania governors, who had received the power to pardon in 1790, were "susceptible," it was feared, "to deception, false sympathetic evidence, and the obligations of feelings of friendliness founded upon political and personal considerations."[256] These were the tones of an enduring theme in American culture, rarely heard in Europe.[257] Pardons, it was argued, were inevitably *inegalitarian*. The same anxieties remained strong throughout the nineteenth century. Americans frequently voiced the suspicion that pardons only benefited persons of relatively secure social status. As Gershom Powers, agent and keeper at Auburn Prison in New York, put it:

> Is it the poor and friendless, whose misfortunes may have rendered them desperate and driven them over the bounds of moral rectitude; who, in moments of frenzy, have committed crimes that under the circumstances they would contemplate with horror: is it this class whose prayer and tears are known beyond their prison walls, and who become the favored recipients of executive mercy? Is it the miserable foreigner, whom oppression may have cast upon our shores, destitute of the means of subsistence, and the knowledge of acquiring it, as well as ignorant of our laws, who has misapplied the principle of self-preservation, by supplying his immediate wants from another's property, without consent: is it such a one whose groans reach the ear of the executive? No: they are the rich, the intelligent, the powerful villains to whom the boon of mercy is generally extended. They have friends; employ agents: property, talents, and influence, are part in requisitions; the executive is deceived, and the prison doors are opened.[258]

This belief that it was the well-connected who benefited from pardons was in fact false[259]—which only makes the strength of the belief more striking. Americans were convinced that "people with money or political connections had an obvious advantage in securing pardons."[260] This conviction, moreover, had to do not only with social status, but also with race. Thus in a passage in his 1844 novel *The Quaker City: Or the Monks of Monk Hall*, George Lippard suggested that pardons were used to benefit antiblack rioters:

> Why you see, a party of us one Sunday afternoon had nothin' to do, so we got up a nigger riot. We have them things in Phi'delphy, once or twice a year. I helped to burn a nigger church, two orphans' asylums and a school-house and happenih' to have a pump-handle in my hand, I askedentally hit an old nigger on the head. Konsekance was he died.
>
> And was you tried for this little accident?
>
> Yes, I was. Convicted, too. Sentenced in the bargain. But the Judge and the jury had the lawyers, on both sides, signed a paper to the Governor. He pardoned me.[261]

This insinuation, sadly, was not always fiction, and it was not limited to the 1840s. In Kentucky during the two years from 1879 to 1890, no few than 390 persons were pardoned for "kukluxing," upon request of their judge.[262] In these cases, pardoning was indeed used to benefit the high over the low. At any rate, unease over the danger of favoritism in pardoning coexisted with classic Beccarian objections to pardons, as expressed for example by Dorothea Dix[263] or Farnham of the female wing at Sing Sing.[264] It continued throughout the century,[265] as the same sort of dissatisfaction would be expressed all over the country, from California to Illinois to Kentucky.[266] This tradition continued into the early twentieth century, as it has continued into the present. One philosopher, writing in 1910, picked up on the long American tradition of suspicion of the pardoning power: pardons, he held, were closely akin to bribes—they represented an individual misuse of official power.[267] Inegalitarianism again. Another philosopher, writing in the same year, argued that pardoning should be used in no more arbitrary a way than the power to call up the militia.[268] No toleration for individualized grace. When Orlando Lewis wrote his pioneering study of American prison history in 1922, he, too, saw things the same way: "In the granting of pardon . . . there lies inherent the great possibilities of apparent favoritism."[269] The pardoning power has simply never had the kind of public acceptability in America that it had, and still has, in Europe.

Certainly it did not stir the kind of awe that it would in the European twentieth century. In twentieth-century France and Germany, as we have seen, much of the old idea of the quasi-sacred exercise of state sovereignty continued to surround the power of grace. During the Weimar and the fascist periods, the power of grace had a host of associations with the charismatic power of the state—of the abrupt, individual, and inexplicable touch of the finger of sovereign mercy; and in France down to this day a change of presidential regime brings with it a general amnesty, just as it did during the ancien régime.

That sort of attitude is alien to the United States; and its alienness is reflected in the development of constitutional thought about the pardoning power. European ideas of the majesty of the personal mercy in the pardoning power died slowly. The leading nineteenth-century case on the pardoning power had, indeed, a strongly European tinge to it. The issue in the case, *United States v. Wilson*, decided in 1833, was whether the beneficiary of a presidential pardon could refuse to accept it for tactical reasons. The Supreme Court, per Chief Justice Marshall, held that the beneficiary could indeed refuse, on the grounds that a pardon was a kind of personal gift from the president:

> As this power has been exercised from time immemorial by the executive of that nation whose language is our language, and to whose judicial institutions ours bear a close resemblance; we adopt their principles respecting the operation and effect of a pardon, and look into their books for the rules prescribing the manner in which it is to be used by the person who would avail himself of it. . . .
>
> A pardon is an act of grace, proceeding from the power entrusted with the execution of the laws, which exempts the individual, on whom it is bestowed, from the punishment the law inflicts for a crime he has committed. It is the private, though official act of the executive magistrate.[270]

The individual touch of the finger of sovereign mercy was still there for the Supreme Court. Pardoning was still understood in its "immemorial" way as an exercise of personal sovereign grace—much though figures like Jefferson and Lieber might object to the idea that any such power could survive in the American republic. This doctrine went unchallenged right through the nineteenth century, despite all of the traditions of doubt about pardoning.

Such a classic conception of the pardon as an act of individual grace could not survive in twentieth-century America, though. A series of decisions weakened and then eliminated it—and did so, strikingly enough, precisely during the period when German law in particular was succumbing to a deepening fascination with the magic of mercy. The doctrine of the individual grace of mercy was at stake in 1915, in *Burdick v. U.S.* This was the case of a muckraking reporter who refused to accept a pardon that would have forced him to testify. Following nineteenth-century precedent, the Supreme Court allowed him to do so.[271] By the 1920s, though, the Supreme Court's view had shifted too. *Biddle v. Perovich*, decided in 1927,[272] involved a man condemned to death who wished to refuse his commutation to a life sentence. In this charged case, Justice Holmes held that a pardon could not in fact be refused, and he did so on the grounds that the traditional concept of a pardon as an act of grace no longer held good: "A pardon in our days in not a private act of grace from an individual happening to possess power." No more individualized touch of the finger of sovereign mercy. This was written by Holmes, arguably the leading figure in American legal thought, at the very moment that Radbruch, arguably the leading figure in German criminal-law thought, was insisting on the sacred magic of grace. A "private act of grace" is exactly what Germans working under the spell of Weber thought that a pardon was. It was not a notion that could mean much at all to Americans.

Conclusion

By the end of the nineteenth century, as Kropotkin arrived at Clairvaux and the great modernist reforms began to sweep the Western world, both the old traditions of status differentiation and the old traditions of mercy had faded into relative insignificance in America.

The old traditions of status were not entirely forgotten. In particular, the Supreme Court showed a clear understanding of them when it grappled with the Fifth Amendment. "Infamous" crimes, according to the Fifth Amendment, required presentment before a grand jury. What were they? In a fine scholarly decision of 1885, the Supreme Court did a study of early modern punishment traditions in an effort to answer that question. "Infamy," the court correctly noted, had had two effective meanings in the eighteenth century. The commission of certain crimes, like perjury, had rendered the offender incompetent to testify in court. That sort of infamy could hardly provide the meaning of the Fifth Amendment. But eighteenth-century infamy had also been the consequence of being subjected to an "infamous" punishment—in particular being whipped, mutilated, or subjected to hard labor (though the court noted variations in the perception of these). This was correct: as we have seen, early modern lawyers on both sides of the channel had viewed infamy as the consequence, not of the commission of a crime as such, but of being subjected to a low-status punishment. From these premises, the court drew the conclusion that "infamous" crimes, for purposes of the Fifth Amendment, were those that carried an "infamous" penalty. It further concluded, with perfect justice, that imprisonment at hard labor would have qualified as an infamous punishment in the mind of the eighteenth century.[273]

This was an entirely faithful reading of Fifth Amendment; but what did it imply? It did not lead the court in anything like the direction contemporary continental law was taking. Nothing in the court's reasoning implied that low-status punishments should be abolished in the United States. Decisions of the subsequent decade extended that reasoning a bit, holding that any sentence to a penitentiary counted as "infamous"[274] and further holding that illegal aliens held pending expulsion could not be subjected to hard labor without a trial. The latter decision, *Wong Wing v. United States*,[275] had real significance for the lot of aliens in the United States down to this day. But the sum of these decisions did not add up to anything like the continental commitment to end low-status treatment.

For a while, during the following century of reform, Supreme Court jurisprudence was more adventurous, making efforts to update the Eighth Amendment's ban on "cruel and unusual punishment" in ways that would leave the eighteenth century behind. In 1910, the court declared in *Weems v. United States* that the phrase "cruel and unusual punishment" was not to be interpreted in a backward-looking way, and over the subsequent seventy years, the court generally tried to gear the interpretation of the Eighth

Amendment to "evolving standards of decency."[276] This was an attitude that would effectively perish with the decline of reformist sentiment of the last quarter-century, but it was an attitude that brought some real change to American punishment for a time. It never brought change of the continental kind, though. If American courts tried to construe the Eighth Amendment in light of the more liberal views of their own twentieth century, they nevertheless betrayed none of the powerful continental sense that historically degrading punishments were incompatible with true republican forms. In particular, flogging and deliberately harsh coerced labor did not end: the sorts of practices that Kropotkin complained about in the 1880s continued in use in the United States into the 1960s.

Flogging makes an especially revealing study—in Arkansas, for example. Arkansas was one of the southern states whose prisons systems were massively reformed in the 1960s, with immensely beneficial results for Arkansan convicts. Strikingly, though, the district court that was responsible for this reform could not see its way to any outright ban on flogging under American constitutional norms. It managed to hold only that flogging had to be subject to "recognizable standards." In a way wholly typical of American tradition, the court put procedural limits on punishment, not substantive ones of the continental kind:

> There are no written rules or regulations prescribing what conduct or misconduct will bring on a whipping or prescribing how many blows will be inflicted for a given act of misconduct. The punishment is administered summarily, and whether an inmate is to be whipped and how much he is to be whipped are matters resting within the sole discretion of the prison employee administering the punishment, subject to the present informal requirement of respondent that the blows administered for a single offense shall not exceed ten. . .
>
> Petitioner Talley has been whipped on a number of occasions by Assistant Warden Harmon both for infractions of discipline and for insufficient work. Hash has been whipped at least once by Assistant Warden Chadick.
>
> The evidence is sharply conflicting as to how many times Talley has been whipped since he came to the Penitentiary about 1961. He says that he has been whipped about 70 times. Harmon says that Talley has been whipped only six or seven times. Talley probably exaggerates; Harmon probably minimizes. In the Court's eyes that conflict in the testimony is not material. . .
>
> The evidence also discloses that on two occasions Talley has been assaulted and beaten by James Pike, the line rider [i.e. an inmate supervisor] assigned to Talley's long line. Pike, an illiterate, is a convicted murderer serving a sentence for beating to death a warden at the Mississippi County Penal Farm where Pike was formerly confined on a misdemeanor charge.
>
> The evidence is conflicting as to the reasons for the assaults of Pike on Talley and as to the extent of the injuries inflicted upon the latter. Again the Court finds it unnecessary to resolve those conflicts. Regardless of why or how severely Pike beat Talley, the Court finds that the assaults were committed by Pike in his capacity as line rider and were for the purpose of disciplining Talley. In connection with the first beating Talley unquestionably received injuries to his teeth which necessitated the furnishing to him of a partial denture.

> Still further disclosed by the evidence is the fact that on occasions Talley has been whipped by Harmon on the report of Pike that Talley had done insufficient work. Pike's reports seem to have been acted upon by Harmon automatically and without investigation.
>
> It is contended by petitioners that the infliction of corporal punishment in any degree and in any circumstances upon an adult human being, either as an initial punishment for crime or as punishment for an infraction of prison discipline by a convict, is abhorrent to the modern mind, and that whatever view of it may have been taken in times past it is today a cruel and inhuman punishment prohibited by the Constitution.
>
> In evaluating that contention it should be said first that in present context it is beside the point whether the use of such punishment is good or bad penology, or whether its infliction is necessary to control Arkansas convicts or to run the Penitentiary efficiently, or whether the Judge of the Court, as an individual, approves of such punishment. The question is whether the use of the strap at the Arkansas Penitentiary is a cruel and unusual punishment in the constitutional sense.
>
> The criminal code of Arkansas does not prescribe whipping as a punishment for any crime, and as early as 1884 the Supreme Court of Arkansas deprecated the whipping of convicts and refused to presume that the then Penitentiary Board had authorized it. *Werner v. State, 44 Ark. 122.* And the infliction of such punishment has been banned in many jurisdictions. It must be recognized, however, that corporal punishment has not been viewed historically as a constitutionally forbidden cruel and unusual punishment, and this Court is not prepared to say that such punishment is per se unconstitutional. See 18 C.J.S. Convicts § 11; *State v. Revis, supra; Balser v. State (Del.), 57 Del. 206, 195 A.2d 757; State v. Cannon (Del.), 55 Del. 587, 190 A.2d 514; United States v. Jones, S.D.Fla., 108 F. Supp. 266, 270.*
>
> But, the Court's unwillingness to say that the Constitution forbids the imposition of any and all corporal punishment on convicts presupposes that its infliction is surrounded by appropriate safeguards. It must not be excessive; it must be inflicted as dispassionately as possible and by responsible people; and it must be applied in reference to recognizable standards whereby a convict may know what conduct on his part will cause him to be whipped and how much punishment given conduct may produce.[277]

A more aggressive approach was taken by the court in *Jackson v. Bishop,* in 1968.[278] This court enjoined the barebacked whipping of inmates by guards subject to no controls, and did its best to hold flogging generally unconstitutional—though doubts can be raised about how far its decision reached.[279] At any rate, this decision was something of an outlier. Most important, the Delaware Supreme Court, in a pair of 1963 opinions, declined to eliminate whipping as a punishment in that state.[280]

To be sure, the Delaware court invited the state legislature to abolish the punishment of whipping as inconsistent with contemporary mores—something the legislature eventually did, in 1973.[281] And to be sure, even in the harsh climate of the late 1980s, as firm as believer in original intent as Justice Scalia admitted that flogging had become too uncomfortable a practice not to be banned.[282] Nevertheless, it is remarkable how difficult American lawyers have found it to uncover some clear argument against the practice of flogging, even at the height of the era of prison reform. Something is missing in our reasoning—at least by contrast with continental European reasoning. We have lost all sense of the social dynamic of degradation in punishment.

This absence could be felt most palpably in the Ninth Circuit's 1994 decision in *Campbell v. Wood*, which considered a challenge to hanging. This was a case in which Judge Reinhardt, a judge nationally known for his unusual willingness to cling to largely forgotten liberal values, struggled in dissent to articulate the dignitary harm in hanging. He wrote: "Although indignity may stem from the needless infliction of pain, it can also arise from the relatively painless infliction of degradation, savagery, and brutality. Cruelty does not necessarily involve pain. Indignities can be inflicted even after a person has died. For example, there can be little doubt that the Eighth Amendment prohibits the public exhibiting of carcasses on yardarms, and the stringing up of bodies in public squares."[283] None of this was persuasive to the majority in the decision, which saw only the infliction of pain as raising any possible Eighth Amendment difficulties. "Dignity" and "degradation" as such fall on deaf ears in American legal culture—just as they already did in the nineteenth century.

Conclusion

Two Revolutions of Status

When Tocqueville and Beaumont returned from America in 1832, eager to introduce American cellular imprisonment into France, they were troubled by the American indifference to "infamy," as we have seen. Typical post-1830 French reformers that they were, Tocqueville and Beaumont thought that low-status punishment had no place in a civilized society. They feared that "public opinion" in France might not accept American models that included such practices as flogging inmates, and they hoped fervently that Americans might overcome their backwardness in this respect.[1] Flogging and the like have disappeared from American prisons today, of course—even if there are Americans today who want to bring back them back. Nevertheless, the differences in "public opinion" identified by Tocqueville and Beaumont survive, in the very different worlds of punishment on either side of the Atlantic. It remains the case that Americans care far less than continental Europeans do about what the nineteenth century called "infamy." Continental practices have been shaped by a long effort to end low status in punishment; American practices have not.

Why is this? It has a great deal to do with what Tocqueville himself talked about: our "point de départ," our starting point.[2] From a very early date, we had nothing like the system of high status that existed in continental Europe. This struck Tocqueville, of course, just as it later struck American commentators such as Hartz and Lipset: we began essentially without Tocqueville's "aristocratic element";[3] and our practices have never reflected the strong urge to generalize high-status treatment that is so noticeable in the history of continental punishment. In continental Europe, by contrast, old high-status norms of punishment have gradually, though incompletely, been generalized. Equality in modern continental Europe has meant conferring on all, to the extent possible, what were once the exclusive privileges of high status. As Heinrich Heine put in 1828, with his characteristic arch snideness, "If the unwashed commoners took the liberty of beheading the high nobility, this was perhaps less in order to inherit their wealth than inherit their ancestors—in order to replace bourgeois inequality with aristocratic equality."[4] A yearning for "aristocratic equality" is indeed a constant in continental Europe. One of the most famous claims of Montesquieu deserves to be remembered here too: the claim that the "principle" of monarchical-aristocratic societies is *honor*.[5] Continental societies are by no means "aristocratic" in the Montesquieuian sense today. But the idea hangs on that "honor" is of central importance, and the commitment to equality on the continent is partly a commitment to generalizing honor to all.

These are simply two different roads, to two different forms of equality. Tocqueville was not unaware that these different forms could exist. As he wrote, in a nearly Nietzschean vein: "There is in effect a manly and legitimate passion for equality that excites men to desire that they should all be strong and esteemed. This passion tends to elevate the small to the rank of the great; but there is also found, in the human heart, a depraved taste for equality, which leads the weak to desire to draw the strong down to their level, and which reduces men to preferring equality as slaves to equality in freedom."[6] What we see in continental European punishment today is Tocqueville's "manly and legitimate passion for equality"; in America we see something else. In this we have at least part of the answer to the question that Tocqueville himself was never able to resolve: the question of how to distinguish between democracy *in America* and democracy elsewhere.[7] Democracy in the continental European countries has taken a different form.

The most dramatic symbols of these very old differences remain the traditional modes of execution. After the eighteenth century, the lands of continental Europe became lands of beheading, while America became a land of hanging. Of course, these old modes of death are gone on both sides of the Atlantic. Nevertheless they remain unmatchable as symbols of a much grander difference in status traditions. The difference was already fixed by 1878, when the United States Supreme Court matter-of-factly declared that beheading was unacceptable in the civilized world[8]—at a time when both France and Germany routinely beheaded condemned offenders. This profound clash of attitudes was not the result of some difference in the degree of "civilization" on either side of the Atlantic. It was a result of differences in traditions of status. By the middle of the nineteenth century, beheading was generalized for persons of all statuses in continental Europe; and by the end of the twentieth, old high-status modes of punishment had become the norm in every respect. By the middle of the eighteenth century, hanging was generalized in the America, and we are still living with the long-term decline of high-status treatment. Equality came to both sides of the Atlantic, that is, but it came on different terms.

Of course, the differences in punishment practice between the United States and Europe seemed to be vanishing for a long time. Until about 1975, there was something of an international orthodoxy, founded in an international triumph of modernist programs of rehabilitation. For a good century, punishment professionals everywhere in the West believed that individualized punishment, founded in social scientific and psychotherapeutic techniques, had permanently displaced older ideas of retribution. But very suddenly, around 1975, they ceased to believe this.[9] The orthodoxy did not collapse everywhere in equal measure: as we have seen, programs of rehabilitation in fact survived in continental Europe. Punishment professionals in continental Europe stopped maintaining that they could really change offenders after the mid-1970s, but they never stopped applying the rehabilitative techniques that were a part of their training and their professional tradition. Bureaucratic momentum kept rehabilitation alive in continental Europe. Nevertheless, if rehabilitation survived, it is certainly true that punishment policy came to seem up for grabs in continental Europe just as it did in the United States. The sense that there was an unchallengeable orthodoxy vanished there just as it vanished here. In consequence, there was a period of real ferment on both sides of the Atlantic.

This period produced very different results, though. We have seen what happened in both France and Germany. Amidst nasty prison riots in both countries, punishment practices were shaken up in the late 1960s and early 1970s. But in both, the consequence was that long-standing ameliorative tendencies were *strengthened*. In both countries, low-status punishment, which had been being gradually dismantled since the early nineteenth century, was finally definitively ended in the prisons. The upheavals of the 1960s in France resulted in the effective extension of "political prisoner" status to all inmates; while in Germany, *Zuchthaus* was definitively abolished, and all inmates were subjected to one form or another of *Einschließung*, the descendant of fortress confinement. Both countries did introduce harsher punishment in some ways, with longer sentences. A determination to crack down on terrorists brought some particularly harsh legislation in the 1970s. Nevertheless, in both France and Germany, tendencies toward effective decriminalization and mildness in sentencing practices continued. The consequence was that while a certain target population of offenders was hit harder in both France and Germany, in both countries that target population was shrinking over the last quarter of the twentieth century. To put it in a formula that simplifies a lot of history, in the aftermath of the sixties, northern continental Europe moved to the left.

The same period of ferment produced very different results in the United States. In our country, which saw its own prison riots and its own resulting crisis,[10] the shift of the mid-1970s brought a return to a historic American Beccarianism—to an attachment to formal equality that reflected a deep American distrust of status differentiation. This return to formal equality affected both sentencing, and attitudes toward the liability of new classes of persons. The shift of the mid-1970s also brought the return of a style of retributivism that, in American practice, is closely associated both with populist justice and with deep-seated Christian sentiment—much though the academic philosophers who advocated retributivism at the same time may have hoped to encourage a kind of gentler Kantianism.

On both sides of the Atlantic, in short, the collapse of the aspirations of modernist jurisprudence brought a return to older historic patterns. And on both sides of the Atlantic, those patterns had to do largely with traditions of social status. France and Germany, as I have tried to show, returned to a peculiar kind of egalitarianism that is also to be found in other areas of their law: an egalitarianism that aims to accord high status to everybody. This continental variety of egalitarianism, the egalitarianism of the guillotine, had had a real impact on continental punishment practices for a long time. It had a renewed impact after the crisis of the late 1960s and early 1970s. American equality, after the early 1970s, revealed itself to be a different beast. With the return to traditional American egalitarianism came something that social scientists once believed to be impossible: increasing harshness in a "modern" country.

Wrestling with Durkheim (and Marx)

Indeed, the most arresting way to view American developments, as I have described them in this book, is to measure them against the optimistic predictions of late nineteenth and early twentieth-century sociologists—and especially of the greatest of theoretical sociologists, Durkheim. Sociologists of a century ago took it for granted that growing "modernity" meant growing mildness in punishment. They lived in a world in which the brutal and garish punishments of the premodern world—mutilations, beatings, brandings, condemnations to the galleys or the mines—had all gradually been abolished. The more seemingly humane punishment of imprisonment had spread everywhere by the middle of the nineteenth century, in both America and Europe. Flogging and the like had vanished from French prisons, if not from American and British ones. Moreover, imprisonment too seemed to be giving way, by the end of the nineteenth century, yielding pride of place to yet milder forms of punishment: fines and probation.

As he surveyed this world at the turn of the last century, Durkheim, like other contemporaries, thus found it natural to assume that, as societies made the transition from primitive to modern social structures, punishment would *always* grow milder. And he offered an explanation for this that is all the more revealing for being so dramatically wrong about America. Premodern punishment, in Durkheim's turn-of-century view, had been harsh in a particular way, and for a particular reason. It had been a retributive harshness, with roots in human instincts toward vengefulness; and it had served the function of creating and reinforcing social cohesiveness. Primitive criminal law revolved around the punishment of activities that mobilized retributivist communal resentment—especially sexual, religious, and other morals infractions. By punishing such acts, premodern groups were able to develop and consolidate a sense of community that they would otherwise lack or easily lose. What we might call the "retributive temper" thus served to create solidarity. To Durkheim, it seemed clear that modern societies had a diminished need for punishment that created that kind of group solidarity; for group solidarity of the communal premodern kind was gone. Modern societies were looser organizations, held together principally through the disengaged means of contract. Marketplace and other contractual relations were adequate to form modern human relations, and there was no need for charivarilike public punishment of "immorality" to keep society together. The rise of the *contractualization* of human relations, that is to say, necessarily brought with it the decline of the *penalization* of human relations; and modern punishment would inevitably become milder.[11]

Well, continental European punishment *has* continued to grow milder; but American punishment has not. Indeed, post-1975 developments in America are exceedingly strange, from the Durkheimian point of view. They include, as we have seen, a great resurgence of retributivism—not just in legal theory but in the practice of punishment as well. They also include the completely unexpected comeback of festive public punishments that not only resemble premodern shaming practices, but deliberately set out to revive the premodern culture of stocks and shackles.

This great divide has opened up between Europe and America *not* (as Durkheim supposed) because human relations are growing more contractualized in Europe. There can hardly be any doubt that it is the United States that has the more "contractualized" society.[12] The critical question is not one of contract, but of status.

More particularly, the critical question is one of the *distribution* of status. The three societies discussed in this book are all the products of what we should think of as revolutionary egalitarian traditions. But their revolutionary traditions are not well understood if we think of them only in classic Marxian terms, as springing from conflicts of economically defined "class." What is at work in the patterns I have traced is not so much class conflict as status conflict. Punishment in all three countries reflects revolutionary traditions of honor, traditions in which, as T. H. Marshall put it, "equality of status is more important than equality of income."[13] Or to quote Gordon Wood once more, "one class did not overthrow another; the poor did not supplant the rich" in any of these countries over the course of the last two revolutionary centuries. "But social relationships—the way people were connected one to another—were changed, and decisively so" in all of them.[14] This is not to deny that there has been real economic conflict, and some redistribution of wealth, in all three societies. It is only to say that what is most striking from the point of view of the development of punishment—and many cognate social relations—is the redistribution of status. These countries have all had revolutions of *social honor*. But the revolution in the United States has been very much one against social honor, against high status; whereas in continental Europe it is been a revolution in favor of social honor, in favor of generalizing high status.

As I have tried to demonstrate in this book, this difference in traditions of the distribution of status has had far-reaching consequences for the shape of criminal punishment. European punishment has been growing milder because, during two centuries of the breakdown of a highly articulated hierarchical order, European status has taken on a certain leveling-up dynamic. The politics of dignity in both France and Germany, conditioned by long historical experience, has become a politics that aims to extend membership in the highest social strata to everybody; the commitment to egalitarianism in these countries is a commitment to a *leveling up*, to a high-status egalitarianism. Where there used to be high and low, everyone in these societies is now supposed to be high. This leveling-up drive is extremely powerful in Germany and France—so powerful that is has swept up even criminal offenders with it. This reflects in particular the continental history of imprisoning political dissenters and other "honorable" persons. There have always been specially defined categories of high status in Europe, special classes of persons in prison who are not "really" criminals. This is a fact that is inextricably connected with the relative strength of European states; and it means that a developed cultural tradition of honorable punishment has survived on the continent. This cultural tradition has come to benefit all offenders. Criminals too have been brought up in status; they too are increasingly treated as honorable persons. Correspondingly, the forms of dignity in punishment, in France and Germany both, with their horror of public exposure and forced labor, and their tendency to gravitate toward dignified terms of imprisonment, hearken back to the high-status punishments of the premodern world. Even in the relatively egalitarian worlds of contemporary France and Germany, the *memory* of status thus continues to matter.

The United States is very different—but not because we have less Durkheimian "contractualization." It is rather that we revolted against a different, and weaker, tradition of articulated status differentiation. Our society was never stratified in the classic ancien régime way. Although there were pockets of old-world ways of doing things in colonial Virginia or in Brahmin Boston, we never had anything like the state of Louis XIV or of Suleyman the Magnificent or of Aurangzeb or of the Qianlong emperor. Except in the slaveholding South, we never had a society in which there were highly articulated status differences, marked by such things as legally compelled differences in dress and in forms of address. We never had a royal court with truly elaborate hierarchical etiquette. We never had one of those great ramifying social pyramids that were so widespread in the human world of the seventeenth or eighteenth centuries, and that so much had the look of a human version of the hierarchical orders we also discover in other primates.

The consequence is that our collective memory of past status degradation is different and weaker. That does not mean that we have never had status differences in punishment. Highly placed Americans have always been able to expect milder punishment. We have our "club feds," our minimum-security facilities. What is missing in America is not high status, but the drive to lift everybody up to high status. What is missing is what we see in the German Code of Punishment: the declaration that *everybody* is presumed to deserve placement in a halfway house.[15]

This reflects the fact that we, unlike our continental kin, have never systematically imprisoned any class of high-status persons. Neither political dissenters nor debtors have routinely gone to prison in America; and in consequence we do not have anything like the developed cultural tradition of "honorable" punishment that reigns in Europe. Tocqueville thought that the absence of political prisoners in America was the most benign feature of American justice.[16] This may have been a fair enough observation in the 1830s; but over time, leaving political dissenters alone has had a paradoxical consequence: we have never felt the continental urge to generalize "honorable" punishment.

Quite the contrary: most of the time, like most human societies, we degrade our offenders. To quote Bentham once again, "legislators and men in general are naturally inclined" to excessive harshness, since "antipathy, or a want of compassion for individuals who are represented as dangerous and vile, pushes them onward to an undue severity."[17] We do indeed tend to regard offenders as "dangerous and vile" and to treat them accordingly. A striking recent article in *The New York Times* helps bring out the some of the depth of the drive, in American punishment, to reduce offenders to a low status. The scene is laid in a North Carolina slaughterhouse, where jobs are assigned according to the great American status-marker, race. The worst jobs, on the assembly line, are assigned almost exclusively to Mexicans—and to one other class: prisoners, permitted to leave prison to work in the slaughterhouse. One white prisoner is astounded to find himself assigned to this low-status work:

> With less than a month to go on his sentence, [Billy] Harwood took the pork job to save a few dollars. The word in jail was that the job was a cakewalk for a white man.
>
> But this wasn't looking like any cakewalk. He wasn't going to get a boxing job like a lot of other whites. Apparently inmates were on the bottom rung, just like Mexicans. . . .
>
> The convict said he felt cheated. He wasn't supposed to be doing Mexican work. After his second day he was already talking of quitting. "Man, this can't be for real," he said, rubbing his wrists as if they'd been in handcuffs. "This job's for an ass. They treat you like an animal."[18]

In every human society the urge is strong to assign criminals to the lowest social rung, however the social ladder is defined, and if there are no countervailing tendencies, degradation is the ordinary form that human punishment takes. In the United States, in which membership in disfavored races carries, for many people, a quality of pollution, it is not surprising to see a convict assigned to "Mexican work." In *both* the United States and continental Europe, punishment is status-oriented. Pace Durkheim, punishment is not just about creating homogeneous social cohesion; punishment, at least in its most unbridled form, is also about affirming that some persons stand on a higher rung than others.

One might well press the question of why things have not turned out differently in America. If the roots of respect for persons in Europe lie in distinctive traditions of social stratification, it is not the case that we have *no* traditions of social stratification of our own in the United States. There *is*, to come back to it again, race. Indeed, Americans do have one highly articulated status order in their past, and it is one that plays a large role in national consciousness: the status order of the slaveholding South. One might expect, or hope, that the memory of the slaveholding South would serve to push American legal culture in the direction of a dignitary evolution like that of Europe. Indeed, in one notable instance, American lawyers did try to build on the history of slaveholding in order to reform American punishment practice. This was the leading early prison reform decision in the United States, Judge Henley's *Holt II* decision of 1970. In that case, lawyers raised a constitutional claim, founded in the Thirteenth Amendment, that challenged forced labor on the grounds that it was a form of slavery. Yet Judge Henley, who accepted all of the other constitutional arguments offered to him, rejected that one—and this in Arkansas, a state in which the association between slavery and imprisonment was historically close.[19] If ever there was a case in which American punishment law might have seen a leveling up pattern like that of Europe, this was it.

But the fact is that the history of slave-society just does not have the same resonance in American society that the history of ancien régime Europe does in France and Germany. For Europeans, it is an imperative consequence of the abolition of the ancien régime that dignity must be extended to all. We do not draw the same conclusion from our own abolition of slavery. It the end, this is perhaps not very surprising. For, on the deepest level, what must drive continental European sensibilities is the natural identification that most Europeans are able to feel with their low-status ancestors. *We were all*, most of them can say, *once at the bottom*. It is precisely the nature of American slaveholding that we Americans were not all once at the bottom; most Americans do not by any means identify with African slaves. Our memories are different; and the pattern of American egalitarianism is correspondingly far from the pattern of European egalitarianism. Slavery means too little to most of us—as Justice Stevens observed with great rhetorical force in his dissent in *Hudson v. Palmer*, the 1984 case that put an effective end to any reform efforts that might guarantee prison inmates' privacy in the United States. Stevens's dissent would still have permitted many more limitations on inmate privacy than are considered acceptable in continental Europe. But it did express something like the European sensibility in one passage. The Supreme Court, he observed, had effectively held "that the prisoners are entitled to no measure of human dignity or individuality—not a photo, a letter, nor anything except standard-issue prison clothing would be free from arbitrary seizure and destruction. Yet that is the view the Court takes today. It declares prisoners to be little more than chattels, a view I thought society had outgrown long ago."[20] The majority sees it differently from Justice Stevens—the majority of the court, and, presumably, majority American culture as well.

Strong States Can Make for Mild Punishment

Traditions of social hierarchy are thus a large part of what makes France and Germany different, in their punishment practices, from the United States. The power and autonomy of the French and German states are another part.

This is true, first of all, because the power and autonomy of continental states helps explain the French and German resistance to the secular shift in the American public mood: the shift to the sort of retributivism that Durkheim regarded as "primitive." Why has American politics turned to the kind of retributivism that both French and German politics generally resists? The answer is, in part, a Durkheimian one: retributivism does indeed mobilize social cohesion. In the United States, though, what the retributive temper primarily does is to mobilize cohesive support *in democratic politics*.[21] It is surely the case that Americans punish more harshly because the management of the punishment system in the United States is more given over to democratic politics—which is often to say demagogic politics. Every commentator who tries to explain punishment in America points to the character of its politics—of a politics that led Mario Cuomo, for example, to build unprecedented numbers of prisons in order to shield himself from criticism for his opposition to the death penalty;[22] or of Bill Clinton to interrupt his campaign schedule in 1992 to deny clemency to another death row inmate. The same is patently true of the new shame sanctions, which also have an immense power to mobilize popular sentiment. "Explicit attempts to express public anger and resentment," writes David Garland, are "a recurring theme of the rhetoric that accompanies penal legislation decision-making"; we have "politicization" and a "new populism."[23] We have, as Samuel Walker entitles his brief history of American crime and punishment, "popular justice" in the United States, and this is often a very harsh business.[24]

Conversely, it is manifest that part of the reason that the retributive temper has not established itself in France and Germany is that democratic politics has much less impact on criminal justice in Europe than it does in the United States. The European media report on horrible crimes just as the American media do; but continental politicians do not have the success of American ones in playing on the fear of crime. European state apparatuses remain highly *autonomous*, largely steered by bureaucracies that are far more insulated from democratic pressures than are American bureaucracies. Continental states simply are not seeing the kind of politics that produced California's "Three-Strikes-and-You're-Out" legislation—politics, as Frank Zimring observes, of "populist preemption of criminal justice policy making," "almost entirely devoid of expert scrutiny from governmental specialists or from scholars."[25] The kind of politics that goes over well in American mass democracy goes over much less well in the bureaucrat-heavy world of continental Europe; the French prison scandal of 2000 is only the most recent example. The "openly avowed expression of vengeful sentiment," to quote Garland again, remains "taboo" in these historically much more bureaucratized cultures.[26]

One consequence is simply that criminological theories remain much more influential in continental Europe, as Zimring and other specialists like Samuel Pillsbury would hope they might.[27] But there are also consequences for the general psychology of punishment—for, as it were, the mood. Bureaucracies tend to have just what Weber said that they have: a routinized attitude that prevents them from getting all that worked up. The sort of unbridled punitiveness in punishment that has become a part of American legal culture does not arise easily or often among bureaucrats. Even in America, professionals tend to see criminal justice issues in a relatively tepid, routinized way—like the head of the New York Correctional Association, who opposed Cuomo's prison building program.[28] To the extent officials have absorbed the bureaucratic ethos, they tend to "go by the book"—to follow rules rather than impulses toward the exercise of petty authority. This has an impact on their behavior on the job. Tepid bureaucratic routinization of criminal law is an important barrier to the kind of overheated democratic retributivism that has come to America.[29]

And tepid bureaucratic routinization sets much of the critical tone in German and French punishment. It is because of the strength of the bureaucratic tradition that prison guards are trained civil servants. Moreover, it is worth reiterating that where there are scandals in German and French prisons, they overwhelmingly involve the institutions that most easily escape bureaucratic control. The jails in which investigative custody prisoners are held are difficult places to manage. Their personnel have no control over the persons delivered to them, in unpredictable numbers, from day to day and night to night, and the inmates delivered are often persons for whom there is no data, no dossier—persons whom even bureaucrats of the greatest skill and the best will cannot keep under proper wraps. This tells on the lot of investigative custody detainees, who are often mixed in overcrowded cells without adequate measures to separate the violent from the passive.

Where bureaucracy works, though, it works both to shield the state from the pressures of democratic politics and to manage prisons and other punishments in a sober and disciplined way. And in Germany and France, bureaucracy often works. To be sure, there are elections in Europe, and there are politicians. Nevertheless, the bureaucrats of Europe have a surprising capacity to set the tone even of political debate. The death penalty makes perhaps the most striking example. As Zimring and Hawkins observe in their study of the death penalty in American politics, there is always majority opposition to abolition of the death penalty in every country: America is not distinctive in this. What sets America apart is the relatively easy translation of majority sentiment into policy. In other countries—including those of continental Europe—government actors initiate abolition and slowly manage to bring public opinion around.[30] The bureaucrats continue to hold the reins of leadership must more tightly in Europe, just as they have for generations.

The strength of the bureaucratized European state also helps explain another crucial aspect of mildness in French and German punishment: the capacity of French and German law to define some forbidden acts as something less awful than "crimes"—as mere *contraventions* or *Ordnungswidrigkeiten*. When European jurists define these species of forbidden conduct, they are able to make use of terms and concepts that would trouble Americans. The justification for punishing *Ordnungswidrigkeiten*, according to standard texts, lies in the pure sovereign prerogative of the state. Because the state is sovereign, the state may declare certain types of behavior impermissible.[31] Americans will instinctively rebel against this characteristically continental attitude toward state power; very few American legal syllogisms begin with the major premise, "the state has sovereign power to act." But it is important to recognize what Europeans gain by pursuing this form of analysis. Because they are able to defer to state power, they are able to treat some offenses as merely forbidden, rather than as evil—as *mala prohibita* rather than *mala in se*. The contrast with the United States is strong: our liberal, antistatist tradition leads us to conclude that nothing may be forbidden by the state unless it is *evil*; otherwise the state would have no right to forbid us to do it.[32] Indeed, we still have much of the quasi-Christian attitude that David Rothman identified in describing the prerevolutionary American world: "The identification of disorder with sin," he writes, "made it difficult for legislators and ministers to distinguish carefully between major and minor infractions."[33] Rothman treats this attitude as one that vanished with the nineteenth century; but it is manifestly still with us. In consequence we have a harder time than Europeans do thinking of some acts as not permitted, but nevertheless not terribly serious. This matters a great deal: as we have seen, the classification of offenses as something less than criminal is an important predicate for the mildness of punishment in France and Germany. Because no one doubts the power of the state to forbid behavior, it is possible for European jurists to proscribe some forms of conduct without stigmatizing those forms of conduct as "evil" and without harshly punishing those who engage in those forms of conduct.

The power and autonomy of the state thus have a great deal to do with the relative mildness of criminal justice in France and Germany. A relatively weak state, like the American one, is much more prey to a harsh retributive politics than these continental states are, and less able to forbid acts without branding them as evil.

Finally, the power of continental states has brought with it a lasting attachment to the values of mercy. As we have seen, the exercise of grace has been exceedingly important all through the twentieth century in Europe, and that fact is a clue to a last critically important difference between the traditions of the European and American state apparatuses. Mercy matters in Europe, sometimes in the literal form of amnesties, sometimes in a vaguer proneness to individualize justice. The European states are still, at a very distant remove, the successors of the quasi-sacral monarchical states of the early modern period. They still maintain their public legitimacy, in part, in the way that they did in the early modern period, and indeed the Middle Ages: by bestowing grace and mercy. This tradition has done very valuable things for European offenders.

That kind of strong, indeed sacral, state tradition is absent in the United States—as two centuries of American discomfort with the pardoning power suggests. Technically the "pardoning power" and the parole power are understood as hanging together in the United States, just as they are in Europe. But by contrast with Europe, the tradition of pardoning in America is weak, and perennially endangered. The weakness of a pardoning tradition is the weakness of a larger tradition of a kind of seigneurial mildness. European state officials continue to behave in some measure like indulgent *seigneurs*—or indeed, like Roman jurists, who used to show "liberality" and "benevolence" in giving justice just as they showed "liberality" and "benevolence" in giving dinner parties, and this helps to keep European punishment practice mild. Our style of egalitarianism leaves little room for that sort of liberality.

All this is not to deny that European traditions of state power can have aspects that seem fearsome to Americans. Our kind of bred-in-the-bone suspiciousness of state power is absent in Europe, and the tradition of strong procedural protections against the workings of the criminal justice system remains weaker there. There is perhaps no example more striking to Americans than the *Meldepflicht*, the German obligation to be registered with the authorities. The effort to introduce any such obligation in the United States would undoubtedly stir up massive resistance. Nevertheless, even with regard toward procedural protections, Europeans have been pressing toward *mildness*: France has its new "law on the presumption of innocence"; Germany has many restrictions on the use of investigative custody. Europeans have never cared as much about procedural protections as Americans, but they care more and more. The drive in continental Europe is toward mildness, and this means that the relatively mild and indulgent aspects of continental state power can come increasingly to the fore.

The Nazi Parallel

Let me now turn to what has been a persistent subterranean theme of this book: the resemblance between the criminal justice of the United States today and the criminal justice of the fascists, and in particular of the Nazis.

This is an extremely delicate point. Let me emphasize that I do not want to say something that only the stupid and ignorant would say: that we have fascism in America. Nevertheless, when the topic is "primitive" retributivism, the resemblance between fascist and contemporary American punishment practices is too close, and too disturbing, not to be discussed. We do not have programmatic racism in American criminal punishment, and we certainly do not have anything like the Nazi program of sterilization. And yet, two major

Western legal traditions have abandoned individualization in favor of retributivism, and done so amidst strikingly similar declarations: the United States, beginning in the mid-1970s, and the Nazis, beginning in 1933. Two major legal traditions have devoted themselves to the permanent elimination of habitual offenders, through both life and death sentences: the United States, beginning in the mid-1970s, and the Nazis, beginning in 1933. Two major Western legal traditions have experimented with reviving public shame sanctions: the United States, beginning in the mid-1970s, and the Nazis, beginning in 1933. Does this signify anything?

It does not signify that the United States is fascist; there was a lot more involved in being fascist than that. What it does signify is something that we can see in many other aspects of the comparison between twentieth-century America and fascist Europe. Fascism was, in a sense, exactly what it claimed to be: a "truly" democratic system—or at least, a system truly founded on techniques of mass mobilization. Now, the techniques of mass mobilization, at least in criminal justice, are few. They mostly have to do with making appeals to the same ugly stirrings that are to be found in human beings everywhere, whether they are Americans of the 1990s or Germans of the 1930s. Retributive politics of criminal justice are in this sense not different from radio addresses and mass rallies: all of these techniques lend themselves naturally to mobilizing mass support. This means that in the absence of some countervailing tendency—such as the leveling up tendency in Europe, such as the bureaucratic tradition—politics of mass mobilization are likely to produce a very harsh kind of retributive criminal justice.

The irony, of course, is that certain countervailing tendencies *were* present in Nazi Germany—and to that extent, there was a shade *more* of a drive toward dignity, and even mildness, in punishment in Nazi Germany, at least for ordinary criminals, than there is in America today. This has to do, as we seen, primarily with traditions of mercy. The drive toward mildness in Nazi criminal justice grew largely out of the politics of *grace*. This is something essentially missing in the United States. We are like the Nazis up to a point. Like the Nazis, we too have become committed to the proposition that punishment should be an "empfindliches Übel"—"something nasty enough to make them hurt." But for the Nazis the underlying traditions of de haut en bas indulgence remained strong and tended to cabin somewhat the drive toward harshness. There is, by contrast, little that holds us back.

The Sociology of "Modernity" and the Diversity of Legal Cultures

Criminal punishment in America, France, and Germany is deeply different; and this should be enough to make us skeptical of any sociology that claims that some single "modernity" is likely to engulf the entire human world.

That hardly means that our theoretical sociology is all wrong. On the contrary, there is a great deal of wisdom to be drawn from it—as long as we are careful to resist overgeneralizing its conclusions, and as long as we remember the importance of status in punishment. In particular, there is a great deal of wisdom to be drawn from the ideas of Durkheim and of Norbert Elias, and of David Garland as well; and not least from the ideas of Gustav Radbruch.

First of all, Durkheim. Durkheim has experienced a revival of late, and for good reason. Criminal punishment does indeed have the quality that Durkheim, like George Herbert Mead, emphasized most: its capacity to stir collective emotion.[34] This is something that we see very clearly in the United States today. But it deserves emphasizing how much less clearly we see the same phenomenon in Europe. It is not the case that the Durkheimian dynamic is equally present in all "modern" societies. On the contrary, there are striking divergences—divergences that have to do with the fundamental differences I have discussed in this book. Collective emotion is stirred in the process of American democracy; by contrast, democratic politicking simply does not shape criminal justice in Europe in the same way. Collective emotion is also stirred by degradation: part of what excites people is the degradation of offenders. There too the United States is different. No account of Durkheim that failed to take account of these differences could be adequate.

Something similar is true of Elias. My arguments in this book run closely parallel to some of Elias's arguments—though not to the arguments of Elias that have made the most headway in the literature on punishment. Elias argued that modern societies had been formed by a "civilizing process." This civilizing process began, according to Elias, in court society—among court aristocrats, who were the first class of persons compelled to curb their grosser and more violent instincts. Norms of "civilized" behavior that first established themselves in court politesse were gradually extended throughout society, so that decent and peaceable behavior became standard throughout all orders of society. These claims have been embraced by some of our shrewdest historians of punishment—most notably Pieter Spierenburg.[35] Both the decline of violence in society at large, and the decline of corporal violence in criminal punishment, has been attributed to the progress of an Eliasian "civilizing process."

I have expressed some doubts about Elias's claims elsewhere.[36] Nevertheless, the notion that such a "civilizing process" has been at work seems to me clearly correct, and so does the notion that norms have spread from the higher orders of society to the lower. Indeed, it is not just that norms of *comportment* have spread from court society; norms of *treatment* have spread from court society too—so that in continental Europe, as I have argued at length, there is strong drive to treat all persons as though they were persons of high status. Much is thus true about what Elias says. But what is true about Elias is *primarily true about continental Europe*: his claims apply much more poorly to the United States. Rates of violence are higher in the United States—just as traditions of politesse are weaker. As for norms of high-status treatment, they simply have not established themselves here in the way that they have in Europe. Elias's sociology makes for a brilliant, and endlessly fertile, account of continental Europe. It does not qualify, though, as a sociology of some uniform world "modernity."

Nor does the sociology of David Garland. Garland has written shrewdly about the functioning of the penal system within the welfare state. Criminal offenders, he observes, generally belong to the same broad swathe of low-income citizens who are cared for by states with social welfare policies. Correspondingly, classic rehabilitationist approaches resemble other social welfare policies. Inmates are low-income clients, served by social welfare professionals just as other low-income clients are. This seems to me entirely correct, at least as an account of France and Germany. Indeed, we cannot understand current continental prison practices if we do not recognize that they are integrated into the social welfare order of their societies. But once again, if it is correct as an account of continental Europe, it does not describe the United States well at all. France and Germany cling to their social welfare states, and they cling to rehabilitationist practices as well. This is not well explained by describing them as "modern." It better explained by observing they have stronger state traditions than ours. It is also, I would suggest, better explained by observing they have stronger traditions of de haut en bas mercy. These are countries with a history of noblesse oblige, in a word—countries in which it has been a part of high status to show condescending care for one's inferiors for a long time. This shows in continental prisons, just as it shows in continental welfare states.

Finally, let me turn from sociology to legal history, and in particular to Gustav Radbruch's account of the origin of punishment. Radbruch, to reiterate, thought that criminal punishment in Germany had originated in the punishment of slaves—that low-status treatment had crept up the status ladder. This was a powerful analytic claim, and this book is meant in many ways as an extension of its core insight that the history of punishment is intimately connected with the history of social status. In this as in other ways, Radbruch is something of the hero of this book. But we have to be careful in generalizing Radbruch's claim. In particular, we have to resist Sellin's way of using Radbruch. Sellin thought that *all* criminal punishment had grown out of low-status treatment. This is not quite what Radbruch claimed—his focus was on medieval Germany, and in a sense, on Nazi Germany—and it is not so. All criminal punishment does *not* grow out of low-status treatment. What is true is that all criminal punishment has *something* to do with status; but it is a mistake to imagine that that something is always the same.

This brings me, finally, to the narrowness of my own claims. This book is about three societies and three societies alone. I do not mean to repeat the errors of earlier generations by claiming to have identified uniform "laws of penal evolution." There is no reason to expect that other societies will all take the same turns that the United States, Germany, or France have taken. There is nothing inevitable about either the American path or the continental one. Neither is "the" modern path. In particular, I am *not* claiming, in this book, that all societies with sharply defined status hierarchies necessarily evolve into countries with mild punishment practices. That claim would be manifestly false—as the case of China, for example, strongly suggests. Nor am I claiming that strong states always produce mild punishments. That too would be a manifestly false claim.[37]

What I am claiming is something else: not that all societies must take the same path, or even one of two paths. I am claiming that questions of the traditions of status, and of the traditions of state authority, always matter. The history of the growing divide in the Atlantic world of the last quarter century does not tell us how punishment always evolves, but it does suggest what forces are always at work. Traditions of status hierarchy do not always produce mild punishment; but traditions of status always affect the trajectory of the development of punishment. They do so, however, in different and unpredictable ways. Thus we can guess that broadly similar Confucian traditions of status hierarchy stand in the historical background of contemporary realities in both Japan (a place of proverbially mild practices) and China (a place of fearsomely harsh ones). The Confucian tradition certainly does not dictate any single contemporary result, but it surely consistently plays some role. By the same token, traditions of state authority and autonomy can play very different roles, but they always play *some* role. Both degradation and state power are always at stake in criminal punishment. How degradation and state power play themselves out in any given society depends, though, on unpredictable currents in the traditions of authority—both of the authorities of social status and of the authority of the state.

Degradation and Mercy

At its core, indeed, the difference between the United States and northern continental Europe is a difference in traditions of *authority*, for both degradation and state power are about authority. It is fifteen years since Mirjan Damaska analyzed the structures of authority that underlay American and continental procedure in his celebrated book *The Faces of Justice and State Authority*.[38] Continental justice, he argued, displayed hierarchical authority where American justice displayed coordinate authority. Damaska offered this as a claim about procedure, but the same claim can be made about the spirit of these systems much more broadly. The European systems do indeed show the traces of a deeply hierarchical concept of authority—both of the hierarchical personal authority that surrounds status, and of hierarchical authority of the state.

That is not to say that French and German societies are in any simple way "hierarchical." On the contrary, both societies have changed profoundly since the hierarchical eighteenth century. Rather, it is to say that, over two centuries of revolutionary change, the legal traditions of both societies have been wrestling with the same deep-seated assumption: the assumption that human relations fall naturally into hierarchical patterns. Continental jurists have always assumed that the tenacity of the hierarchical impulse in human society means that degradation is an ever-present danger. They have also always assumed that the state had a kind of natural authority over its subjects. In the United States, we have never worked with the assumption that there is anything natural about hierarchy. As Lawrence Friedman puts it, in a formula that echoes Damaska's, we are attached, broadly speaking, to the values of a "horizontal" society.[39]

This has ultimately led us to different, and harsher, attitudes toward criminal punishment. *Our* traditions of authority—really, our traditions of opposition to authority—have given us a criminal justice system long on degradation and short on mercy. This may be the way we want it. If it is not, there is certainly nothing to stop us from trying to overcome the traditions that have brought us to this point—though it is hard to be confident that we can really transcend them. If mildness comes to America, it seems more likely to come from a different quarter entirely: from our Christian tradition. What Tocqueville and Beaumont observed a hundred and seventy years ago has the ring of truth once again: "In America, the movement that has shaped reform has been essentially religious,"[40] and any progress of reform in the immediate future is likely to be Christian in tone. Certainly the Christian tradition has its own resources of dignity and mercy: Christianity has a long history of declaring that the aim of punishment is to *chastise* rather than to *avenge*.[41] To paraphrase the leading French criminal lawyer of the years before the French Revolution: "Following the maxims of canon law, one can take the attitude of a stern but caring father, never forgetting that if human beings are prey to weaknesses, they nevertheless remain human beings."[42] The idea of a Christianized America carries its own discomforts, though, and *chastisement* in the practice of punishment carries its own dangers. For the moment, in any case, real change does not loom; and real change would mean change, not just in punishment practices but in much grander American cultural traditions. It would be foolish to think that such change is coming soon.

Notes

Introduction

1 "U.S. Population behind Bars Reaches Record Two Million," Agence France Presse, Aug. 13, 2001. Counting noncustodial supervision, the figures are far higher. See "National Correctional Population Reaches New High," U.S. Newswire, Aug. 26, 2001.

2. "Police Arrest Smokers in Subways, and Lawyers Object," *New York Times*, June 11, 2000, 48; "A New Subway Unit Tickets 2,143 Riders in Drive on Smokers," *New York Times*, April 29, 1983.

3. *Atwater v. City of Lago Vista*, 121 S. Ct. 2450; 150 L. Ed. 2d 709 (2001).

4. Quoted and discussed, along with other examples, in Craig Haney, "Riding the Punishment Wave: On the Origins of Our Devolving Standards of Decency," *Hastings Women's Law Journal* 9 (1998): 27, 32.

5. M. Tonry, Preface, in Tonry, ed., *The Handbook of Crime and Punishment* (Oxford, 1998), v.

6. For e.g., Pakistan: A. Jahangir and H. Jilani, *The Hudood Ordinances: A Divine Sanction*? (Lahore, 1990), 23–25. For a moving description of the shifts of the post-1975 period in Egypt, see K. Abou El Fadl, *And God Knows the Soldiers: The Authoritative and Authoritarian in Islamic Discourses* (Lanham/New York/Oxford, 2001), 1–22.

7. British parallels to American practice are traced in much detail by David Garland, *The Culture of Control: Crime and Social Order in Contemporary Society* (Chicago, 2001). Yet Garland acknowledges that the United States has "gone further" at, e.g., 7, 258 n.5. For the comparison, see also ibid., 9, 14, 168 and often. Some of the parallels in historical development are discussed in chapter 5 of this book.

8. E.g., "La justice américaine est plus sevère que jamais," *Le Monde*, Nov. 15, 1999. Cf. S. Body-Gendriot, "La politisation du thème de la criminalité aux États-Unis," *Déviance et Société* 23 (1999): 75–89.

9. E.g., "New Drug-Offender Program Draws Unexpected Clients," *New York Times*, Sept. 29, 2001, A6; "Court Rejects 3-Strikes Term for Shoplifter," *New York Times*, Nov. 3, 2001, A8; "13 States see Decline in Prison Population," *New York Times*, Aug. 13, 2001; "States Ease Laws on Time in Prison," *New York Times*, Sept. 2, 2001, A1.

10. See chapter 2 of this book.

11. "U.S. Population Behind Bars Reaches Record Two Million," Agence France Presse, Aug. 13, 2001; The Sentencing Project, "New Prison Population Figures Show Slowing of Growth But Uncertain Trends," Briefing Sheet #1044, available at http://www.sentencingproject.org/brief/pub1044.pdf, downloaded November 6, 2001).

12. See, e.g., "Man Accused of Illicit Sex Paraded Through Kabul Streets," Agence France Presse, Dec. 14, 1996, available in LEXIS, News Library, AFP File; "Taliban Parade Arrested Gamblers in Public with Blackened Faces," Agence France Presse, Nov. 30, 1996, available in LEXIS, News Library, AFP File.

13. See chapter 4 of this book.

14. Today, the literature is ordinarily broken down into four principal traditions: the Marxian, the Durkheimian, the Foucauldian, and the Eliasian. See esp. Garland, *Punishment and Modern Society: A Study in Social Theory* (Oxford, 1990). All four of these can be charged, in various ways and degrees, with postulating too uniform a "modernity." I will discuss all four in more detail in the conclusion to this book. The most imposing recent contributions to this literature come from Garland and Loïc Wacquant. Garland, *The Culture of Control*, is a study of "late modernity." Garland acknowledges that there are real variations, but sees those same forces at work everywhere. See *Culture of Control*, 201–202. Wacquant, *Les Prisons de la Misère* (Paris, 1999) presents the American model as establishing itself rapidly in Europe and elsewhere. Nevertheless he does contend that Europeans systems can still resist it. See ibid., 151. Garland in particular, I should emphasize, brings a learned skepticism to the claims of his predecessors in theoretical sociology. E.g., Garland, *Culture of Control*, 3: "Not even the most inventive reading of Foucault, Marx, Durkheim, and Elias could have predicted these recent developments."

15. E. Sutherland and D. Cressey, *Principles of Criminology*, 7th ed. (Philadelphia, 1966), 363.

16. See for example D. Nelken, "Whom Can You Trust? The Future of Comparative Criminology," in Nelken, ed., *The Futures of Criminology* (London, 1994), 220–243; D. Downes, *Contrasts in Tolerance* (Oxford, 1988); D. Foote, "The Benevolent Paternalism of Japanese Criminal Justice," *California Law Review* 80 (1992): 317. Lawrence Friedman, "Dead Hands: Criminal Justice Policy Past and Present," 27 *Cumberland Law Review* 27 (1996): 903, engages in a sustained, and fascinating, comparison of the United States with Japan. For a noble effort to explain differences in incarceration rates, though not other aspects of American harshness, see John Sutton, "Imprisonment and Social Classification in Five Common-Law Democracies, 1955–1985," *American Journal of Sociology* 106 (2000): 350–386. There is also a literature devoted to "learning across jurisdictional boundaries," in Michael Tonry's phrase. Tonry, *Sentencing Matters* (Oxford, 1996), 182. See, e.g., ibid., 174–189; Gary Friedman, Comment, "The West German Day-Fine System: A Possibility for the United States?" *University of Chicago Law Review* 50 (1983): 281. This literature focuses on seeking inspiration rather than explaining differences, however. Even studies rich on data about differ-

ences between Europe and America tend to focus on their commonalities—on overcrowding, in particular, as a common problem in Western prisons. See esp. M. Tonry and K. Hatlestad, eds., *Sentencing Reform in Overcrowded Times: A Comparative Perspective* (Oxford, 1997). It should be emphasized that the search for a single modernity in theoretical sociology is in some ways relatively recent. Scholarship of the period between roughly 1930 and 1970 was more concerned with explaining differences—an attitude that perhaps reflects the preoccupation of authors of that era with the problem of understanding fascism and communism. Among important efforts to explain different patterns of punishment in this middle period of the twentieth century was Pitirim Sorokin's proposed law of heterogeneity, which made severity in punishment a function of the degree of "ethicojuridical heterogeneity and antagonism" in a given society. See Sorokin, *Social and Culture Dynamics* (New York, 1962), 2:595. Also a product of the same era was G. Rusche and O. Kirchheimer's well-known *Punishment and Social Structure* (repr. New York, 1968; orig. 1939), which attempted to link differences in modern punishment to conditions in the labor market. Of these, Rusche and Kirchheimer's analysis remains by far the more vigorous in the current literature. See, e.g., Jonathan Simon, "Power without Parents: Juvenile Justice in a Postmodern Society," *Cardozo Law Review* 16 (1995): 1363, 1366, who observes that growing punitiveness toward teenage males grows partly from loss of "labor market and working-class culture (toward which the juvenile court once aimed at steering troubled youth)"; D. Melossi and M. Pavarini, *Carcere e fabbrica : alle origini del sistema penitenziario (XVI–XIX secolo)*, 3d ed. (Bologna, 1982). For a recent defense of their hypothesis, see T. Chiricos and M. Delone, "Labour Surplus and Punishment," *Social Problems* 39, no. 4 (1992): 421–446; for a recent expression of doubt, see Garland, *Punishment and Modern Society*, 107–109. For a plague-on-all-your-houses view of the success of sociological efforts to account for American incarceration, see M. Tonry and J. Petersilia, "American Prisons at the Beginning of the Twenty-First Century," in Tonry and Petersilia, eds., *Prisons, Crime, and Justice: A Review of Research* 26 (1999): 1–2.

17. For a start on this topic, see F. Zimring and G. Hawkins, *Crime is Not the Problem: Lethal Violence in America* (New York, 1997); J. Lynch, "A Comparison of Prison Use in England, Canada, West Germany, and the United States: A Limited Test of the Punitive Hypothesis," *Journal of Criminal Law and Criminology* 79 (1988): 180–217. Adequately analyzing comparative violence would take us well beyond what criminal statistics would tell us, since it would have to include such questions as child- and spouse-beating, school discipline, and more. This is project I do not tackle in this book.

18. Alexis de Tocqueville, *De la Démocratie en Amérique* (Paris, 1981), 1:114; S. Lipset, *It Didn't Happen Here: Why Socialism Failed in the United States* (New York, 2000), 28–31; L. Hartz, *The Liberal Tradition in America* (New York, 1955).

19. Tocqueville, *De la Démocratie en Amérique*, 2:205, 209.

20. See the fuller discussion of Durkheim in the conclusion of this book.

21. James Whitman, "Enforcing Civility and Respect: Three Societies," *Yale Law Journal* 109 (2000): 1279–1398.

22. R. Jhering, *Der Zweck im Recht* (repr. Hildesheim, 1970), 2: 524; N. Elias, *Über den Prozess der Zivilisation. Soziogenetische und Psychogenetische Untersuchungen*, 2 vols. (Frankfurt a. M., 1997); P. Bourdieu, *La Distinction: Critique Sociale du Jugement* (Paris, 1979). Jhering's great work on manners deserves far more attention than it receives.

23. Montesquieu, *De L'Esprit des Lois* (Paris, 1979), 1:210–211 (Bk. VI, Chap. IX). There is a kinship, of course, between Montesquieu's ideas and those of Tocqueville.

For the shared intellectual project of the two in analyzing "democratic republics," see M. Richter, "The Uses of Theory: Tocqueville's Adaptation of Montesquieu," in Richter, ed., *Essays in Theory and History: An Approach to the Social Sciences* (Cambridge, 1970), 83–87, 95–97; and for their shared "inspiration libérale," see J.-C. Lamberti, *Tocqueville et les deux Démocraties* (Paris, 1983), 30–32.

24. Durkheim, "Two Laws of Penal Evolution," in M. Gane, ed., *The Radical Sociology of Durkheim and Mauss* (London, 1992), 21.

25. This is the background problematic, for example, of N. Lacey, *State Punishment: Political Principles and Community Values* (London, 1988); see also Garland, *Punishment and Modern Society*, 39.

26. See R. H. Helmholz, "The Privilege and the *Ius Commune*: The Middle Ages to the Seventeenth Century," in Helmholz et al., eds. *The Privilege Against Self-Incrimination: Its Origins and Development* (Chicago, 1997), 17–46.

27. Kant, *Metaphysische Angfangsgründe der Rechtslehre*, ed. B. Ludwig, 2d ed. (Hamburg, 1998), 155. Kant's philosophy of punishment is considerably more elusive than the quotation of this one passage suggests. See J. Murphy, "Does Kant have a Theory of Punishment?" *Columbia Law Review* 87 (1987): 509–532.

28. Garland, *Culture of Control*, 9, 13–14; S. Walker, *Popular Justice: A History of American Criminal Justice*, 2d ed. (New York, 1998).

Chapter 1

1. See, e.g., *Soering v. United Kingdom*, 161 Eur. Ct. H.R. (ser. A) (1989), reprinted in 11 Eur. Hum. Rts. Rep. 439 (1989), 28 ILM 1063 (1989); *Ireland v. United Kingdom*, 25 Eur. Ct. H.R. (ser. A) (1978); and, more recently, *Prosecutor v. Furundzija*, 38 I.L.M. 317 (1999).

2. In *Denmark v. Greece* (1972), 12 Yearbook 186, the European Commission defined "degrading treatment" for purposes of Article 3 of the Convention for the Protection of Human Rights and Fundamental Freedoms as treatment that "grossly humiliates" an individual, or forces him to act "against his will or conscience." The first of these phrases is of course the one relevant to my discussion here. With its use of the term *grossly* its practical application is inevitably unpredictable. The Convention Against Torture and Other Cruel, Inhuman or Degrading Treatment does not undertake to define "degradation."

3. This corresponds to the first part of the definition in Article 1 of the Convention Against Torture and Other Cruel, Inhuman or Degrading Treatment: "the term 'torture' means any act by which severe pain or suffering, whether physical or mental, is intentionally inflicted on a person for such purposes as obtaining from him or from a third person information or a confession, punishing him for an act he or a third person has committed or is suspected of having committed, or intimidating or coercing him or a third person, or for any reason based on discrimination of any kind, when such pain or suffering is inflicted by or at the instigation of or with the consent or acquiescence of a public official or other person acting in an official capacity."

The definition explicitly makes exception for "pain or suffering arising from, inherent in or incidental to lawful sanctions." The definition adopted by Congress in 18 U.S.C. § 2340 (1), which implements the same Convention in the United States, is strikingly different: "'torture' means an act committed by a person acting under the color of law specifically intended to inflict severe physical or mental pain or suffering (other than pain or suffering incidental to lawful sanctions) upon another person within his custody or physical control." Americans have little sense of the technical meaning of "torture." This may in part reflect the differences in a European tradition that developed in reaction to the practices of torture still current in the eighteenth century on the continent: Europeans have a more lively memory of the uses of torture than Americans do.

4. E.g., P. Farinaccius, *Tractatus Integer de Testibus* (Osnabrück, 1677), 644 (q. 79. nu. 60); G. MacCormack, *The Spirit of Traditional Chinese Law* (Athens, 1996), 229 n. 5; M. Halm-Tisserant, *Réalités et imaginaire des supplices en Grèce ancienne* (Paris, 1998), 111–119; P. Garnsey, "Why Penalties Become Harsher: The Roman Case, Late Republic to Fourth Century Empire," *Natural Law Forum* 13 (1968): 151.

5. H. Popitz, *Phänomene der Macht*, 2d. ed. (Tübingen, 1992), 45–46.

6. M. Duncan, *Romantic Outlaws, Beloved Prisons* (New York, 1996), 121–187.

7. T. Des Pres, *The Survivor: An Anatomy of Life in the Death Camps* (New York, 1976), 52–71.

8. H. Garfinkel, "Conditions of Successful Degradation Ceremonies," *American Journal of Sociology* 61 (1956): 420–424.

9. E. Goffman, *Asylums: Essays on the Social Situation of Mental Patients and Other Inmates* (New York, 1961), 14-74.

10. Cf. M. Douglas, *Purity and Danger: An Analysis of Concepts of Pollution and Taboo* (London, 1978); L. Dumont, *Homo Hierarchicus: Le Système des Castes et ses Implications* (Paris, 1979). See also the useful account in L. de Heusch, préface to Douglas, *De la Souillure: Essais sur les Notions de Pollution et de Tabou*, trans. A. Guérin (Paris, 2000).

11. F. Nietzsche *Zur Genealogie der Moral. Eine Streitschrift, Erste Abhandlung*, Paragraph 15, in Nietzsche, *Kritische Studienausgabe*, eds. G. Colli and M. Montinari (Berlin, 1999), 5: 283–285.

12. J. Hampton and J. Murphy, *Forgiveness and Mercy* (Cambridge, 1988), 125.

13. Ibid., 130.

14. J. Hampton, "An Expressive Theory of Retribution," in W. Cragg, ed., *Retributivism and its Critics* (Stuttgart, 1992), 14, 16.

15. D. Allen, *The World of Prometheus: The Politics of Punishing in Democratic Athens* (Princeton, 2000), 70; for Hampton's invocation of this concept, see "Expressive Theory of Retribution," 18 and 25 n. 26.

16. See the discussion in Allen, *World of Prometheus*, 69–70.

17. K. J. Dover, "Fathers, Sons and Forgiveness," *Illinois Classical Studies* 16 (1991): 177.

18. See M. MacKenzie, *Plato on Punishment* (Berkeley, 1981), 106–120, 179–206.

19. Matthew 25:46.

20. Clement of Alexandria, *Miscellanies*, Book VII, ed. J. Hart and J. Mayor (New York and London, 1987), 180.

21. Augustine, Epistle 133, in J.-P. Migne, *Patrologia Latina* (repr. Turnhout, 1983), 33: col. 509.

22. See K. Bradley, *Slavery and Society Rome* (Cambridge, 1994), 28–29; R. Saller, "Corporal Authority, Punishment, Authority and Obedience in the Roman Household," in B. Rawson, ed., *Marriage, Divorce and Children in Ancient Rome* (Canberra/Oxford, 1991), 157–160.

23. For a Catholic example: Muyart de Vouglans, *Institutes au Droit Criminel ou Principes Généraux sur ces Matières* (Paris, 1768), 281; for the Protestant world, the image of "castigatio" at the entrance to the Amsterdam *rasphuis*, described in P. Spierenburg, *The Prison Experience: Disciplinary Institutions and Their Inmates in Early Modern Europe* (New Brunswick, N.J., 1991), 88.

24. Jefferson, *Notes on the State of Virginia*, ed. W. Peden (Chapel Hill, 1955), 162. For similar sentiments from Brissot de Warville and Francis Wayland, see A. Hirsch, *The Rise of the Penitentiary: Prisons and Punishment in Early America* (New Haven, 1992), 73 and 198 n. 23.

25. Cf. [Theodore Weld,] *American Slavery As It Is: Testimony of a Thousand Witnesses* (New York, 1839) (repr. 1968), 187–188.

26. William Shakespeare, *Measure for Measure*, ed. B. Gibbons (Cambridge, 1990), 2:2, 122–124. I have reversed the order of these famous lines.

27. Bentham, *Principles of Penal* Law, in *The Works of Jeremy Bentham*, ed. J. Bowring, 11 vols. (Edinburgh: William Tait, 1843), 1:401.

28. E.g., E. Beardsley, "A Plea for Deserts,"*American Philosophical Quarterly* 6 (1969): 36; J. Weiler, "Why Do We Punish? The Case for Retributive Justice," *University of British Columbia Law Review* 12 (1978): 295–319, esp. 310–316 (1978); S. Gendin, "A Plausible Theory of Retribution," *Journal of Value Inquiry* 5 (1970): 1; J. Finnis, "The Restoration of Retributivism," *Analysis* 32 (1972): 131; generally, A. von Hirsch, *Censure and Sanctions* (Oxford, 1993).

29. A. von Hirsch and U. Narayan, "Degradingness and Intrusiveness," in Hirsch, *Censure and Sanctions*, 80–87, provides, as the authors note "more questions than answers," Ibid., 87. Murphy, "Cruel and Unusual Punishment," in Murphy, *Retribution, Justice and Therapy* (Dordrecht, 1979), 233–249, makes a more sustained Kantian effort to reject degradation.

30. For a statement of this critique, see D. Garland, "Philosophical Argument and Ideological Effect: An Essay Review," *Contemporary Crises* 7 (1983): 79–85.

31. Braithwaite, *Crime, Shame, and Reintegration* (Cambridge, 1989).

32. Kahan, "What do Alternative Sanctions Mean?" *University of Chicago Law Review* 63 (1996): 591.

33. I have offered this argument at greater length in Whitman, "What is Wrong with Inflicting Shame Sanctions?" *Yale Law Journal* 107 (1998): 1055–1092.

34. In American military law, this is no longer the case: except in wartime, and except by special order of the relevant cabinet official, officers may no longer be reduced in rank. See "Rules for Courts-Martial," 1003 (c) (2) (A) (i)—though enlisted men may still be reduced in rank. "Rules for Courts-Martial," 1003 (b) (4). Nevertheless, some of the old sensibility survives in the prohibition on "hard labor without confinement" for officers. "Rules for Courts-Martial," 1003 (c) (2) (A) (iii). For the older state of affairs, with the tradition of reduction in rank for officers, see E.g., *A Manual for Courts-Martial* (Washington, 1920), 249–250.

35. For Byzantine dignities, in general, often symbolized by a device called a "brabeion": N. Oikonomides, *Les Listes de préséance byzantines du IXe et Xe siècle* (Paris, 1972); for illustrations of Chinese rank dress, C. Roberts, ed., *Chinese Dress, 1700s–1900s* (Sydney, 1997), 32–33; and for a general account, A. C. Scott, *Chinese Costume in Transition* (Singapore, 1958), 11–28.

36. For deprivation of rank in Byzantium, see R. Guilland, *Recherches sur les Institutions Byzantines* (Berlin, 1967), 1:38–39. It is worth noting that mere deprivation was not the only sanction. Byzantine dignities were "sticky": It was not easy to strip their holder of them. Consequently, within the elaborate Byzantine system, *dilution* of status also worked as a punishment: new titles and offices could be created that diminished the relative precedence of the punished or disfavored person. See ibid. For reduction in rank in China, D. Bodde and C. Morris, *Law in Imperial China* (Philadelphia, 1967), 80; A.F.P. Hulsewé, *Remnants of Han Law* (Leiden, 1955), 1: 204, 216–222. In Chinese practices, deprivation of the dress and courtesies of rank was inflicted even

on the Song emperors after their defeat by the Jin. See F. W. Mote, *Imperial China, 900–1800* (Cambridge, Mass., 1999), 197. For examples from more familiar Western societies: in France, F. Serpillon, *Code Criminel our Commentaire sur l'Ordonnance de 1670* (Lyon, 1767), 680 and 1524 n.; for England, the case of Titus Oates, discussed in chapter 5 of this book.

37. James Wilson, "Lectures in Law," in Wilson, *Works*, ed. R. McCloskey (Cambridge, MA, 1967), 1:403 (orig. 1792).

38. For the five types of punishment in traditional Chinese law (which were quite close in character to the early modern continental European punishments), see Bodde and Morris, *Law in Imperial China*, 76–112; for their continental counterparts, see chapter 4 in this book. China has a complex history. I hope it will be obvious that this book does not offer any but the most cursory and inadequate discussion of Chinese punishment.

39. For the shaved head in Germanic law, J. Thorsten Sellin, *Slavery and the Penal System* (New York, 1976), 38; in ancient China, A. F. P. Hulsewé, *Remnants of Ch'in Law* (Leiden, 1985), 14–16; this was broadly true, in the ancient world, not only of slaves, but also of persons deformed by birth or accident. Persons with imperfect bodies were generally not permitted to participate directly in the religious rituals that were the principal public markers of high status. See my discussion in Whitman, "At the Origins of Law and the State: Supervision of Violence, Mutilation of Bodies, or Setting of Prices?" *Chicago-Kent Law Review* 71 (1995): 41, 77–79.

40. There are complexities of the psychology of these punishments that I cannot discuss in the text. In particular, the psychologies both of disgust and of humiliation are of central importance. The importance of disgust as an element of some degrading punishments shows particularly clearly in the case of mutilation. Most of us, when we encounter a mutilated person, are overcome by feelings of disgust or horror. (This is more true today than it was in the premodern world; but it was true in the premodern world as well.) A person who has been mutilated is commonly a person who has been made *repulsive*. These feelings of disgust and horror are not unrelated to the structure of human status hierarchy, as Mary Douglas argues. Mutilation is thus only typical of a much larger class of punishments: of punishments that diminish the standing of the offender by associating him with the degradation of the disgusting and horrific. For a brilliant effort to draw the connections between disgust and the social order, see W. Miller, *The Anatomy of Disgust* (Cambridge, 1997).

Spanking and comparable punishments also operate in ways that are more complex than any simple symbolic rank-marking. What predominates in spanking and the many other punishments that involve baring the buttocks is not so much *disgust*, however, as *humiliation*. Spanking and the like belong to a large class of punishments that involve stripping the offender naked or compelling the offender to defecate symbolically. These sorts of punishments tend to focus on the offender's lower functions: on sex and excretion. Such punishments almost always involve public display of the offender—though they typically do not mark the offender permanently. What they publicly display, however, is not precisely the offender's *low social rank*. Rather, what they display (as I have argued at length elsewhere; see Whitman, "What is Wrong with Inflicting Shame Sanctions?") is the offender's *animal nature*. They tend to humiliate the offender by publicly exposing him as a mere body. This too is a form of degradation—a form of degradation that, in an attenuated way, appears in all public shaming penalties. We can think of it, in its own way, as a rank-oriented form of degradation, if we think of humans as being more highly ranked than animals.

41. Halm-Tisserant, *Réalités et imaginaire des supplices*, 119–138. There are exam-

ples of status-marking in which higher-status persons are treated *more* harshly: See, e.g., Bodde and Morris, *Law in Imperial China*, 135. I leave this issue for another occasion.

42. See M. Hall, "Sanctions in Athens," in L. Foxhall and A. Lewis, *Greek Law in its Political Setting* (Oxford, 1996), 83. There may have been something of a tradition of thinking such status abuse was appropriate for plotters of tyranny: Cf. Plato, *Gorgias*, 472: "If a man is caught in a criminal plot to make himself tyrant, and when caught is put to the rack and mutilated and has his eyes burned out and after himself suffering and seeing his wife and children suffer many other signal outrages of various kinds is finally impaled or burned in a coat of pitch," trans. W. D. Woodhead, in E. Hamilton and H. Cairns, eds., *The Collected Dialogues of Plato* (Princeton, 1961), 255.

43. For a survey of European jurisprudence, J. Döpler, *Theatrum Poenarum, Suppliciorum et Executionum Criminalium, oder Schau-Platz derer Leibes- und Lebensstraffen* (Sondershausen: In Verlegung des Autoris, 1693–1697), 1:113–1140.

44. This was by no means forgotten in the early modern period. Indeed, hanging, shameful punishment that it was, was sometimes directly related to crucifixion. See B. Carpzov, *Practica Nova Imperialis Saxonica Rerum Criminalium* (Wittenberg: Mevius and Schumacher, 1677), 3:242.

45. R. MacMullen, "Judicial Savagery in the Roman Empire," in MacMullen, *Changes in the Roman Empire: Essays in the Ordinary* (Princeton, 1990), 211. This tendency of punishment to creep up the status ladder predated these famous late antique abuses of high-status persons. Relatively low-status free persons—so-called "humiliores"—were already subjected to the sharply degrading punishments of being thrown to the beasts in the principate. See L. Friedländer, *Roman Life and Manners under the Early Empire*, trans. L. Magnus (New York, 1965), 2:44.

46. Garnsey, *Why Penalties Become Harsher*, 152–153; and for a careful and wide-ranging discussion, D. Grodzynski, "Tortures Mortelles et Catégories Sociales," in *Du Châtiment dans la Cité* (Rome, 1984), 382–403.

47. See Hulsewé, *Remnants of Ch'in Law*, 7–8 for this (only partially realized) leveling ambition, and passim for the character of Qin punishment.

48. E.g., B. Schwartz, *The World of Thought in Ancient China* (Cambridge, 1985), 332–333; J. Gernet, *A History of Chinese Civilization*, 2d ed., trans. Foster and Hartman, (Cambridge, 1996), 73–77, 90–93.

49. T. H. Marshall and T. Bottomore, *Citizenship and Social Class* (London, 1992), 33.

50. G. Lenski, "Status Crystallization: A Non-Vertical Dimension of Social Status," *American Sociological Review* 19 (1954): 405–413.

51. Ibid., 412–413.

52. The original version of Radbruch's argument appeared in his "Stand und Strafecht," *Schweizerische Zeitschrift für Strafrecht* 49 (1935): 17–30. The context of this article in the Nazi period deserves more attention than it has received. That Radbruch had his eye on Nazi law is clear enough from the closing passage in the article, which cites Schaffstein, a leading Nazi jurist, on the importance of dishonor in punishment. Radbruch's argument also bore on Nazi ideas in more complex ways. The burden of the argument was that the history of punishment should revolve, not around blood feud and dueling, but around state-imposed discipline and mutilation. This constituted an important assault on Nazi ideas—as well as on the legal-historiographical tradition on which the Nazis drew. Nazi jurists were very fond of insisting on the centrality of blood-feud and duel in the history of criminal law—and in their own society. It was Radbruch's claim that blood-feud and duel were institu-

tions meaningful only between status-equals, while criminal punishment assumed a disparity of status between state and offender.

53. Radbruch, "Der Ursprung des Strafrechts aus dem Stande der Unfreien," in Radbruch, *Elegantiae Juris Criminalis* (Basel, 1950) (orig. 1938), 11–12. I have slightly altered the translation in Sellin, *Slavery and the Penal System*.

54. Nietzsche, "Der Wille zur Macht. Versuch einer Umwertung aller Werte," eds. P. Gast and E. Förster-Nietzsche, in *Sämtliche Werke in Zwölf Bänden* (Stuttgart, 1964), 9: 498: "Das Beschimpfende ist erst so in die Strafe gekommen, daß gewisse Bußen an verächtliche Menschen (Sklaven z.B.) geknüpft wurden. Die, welche am meisten bestraft wurden, waren verächtliche Menschen, und schließlich lag im Strafen etwas Beschimpfendes." This is Aphorism 741, not 471 as stated by Radbruch, who quoted it at the end of his 1938 article.

55. Sellin, *Slavery and the Penal System*.

56. There have been plenty of societies in which death was regarded as milder than public shame. See, e.g., Matthias Calonius, "Dissertatio Juridica de Delinquentium ad Publicam Ignominiam Expositione," in Calonius, *Opera Omnia*, ed. Adophus Iwarus Arwidsson (Holm, 1830), 2: 240: "publicam contumeliam . . . haud raro morte acerbiorem." Coming close to home: For the case of Philadelphia man who slit his throat rather than undergoing humiliating punishment at the whipping post, see Meranze, *Laboratories of Virtue: Punishment, Revolution, and Authority in Philadelphia, 1760–1835* (Chapel Hill, 1996), 47, citing Scharf and Westcott, *History of Philadelphia*, 2: 857. Moreover, for many Christians in particular, the death penalty seems to confer a kind of near-benefit on the offender: by concentrating the offender's mind, the death penalty helps bring the offender into a profitable state of repentance. Indeed, prosecutors in American courts have been able to rely precisely on this Christian argument to claim that the death penalty is *good* for the offender—a claim that at least some American jurors have presumably accepted. For a recent opinion forbidding this practice, see Sandoval v. Calderon, 241 F.3d 765, 776 (9th Cir. 2000). The fact that perceptions vary in this way does not mean that we are wrong if we choose on moral grounds to condemn the death penalty. But it does mean that we are mistaken if we think we can accurately characterize the death penalty as always *harsh*. Societies or persons that inflict the death penalty are by no means clearly "cruel" or "harsh" in their underlying sensibility; the matter is more complicated than that. Harshness must be understood as harshness within a particular cultural world. Indeed, even the most heartfelt contemporary opposition to the death penalty must be understood as the product of a particular pattern of cultural beliefs and practices: persons who view the death penalty as paradigmatically harsh tend to be persons who come from cultures that have abandoned the panoply of religious rites that once gave death meaning. It is above all in secularized northern Europe, in which faith has faded in the old Christian ceremonies that surrounded the passage from life to death, that the death penalty has come to seem meaningless and horrible. In America, where religious belief is stronger, the death penalty has held on. For a famous statement connecting the decline of religious faith with opposition to the death penalty, see A. Camus, *Refléxions sur la guillotine*, in A. Koestler and A. Camus, *Réflexions sur la Peine Capitale* (n.p., 1957), 159–167.

57. Durkheim, *Division of Labor in Society*, trans., W. D. Halls (New York, 1984), 28.

58. Compare H. L. A. Hart's doubts about Durkheim's conceptions in "Social Solidarity and Morality," in Hart, *Essays in Jurisprudence and Philosophy* (Oxford, 1983), 253–254.

59. For an effort to reconceptualize white-collar crime as involving a type of offense, rather than a type of offender, see S. Shapiro, "Collaring the Crime," *American Sociological Review* 55 (1990): 346–365. Shapiro aims to recharacterize white-collar crime as what Europeans call "Untreue" or disloyalty. On this European conception, see chapter 3 of this book.

60. This measure of harshness has been often neglected by specialists in criminal law, and therefore deserves special emphasis. The nature of the application of punishment is central to the dynamic of the criminal law itself. Defendants who are faced with really bad conditions of punishment are, after all, more likely to cooperate with authorities than defendants who are not: bad prison conditions can thus be viewed as torture, in the technical sense, to the extent they are used—as one suspects they are by both European and American police and prosecutors—to induce confession or cooperation.

Chapter 2

1. Blackstone, *Commentaries on the Laws of England,* 4 vols. (Chicago, 1979), 4:370–371 (hereinafter Bl.Comm.).

2. See Acts 10:34; Romans 2:11; Colossians 3:25; James 2:1 and 2:9. On the early Christian rejection of values of honor and deference, see more generally W. Meeks, *The Origins of Christian Morality: The First Two Centuries* (New Haven, 1993), 46–47, 62–63, 86–87, 96.

3. See Michael H. Dessent, "Weapons to Fight Insider Trading in the 21st Century: A Call for the Repeal of Section 16(b)," *Akron Law Review* 33 (2000): 481; Elizabeth Szockyi, *The Law and Insider Trading: In Search of a Level Playing Field* (Buffalo, 1993); and also J. Stewart, *Den of Thieves* (New York, 1991).

4. Comprehensive Crime Control Act of 1984, Pub. L. 98–473, October 12, 1984.

5. Quotes taken from O. Obermaier and R. Morvillo, *White Collar Crime: Business and Regulatory Offenses* (New York, 1990), 3–2, 4–12–4–13, 5–12.

6. See *Wall Street Journal,* "Securities Fraud Penalties Stiffen," April 5, 2001, p. C1; "ADM Ex-Officials Get 2 Years in Jail in Sign of Tougher Antitrust Penalties," *Wall Street Journal,* July 12, 1999, A4. Securities-fraud offenders continue to receive lighter treatment than offenders such as drug dealers. See the report in the *Wall Street Journal,* "Stock-Fraud Cases Sometimes Lose Their Sting," June 27, 2000. That report observes that "only" half of the offenders in one case received prison sentences ranging from 3 to 71 months. By contrast with European standards, this probably remains relatively stern punishment; and the bringing of these highly publicized prosecutions still reflects the changing atmosphere of American law enforcement even where convictions do not result. As the same report notes, prosecutors eagerly seek "publicity about mass arrests."

7. See J. Arlen, "The Potentially Perverse Effects of Corporate Criminal Liability," *Journal of Legal Studies* 23 (1994): 833, 838–839.

8. Carol E. Jordan et al., "Stalking: Cultural, Clinical, and Legal Considerations," *Brandeis Law Journal* 38 (2000): 513; U.S. Dept. of Justice, Office of Justice Programs, Violence Against Women Grants Office, *Stalking and Domestic Violence: The Third Annual Report to Congress Under the Violence Against Women Act,* available at http://www.ojp.usdoj.gov/vawo/grants/stalk98/stalk98.pdf (1998).

9. Jill Elaine Hasday, "Contest and Consent: A Legal History of Marital Rape," *California Law Review* 88 (2000): 1373, 1376.

10. E.g., Walker, *Popular Justice,* 234–236.

11. See, for example, 1973 N.Y. Laws 1040–80, 2190–239, 3023–31 (codified throughout sections 220.00–.65, and 221.00–.55 of the N.Y. Penal Law and known collectively as the Rockefeller Drug Laws) and *Harmelin v. Michigan*, 501 U.S. 957 (1991). See, more generally, J. Gray, *Why Our Drug Laws Have Failed and What We Can Do About It: A Judicial Indictment of the War on Drugs* (Philadelphia, 2001), I. Glasser, "American Drug Laws: The New Jim Crow," *Albany Law Review* 63 (2000): 703; Michael Tonry, "Race and the War on Drugs," *1994 University of Chicago Legal Forum* (1994): 25; and D. Husak, *Drugs and Rights* (Cambridge, 1992). For the history of antidrug legislation, see David F. Musto, *The American Disease: Origins of Narcotic Control*, 3d ed. (New York, 1999).

12. See the fine brief account in Garland, *Punishment and Modern Society*, 29–41.

13. Cf. P. Robinson and J. Darley, "The Utility of Desert," *Northwest University Law Review* 91 (1997): 453, 473–474.

14. Or, in some instances, simply to harshen the practice of the juvenile courts themselves. See Jonathan Simon, "Power without Parents: Juvenile Justice in a Postmodern Society," *Cardozo Law Review* 16 (1995): 1363. For discussions of recent developments, see Martha Minow, "What Ever Happened to Children's Rights," *Minnesota Law Review* 80 (1995): 267; Susan Guarino-Ghezzi and Edward Loughran, *Balancing Juvenile Justice* (New Brunswick/London, 1996), 14–25, 101–109. Of special importance on the federal level is the Comprehensive Crime Control Act of 1984, which put an end to the short-lived liberalism of the Juvenile Justice and Delinquency Prevention Act of 1974. For a brief account of federal standards with regard to the trial of minors, see Abraham Abramovsky, "Trying Juveniles as Adults," *New York Law Journal* 219 (June 8, 1998), 3, col. 1.

15. Floyd Feeney, *German and American Prosecutions* (Washington, D.C, 1998).

16. In France, punishment may, in exceptional circumstances, be imposed on minors over the age of thirteen. P. Poncela, *Droit de la Peine*, 2d ed. (Paris, 2001), 186. As in the United States, there has been considerable concern about the problem of criminal justice and minors since the mid-1970s. Nevertheless, the drift has not been toward increased severity of "punishment" rather than education. See chapter 3 of this book.

17. See, e.g., "À 11 ans, menotté et détenu à Denver. Son inculpation pour inceste révèle la dureté de la justice américaine des mineurs," *Libération*, 29 October 1999; "Angeklagt," *Frankfurter Allgemeine Zeitung*, 23 October 1999. Raoul's subsequent release did not calm the waters of European commentary. See "Les États-Unis libèrent le petit Raoul," *Libération*, 12 November 1999; "La justice américaine est plus sévère que jamais," *Le Monde*, 15 Novembre 1999; "Verfahren gegen elfjährigen Raoul schnell und ohne Auflagen eingestellt," *Frankfurter Allgemeine Zeitung*, 12 November 1999.

18. E.g., "U.S. Throws 'Predator' Kids to the Wolves; Juvenile Offenders Increasingly Ending Up in Adult Prisons, Jails"; "Rehabilitation Ignored as Americans Run Scared of Juvenile Crime," *The Guardian* (London), March 17, 2000, 19.

19. See experts: "Boy Shouldn't Be Charged," *Detroit News*, March 2, 2000. For further literature: A. Abramovsky, "Trying Juveniles as Adults," *New York Law Journal*, June 8, 1998, p. 3.

20. See *New York Times*, "Young and Condemned," Aug. 22, 2000; cf. *Washington Post*, "Meting Death to Juvenile Criminals," Dec. 8, 2000; Human Rights Watch, Press Release, "Missouri Gov. Urged Not to Execute Juvenile Offender With Mental Retardation," March 5, 2001.

21. *Eddings v. Oklahoma*, 455 U.S. 104 (1982); *Thompson v. Oklahoma*, 487 U.S. 815 (1988).

22. See generally P. Elikann, *Superpredators: The Demonization of Our Children by the Law* (New York, 1999), 151–152.

23. For the contrast between African-Americans, Cambodians, and others, see Elikann, *Superpredators*, 114–116; Jonathan Simon, "Power without Parents," 1363, 1367.

24. See chapter 3.

25. *Atwater v. City of Lago Vista*, 121 S. Ct. 2450; 150 L. Ed. 2d 709 (2001).

26. Or indeed, at the other end of social spectrum, inmates who are held liable for back child support payments after their release. See *New York Times*, "Prison Offers No Escape from Paying Child Support," September 17, 2000, p. 35.

27. "Boy Who Killed a Teacher Gets 28 Years and No Parole," *New York Times*, July 28, 2001, A7.

28. Minow, "What Ever happened to Children's Rights?" 295.

29. See also Paul E. Peterson, "An Immodest Proposal," *Daedalus* 121 (1992): 151–159; Steven Drizin of Northwestern Law School, quoted in "La Justice américaine est plus sévère que jamais pour les mineurs délinquants," *Libération*, 13 November 1999.

30. Braithwaite, "White Collar Crime," *Annual Review of Sociology* 11 (1985): 1. This article offers a fine critical account of the uncertainty of the "white-collar crime" concept.

31. Sutherland, "White-Collar Criminality," in *American Sociological Review* 5 (1940): 1.

32. D. Weisburd, S. Wheeler, E. Waring, and N. Bode, *Crimes of the Middle Classes* (New Haven, 1991), 5.

33. Ibid., 6–7.

34. E. Symons and J. J. White, *Banking Law*, 3d ed. (St. Paul, 1991), 330.

35. Wesiburd et al., *Crimes of the Middle Classes*, 171.

36. For a sensitive discussion of the complexities, see S. Wheeler, K. Mann and A. Sarat, *Sitting in Judgment: The Sentencing of White Collar Criminals* (New Haven, 1988).

37. For the importance of the shift in perceptions in the 1970s, see also J. Coleman, *The Criminal Elite: The Sociology of White Collar Crime* (New York, 1985), vii.

38. Ilene Nagel Bernstein, William Kelly, and Patricia Doyle, "Social Reaction to Deviants: The Case of Criminal Defendants," *American Sociological Review* 42 (1977): 743–795; for this commonplace in the historical literature, E.g., J. Chiffoleau, *Les Justices du Pape. Délinquance et Criminalité dans la Région d'Avignon au XIVe siècle* (Paris, 1984), 243–260.

39. Barry C. Feld, "Criminalizing the American Juvenile Court," *Crime and Justice: A Review of Research* 17 (1993) 197; Feld, "The Juvenile Court Meets the Principle of Offense: Punishment, Treatment, and the Difference It Makes," *Boston University Law Review* 68 (1988): 821; Guarino-Ghezzi and Loughran, *Balancing Juvenile Justice*, 101: "Juvenile courts became more offense-oriented and less offender-oriented, and responding to the 'needs' of the child was no longer the first priority. The courts began to rely on offense criteria in making decisions far more often than the philosophy of rehabilitation would [dictate]."

40. Interestingly, Judge Frankel's commitment to equality in sentencing led him to suspend the prison sentence of one offender in the wake of President Ford's pardon of Richard Nixon. See *United States v. Braun*, 382 F Supp 214 (S.D.N.Y. 1974). Our opposition to status *immunities* represents, as it were, the obverse of the coin our opposition to status *offenses*. Especially since the liberal era of the early 1960s, the Supreme

Court has condemned the notion that persons can be prosecuted for who they are rather than what they do—for being narcotics addicts, see *Robinson v. California*, 370 U.S. 660 (1962), for example, or for being homeless. *Pottinger v. City of Miami*, 810 F. Supp. 1551 (S.D. Fla. 1992). This is a jurisprudence that probably sets few effective limits today, see esp. *Powell v. Texas*, 392 U.S. 514 (1968)—but that is not the point. What matters is that American criminal law today is rife with the notion that no person should either be condemned *or* be acquitted on account of status—even the status of being a minor.

41. See, e.g., H. Josephs, "The Upright and the Low-Down: An Examination of Official Corruption in the United States and People's Republic of China," *Syracuse Journal of International Law and Commmerce* 27 (2000): 269, 277.

42. Beccaria, "Dei Delitti e delle Pene," in *Edizione Nazionale delle Opere di Cesare Beccaria*, ed. L. Firpo (Milano, 1984), pp. 40–46 (=§§ VI–VII).

43. Montesquieu, *De l'Esprit des Lois*, 1: 301 (Bk. XI, Chap. VI).

44. Beccaria, "Dei Delitti e delle Pene," 46 (=§VII).

45. Ibid., 29 (=§II), quoting Montesquieu, Esprit, XIX, 14.

46. Ibid., 83–86 (=§XXVII)

47. Ibid., 86–95 (=§XXVIII).

48. For the standard view, see e.g., M. Wolfgang, "Beccaria: Precursor of Modern Criminology," in D. Rössner and J.-M. Jehle, eds., *Beccaria als Wegbereiter der Kriminologie* (Mönchengladbach, 2000), 32–33; H.-D. Schwind, "Beccaria als Pionier moderner Kriminalpolitik," in G. Deimling, ed., *Cesare Beccaria. Die Anfänge moderner Strafrechtspflege in Europa* (Heidelberg, 1989), 8.

49. "Dei Delitti e delle Pene," 73–75 (§XXI).

50. Brockway, "The Idea of a True Prison System for a State," in E. C. Wines, ed., *Transactions of the National Congress on Penitentiary and Reformatory Discipline* (Albany, 1871): 38–65. See generally Friedman, *Crime and Punishment*, 159–163.

51. Liszt, *Lehrbuch des deutschen Strafrechts*, 20th ed. (Berlin, 1914), 69–91; Saleilles, *The Individualization of Punishment*, trans. R. Jastrow (Boston, 1911) (orig. 1898).

52. For a survey of the German tradition, see R. Wetzell, *Inventing the Criminal: A History of German Criminology, 1880–1945* (Chapel Hill, 2000). For the American version of this line of thought, see Friedman, "Dead Hands," 907–908, and the literature cited there.

53. By the mid-1960s, retributivism had essentially vanished from the programs of criminology. To criminologists, it seemed clear that "the modern behavioral sciences have shown that arm-chair abstractions about the 'justice' of retribution by philosophers who reject human experience are sadly defective in human understanding, not to say human sympathy." Henry Weihofen, quoted and discussed in Kathleen Moore, *Pardons: Justice, Mercy, and the Public Interest* (New York, 1989), 60. See generally Francis Allen, *The Decline of the Rehabilitative Ideal: Penal Policy and Social Purpose* (New Haven, 1981). Philosophers had more nuanced views. See esp. H. L. A. Hart, *Punishment and Responsibility: Essays in the Philosophy of Law* (New York, 1968), 1–27, for a defense of a mixed philosophical approach.

54. Sentencing Reform Act of 1984, held constitutional in *Mistretta v. United States*, 488 U.S. 361 (1989). The impact of the Supreme Court's 2000 decision in *Apprendi* remains to be determined. In any case, that decision does not depart from the broad American commitment to the determinate sentencing program. *Apprendi v. New Jersey*, 530 U.S. 466 (2000).

55. The rise of determinate sentencing laws in the states begins with Maine

(1976); California, Illinois, and Indiana (1977); and especially Minnesota (1980). For the state of play in the mid-1990s, see Richard Frase, "Sentencing Guidelines, Still Going Strong," in *Judicature* 78 (1995): 173–179; K. Reitz, "The Status of Sentencing Guidelines in the U.S.," *Overcrowded Times* (December 1999): 8–10.

56. Under the federal guidelines, judges retain discretion to consider "aggravating or mitigating circumstance[s] of a kind, or to a degree, not adequately taken into consideration by the Sentencing Commission." 18 U.S.C. § 3553 (b). In practice, courts hold that this leaves judges effectively without discretion on matters considered at all by the Commission. But see *Koon v. United States*, 518 U.S. 81 (1996).

57. The federal guidelines in particular require the inmates serve 85 percent of their sentences. To be sure, not everything has changed in American sentencing. If parole is on the wane, probation has survived: roughly 80 percent of offenders still receive sentences of probation in the United States—though here too, the immense volume of probation orders (vastly larger than anything to be found in Europe) threatens to overwhelm the capacities of the American system. See J. Byrne, A. Lurigio, and C. Baird, "The Effectiveness of the New Intensive Supervision Programs," *Research in Corrections* 2 (1989): 1–15.

58. American Friends Service Committee, *The Struggle for Justice* (New York, 1971).

59. Von Hirsch, *Doing Justice* (New York, 1976).

60. Marvin Frankel, *Criminal Sentences: Law without Order* (New York, 1973).

61. *Furman v. Georgia*, 408 U.S. 238 (1972). Nevertheless, it is in death penalty litigation that individualization has since been most concertedly cultivated, with the requirement, under *Gregg v. Georgia*, 428 U.S. 153 (1976), of a death penalty sentencing phase dedicated to circumstantial consideration of the case.

62. E.g., Tonry, *Sentencing Matters*, 57—though guessing that state enactments may have had more success than federal at 44; L. Farabee, "Disparate Departures under the Federal Sentencing Guidelines," *University of Connecticut Law Review* 30 (1998): 569; K. Stith and J. Cabranes, "Judging under the Federal Sentencing Guidelines," *Northwestern Law Review* 91 (1997): 1247, 1273; D. Mustard, "Racial, Ethnic, and Gender Disparities in Sentencing," *Journal of Law and Economics* 45 (2001): 285–314.

63. Cf. Garland, *Culture of Control*, 11, 121–22.

64. Esp. James Q. Wilson, *Thinking about Crime* (New York, 1975). See generally Pamela Griset, *Determinate Sentencing: The Promise and Reality of Retributive Justice* (Albany, 1991). For the alliance of liberals and conservatives, K. Stith and S. Yoh, "The Politics of Sentencing Reform: The Legislative History of the Federal Sentencing Guidelines," *Wake Forest Law Review* 28 (1993): 223; and the excellent account in Garland, *Culture of Control*, 53–73.

65. Dershowitz, "Indeterminate Confinement: Letting the Therapy Fit the Harm," *Pennsylvania Law Review* 193 (1974): 304. See also the brief memoir of Stanton Wheeler in *Criminal Justice Ethics* (Summer/Fall 1997): 50.

66. For aspects of the guidelines that could lead to longer sentences, see, e.g., G. Heaney, "The Reality of Guidelines Sentencing: No End to Disparity," *American Criminal Law Review* 28 (1991): 161; J. Weinstein and F. Bernstein, "The Denigration of Mens Rea in Drug Sentencing," *Federal Sentencing Reporter* 7 (1994): 121.

67. See R. Conaboy, "The United States Sentencing Commission: A New Component in the Federal Criminal Justice System," *Federal Probation* 61 (1997): 58, 62. This does not mean that they are in fact insulated. Cf. Stith and Cabranes, *Fear of Judging: Sentencing Guidelines in the Federal Courts* (Chicago, 1998), 48–49; A. Alschuler, "The Failure of the Sentencing Guidelines: A Plea for Less Aggregation," *University of Chicago Law Review* 58 (1991): 935–936.

68. See A. Payne, "Does Inter-Judge Disparity Really Matter? An Analysis of the Effects of Sentencing Reforms in Three Federal District Courts," *International Review of Law and Economics* 17 (1997): 337, 338.

69. As the Federal Courts Study Committee noted, it also engendered a shift from the discretion of judges to the discretion of prosecutors. This too can be seen in the same light, to the extent that American prosecutors make political and quasi-political plays for public favor.

70. Compare the analysis of F. Zimring, "Populism, Democratic Government, and the Decline of Expert Authority: Some Reflections on 'Three Strikes' in California," *Pacific Law Journal* 28 (1996): 243; and J. Braithwaite and P. Pettit, *Not Just Deserts: A Republican Theory of Criminal Justice* (Oxford, 1990), 2–5. Cf. B. Burns and B. Elden, "We Make the Better Target (But the Guidelines Shifted Power from the Judiciary to Congress, not from the Judiciary to the Prosecution)," *Northwestern University Law Review* 91 (1997): 1317.

71. Montesquieu, *De l'Esprit des Lois*, 1: 223 (Bk. VI, Chap. XXI).

72. Last of all, I think something else is at work in the harshness of the guidelines regime too. Their harshness is typical of a much larger pattern in American law. Equality in America tends *generally* to be harsh equality; there is nothing exceptional about the American law of punishment. And it tends to be harsh equality precisely because we do not distinguish clearly between the two types of rejection of *respect for persons* with which I began. Judge Frankel and Professor Dershowitz wanted to create a world that made no distinctions between persons. Accordingly they did not want a law that entrusted the officers of the state with the authority to show individualized concern for particular offenders, lest white offenders receive more concern than black ones. There would have been nothing harsh about this program if the legislators, judges, and guards who carried it out had responded by showing uniformly *high* concern for each offender. But it is wholly characteristic of the United States *not* to show high concern in this way, not to generalize norms of respect. We do not show uniformly high concern in the workplace; we do not show it in the realms of concern to the law of privacy; and we do not show it in punishment either. In the American cultural climate, in which values of respect are so much absent, the makers of the sentencing guidelines succeeded only in contributing to the making of a law of punishment that shows obstinately *little* concern for the personhood of offenders. It is indeed a law that tends to treat offenders as something closer to animals than humans, and that has correspondingly sought, more and more frequently, simply to lock them away.

73. Garland, *Culture of Control*, 13–14.

74. On these, see Walker, *Popular Justice*, 222. See E.g., Eric Schlosser, "The Prison-Industrial Complex," *Atlantic Monthly* at http://theatlantic.com/issues/98dec/prisons.html, 5–6. This is a matter of great importance: under "three-strikes-and-you're-out" laws, every felony typically counts as a strike. Much hangs, accordingly, on the definition of "felony."

75. The difficulty in analysis has to do with the fact that drug offenses are relatively easy to prove, and sentences are long. This means that prosecutors may have little incentive to charge other offenses. In consequence, it is difficult to know how many convicts serving time for drug offenses have also committed some other offense.

76. N. Genscher, *Boot Camp-Programme in den USA : ein Fallbeispiel zum Formenwandel in der amerikanischen Kriminalpolitik* (Mönchengladbach, 1998), 10; Schlosser, *Prison-Industrial Complex*, 3–4. The contribution of drug offenses in particular for the period 1980–96 is put at 45 percent by A. Blumstein and A. Beck, "Population Growth

in U.S. Prisons," in M. Tonry and J. Petersilia, eds., *Prisons, Crime, and Justice: A Review of Research* 26 (1999): 21.

77. Elikann, *Superpredators*, 120–122.

78. See Genscher, *Boot Camp Programme*, 31. Particularly famous in American history was New York's "four-strikes-and-you're-out" Baumes law of the Prohibition Era. See Friedman, "Dead Hands," 910.

79. John Clark, James Austin, and D. Alan Henry, "Three Strikes and You're Out: A Review of State Legislation," National Institute of Justice, 1997.

80. Eric Slater, "Pizza Thief Gets 25 Years to Life," *Los Angeles Times*, March 3, 1995, B3. Walker, *Popular Justice*, 211.

81. Greg Krikorian, "Judge Slashes Life Sentence in Pizza Theft Case," *Los Angeles Times*, Jan. 29, 1997, A1.

82. See, for example, the EU Charter of Fundamental Rights of the European Union, Chapter VI, Art. 49, Principles of Legality and Proportionality of Criminal Offences and Penalties, which declares that "the severity of penalties must not be disproportionate to the criminal offence," in *The Bulletin of the European Union*, (December 2000), Part 2, Section 2.

83. Cal. 3d. 410 (1972). Contrast *People v. Levy*, 151 Cal. App. 2d 460 (1957).

84. See, e.g., *People v. Marshall*, 13 Cal. 4th 799, 919 P.2d 1280 (1996), *People v. Lucero*, 23 Cal.4th 692 (2000); *People v. Kipp*, Cal. LEXIS 7132 (2001).

85. U.S. 957 (1991). Still not overruled, but of very uncertain reach, is the Supreme Court's earlier decision endorsing a larger measure of proportionality, *Solem v. Helm*, 463 U.S. 277 (1983).

86. Courts have struggled with proportionality after *Harmelin*, keeping a proportionality jurisprudence alive while permitting sentences that would be impossible in continental Europe. See E.g., *Hawkins v. Hargett*, 200 F. 3d 1279 (10th Cir. 1999); *State v. DePlano*, 926 P.2d 494 (Ariz, 1996); *Henderson v. State*, 322 Ark. 402, 910 S.W.2d 656 (1995).

87. See chapter 3 in this book.

88. See, e.g., "U.S. Prison Population hits the 2 Million Mark," *International Herald Tribune*, February 16, 2000. As has been repeatedly observed, this growth has come during a period when crime rates have remained constant or fallen. E.g., Thomas Arvanides, "Increasing Imprisonment: A Function of Crime or Socioeconomic Factors?" *American Journal of Criminal Justice* 17 (1992): 19–38.

89. See U.S. Department of Justice, Bureau of Justice Statistics, Jail Statistics, http://www.ojp.usdoj.gov/bjs/jails.htm, downloaded November 27, 2001. The frequently cited figure of 460 per 100,000 is, importantly, a measure of the *prison* population—that is to say, of those serving more than a year. If we include the *jailed* population, we get the higher figure. See further The Sentencing Project, "U.S. Surpasses Russia as World Leader in Rate of Incarceration," available at http://www.sentencingproject.org/brief/usvsrus.pdf, downloaded November 27, 2001; International Centre for Prison Studies, http://www.prisonstudies.org/ (last visited November 27, 2001). On South Africa, see Susan Rhodes, "Democratic Justice: The Responsiveness of Prison Population Size to Public Policy Preferences," *American Politics Quarterly* 18 (1990): 337–375.

90. France is 78 per 100,000 as of July 2001; Germany is 97 as of mid-2000; U.K. (England and Wales only) is 127 as of mid-2001; Belgium is 85 as of mid-2000; Switzerland is 89 as of the beginning of 2000; Spain is at 118 as of early 2001; Denmark is 62 as of the beginning of 2000; Sweden is 64 as of 2000; Italy is 93 as of mid-2000. International Centre for Prison Studies, http://www.prisonstudies.org/, downloaded November 27, 2001.

91. Experimentation with boot camps has taken place in at least twenty-four states: *Juvenile Boot Camps and Military Structured Youth Programs: 2000 Directory* (Topeka, 2000). It was expressly encouraged by Congress in the Violent Crime Control and Law Enforcement Act of 1994. For fuller discussion of this and other so-called "intermediate sanctions," see Norval Morris and Michael Tonry, *Between Prison and Probation: Intermediate Punishments in a Rational Sentencing Structure* (New York, 1990); Dale Parent, Terrence Dunworth, Douglas MacDonald, and William Rhodes, *Intermediate Sanctions* (National Institute of Justice, 1997). Note, however, that the U.S. Justice Department is pulling back from its early support of juvenile boot camps: "U.S. Justice Department Says Boot Camps Do More Harm than Good," Associated Press, June 1, 1998.

92. See "Parading of Suspects is Evolving Tradition," *New York Times*, Feb. 7, 1999, B1.

93. See Lynn M. Burley, "History Repeats Itself in the Resurrection of Prisoner Chain Gangs: Alabama's Experience Raises Eighth Amendment Concerns," *Law and Inequality* 15 (1997): 127; Neal R. Pierce, "But in Its Prisons, Georgia Has Reverted to the Bad Old Days," *Philadelphia Inquirer*, July 19, 1996, A19 (concerning the reintroduction of chain gangs in several states); and Rick Bragg, "Chain Gangs to Return to Roads of Alabama," *New York Times*, Mar. 26, 1995, 16 (describing the return of chain gangs in Alabama). See also "Alabama to Make Prisoners Break Rocks," *New York Times*, July 29, 1995, 5; Sam Grossfeld, "Upon This Rock: Working on the Chain Gang in Alabama," *Boston Globe*, Aug. 27, 1995, 66; Brent Staples, "The Chain Gang Show," *New York Times Magazine*, Sept. 17, 1995, 62; and Stephen Goode, "Chain Gangs Are Good, Say Citizens," *Washington Times*, Mar. 31, 1997, 4. For a history of chain gangs, see Mark Colvin, *Penitentiaries, Reformatories, and Chain Gangs: Social Theory and the History of Punishment in Nineteenth-Century America* (New York, 1997).

94. F. Serpillon, *Code Criminel ou Commentaire sur l'Ordonnance de 1670* (Lyon, 1767), 1071.

95. *Harmelin v. Michigan*, 501 U.S. 957, 967–968 (1991).

96. For example, S. Turow, *Presumed Innocent* (New York, 1987), 228–231.

97. R. Pack, "Artemidorus and his Waking World," *Transactions of the American Philological Association* 86 (1955): 283 n. 9, as discussed in MacMullen, *Judicial Savagery*, 207.

98. For the history, along with the very tentative beginnings of court intervention before the mid-1960s, see M. Feeley & E. Rubin, *Judicial Policy Making and the Modern State: How the Courts Reformed America's Prisons* (Cambridge, 1998), 30–50.

99. See J. DiIulio, ed., *Courts, Corrections, and the Constitution: The Impact of Judicial Intervention on Prisons and Jails* (New York, 1990); B. Crouch and J. Marquart, "Resolving the Paradox of Reform: Litigation, Prisoner Violence, and Perceptions of Risk," *Justice Quarterly* 7 (1990): 103–123; W. Taggart, "Redefining the Power of the Federal Judiciary: The Impact of Court-Ordered Prison Reform on State Expenditure for Corrections," *Law and Society Review* 23 (1989): 241–272; M. Feeley, "The Significance of Prisons Conditions Cases: Budgets and Regions, *Law and Society Review* 23 (1989): 273–282; R. Hanson and H. Daley, *Challenging the Conditions of Prisons and Jails* (Washington, D.C. 1996); M. Mushlin, *Rights of Prisoners*, 2d ed. (Colorado Springs, 1993), 12–17.

100. *Ruffin v. Commonwealth*, 62 Va (21 Gratt) 790, 796 (1871). See the discussion in Mushlin, *Rights of Prisoners*, 7, 12.

101. Mushlin, *Rights of Prisoners*, 41 and passim; Bradley Chilton, *Prisons under the Gavel: The Federal Takeover of Georgia Prisons* (Columbus, 1991).

102. *DeShaney v. Winnebago County Dept. of Social Servs.*, 489 U.S. 189, 200 (1989).

103. See, e.g., "Louisiana Settles Suit, Abandoning Youth Prisons," *New York Times*, September 8, 2000, p. A14.

104. K. Pyle, "Note: Prison Employment, A Long-Term Solution to the Overcrowding Crisis," *Boston University Law Review* 77 (1977): 151, 152 n. 12. Walker, *Popular Justice*, 223.

105. Feeley and Rubin date the beginning of the disengagement of the courts to *Bell v. Wolfish* (1979) and its full-scale "retreat" to 1986, with the Supreme Court's decision in *Whitley v. Albers. Judicial Policy Making*, 46–48.

106. See U.S. Department of State, "Initial Report of the United States of America to the UN Committee Against Torture," Annex I.

107. A standard already adumbrated in Justice Marshall's opinion in *Estelle v. Gamble*, 429 U.S. 97 (1976), which extended the jurisprudence of the Eighth Amendment to prison conditions in a case involving denial of medical care.

108. In this, the court retreated somewhat from an earlier, arguably stiffer, standard: as the court held in a case involving an inmate shot by a prison guard, the shooting was not actionable under the Eighth Amendment unless done "maliciously and sadistically for the very purpose of causing harm." *Whitley v. Albers*, 475 U.S. 312, 320 (1986).

109. *Wilson v. Seiter*, 501 U.S. 294 (1991).

110. *Turner v. Safley*, 482 U.S. 78 (1987), and the discussion in Mushlin, *Rights of Prisoners*, 14–15.

111. See Mushlin, *Rights of Prisoners*, 32.

112. *Hudson v. McMillian*, 503 U.S. 1 (1992).

113. *Helling v. McKinney*, 509 U.S. 25 (1993).

114. Feeley and Rubin, *Judicial Policy Making*, 50.

115. Schlosser, *Prison-Industrial Complex*, 4–5.

116. See A. Bottoms, "Interpersonal Violence and Social Order in Prisons," *Crime and Justice* 26 (1999): 205, 268–272; S. Sowle, "A Regime of Social Death: Criminal Punishment in the Age of Prisons," *New York University Review of Law and Social Change* 21 (1994): 497.

117. See W. Davies, "Violence in Prisons," in P. Feldman, ed., *Developments in the Study of Criminal Behavior* (Chichester, 1982), 2:150.

118. See, e.g., Human Rights Watch, *No Escape: Male Rape in U.S. Prisons* (New York, 2001). It is indeed possible that the sheer horror of prison conditions in the United States has changed the very dynamic of criminal prosecution. Prosecutors may be able to hope that their targets will cooperate out of sheer fear of the hellishness of an American prison term. Some defendants have indeed claimed that prosecutors have threatened them, directly or indirectly, with inhumane prison conditions. If prosecutors have in fact done so, they have committed a manifest ethical violation. Even if prosecutors do no more than rely on the common knowledge, and the common terror, of prison conditions in America, they have in any case done something that reveals what a far-reaching systemic impact punishment practices can have on the workings of criminal law. Defendants who fear really horrific punishment will inevitably act differently from defendants who do not.

119. See the discussion in Mushlin, *Rights of Prisoners*, 52–53.

120. Even in New York City, for example, where corrections officers are relatively well paid and are subjected to a civil service examination, their formal training lasts fifteen weeks. See http://www.nyc.gov/html/jobs.html#apply. For the European contrast, see chapter 3.

121. See *Kennibrew v. Russel*, 578 F. Supp 164 (ED Tenn 1983) (firearms); *State v. Rhea*, 608 P 2d 144 (NM 1980) (jailer a peace officer).

122. *Soto v. Dickey*, 744 F 2d 1260 (7th Cir 1984) and the discussion in Mushlin, *Rights of Prisoners*, 56–57.

123. E.g., Lezin, "Life at Lorton: An Examination of Prisoners' Rights at the District of Columbia Correctional Facilities," *Boston University Public Interest Law Journal* 5 (1996): 190–192.

124. For a typical recent exposé, see "14-Month Federal Study Denounces Cruel Conditions at the Nassau County Jail," *New York Times*, September 16, 2000, B5.

125. See D. McDonald, "Medical Care in Prisons," in Tonry and Petersilia, eds., *Prisons*, 427–478.

126. See Stephen S. Sypherd and Gary M. Ronan, *Thirtieth Annual Review of Criminal Procedure: Introduction and Guide for Users: VI. Prisoners' Rights: Substantive Rights Retained by Prisoners*, 89 Geo. L.J. 1897 (2001); *Meachum v. Fano*, 427 U.S. 215 (1976).

127. *Rhodes v. Chapman*, 452 U.S. 337, 347 (1981). Nevertheless, some lower courts have acted in a number of cases—though others have not. See the discussion and citations of Mushlin, *Rights of Prisoners*, 101 and 101 n. 520 and 102 n. 523.

128. Quoted and discussed, along with other examples, in Craig Haney, "Riding the Punishment Wave," 27, 32.

129. Cf. Tonry and Morris, *Between Prison and Probation*.

130. This can help us understand a mystery. The new shame sanctions, as Dan Kahan has suggested, have thus not served as *alternative* sanctions, inflicted on persons who would otherwise be imprisoned. Instead, they have arguably served as *signaling* sanctions, marking persons who have become newly susceptible to criminal liability in a society in which the boundaries of the criminal are expanding. There are other aspects of the new sanctions that should be viewed in the same light—most notably boot camps, which can be thought of as providing, like shame sanctions, a kind of rite of potential passage, of looming status-change. At the same time, it should be emphasized that the "expressive" function of shame sanctions, praised by Dan Kahan in his well-known article, "What do Alternative Sanctions Mean?" *University of Chicago Law Review* 63 (1996): 591, is thus not quite what Kahan says it is. According to Kahan, shame sanctions express social condemnation of forbidden acts. It is better to say that what those sanctions signal is not an *existing* consensus that those acts are wrong, but a *developing* practice of criminalizing them.

131. In particular, the Model Penal Code makes the important declaration that all offenses with any element of strict liability must be treated as "violations," the lowest grade. MPC § 2.05. For American law more broadly, see *Wharton's Criminal Law*, 15th ed. (Deerfield, 1993), 1:105–107

132. See L. Beres and T. Griffith, "Do Three Strikes Laws Make Sense? Habitual Offender Statutes and Criminal Incapacitation," *Georgetown Law Journal* 87 (1998): 103; Markus Dubber, "Recidivist Statutes as Arational Punishment," *Buffalo Law Review* 43 (1996): 689.

133. B. Liang and W. MacFarlane, "Murder by Omission: Child Abuse and the Passive Parent," *Harvard Journal on Legislation* 36 (1999): 397.

134. This too has a complicated jurisprudence, which I pass over here; technically the second form described in the text is not an "enhancement." See B. Witkin and N. Epstein, *California Criminal Law*, 2d ed.. (1989), § 1509 and relevant pocket part.

135. See, e.g., Del. Code Ann. tit. 11, 1304(a)(2) (1998); Minn. Stat. Ann. 609.749 (West 2000). Enhancements are the subjects of some complicated Supreme Court ju-

risprudence, which I do not discuss here. See *Deal v. United States*, 508 U.S. 129 (1993); *Jones v. United States*, 526 U.S. 227 (1999). I also leave aside the question of the treatment of prior convictions under the federal sentencing guidelines, which can have much the same effect. See generally R. Haines and F. Bowman, *Federal Sentencing Guidelines Handbook*, November 1999 ed., §§ 1B1.1, 4A1.2. For further cases, see Annotation. *Imposition of Enhanced Sentence under Recidivist Statute as Cruel and Unusual Punishment*, 27 A.L.R. Fed 110 (2000).

136. For recent efforts in New York City, see Bernard E. Harcourt, "Reflecting the Subject: A Critique of the Social Influence Conception of Deterrence, the Broken Windows Theory, and Order Maintenance Policing New York Style," *Michigan Law Review* 97 (1998): 291. For the role of new forfeiture laws in the crackdown on prostitution, see Shirley W. Whittle, "New York's Property Clerk Forfeiture Act—Can They Do That?," *Washington University Journal of Law and Politics* 4 (2000): 361; and George E. Ward, "Bennis and the War on Drugs," *Catholic University Law Review* 46 (1996): 109. For the use of community policing programs in the crackdown on prostitution (especially in New York City), see Sarah E. Waldeck, "Cops, Community Policing, and the Social Norms Approach to Crime Control: Should One Make Us More Comfortable with the Others?" *Georgia Law Review* 34 (2002): 1253. For the role of loitering laws in the crackdown on prostitution, see Peter W. Poulos, "Chicago's Ban on Gang Loitering: Making Sense of Vagueness and Overbreadth in Loitering Laws," *California Law Review* 83 (1995): 397.

137. "Skier found guilty of homicide: Jury finds man criminally negligent in fatal slope crash," Associated Press, Eagle, Col., Nov. 17, 2000. The Colorado Supreme Court confirmed the sufficiency of the prosecution in *People v. Hall*, 999 P.2d 201, 2000 Colo J. C.A.R. 1738.

138. Friedman, *Crime and Punishment*, 280–281.

139. E.g., David P. Bryden and Sonja Lengnick, "Rape in the Criminal Justice System," *Journal of Criminal Law and Criminology* 87 (1997): 1194.

140. Though arguably even here we have seen some increasing harshness in the Supreme Court's confusing jurisprudence on burdens of proof. In 1975, at the very beginning of the era of increasing harshness, the court issued *Mullaney v. Wilbur*, 421 U.S. 684 (1975), which placed the burden of proof with regard to a "heat of passion" defense of provocation on the prosecution. The court retreated within two years in *Patterson v. New York*, 432 U.S. 197 (1977), in ways that baffled commentators. For later cases, see *Martin v. Ohio*, 480 U.S. 228 (1986); *Montana v. Englehoff*, 518 U.S. 37 (1996). This is a difficult jurisprudence to interpret, though, and I leave it to the side here.

141. Cf. Schlosser, *The Prison-Industrial Complex*, 2: "In Bare Hill Correctional Facility [in upstate New York] . . . most of the inmates, . . . are housed in dormitories, not cells. The dormitories were designed to hold about fifty inmates, each with his own small cubicle and bunk. . . . [As of 1998] every dormitory at Bare Hill houses sixty inmates, a third of them double-bunked. . . . The low walls of the cubicles . . . allow little privacy. . . . Twenty-four hours a day a correctional officer sits alone at a desk on a platform that overlooks the dorm."

142. *Hudson v. Palmer*, 468 U.S. 517, 526 (1984).

143. "Prison clothing, drab and unindividualized, is still the order of the day in many [American] penitentiaries." Mushlin, *Rights of Prisoners*, 415, citing Ala Code § 14-3-44 1982. For the prominence of the experience of the uniform in one prison, see Katya Lezin, "Life at Lorton," 165, 171–172. For a failed challenge to a denial to wear civilian clothing, under a California statute that permitted a prisoner to choose his

own clothing except where doing so interfered with prison security concerns, see *In re Alcala*, 222 Cal App 3d 345, 271 Cal Rptr 674 (1990), interpreting a statute passed in 1975.

144. Mushlin, *Rights of Prisoners*, 414–420, noting religious exemptions in some cases on 419.

145. *Lamb v. Maschner*, 633 F Supp 351 (D Kan 1986).

146. Goffman, *The Presentation of Self in Everyday Life* (Woodstock, N.Y., 1973).

147. No in Lorton, Lezin, "Life at Lorton," 177; yes in the super-maximum security federal prison at Marion: Feeley & Rubin, *Judicial Policy Making*, 133.

148. E.g., again, Lezin, "Life at Lorton," 172.

149. See *Biejol v. Nelson*, 579 F2d 423 (7th Cir 1978); and further the discussion in Mushlin, *Rights of Prisoners*, 83. Free exercise of religion rights are an exception.

150. *Robbins v. South*, 595 F Supp 785 (D Mont. 1984); *Rutherford v. Pitchess*, 457 F. Supp 104, 116 (CD Cal, 1978). Some courts have condemned diets of bread and water, but the question remains an open one in American jurisprudence. *Jenkins v. Weger*, 564 F Supp 806 (D Wyo 1982); *People v. Joseph*, 434 NE2d 453 (Ill Ct App 1982); *Landman v. Royster*, 333 F Supp 621, 647 (ED Va 1971) (partial condemnation of bread and water); and the discussion in Mushlin, *Rights of Prisoners*, 84.

151. "Hatred, fear or contempt": J. Feinberg, *Doing and Deserving: Essays in the Theory of Responsibility* (Princeton, 1970), 100.

152. Shackling is still routine in some circumstances in many American prisons. For the general state of the law, see Mushlin, *Rights of Prisoners*, 52 and note 205. See also Lezin, "Life at Lorton," 195 (shackling of inmates awaiting medical care). Chaining by the neck has in some instances (but only some) been banned. *Spain v. Procunier*, 600 F2d 189 (9th Cir 1979); Cal Penal Code §2652.5. At least one court found it "excessive" to chain an inmate who was seeking medical care spread-eagled to a bed for more than twenty hours. *Ferola v. Moran*, 622 FSupp 814 (DRI 1985). Shackling also goes on Europe. But I will wager that it is a much more humiliating and frequent practice in the United States.

153. See, e.g., "Felony Costs Voting Rights for a Lifetime in 9 States," *New York Times*, November 3, 2000, A18; "Felony convictions keep 13% of Black Males from Voting," *Chicago Tribune*, Sept. 22, 2000, 10.

154. Schlosser, *Prison-Industrial Complex*, 6; Haney, "Riding the Punishment Wave," 35–36.

155. *Hudson v. Palmer*, 468 U.S. 517, 527 (1984).

156. Mushlin, *Rights of Prisoners*, 361–362.

157. Ibid., 362–370.

158. Ibid., 408–414.

159. *Bell v. Wolfish*, 441 U.S. 520 (1979).

160. E.g., *Loden v. State*, 199 Ga App 683, 406 SE 2d 103 (1991).

161. Mushlin, *Rights of Prisoners*, 373 n. 54, citing *United States v. Stumes*, 549 F2d 831 (8th Cir 1977); *State v Bishop*, 137 Ariz 361, 670 P 2d 1185 (Ct App 1983).

162. *Hudson v. Palmer*, 468 U.S. 517 (1984). The same generally holds of the homes and effects even of parolees and probationers. Mushlin, *Rights of Prisoners*, 374.

163. G. Sykes, *Society of Captives: A Study of a Maximum-Security Prison* (Princeton, 1971), 75.

164. *Griffin v. Michigan Department of Corrections*, 654 FSupp 690 (E.D. Mich. 1982).

165. *Delgado v. Cady*, 576 FSupp 1446, 1448 (ED Wis 1983).

166. Mushlin, *Rights of Prisoners*, 380–401.

167. *Hudson v. Palmer*, 468 U.S. 517, 530 (1984), and the discussion of Lezin, "Life at Lorton," 183–184. Eavesdropping on inmates' conversations is permitted, see the discussion in Lezin, "Life at Lorton," 181; as is reading of their personal mail. Mushlin, *Rights of Prisoners*, 401–404. These practices are also present in European law, though. See below.

168. Generally S. Garvey, "Can Shaming Punishments Educate?" *University of Chicago Law Review* 65 (1998): 733.

169. *Paul v. Davis*, 424 U.S. 693 (1976).

170. See "Hoping People Watch Jail and Won't Want to Visit," *New York Times*, August 24, 2000, G10. For a survey of American practices, see A. Book, "Shame on You: An Analysis of Modern Shame Punishment as an Alternative to Incarceration," *William and Mary Law Review* 40 (1999): 653–686.

171. Elikann, *Superpredators*, 143 and generally 142–145.

172. This is a topic I leave for fuller exploration later, but see J. Hauch, "Protecting Private Facts in France: The Warren and Brandeis Tort is Alive and Well and Flourishing in Paris," *Tulane Law Review* 68 (1994): 1219.

173. Moore, Pardons, at E.g., 8, 82; M. Love, "Politics and Collar Buttons: Reflections on the President's Duty to Be Merciful," *Fordham Urban Law Journal* 27 (2000): 1483, 1488–1494; "Access to the White House Opened Door to Clemency," *Washington Post*, February 8, 2001, A14.

174. E.g., "Getting Wise to Stupid Drug Laws," *Washington Post*, March 30, 2001.

Chapter 3

1. For the most recent presidential campaign in France, for example, see "Deux Projets au banc d'essai, Libération," 27 Janvier 2002, 10–11; and for developments since 1970, P. Poncela, *Droit de la peine*, 71; for Germany, C. Prittwitz, "Positive Generalprävention und 'Recht des Opfers auf Bestrafung des Täters?' " in *Kritische Vierteljahresschrift für Gesetzgebung und Rechtswissenschaft. Sonderheft: Winfried Hassemer zum sechzigsten Geburtstag* (2000): 162–175.

2. After the election of 1978, objections to the French system of parole led to the passage of a law limiting the discretion of officials to alter terms of imprisonment. Loi du 22 Novembre 1978 (art. 720–2 to 720–4 CPP); for the political context, see J. Léauté, *Les Prisons*, 2d ed. (Paris, 1990), 53–60. This movement showed some of the same concern for equality in punishment as its American parallel. See Pradel, "Vers un retour à une plus grande certitude de la peine," *Recueil Dalloz Sirey de Doctrine, de Jurisprudence et de Législation* (1987): 5–10.

3. Lois du 2 Février 1981, 10 Juin 1983, 9 Septembre 1986, 1 Février 1994. This was not the first time such a movement appeared in French law. The Law of 27 Mai 1885 also aimed to condemn incorrigible criminals to life confinement in Guyane. A certain French desire for greater harshness has most recently made itself felt in the new French Criminal Code of 1994, which specifies longer terms where it requires imprisonment. See Poncela, *Droit de la peine*, 124.

4. "Aménagements des peines et libérations conditionelles," *Le Monde*, 19 Juillet 1999. The prison population in France roughly doubled, from 26,000 in 1975 to 51,600 in 1995.

5. Poncela, *Droit de la peine*, 189.

6. For discussion and references, see Prittwitz, "Positive Generalprävention und 'Recht des Opfers auf Bestrafung des Täters?' "

7. A series of semiofficial and official drafts of the late 1980s endorsed the idea of

gearing punishment to the measure of guilt in individual cases, rather than to the general policy of resocialization. Discussed in Klaus Laubenthal, *Strafvollzug*, 2d ed. (Berlin, 1998), 72–73. In particular, an important appellate decision of 1977 confirmed a decision to deny a 69-year-old Nazi war-criminal, condemned to life imprisonment, temporary release [Hafturlaub], on the grounds that the severity of his crime justified unusually restrictive measures. OLG Karlsruhe, JR 1978, 213. Child molesters too have been hit harder. See " 'Wegsperren' und Zwangstherapie," *Frankfurter Allgemeine Zeitung*, 11 Feb. 2000, 10.

8. Figures in Laubenthal, *Strafvollzug*, 21.

9. For examples, see the website of the Bundesjustizministerium, www.bmj.bund.de, under the rubric "Opferschutz."

10. See StGB § 46a, and generally B.-D. Meier, *Strafrechtliche Sanktionen* (Berlin, 2001), 309-336, which notes, at 310, that this procedure is rarely used.

11. Ministère de la Justice. Direction de l'Administration Pénitentiaire, "Les chiffres clés de l'administration pénitentiaire," May 2000, p. 4.

12. Bureau of Justice Statistics. "State Court Sentencing for Convicted Felons," 1996, p. 4, table. 1.5. On Internet at http://www.ojp.usdoj.gov/bjs/pub/pdf/scsc9601.pdf.

13. Bureau of Justice Statistics. Felony Sentences in the United States, 1996, p. 9. Table 11. On internet at http://www.ojp.usdoj.gov/bjs/pub/pdf/fsus96.pdf.

14. Rather than tallying statistics by sentence imposed, the Statistisches Bundesamt provides a snapshot of the prison population on a given day, which inevitably overstates the relative proportion of inmates serving longer sentences.

15. StGB § 47.

16. Only in theory, because, under the day fine system (see below), convicts who fail to pay their fines are jailed. It is widely believed in Germany that many convicts, especially in the former East German states, effectively choose prison rather than pay their fines. Here too, though, firm statistics are not available.

17. Bundesjustizministerium, Reform des Sanktionensystems, 8 Dec. 2000. German law has also seen efforts to safeguard privacy in criminal prosecutions. See K. Brodersen, "Das Strafänderungsgesetz 1999," *Neue Juristische Wochenschrift* (2000): 2536–2542.

18. "Les juges semblent resserer le recours à l'emprisonnement ferme en le cantonnant de plus en plus à des affaires de violence, d'immigration clandestine ou de stupéfiants. Mais quand ils y recourent, c'est pour des durées longues à très longues. La part de l'amende a profondément régressé en matière correctionnelle et l'on assiste à une remarquable percée des sanctions intermédiaires—sursis, mise à l'épreuve, travail d'intérêt géneral." P. Robert et al., *Les Comptes du Crime*, 2d ed. (Paris, 1994), 160.

19. Thus while it is true that French laws have cut back on individualization, they have done so only for crimes involving serious violence, sexual abuse of minors, and treason. Most luridly, it has become French law that murderers who have raped, tortured, or committed barbaric acts on victims younger than sixteen must suffer mandatory life imprisonment. Loi du 1er Février 1994 (art. 221–3, 221–4 NCP).

20. See Loi no. 2000–516 du 15 Juin 2000 renforçant la protection de la présomption d'innocence et les droits des victimes, § 57.

21. The contrast is noted even in some basic American texts on criminology. See, e.g., David Neubauer, *America's Courts and the Criminal Justice System*, 6th ed. (Belmont, Calif., 1999), 387, observing that while fines are often imposed in the United States, European practice is far more thoroughgoing. For investigations of the possibility of importing the day fine system into the United States, see Bureau of

Justice Statistics, *How to Use Structured Fines (Day Fines) as an Intermediate Sanction* (1996).

22. In Germany, the history of fines as a primary punishment is very long, reaching back to the end of the nineteenth century. See chapter 4 of this book.

23. France: Loi du 10 Juin, 1983; Poncela, *Droit de la Peine*, 129–130; G. Friedman, Comment, "The West German Day-Fine System: A Possibility for the United States?" *University of Chicago Law Review* 50 (1983): 281.

24. See chapter 4 of this book.

25. For the general state of affairs in Germany, see the contributions of T. Weigend and H.-J. Albrecht, "West Germany," in M. Tonry and K. Hatlestad, eds., *Sentencing Reform in Overcrowded Times: A Comparative Perspective* (Oxford, 1997), 177–187. The prevailing German attitude is described in an introductory text as follows: "Eine nicht erforderliche zwangsweise Ausgliederung von Personen aus ihrer gewohnten sozialen Umwelt und ihre Unterbringung in Vollzugsanstalten als mehr oder weniger gesellschaftlich isolierte Verbüßungsstätten, tangiert bereits die Würde des Menschen. Freiheitsentzug ist daher vor allem bei schweren Delikten—insbesondere Gewaltverbrechen—oder bei wiederholt rückfälligen Verhalten zur Aufrechterhaltung der Generalprävention und Bewahrung der öffentlichen Sicherheit vor weiteren Taten eines Straffälligen unentbehrlich. Allerdings muß dann ihre Dauer auch auf das generalpräventiv Notwendige beschränkt bleiben und darf sich spezialpräventiv nicht schädlich auswirken." Laubenthal, *Strafvollzug*, 1. Thus convicts who are sentenced to serve time in Germany can still ordinarily expect to be released on parole after two-thirds, and sometimes less, of their sentence has been served. § 57 StGB.

26. See "Seles-Attentäter Parche Verurteilt," *Frankfurter Allgemeine Zeitung*, Oct. 14, 1993. On the European level, too, a 1992 recommendation of the Council of Europe pushes for limiting imprisonment as a penalty. Rec. 92/17.

27. Poncela, *Droit de la peine*, 133–144.

28. Ibid., 393.

29. Ibid., 130.

30. Loi no. 2000–516 du 15 Juin 2000 renforçant la protection de la présomption d'innocence et les droits des victimes, § 57.

31. "Bundesjustizministerium, Reform des Sanktionensystems," 8. Dec. 2000. See "Strafen mit Fantasie," *Die Zeit*, 19 April 2000, 4.

32. Patrick Langan and Jodi Brown, *Felony Sentences in State Courts, 1994*. (Washington, D.C., 1997).

33. Possession of drugs brought a term of prison or jail for 66 percent of defendants in American state courts in 1994. Langan and Brown, *Felony Sentences in State Courts, 1994*.

34. For German law: §29 Betäubungsmittelgesetz, and H. Körner, ed., *Betäubungsmittelgesetz*, 5th ed. (Munich, 2001), § 29, Rdn. 13; for French law: F. Caballero and Y. Bisiou, *Droit de la Drogue*, 2d ed. (Paris, 2000), 549. Under a 1970 statute that has resisted many efforts at reform, drug consumption remains illegal in France. Nevertheless, where there is intervention at all, it is generally in the form of court-ordered treatment. See ibid., 549–550.

35. For the decline in admissions (1980: 97,000; 1996: 80,000) see "Un groupe d'experts propose une refonte de la politique d'aménagement des peines," *Le Monde*, 19, Juillet 1999.

36. Poncela, *Droit de la peine*, 182–183.

37. Departing from long tradition, the new code has, in classic individualizing fashion, tended to eliminate extenuating circumstances, and defenses such as provoca-

tion, entirely as a codified doctrine. Poncela, *Droit de Peine*, 201–202, for general account. Instead, the new code generally limits itself to only maximum penalties, leaving it to the discretion of judges to set lower penalties where they see fit. The code does also specify certain minimum penalties in Art. 132–18, though they themselves testify to a spirit of leniency. If the maximum penalty is life in prison, the minimum that must be ordered is ten years, and otherwise the minimum is of one year. Note Art. 132-19, al. 2, NCP, which requires judges to give particular reasons any time they choose *not* to parole the accused.

Within the French prisons, a system of individualization remains quite well entrenched, despite all of the agitation of the last twenty years. Special "juges de l'application des peines," charged with supervising convicts, have a wide range of options for easing the lot of prisoners, and particularly for granting them various forms of semiliberty. Generally Poncela, *Droit de la Peine*, 252–269. For an account by one of them emphasizing the depth of their duties, see X. Lameyre, "Pour une éthique des soins pénalement obligés," *Médecine et Droit* 34 (2000): 1–23. Normally, the period of fixed penalty in France is half of the statutory sentence, though extension of the sentence is also possible. In most cases, it remains possible even for French inmates sentenced to fixed terms to enjoy early dispensation, if they show "gages sérieux de réadaptation sociale"—the classic individualizing test. To be sure, limitations remain. See "La chute des libérations conditionnelles accroît la désespérance des détenus," *Le Monde*, 19 Juillet 1999, giving figures. The decline in grants of parole also reflects the tightness of the French job market, since inmates must demonstrate "gages sérieux de réadaptation sociale" that ordinarily include the prospect of employment.

38. E.g., G. Kaiser, H.-J. Kerner, and H. Schöch, *Strafvollzug. Eine Einführung in die Grundlagen* (Heidelberg, 1991), 24–28.

39. For the contemporary view, E.g., R. Badinter, *La Prison (1871–1914)* (Paris, 1992), 181–182.

40. Saleilles, *The Individualization of Punishment*, trans. R. Jastrow (Boston, 1911), 60; and, in the Marxist tradition, E.-B. Pashukanis, *La Théorie Générale du Droit et le Marxisme*, trans. J.-M. Brohm (Paris, 1970), 162–163. For the leading modern American economic analysis of the same issue, see R. Cooter, "Prices and Sanctions," *Columbia Law Review* 84 (1984): 1523–1560.

41. For an early statement of continental dissatisfaction with Beccaria, see C. J. A. Mittermaier, *Über den neuesten Zustand der Criminalgesetzgebung in Deutschland* (Heidelberg, 1825), 9–10. For the turn to doctrines of extenuating circumstances in France after 1830, see chapter 4.

42. It is worth noting that the idea of depravity egalitarianism, like the idea of act egalitarianism, can of course itself be viewed as a Christian philosophy of punishment.

43. For the contrast with Anglo-American law, see the report of M. Kilchling, "Tatproportionalität in den theoretischen und empirischen Grundlagen der Strafzumessung," *Monatsschrift für Kriminologie und Strafrechtsreform* 83 (2000): 30–31.

44. Dienst- und Vollzugsordnung of 1961. This came a little bit later, that is, than the rise of modern German *Persönlichkeitsschutz*. The reigning doctrine of the 1950s held that inmates, along with other dependent persons such a schoolchildren, soldiers, and functionaries, stood in a "besonderes Gewaltverhältnis," a special relationship of subjection. For this, and its breakdown, see W. Loschelder, "Staatseingliederung als Institutionalisierungsproblem. Zur Entwicklung und Krise des besonderen Gewaltverhältnisses," in D. Merten, ed., *Das besondere Gewaltverhältnis* (Berlin, 1985), 9–32.

45. Kaiser et al., *Strafvollzug*, 46, with references to further literature.

46. BVerfGe, *Neue Juristische Wochenschrift* (1972): 811: "Abschied vom besonderen Gewaltverhältnis."

47. Cf. J. Baumann et al., eds., *Alternativ-Entwurf eines Strafvollzugsgesetzes* (Tübingen, 1973).

48. See C. Messner and V. Ruggiero, "Germany: The Penal System between Past and Future," in V. Ruggiero, M. Ryan, and J. Sim, eds., *Western European Penal Systems* (London, 1995), 128–148

49. See chapter 4.

50. See, e.g., Observatoire International des Prisons, Section Française, *Prisons: Un État des Lieux* (Paris, 2000); and the two legislative reports of 2000, cited and discussed below.

51. See "Les Prisons: Une Humiliation pour la République." Rapport du Sénat no. 449 (2000), 80–92; for improvement efforts over the last decade, see M. Colin and J.-P. Jean, "La Prison, Parlons-en," *Libération*, Feb. 15, 2000. Minister Elisabeth Guigou announced a plan to build seven new prisons in January of 2000.

52. Cf. Mushlin, *Rights of Prisoners*, 66 n. 296.

53. Cf., e.g., "Trois surveillants de la Prison de Fleury-Merogis condamnés pour agressions sexuelles sur des travestis," *Le Monde*, 03.02.99.

54. As in American prisons, French prisons are regarded as being troubled by the problem of homosexual rape. See Léauté, *Les Prisons*, 80. For one recent French exposé by a prison guard describing the rape of one inmate by another, see Christophe Lambert, *Derrière les Barreaux* (Paris, 1999); and for a recent scandal, "Un détenu, terreur des cellules, frappe deux fois," *Libération*, 12 Juillet 2000, 17.

55. K. Weis, "Die Subkultur der Strafgefangenen," in H.-D. Schwind and G. Blau, eds., *Strafvollzug in der Praxis*, 2d ed. (Berlin, 1988), 246–249. When I asked the director of one German facility about the problem of homosexual rape, he averred that there was undoubtedly far more of it than came to the attention of authorities.

56. Some discussion, without any investigation of empirical circumstances, in Laubenthal, *Strafvollug*, 139–140 (focusing on language difficulties and impossibility of preparing foreigners for social integration when they will generally be deported upon release.) See also ibid., 351, for the problems arising from housing deportees in the same institutions with other inmates.

57. V. Vasseur, *Médecin-Chef à la Prison de la Santé* (Paris, 2000). Dr. Vasseur did not make it clear until the end of her sensational text that she had worked in an investigative custody facility—a point of great significance. For controversy between Dr. Vasseur and internal gatherers of statistics, see "Polémique sur le nombre de tentatives de suicide à la Prison de la Santé," *Le Monde*, May 5, 2000.

58. For the background: "Les Députés votent à l'Unanimité la Création d'une Commission d'Enquête sur les Prisons," *Le Monde*, Feb. 5, 2000.

59. "L'enfer carcéral secoue la République," *Libération*, 6 Juillet 2000, 2. Cf. "Voyage au bout de l'horreur dans les prisons françaises," *Le Monde*, 5 Feb. 2000: "indigne d'une démocratie."

60. As two French magistrates put it: "Les prisons sont l'image de notre démocratie, et doivent proposer un contre-modèle à celui de la société sécuritaire des États-Unis." Colin and Jean, *Libération*, Feb. 15, 2000. The reforms have brought important changes to internal prison discipline, much resisted by guards. See "Les avocats admis au 'prétoire' des prisons," *Le Monde*, 16 Octobre 2000, 32; "Les premier fruits de la réforme du régime disciplinaire des détenus," *Le Monde*, 10 Juillet 1999.

61. For similar reform movements in Germany under the current government, see

"Schwitzen statt Sitzen," *Die Zeit*, Nov. 28, 2000, 1, and interview with Herta Däubler-Gmelin, ibid., 8–9.

62. E.g., "2000 personnes manifestent leur colère contre la justice," *Libération*, May 28, 2001, 16; "Ein Fingerabdruck führte die Polizei zum Täter," *Frankfurter Allgemeine Zeitung*, March 30, 2001, 9; "Schmökel bleibt noch in Bautzener Klinik," *Süddeutsche Zeitung*, November 9, 2000, 16; "Traf sich Jessica mit ihrem Mörder?" *Frankfurter Allgemeine Zeitung*, January 13, 1999, 9; "Zwei Kindermörder noch auf freiem Fuss," *Frankfurter Allgemeine Zeitung*, May 15, 1998, 13.

63. Other reform efforts are also afoot in France—in particular a new guarantee of legal representation for convicts at their disciplinary proceedings. See Commission National Consultative des Droits de l'Homme, "Avis Portant sur le Régime Disciplinaire des Détenus," June 17, 1999; "Les avocats admis au 'prétoire' des prisons," *Le Monde*, Oct. 16, 2000. When I spoke with prison officials about these efforts in 2000, though, it was clear that they faced considerable resistance from guards.

64. For the importance of the applicability of international norms in France since 1975, M. Hezog-Evans, "Vers une Prison Normative?" in C. Veil and D. Lhuilier, *La Prison en Changement* (Ramonville-Saint-Agne, 2000), 47–48; and for a simple account familiarizing inmates with the law, B. Boze et al., *Le nouveau Guide du Prisonnier* (n.p., 2000), 383–391. The norms are not directly applicable in Germany, but have an important and growing influence nevertheless. See, R.-P. Calliess and H. Müller-Dietz, *Strafvollzugsgesetz*, 9th ed. (Munich, 2002), introduction, 30.

65. This is simply typical of a more general difference: specialized training is the norm in France, by contrast with the United States, not only for guards but also for such actors as prosecutors, judges and law professors. Cf. R. Frase, "Comparative Criminal Justice as a Guide to American Law Reform: How Do the French Do It, How Can We Find Out, and Why Should We Care?" *California Law Review* 78(1990): 542, 564.

66. "Eric, La nouvelle vie d'un patron fraîchement sorti de prison," *Le Monde* 19.07.99: "En maison d'arrêt, c'est le caïdat qui régule la prison. J'ai assisté à plusieurs tabassages, des règlements de comptes, deux morts . . . [at Fresnes] Ça a été un vrai soulagement pour moi, je rencontrais enfin des gens qui nous traitaient humainement, individuellement." One is placed ordinarily in a maison d'arrêt as a "prévenu"—that is to say, a person inculpated by a "juridiction d'instruction et incarcérée en vertu d'un mandat de cette juridiction." For the establishment of different classes of prisons depending on length of sentence, see Léauté, *Les Prisons*, 104–107.

67. See "U.S. Fugitive is Sentenced to Three Years in Germany," *New York Times*, June 22, 2000, C4.

68. Frase, "Comparative Criminal Justice," 574–611.

69. For overcrowding in investigative custody in France, see "Prisons: Une Humiliation pour la République," 116–126, and "La France face à ses Prisons," Rapport de l'Assemblée Nationale no. 2521 (2000), 21–44. See also E.g., "Trois Détenus pour 9 mètres carrés," Sud-Ouest," Mar. 9, 2000; "Viols à la prison de Gradignan," Sud-Ouest, Mar. 7, 2000.

70. Loi no. 2000–516 du 15 Juin 2000 renforçant la protection de la présomption d'innocence et les droits des victimes, §48. For earlier efforts, see also Décret no 85–836 du 6 août.

71. E.g., "Les juges, leur malaise et leurs erreurs," *Le Monde*, 20 Jan. 2001.

72. Notably in the form of the *Meldepflicht*, the universal obligation to be registered with the authorities. See Melderechtsrahmengesetz v. 16.8.1980 (BGBl I S. 1430) most recently amended in Zweites Gesetz zur Änderung des Melderechtsrahmengesetzes vom 28.8.2000 (BGBl S. 1302).

73. See StPO § 112, and the comments of R. Schlothauer and H.-J. Weider, *Untersuchungshaft* (Heidelberg, 2001), 186–272.

74. For the situation before and after, see, e.g., "In Germany, Terrorists Made Use of a Passion: An Open Democracy," *New York Times*, Oct. 5, 2001, B6; "U.S. Terror Attacks Galvanize Europeans to Tighten Laws," *New York Times*, Dec. 6, 2001, B1.

75. Robert et al., *Les Comptes du Crime*, 141.

76. Poncela, *Droit de la Peine*, 288.

77. Laubenthal, *Strafvollug*, 139.

78. Reported to me at the time of my visit to the institution.

79. E.g., "Judge Refuses to Void Lawsuit Against INS," *Los Angeles Times*, July 26, 1997, B1.

80. For France: Frase, "Comparative Criminal Procedure," 567–568; for Germany: M. von Galen, "Prostitution and the Law in Germany," *Cardozo Women's Law Journal* 3 (1996): 349.

81. See the literature cited above, note 34.

82. M. Delmas-Marty and G. Giudicelli-Delage, *Droit Pénal des Affaires*, 4d ed. (Paris, 2000), 16–17.

83. See chapter 4.

84. For imprisonment for debt in Germany: ZPO §§ 916–945; for France, limited to penal debtors since 1867, see Code de Procédure Criminelle, Arts. 749–762.

85. P. Marini, *La modernisation du droit des sociétés* (Paris, 1996).

86. Delmas-Marty and Giudicelli-Delage, *Droit Pénal*, 171–200. In American terms, we would say that French law shows a continuing tendency to abide by the analysis of strict liability offenses classically given in *Morrissette v. United States*, 342 U.S. 246 (1952).

87. Delmas-Marty and Giudicelli-Delage, *Droit Pénal*, 205

88. *Wall Street Journal*, "Europe's Police are Out of Luck on Insider Cases: Convictions are Few Despite Signs Practice has Become Pervasive," August 17, 2000, C1.

89. See the discussion in W. Krekeler, K. Tiedemann, K. Ulsenheimer, and G. Weinmann, *Handwörterbuch des Wirtschafts- und Steuerstrafrechts* ([Heidelberg], 1990), 8.

90. For a general survey of German developments, see H.-B. Wabnitz and T. Janovsky, *Handbuch des Wirtschafts- und Steuerstrafrechts* (Munich, 2000), 19–50.

91. For Germany, StGB §§ 283–283d; for France, J. Larguier and P. Comte, *Droit Pénal des Affaires*, 10th ed. (Paris, 2001), 477–485.

92. Current American law probably shows a greater concern with whether bankruptcy courts can enjoin a criminal proceeding. See e.g., In re Seidelman, 57 B.R. 149, 14 Collier Bankr.Cas. 2d (MB) 1 (D.Md. 1986).

93. For Germany, see StGB §§ 263–266b; for France, NCP Art. 314–1, and E.g., the discussion of Larguier and Comte, *Droit Pénal des Affaires*, 166–212.

94. For this observation, see Wabnitz and Janovsky, *Handbuch des Wirtschafts- und Steuerstrafrechts*, 30.

95. This characterization was however highly problematic. See P. Velten, "Untreue durch Belastung mit Risiko zukünftiger Sanktionen am Beispiel bedeckter Parteienfinanzierung," *Neue Juristische Wochenschrift* (2000), 2852–2856 for a spirited go at the problem.

96. See, e.g., "Kohl zahlte 300,000 Mark wegen des Verdachts auf Untreue," Deutsche Presse-Agentur, June 8, 2001; and Werner Bosshardt, "Kohl–der grosse Schweiger," *Tages-Anzeiger*, February 10, 2001, 4; and Dr. Friedbert Pflüger, "Den Staatsmann Kohl ehren–das 'System Kohl' überwinden," *Frankfurter Allgemeine Zeitung*, April 6, 2000, 10.

97. This defense stirred massive criticism in the German press. See E.g., Volker Skierka, "Der Untersuchungsausschuss verblasste Mythen," *Süddeutsche Zeitung*, February 23, 2001, 14; and Eva Kohlrusch, "Lügen–der neue Gesellschaftssport," Bunte, November 9, 2000, 96; and Ludgera Vogt, "Die verlorene Ehre des Helmut K.," *taz, die tageszeitung*, January 22, 2000, 13.

98. Beaud, *Le Sang Contaminé: Essai Critique sur la Criminalisation de la Responsabilité des Gouvernants* (Paris, 1999).

99. For a success, there is of course the Elf-Aquitaine scandal. For a failure, see "Former French Finance Minister is Acquitted in Forgery Trial," *New York Times*, Nov. 8, 2001, A13. Further accounts: "Court Shields President Chirac from Corruption Inquiries," *New York Times*, Oct. 11, 2001, A3; "French Prime Minister Now has Legal Problems of his own," *New York Times*, November 23, 2001, A9.

100. For the contrast with America, e.g., J. Renucci and C. Courtin, *Le Droit Pénal des Mineurs*, 4th ed. (Paris, 2001), 22.

101. See chapter 4.

102. See generally W. Mitsch, *Recht der Ordnungswidrigkeiten* (Berlin, 1995).

103. See the texts cited above in note 34.

104. Moynihan, "Defining Deviancy Down," *The American Scholar* (1993): 17–30.

105. Compare Garland, *Culture of Control*, 117–119.

106. For an excellent survey of French downgrading, see Frase, "Comparative Criminal Justice," 567–574. The New Criminal Code of 1994 envisages the substitution of fines for imprisonment even in the case of crimes. Poncela, *Droit de la peine*, 120; and the Loi of 15 Juin testifies to a continuing drive to limit imprisonment.

107. Art. 131–16 NCP.

108. Above, n. 37.

109. StGB § 50.

110. See below.

111. Mme. Baste-Morand, in Société Générale des Prisons et de Législation Criminelle, Séance du 13 mars 1982. "Droits sociaux du détenu," *Revue Pénitentiaire et de Droit Pénal* (Juillet-Septembre 1982): 276. The rest:

> Droit à l'information. Les détenus n'ont jamais l'information qui les concerne directement. Il n'existe pas un règlement général et chaque établissement a son règlement particulier que les détenus ne connaissent pas. On ne leur communique jamais les motifs, l'époque et le lieu des transferts.
>
> Hygiène. À Fresnes, les détenus n'ont qu'une douche par semaine, ce qui n'est pas beaucoup.
>
> Travail. Pour un détenu sur deux, ce n'est pas une réalité.
>
> Instruction. Tous les détenus n'y ont pas accès.
>
> Activités physiques. Elles ne sont pas possibles dans les trois-quarts des établissements. Un seul exemple: la superficie très insuffisante de la cour de Fresnes.
>
> Vie privée. Il n'est pas normal que, lorsqu'un détenu écrit à sa femme, n'importe qui puisse lire sa lettre. Cette possibilité ne devrait appartenir qu'au seul service de censure.
>
> Secret médical. À Fleury-Mérogis, un détenu ne peut voir le médecin qu'en présence d'un surveillant. On ne lui communique pas les résultats des analyses médicales.

112. "Prisons: promesses non tenues," *Le Monde*, 9 Juillet 1999. (discussing maison d'arrêt in Beauvais).

113. From the jurisprudence of the European Union, see Yue Ma, "The European Court of Human Rights and the Protection of the Rights of Prisoners and Criminal Defendants under the European Convention on Human Rights," *International Criminal Justice Review* 10 (2000): 54–80.

114. For a fine comparative discussion of German and American law: N. Demleitner, "Continuing Payment on One's Debt to Society: The German Model of Felon Disenfranchisement as an Alternative," *Minnesota Law Review* 84 (2000): 753–804.

115. Some changes are certainly making their way into continental punishment—for example the electronic bracelet, borrowed from American practice. Nevertheless even here, resistance has been notable: a 1997 law introducing the electronic bracelet was simply not put into effect for three years, and then only a very limited basis. See "Des Condamnés vont pouvoir purger leur peine de prison à domicile," *Le Monde*, 13 Mai 2000.

116. See E.g., an English-language guide for prisoners who find themselves in France, R. Vogler, *France: A Guide to the French Criminal Justice System* (Rochdale, 1989), 118.

117. Froment, "Vers une 'prison de droit?'" *Revue de science criminelle et de droit comparé* (Juillet-Sept. 1997): 547.

118. For a general account, see Calliess and Muller-Dietz, *Stravollzugsgesetz*, § 3.

119. For a general description, see C. Bertram, et al., *Kommentar zum Strafvollzugsgesetz*, 3d ed. (Neuwied, 1990), §3. While German inmates can ordinarily possess radios, unlike their French counterparts, they can only exceptionally possess television sets. Laubenthal, *Strafvollzug*, 248.

120. Laubenthal, *Strafvollzug*, 257; § 20 Abs. 1, StVollzG.

121. This is the rule for leisure clothing, see LG Hamburg, 3.10.1989, in NStZ 1990, 255–256, but work uniforms too resemble clothing in the outside world. Prison officials may, in their discretion, allow inmates to wear their own clothes. OLG Karlsruhe, NStZ 1996, 303. Cf. H.-D. Schwind and A. Böhm, *Strafvollzugsgesetz* (Berlin, 1999), § 20 Rdn. 7.

122. *Strafvollzugsgesetz*, § 5. This is intended both to protect the "Intimsphäre" of the inmate and to prevent rapid acculturation to prison subculture. Schwind and Böhm, *Strafvollzugsgesetz*, § 5 Rdn. 2.

123. For further discussion, Schwind and A. Böhm, *Strafvollzugsgesetz*, § 3 Rdn. 14.

124. In other respects, German law resembles French. With the exception of terrorists and drug dealers, German inmates, like French ones, cannot generally be restricted to visits behind glass partitions. Laubenthal, *Strafvollzug*, 210–211. Drug dealers: OLG Koblenz, NStZ 1991, 304

125. See *Hudson v. Palmer*, 468 U.S. 517, 526 (1984) (inmates cannot have the same expectation of privacy as persons in the outside world).

126. *Rhodes v. Chapman*, 452 U.S. 337, 347 (1981).

127. Zakine, in "Société Générale des Prisons et de Législation Criminelle, Séance du 13 mars 1982. Droits sociaux du détenu," in *Revue Pénitentiaire et de Droit Pénal* (Juillet-septembre 1982): 271.

128. Ibid., 268. Zakine's survey included still, remarkably enough, an echo of the late-eighteenth-century concern to spare the families of inmates difficulty. The reform legislation, as he described it, reflected:

—la volonté de politique générale d'étendre à l'ensemble de la population française le bénéfice des prestations de la Sécurité sociale;

—la volonté de ne pas pénaliser les familles des détenus qui doivent déjà surmonter de graves difficultés financières et morales;

—la volonté d'accroître les possibilités de réinsertion des détenus libérés en les mettant eux-mêmes et leurs familles à l'abri des conséquences d'une maladie ou d'un accident.

Ibid., 268–269.

129. Ibid., 1982, 273.

130. Section 2, S. 1 of the 1977 statute on punishment, which requires that punishment make possible a "socially responsible way of life" for convicts, is understood to derive directly from the constitutional sanctifications of human dignity and of the social state principle. Laubenthal, *Strafvollzug*, 8. Necessarily, the Stravollzugsgesetz limits the application of certain constitutional provisions in its § 196 StVollzG.

131. For the requirement, and the practical difficulties in providing work for all, see most recently R.-P. Calliess, "Die Neuregelung des Arbeitsentgelts im Strafvollzug," *Neue Juristische Wochenschrift* (2001): 1693. This raises some uncomfortable problems for European traditions, which, as we shall see, associate forced labor with low-status punishment. Nevertheless, the requirement to work has been deemed acceptable by the German Constitutional Court (see BVerfG 1.7.1998, in *Neue Juristische Wochenschrift* (1998), 3337–3342); and, despite the prohibition on forced labor in the Charter of Fundamental Rights Art. 5, II. See Calliess, ibid.

132. Laubenthal, *Strafvollzug*, 192.

133. "Häftlinge werden besser versorgt als Versicherte," *Süddeutsche Zeitung*, June 20, 2000, 6.

134. Laubenthal, *Strafvollzug*, 168.

135. Calliess, "Neuregelung des Arbeitsentgelts," 1692–1694. These are reckoned in weeks of six days because of the well-established tradition that inmates rest on the sabbath, which extends far back. See A. Klein, *Die Vorschriften über Verwaltung und Strafvollzug in den Preußischen Justizgefängnissen* (Berlin, 1905), 114.

136. Calliess, "Neuregelung," 1694.

137. Froment, "Vers une 'prison de droit?'" *Revue de science criminelle et de droit comparé* (Juillet-Sept, 1997): 547. For further discussion, see Léauté, *Les Prisons*, 62.

138. Whitman, "Enforcing Civility and Respect."

139. CPP D. 249-3-1, 249-3-2, 249-3-3. Discussed in Herzog-Evans, "La réforme du régime disciplinaire dans les établissements pénitentiaires," *Revue pénitentiare et de droit pénal* (1997): 16. Despite changes of regime, the general tendency toward safeguarding "dignity" in prison conditions is continuing in France. Newly announced prison renovations aim (among other things) to establish small apartments without surveillance in which inmates can be visited by their families. See "Mme. Guigou annonce la rénovation de cinq prisons," *Le Monde* 28 Juillet 1999. The law of insult is generally absent in American discussions, though the issue is at least mentioned in one account of current prison conditions: "The inmates [in the District of Columbia prison complex at Lorton] complain that officers can address them in any manner they please, but if an inmate talks back to or disagrees with an officer, he is charged with a violation—disrespect, threatening conduct, or lying—and is punished accordingly." Lezin, "Life at Lorton," 175.

140. BVerfG 14.3.1972, in *Neue Juristische Wochenschrift* (1972): 811–814.

141. ZfStrVO 1995, 207–208. Calliess and Müller-Dietz, *Strafvollzugsgesetz*, § 5 Rdn. 1.

142. Generally Laubenthal, *Strafvollzug*, 207–213, and OLG Bamberg, NStZ 1995, 304. Limited experimentation with conjugal visits (on the American model!) has taken place. Laubenthal, *Strafvollzug*, 212–213.

143. Laubenthal, *Strafvollzug*, 194.

144. Calliess and Müller-Dietz, *Strafvollzugsgesetz*, §7 Rdn. 1.

145. See Bertram et al., *Kommentar zum Strafvollzugsgesetz*, § 10 Rdn. 6.

146. Laubenthal, *Strafvollug*, 161.

147. BVerfG 30.05.1996, in ZfStrVo 1997, 111–113. See further Callies and Müller-Dietz, *Strafvollzugsgesetz*, § 3 Rdn. 3.

148. More broadly, German courts confront numerous questions of the character of inmate dignity that are rich in the odors of German everyday dignitary culture. German jurists face the questions, for example, of whether a violent offender fond of painting violent scenes may be forbidden to paint (yes) (OLG Nürnberg, ZfStrVo 1989, 374); whether a con-man guilty of repeatedly bilking women on a promise of marriage could be forbidden to write letters to potential victims (again yes). These examples are collected and discussed in Laubenthal, *Strafvollug*, 94–97; whether a prisoner serving a life sentence could be forbidden to keep a pet bird (no). See E. Vogelgesang, "Kleintierhaltung im Strafvollzug," in *Zeitschrift für Strafvollzug* (1994), 67–68; whether a prisoner could be forbidden to post an oversize photo of her fiancé, where prison authorities claimed that such photos hampered their security efforts (no without more detailed findings). OLG "Zweibrücken," ZfStrVo (1995): 374–375.

149. See "Dienst und Sicherheitsvorschriften für den Strafvollzug" (DSVollz), I, § 10.

150. BVerfG 12. 9. 1994, in JR 1995, 379–383, with critical commentary by M. Kiesel. For limits, see BVerfG 30.4.1992 in *Neue Juristische Wochenschrift* (1994): 244.

151. While inmates' right to "Persönlichkeitsentfaltung" guarantees them a certain right to freely compose letters, prison officials *are* permitted, under the principles of the "Verhältnismäßigkeitsgrundsatz," to intercept letters that that include "grob unrichtige oder erheblich entstellende Darstellungen von Anstaltsverhältnissen" or that include "grobe Beleidigungen." Laubenthal, *Strafvollzug*, 200. Nevertheless, the Constitutional Court has upheld the right of one inmate to use the phrase "Reichsparteitag-OLG" where prison officials regarded the phrase as a "grobe Beleidigung" (BVerfG, StrVert 1993, 600) and of another inmate to use the phrase "berüchtigter Misanthrop," where the prison censor regarded that phrase as a knowing injury to his honor. BVerfG, ZfStrVo 1996, 111. The special tensions of imprisonment put special pressures on the law of insult. In one case, for example, a law student sent her imprisoned brother a letter that read in part: "Vergiß auch nicht, daß Du fast ausschließlich mit Kretins (Schwachsinnigen) zu tun hast, die auf Beförderung geil sind oder ganz einfach Perverse sind. Denk dabei auch an die KZ-Aufseher und Du weißt, welche Menschengruppe Dich umgibt. Versuche damit, Dein doch sonst immer lebensbejahendes Denken und Dein fröhliches Wesen aufrecht zu erhalten." Intercepted by prison authorities, this letter became the subject of an insult action against its author, who was convicted and fined. The Constitutional Court held, however, that the letter constituted protected expression: insulting though the letter might be, it was a communication within what had to be a protected private sphere within the penal world. For limits on the rights of right radicals, see BVerfG 29.6.1995, in ZfStrVo 1996, 174–178.

152. BVerfG, StrVert 1994, 441.

153. For the primary importance of the Lebach decision, see E.g., Calliess and H. Müller-Dietz, *Strafvollzugsgesetz*, introduction, 14. Lebach has been limited in ways that are not directly relevant in BVerfG, 1 BvR 348/98 vom 25.11.1999, Absatz-Nr. (1–45), http://www.bverfg.de/. For an early effort to analyze German prison law in light of contemporary constitutional norms: A. Krebs, "Entwicklung der Persönlichkeitserforschung im deutschen Gefängniswesen," *Zeitschrift für Strafvollzug* 1954 (4): 241–252.

154. Typically, commentary on this jurisprudence is often framed in Kantian terms, speaking of the imperative of not reducing the convict to an "object." E.g, Laubenthal, *Strafvollzug*, 57, 133. Nevertheless, the background social assumptions show through clearly enough.

155. § 86 StVollzG; see Laubenthal, *Strafvollzug*, 282.

156. This question raises complications that go beyond what can profitably be discussed in this text. In particular, the latest reform on protection of information embodies a complex compromise. See K. Brodersen, "Das Strafverfahrensänderungsgesetz 1999," 2536–2542.

157. Article 9-1 du code civil, introduit par la Loi n° 93-2 du 5 Janvier 1993.

158. For a further move in this direction—aiming to protect not only accused persons but also victims from publicity—see "Elisabeth Guigou tente d'apaiser la polémique sur le droit à l'image," *Le Monde*, Oct. 6, 1999.

159. For a German-language account noting the distinctiveness of French law, see I. Sagel-Grande, "Die Amnestie—ein Rechtsinstitut mit deutscher Zukunft? Überlegungen am Beispiel Frankreich," in *Recht in Ost und West* 34 (1990): 293–298.

160. Though note that "amnistie" (art. 133–9 to 133–11 NCP) is technically different from "grâce" (art. 133–7 to 133–8) in French law.

161. See chapter 4.

162. Amnesties of 16.8.1947, 5.1.1951, 20.2.1953, 6.8.1953, 8.8.1956, 9.6.1958. These have not succeeded in preventing a drastic recent growth in the prison population, though. In particular, the amnesties of 1981, 1988, and 1995, along with other collective pardons, have not stopped the broad rise in the French prison population. See "Aménagements des peines et libérations conditionelles," *Le Monde*, 19 Juillet 1999.

163. E.g., amnesty of 16 juillet 1974 (accession of Président Giscard d'Estaing); amnesty of August 4, 1981 (after accession of Président Mitterand, and made on the symbolic anniversary of the abolition of feudalism, August 4, 1789). For the full terms of such an amnesty, see Loi no. 88–828, du 20 Juillet 1988, Portant amnistie, *Actualité Législative Dalloz Année* (1988): 384–388. For a survey of this history, and an expression of doubt about the wisdom of continuing the old royal tradition, see M.-H. Renaut, "Le droit de grâce doit-il disparaître?" *Revue de Science Criminelle* (July/Sept., 1996), 575–606. For a defense from a standard text, J. Pradel, *Droit Pénal*, 6th ed. (Paris, 1987), 1: 820–821.

164. For a study of the contrasts, see A. Spies, *Amnestiemaßnahmen und deren Verfassungsmässigkeit in Frankreich und Deutschland* (Frankfurt a. M., 1992), 11–82.

165. See J.-G. Schätzler, *Handbuch des Gnadenrechts*, 2d ed. (Munich, 1992), 45–48.

166. Goffman, *Asylums*.

Chapter 4

1. See *Voltaire et l'Europe. Exposition Bibliothèque Nationale de France/Monnaie de Paris* (Paris, 1994), 54.

2. Spierenburg, *The Spectacle of Suffering: Executions and the Evolution of Repression: From a Preindustrial Metropolis to the European Experience* (Cambridge, 1984).

3. For a typical account, see, E.g., A. F. Berner, *Die Strafgesetzgebung in Deutschland vom Jahre 1751 bis zur Gegenwart* (1867) (Repr. Aalen, 1978), 122. A great deal of this literature is surveyed in Whitman, "What is Wrong with Inflicting Shame Sanctions?" 1055–1092.

4. P. Spierenburg, *The Prison Experience.*

5. On this, and on Bérenger, whose father had been rapporteur of the Tocqueville and Beaumont report, see Badinter, *La Prison Républicaine*, 247–266, 41, and often.

6. E.g., M.-L. Rassat, *Droit Pénal* (Paris, 1987), 612–614; R. Charles, *Histoire du Droit Pénal* (Paris, 1976), 98–105; M. Patin, "Du sursis et des circonstances atténuantes, *Revue de Science Criminelle et de droit pénal comparé* (1947): 341–347; C. Germain, "Le sursis et la probation," *Revue de Science Criminelle et de droit pénal comparé* (1954): 629–651.

7. For fines, E.g., Kaiser et al., *Strafvollzug*, 30; for the conditional pardon, below.

8. E.g., Kaiser et al., *Strafvollzug*, 8–9.

9. Especially through the work of Radbruch as Reichsjustizminister—work embodied in the Reichsratsgrundsätze of 1923. See RGBl 1923, 263–282.

10. §48 Verordnung über den Vollzug von Freiheitsstrafen 1934, in RGBl. I 1934, 383: "Durch die Verbüßung der Freiheitsstrafe sollen die Gefangenen das begangene Unrecht sühnen. Die Freiheitsentziehung ist so zu gestalten, daß sie für den Gefangenen ein empfindliches Übel ist and auch denen, die einer Erziehung nicht zugänglich sind, nachhaltige Hemmungen gegenüber der Versuchung, neue Straftaten zu begehen, erzeugt." See also "Strafvollzugsordnung," *Amtl. Sonderveröffentlichungen der deutschen Justiz*, 1940, no. 21.

11. E.g., Kaiser et al., 9–11; H. D. Quedenfeld, *Der Strafvollzug in der Gesetzgebung des Reiches, des Bundes und der Länder* (Tübingen, 1971), 37.

12. M. Broszat, "Nationalsozialistische Konzentrationslager, 1933–1945," in H. Buchheim et al., eds., *Anatomie des SS-Staates* (Olten, 1965) 2:9–160; W. Sofsky, *Die Ordnung des Terrors: Das Konzentrationslager* (Frankfurt a.M., 1993).

13. Léauté, *Les Prisons*, 45. For Vichy harshness more generally: C. Chromienne, "Juger les Juges?" in *Juger sous Vichy* (Paris, 1994), 15–16; A. Bancaud, "La magistrature et la répression politique de Vichy ou l'histoire d'un demi-échec," *Droit et Société* 34 (1996): 557–574.

14. E.g., S. Plawski, "Les droits de l'homme dans le procès et l'exécution des peines," *Revue Pénitentiaire et de Droit Pénal* (1978): 203.

15. Universal Declaration of Human rights (1948), Art. 5; International Covenant on Economic, Social and Cultural Rights (16. Dec. 1966), Art. 7; European Convention on Human Rights (4 nov. 1950) (ratified by Germany in 1952; ratified 1974 by France and permitting individual recourse by French citizens as of 9 Oct. 1981), art. 3 (cf. also art. 8 on privacy); Convention against Torture and other Cruel, Inhuman or Degrading Treatment or Punishment, 10 Dec. 1984 (entered into force in France 01.05.89); Convention on the Rights of the Child, 26 Janvier 1990.

16. Discussed in Léauté, *Les Prisons*, 45. The Code de Procédure Pénale of 1958 aimed to establish resocialization as the principle goal of French punishment practice.

17. E.g., C. Roxin, *Strafrecht: Allgemeiner Teil* (Munich, 1992), 79.

18. E.g., P. Pedron, *La Prison sous Vichy* (Paris, 1993); G. Pauli, *Die Rechtsprechung des Reichsgerichts in Strafsachen zwischen 1933 und 1945 und ihre Fortwirkung in der Rechtsprechung des Bundesgerichtshofes* (Berlin, 1992).

19. R. Mousnier, *Les Institutions de la France sous la Monarchie Absolue, 1589–1789* (Paris, 1974–1980).

20. See, e.g., R. van Dülmen, *Der Ehrlose Mensch: Unehrlichkeit und soziale Ausgrenzung in der frühen Neuzeit* (Cologne, 1999).

21. [P.P.N.] Henrion de Pansey, *Dissertations Féodales* (Paris, 1789), 1:286.

22. Le Roy Ladurie, *Saint-Simon and the Court of Louis XIV*, trans. Goldhammer (Chicago, 2001), 93–119.

23. Esp. his discussion of the German-speaking world in *Prison Experience*, 161–170.

24. See the brief account in Spierenburg, *Spectacle of Suffering*, 66–77.

25. For the savagery of sixteenth-century punishment, see Muchembled, *Le Temps des Supplices: de l'obéissance sous les rois absolus, XVe–XVIIIe siècle* (Paris, 1992), 81–125. For the decline, see Spierenburg, *Spectacle of Suffering*; R. Evans, *Rituals of Retribution: Capital Punishment in Germany, 1600–1987* (Oxford, 1996), 47–48; Sellin, *Slavery and the Penal System*, 43 and the literature cited in 183 n. 2.

26. These quotes from J. Döpler, *Theatrum Poenarum, Suppliciorum et Executionum Criminalium, oder Schau-Platz derer Leibes- und Lebensstraffen* (Sondershausen: In Verlegung des Autoris, 1693–1697), 2:200 (von Aufhencken), 2:73 (von der Hinrichtung mit dem Schwerd).

27. Muyart de Vouglans, *Institutes au Droit Criminel ou Principes Généraux sur ces Matières* (Paris, 1768), 288.

28. The two frequently cited Greek texts were Odyssey 22.462, and the scholiast in W. Dindorf, *Scholia Graeca in Homeri Odysseam* (Amsterdam, 1962), 714, which described beheading as a purer death than hanging; and Xenophon, Anabasis, Bk. II, chapt. 6 for the honorability of beheading. This is nothing simple about interpreting this evidence on its own terms. See the discussion in E. Cantarella, "Per una Preistoria del Castigo," in *Du Châtiment dans la Cité* (Rome, 1984), 41–44; and N. Loraux, "Le corps étranglé," in ibid., 195–218. For various forms of hanging offenders up for display in the Greek world, see Halm-Tisserant, *Réalités et Imaginaires des Supplices*, 168–181. For beheading at Rome, C. Lovisi, *Contribution à l'Étude de la Peine de Mort sous la République Romaine* (Paris, 1999), 158. Undoubtedly the honorability of death by beheading in the occident had something to do with its military associations. Other associations also played a confusing role, though: hanging was sometimes associated with the Crucifixion; and beheading was sometimes associated with the death of John the Baptist.

29. See Evans, *Rituals of Retribution*, 47–48; Hans von Hentig, *Die Strafe* (Berlin, 1955), 1:206.

30. D. Bodde and C. Morris, *Law in Imperial China*, 92. For dishonorable beheading in the Han, see A.F.P. Hulsewé, *Remnants of Han Law*, 1: 110–111.

31. Again, e.g., Muyart de Vouglans, *Institutes au Droit Criminel*, 288.

32. Ulpian in D. 48.19.8.9. For incorporation in early modern law, Langbein, *Torture and the Law of Proof*, 28–29; David J. Rothman, *The Discovery of the Asylum: Social Order and Disorder in the New Republic* (Boston, 1971), chaps. 1 and 2.

33. Convenient illustrated accounts of all these can be found in nineteenth-century standards such as M. B. Saint-Edme, *Dictionnaire de la Pénalité*, 5 vols. (Paris, 1826–1828).

34. Spierenburg, *Prison Experience*, 23–25; for galleys, Langbein, *Torture and the Law of Proof*, 30–39; and the excellent account in R. van Dülmen, *Theater of Horror*, trans E. Neu (Cambridge, 1990), 43–57.

35. Foucault, *Surveiller et Punir* (Paris, 1975), 59, and generally 41–83.

36. For a textbook account, A. Laingui and A. Lebigre, *Histoire du Droit Pénal* (Paris, 1979), 116–119.

37. See esp. the fine account in van Dülmen, *Theater of Horror*, 43–57.

38. E.g., Muyart de Vouglans, *Institutes au Droit Criminel*, 296.

39. Ulrich Huber, *Eunomia Romana, sive Censura Censurae Juris Justinianaei*, ed. Z. Huber (Franeker, 1700), 142–143.

40. See D. 48.19.10. The Roman tradition did create some controversy among early modern jurists. See, e.g., C. Ziegler, *In Hugonis Grotii de Jure Belli ac Pacis Libros Notae et Animadversiones*, 4th ed. (Strasbourg, 1706), 460ff.

41. Spierenburg, *Prison Experience*, 45, 163, 243–246; and for a classic pre-French Revolution discussion, M. Robespierre, "Discours sur les peines infamantes," in *Oeuvres Complètes* (Paris, 1912), 1:20–47. This was sometimes true of traditional Chinese law as well: see Hulsewé, *Remnants of Han Law*, 135.

42. E.g., discussion and citations in Karl Richard Sontag, *Die Festungshaft. Ein Beitrag zur Geschichte des deutschen Strafsystems und zur Erläuterung des Reichsstrafrechts* (Leipzig/Heidelberg: Winter, 1872), 20.

43. Spierenburg, *Prison Experience*, 223–255; R. v. Hippel, *Deutsches Strafrecht* (Berlin, 1925), 1:240–249.

44. See most recently Spierenburg, *Prison Experience*, 13–14; and H. Treiber and H. Steinert, *Die Fabrikation des zuverlässigen Menschen. Über die 'Wahlverwandschaft' von Kloster- und Fabrikdisziplin* (Munich, 1980). Down into the nineteenth century, the principal French prisons were all former monastic institutions. See Badinter, *La Prison Républicaine*, 32.

45. San Michele, once rather neglected in the protestant historiography, has begun to find its place. See E.g., Kaiser et al., *Strafvollzug*, 37.

46. This secularization of monastic discipline probably distinguishes the European Christian tradition from the Buddhist tradition in particular: Buddhism too developed a system of monastic discipline; but Buddhist monastic rules are generally taken never to have become the basis of a secularized legal system in East Asia. This is a comparison that deserves more careful development, though.

47. E.g., Hentig, *Die Strafe*, 1:172–175.

48. E.g., F. v. Holtzendorff and E. Jagemann, eds., *Handbuch des Gefängniswesens* (Hamburg, 1888), 1: 418.

49. For a standard formulation of this "arbitrary" power of the early modern judge, see Benedict Carpzov, *Practica Nova Rerum Criminalium cum Observ. Boehmerii* (Frankfurt, 1758), qu. 1 no. 12: "Regula, quae nobiles mitius quam ignobiles puniri vult, solum procedit in poenis arbitrariis et non uniformibus, quae scilicet ex qualitate personarum distinguendae sunt per judicem." As Boehmer commented (id. Obs. 4, qu. 148): "Neque etiam ejusmodi personas ad operas publicas viliores, sed potius ad ergastulum damnare convenit, nisi forsan ita gratia fiat, ut loco poenae capitalis ad fortalitium remittantur."

50. For eighteenth-century imprisonment: N. Castan, "Le Régime des Prisons au XVIIIe siècle," in J. Petit, ed., *La Prison, le Bagne, et l'Histoire* (Geneva, 1984), 32-33. For the subjection of debtors to the arbitrary power of ancien régime judges, and for the statutory sources, see L. Deymès, *L'Évolution de la nature juridique de la contrainte par corps* (Lavaur, 1942), 49 and 44–48; for the survival of shame sanctions into the eighteenth-century, ibid., 52. For the character of French early-modern shame sanctions against debtors, Whitman, "The Moral Menace of Roman Law and the Making of Commerce: Some Dutch Evidence," *Yale Law Journal* 105 (1996): 1875–1876.

51. Quétel, *De Par le Roy: Essai sur les Lettres de Cachet* (Toulouse, 1981), 206.

52. Spierenburg, *Prison Experience*, 247–248.

53. "Roughly half of all status offender complaints are filed by parents." Guarino-Ghezzi and Loughran, *Balancing Juvenile Justice*, 21.

54. Spierenburg, *The Prison Experience*, 9 and often. Spierenburg shows that imprisonment itself in Amsterdam and urban Germany began in the forlorn effort to shield all offenders from "infamy." Ibid., 43ff., 161ff. The leveling-up pattern that elsewhere belongs to the late eighteenth and nineteenth centuries thus has an older history, which I do not explore here.

55. Outside Paris, religious establishments predominated. See Quétel, *De par le Roy*, 173–188. A list of the so-called "prisons d'état" can be found in C. Desmaze, *Les Pénalités Anciennes: Supplices, Prisons et Graces en France* (Paris, 1866), 266.

56. E.g., N. Castan, "Du grand Renfermement à la Révolution," in J.-G. Petit, N. Castan, C. Faugeron, M. Pierre, and A. Zysberg, *Histoire des Galères, Bagnes et Prisons* (Toulouse, 1991), 51–52. Late medieval statutory antecedents for privileged treatment in prisons is collected in Desmaze, *Les Pénalités Anciennes*, 233–238.

57. Monique Cottret, *La Bastille à Prendre* (Paris, 1986), 63–65. For a vivid account, see B. Strayer, *Lettres de Cachet and Social Control in the Ancien Régime, 1659-1789* (New York, 1992), 59–115.

58. Cottret, *La Bastille à Prendre*, 105–134; Quétel, *De Par le Roy*, 204–226.

59. E.g., Chauveau and Hélie, *Théorie du Code Pénal* (Paris: 1836–1842), 311–312.

60. E.g., P. Lascoumes, P. Poncela and P. Lenoël, *Au Nom de l'Ordre: Une Histoire Politique du Code Pénal* (n.p., 1989), 9; J.-G. Petit, "Politiques, modèles et imaginaires de la prison (1790–1875)," in Petit et al., *Histoire des Galères, Bagnes et Prisons*, 110–111.

61. Robespierre, "Discours sur les peines infamantes," 1:28–29.

62. Ibid., 44.

63. Reform tendencies were of course far older than the eighteenth century. For some of the early Christian reformist programs, see Whitman, "The Opposition to Public Punishment in Germany: The Christian Sources," in R.Helmholz et al., eds., *Grundlagen des Rechts. Festschrift für Peter Landau* (Paderborn, 2000): 759–776; cf. also H. von Weber, "Calvinismus und Strafrecht," in P. Bocklemann and W. Gallas, eds., *Festschrift f. Eberhard Schmidt* (Göttingen, 1961): 39–53. The influence of Beccaria dominated reform ideas in the years immediately before the revolution. See E.g., M. Maestro, *Voltaire and Beccaria as Reformers of Criminal Law* (New York, 1942); J. Imbert, "La Peine de Mort et L'Opinion au XVIIIe Siècle," in *Revue de Science Criminelle et de Droit Pénal*, n.f. 19 (1964): 509–525; R. Badinter, "Beccaria, l'Abolition de la Peine de Mort et la Révolution Française," *Revue de Science Criminelle et de Droit Pénal*, n.f. (1989): 235–251.

64. The entire report is reproduced in G. Michon, *Essai sur l'Histoire du Parti Feuillant: Adrien Duport* (Paris, 1924), 143–147.

65. E.g., Poncela, *Droit de la Peine*, 88.

66. See for example his proposal that all persons be permitted the privilege of having nameplates on their homes, in *Journal de Paris*, 31 Décembre 1789, 1714.

67. E.g., Guillaume, *Addition à la Motion de M. Guillotin, sur les Loix Criminelles* (n.p., n.d. [1789)]), 4, calling for an end to flogging and branding.

68. For an account of these famous antecedents of the guillotine, see e.g., D. Arasse, *La Guillotine et l'Imaginaire de la Terreur* (Paris, 1987), 23–24.

69. Courier Français, 2 December 1789, 501: "un discours touchant & pathétique . . . sur la barbarie des peines imaginées par nos ayeux, & la bizarrerie du préjugé qui couvre d'infamie l'honnête homme qui a le malheur d'avoir pour parent un

scélérat qui a péri sous le glaive de la loi." Despite the poetic phrase "glaive de la loi," this cannot of course refer to beheading.

70. To the apparent uncontrollable hilarity of the Assembly, he described the workings of his machine in staccato periods: "Like thunder, the mechanism falls! The head goes flying! Blood spurts! The man is no more." For a lively discussion, see A. Soubiran, *The Good Doctor Guillotin and His Strange Device*, trans. MacCraw (Aberdeen, 1964), 111–117. For a snide contemporary account of Guillotin's "bad taste," see A. Duquesnoy, *Journal sur l'Assemblée Constituante* (Paris, 1894), 2:119.

71. Quoted in full below n. 77.

72. On Favras, see J. Tulard, J.-F. Fayard, and A. Fierro, eds. *Histoire et Dictionnaire de la Révolution Française* (Paris, 1987), 814–815, and the ongoing reportage in the *Journal de Paris*, E.g., 22 and 27 Janvier, 1, 8, 11, 16, 19, 22, 26 Février, 1790.

73. Desmoulins, *Révolutions de France et de Brabant*, 4th ed. (Paris, 1790), 14:1.

74. See the discussion of A. Kessler, "From Virtue to Commerce: The Parisian Merchant Court and the Rise of Commercial Society in Eighteenth-Century France," Ph.D. diss., Stanford, 2001.

75. For the date of the sentence, see *Journal de Paris*, 22 Janvier 1790, col 87. For the sentence, see *Arret de la cour de Parlement, qui condamne Augustin-Jean Agasse & Anne-Jean-Baptiste Agasse à etre pendus & étranglés . . .* ([Paris: Nyon, 1790]), which includes the original sentence of the Châtelet and the appellate decision modifying it. The modification is reported in *Journal de Paris*, 7 Février 1790, 152, along with an order, never carried out, that the brothers' counterfeited bills be burned.

76. See *Commune de Paris. District de Saint-Jacques-l'Hôpital. Comité civil permanent, séance du Lundi 1er Février 1790. Déliberation relative à Messieurs Agasse*. [Paris: Cailleau, 1790].

77. "Art. 1. Les délits du même genre seront punis par le même genre de peine, quels que soient le rang et l'état des coupables.

Art. 2. Les délits et les crimes étant personnels, le supplice d'un coupable et les condamnations infamantes quelconques n'impriment aucune flétrissure à sa famille. L'honneur de ceux qui lui appartiennent n'est nullement entaché, et tous continueront d'être admissibles à toutes sortes de professions, d'emplois et de dignités.

Art. 3. La confiscation des biens des condamnés ne pourra jamais être prononcée en aucun cas.

Art. 4. Le corps du supplicié sera délivré à sa famille si elle le demande. Dans tous les cas, il sera admis à la sépulture ordinaire et il ne sera fait sur le registre aucune mention du genre de mort."

Quoted and discussed in Arasse, *La Guillotine et l'Imaginaire de la Terreur*, 9–10, 25–27.

78. For the proposal, see again Arasse, *La Guillotine et l'Imaginaire de la Terreur*, 9, 25.

79. Published, along with the text of the law, in *Journal de Paris*, 26 Janvier 1790, 101–103.

80. [Janinet], *Gravures Historiques des Principaux Événemens depuis l'Ouverture des États Généraux de 1789. Tome Premier* (Paris, 1789 [-1791]), Événement du 8 Février, 1790. The text describes the basic series of events. Another print of the return of their bodies can be found in C. Hould, *L'Image de la Révolution Française* (Quebec, 1989), 228.

81. This account in *Courier Extraordinaire, ou Le Premier Arrivé*, 4 Juin 1791, 3.

82. This came in the wake of two kinds of complaints: on the one hand, it was argued that beheading by the sword was messy, with executioners frequently having to

hack repeatedly. (French executioners, it was observed, unlike German ones, had too little experience, since they had only beheaded the occasional noble. See Docteur Louis, "Avis motivé sur le mode de décollation" (1792), appendix to Arasse, *Guillotine et l'Imaginaire de la Terreur*, 209). There was also some concern that commoners, unlike nobles, did not have the necessary fortitude to hold still as the sword swung down. See Arasse, *Guillotine et l'Imaginaire de la Terreur*, 30.

83. E.g., J.-C. Vimont, *Punir Autrement . . . Les Prisons de Seine-Inférieure pendant la Révolution* (Mont-Saint-Aignan, 1989), 35. It is frequently paired with the Code des Délits et Peines of 3 Brumaire An IV. This latter law, it should be observed, while it did briefly regulate prison affairs, Arts. 570–580, retained the basic structure of the Code of 1791. See Arts. 599–605. Its emphasis was not so much on imprisonment as such, as on the development of a system of criminal police. See B. Schnapper, "Les Systèmes Repressifs Français de 1789 à 1815," in X. Rousseaux, M.-S. Dupont-Bouchat, and C. Vael, *Révolutions et Justice Pénale en Europe: Modèles Français et Traditions Nationales* (1780–1830), 27.

84. E.g., Vimont, *Punir Autrement*, 35–36.

85. See J. Godechot, *Regards sur l'Époque Révolutionnaire* (Toulouse, 1980), 39–52.

86. The principle exception was homicide, which was treated with more nuance. See "Decret concernant Le Code Pénal du 25 Septembre 1791," in *Procès-Verbal de l'Assemblée Nationale* (Paris, 1791), 62, Part II, Title II, Section I, Arts. I–VII.

87. Part I, Title I, Art. I.

88. Foucault, *Surveiller et Punir*, 14–15.

89. E.g., Chauveau and Hélie, *Théorie du Code Pénal*, 1:189.

90. See Art. XXXI. The connection with legal infamy is clear on the face of this punishment, and clearer from the provisions of the Article, which require the *greffier* to announce publicly that the offender has been "convaincu d'une action infame."

91. See Part I, Title I, Articles XXVIII – XXXV, subjecting offenders to the several hours of public exposure either in the *carcan* or wearing a sign describing their offense; and Part I, Title IV, describing loss of rights.

92. Part I, Title VII.

93. Part I, Title I, Arts. VI–VIII. The galleys were temporarily suppressed by an act of September 9, 1792, but were quickly reinstated.

94. Ibid., Arts. IX–X.

95. Ibid., Art. XIV.

96. Ibid., Arts. XV–XVII.

97. Ibid., Arts. XX–XXV.

98. Vimont, *Punir Autrement*, 43.

99. Typically sensible discussion in ibid., 43–44.

100. See the discussion of Petit, "Politiques, modèles et imaginaires," in Petit et al., *Histoire des Galères, Bagnes et Prisons*, 112.

101. Code Pénal, Part I, Title II, Sections I–III. False testimony in a civil matter also carried the same penalty: Part II, Title II, Section II, Art. XLVII.

102. Part II, Title I, Section IV, Arts. I, VII.

103. Ibid., Section V, Arts. II, IV, IX

104. Part II, Title II, Section I, Arts. XXI–XXIII; Part II, Title II, Section II, Arts. XXI– XII, XXVI–XXVII; Part II, Title II, Section III, Art. IV.

105. For the huge influx of prisoners during this period, see Petit, *Politiques, modèles et imaginaires*, 118; and for a sensitive account of their treatment, rich in observations on the tradition of political detention in France, Vimont, *Punir Autrement*, 79–89.

106. Citoyen [Pierre] Giraud, *Observations sommaires sur toutes les prisons du Département de Paris* (n.p.: 1793), 14, proposing to convert the Prison de l'Abbaye into a national institution restricted to "criminels d'état."

107. Paganel, *Rapport sur les Prisons, maisons d'arrêt ou de police, de répression, de détention, & sur les hospices de santé* [Paris: 1er Brumaire, An III], 7.

108. Deymès, *Contrainte par corps*, 56–58. Fraudulent bankruptcy was treated as a severe crime, following ancien régime tradition. See Code Pénal, Part II, Title II, Section II, Arts. XXX–XXXI.

109. Deymès, *Contrainte par corps*, 60–61.

110. Ibid., 63–64.

111. See J.-P. Royer, *Histoire de la Justice en France* (Paris, 1995), 456–457 for the importance of this reform year.

112. See the report of M. le comte Treilhard, in *Archives Parlementaires* 10 (1810): 489–490.

113. For a survey of the movements leading up to 1810: Petit, *Ces Peines Obscures*, 122–131.

114. Lascoumes, Poncela, and Lenoël, *Au Nom de l'Ordre*, 179.

115. See the report of M. le comte Treilhard, in *Archives Parlementaires* 10 (1810): 489–493. As the comte explained, the Constituent Assembly, "qui se distingua par tant de *conceptions utiles*, qui détruisit *tant d'abus*, qui avait, sans contredit, pour elle *la pureté des intentions*, ne se tint pas toujours en garde contre l'*enthousiasme du bien*." Ibid., 489.

116. [Target], *Projet du Code Criminel, Correctionel et de Police* (n.p., 1802), xviii. For Target's role, see Lascoumes, Poncela and Lenoël, *Au Nom de l'Ordre*, 204–216, 231; on the law of 23 Floréal, An X, id., 249.

117. See ibid., 490. As Treilhard observed, parents impoverish their children through all sorts of follies; why not through committing crimes as well?

118. Most of the "contraventions" defined in the code were minor public order offenses, but the insult was also included. See §471, no. 11; and the discussion in Whitman, "Enforcing Civility and Respect,"1349–1350.

119. Comte de Treilhard in *Archives Parlementaires* 10 (1810): 491–492.

120. Ibid., 492.

121. E.g., Arts. 110, 115.

122. Generally Bk. III, Title 1.

123. Archives Parlementaires 10 (1810), 650. For translation, further discussion and some literature, see E. Arnold, ed., *A Documentary Survey of Napoleonic France* (Lanham, 1994), 305–310.

124. These "prisons d'état" were condemned in 1814. Poncela, *Droit de la peine*, 86.

125. Charles Monier, quoted in J.C. Vimont, *La Prison Politique: Génèse d'une Mode d'Incarcération Spécifique, XVIIIe – XXe Siècles* (Paris, 1993), 207. For Vimont's research, see further his fine article, "Enfermer les politiques: La Mise en Place Progressive des 'Régimes Politiques' d'Incarcération (1815–1848)," in P. Vigier et al., eds., *Répression et Prisons Politiques en France et en Europe au XIXe Siècle* (Paris, 1990), 189–201.

126. Vimont, *La Prison Politique*, 246.

127. Ibid., 262–263, on this importance of this "scandale Magalon."

128. Ibid., 256–257.

129. For a measured assessment, downplaying the importance of Beccaria, see J. Langbein, *Torture and the Law of Proof: Europe and England in the Ancien Régime* (Chicago, 1977), 27.

130. Guizot, *De la Peine de Mort en Matière Politique* (repr. n. p., 1984).

131. See id., 87: "Je n'espère pas, j'en conviens, que les gouvernemens demeurent convaincus de l'inutilité politique de la peine de mort, encore moins qu'ils renoncent a s'en servir. La vérité se glisse lentement dans l'esprit du pouvoir, et quand elle y entre, ce n'est pas pour y régner aussitôt. Il refuse longtemps de la croire: forcé de la croire, il refuse longtemps de lui obéir. Je n'ai pas besoin d'en dire les raisons.

"Précisément à cause de cela, il faut, quand le pouvoir se trompe, se hâter d'en convaincre le public, d'établir dans l'opinion ce qui ne pénétra que si tard dans les faits. Plus la route est longue, plus on doit se mettre en marche de bonne heure."

132. Deymès, *Contrainte par corps*, 67.

133. Ibid., 68.

134. See generally F. Billacois, *Le Duel dans la Société Française des XVIe–XVIIe Siècles: Essai de Psychosociologie Historique* (Paris, 1986).

135. See Robert Nye, *Masculinity and Male Codes of Honor in Modern France* (Berkeley, 1993).

136. For Tocqueville and Beaumont, along with parallel movements, see Petit, "Politiques, modèles et imaginaires," 130–137; and for Tocqueville's struggles over the two systems, M. Perrot, "Alexis de Tocqueville et les Prisons," in Petit, ed., *La Prison, le Bagne et l'Histoire*, esp. 105–106. For the fate of cellular imprisonment in the later nineteenth century, see Badinter, *La Prison Républicaine*.

137. De Molènes, *De l'Humanité dans les Lois Criminelles* (Paris, 1830), 400–405; A. Chauveau, ed., *Code Pénal Progressif: Commentaire sur la Loi Modificative du Code Pénal* (Paris, 1832), 125; Chauveau and Hélie, *Théorie du Code Pénal*, 22–29, 94–99.

138. G. de Beaumont and A. de Tocqueville, *Du Système Pénitentiaire aux États-Unis, et de son Application en France* (Paris, 1833), 167–168. For these abolitions, E.g., Poncela, *Droit de la Peine*, 103–104.

139. E.g., Molènes, *De l'Humanité*, 405; L.-A.-A. Marquet-Vasselot, *École des Condamnés* (Paris, 1837), 1:52–55; and the general assessment in J.-M. Carbasse, *Introduction Historique au Droit Pénal* (Paris, 1990), 333.

140. Sutherland, *White-Collar Criminality*, 1.

141. Art. 19 [= Code. Art. 20]: "Quiconque aura été condamné à la détention, sera renfermé dans l'une des forteresses—qui auront été déterminées par une ordonnance du Roi."

142. Quoted in Chauveau, *Code Pénal Progressif*, 113–114: "La peine nouvelle de la détention est surtout déstinée à réprimer les attentats politiques. Elle portera aux âges futurs la preuve du haut dégré de civilisation, auquel notre patrie est arrivée."

143. Poncela, *Droit de la peine*, 86–87.

144. Maurice Alhoy, *Les Bagnes. Histoire, Types, Moeurs, Mystères* (Paris, 1845), 392.

145. For an account, see F. Ravello, *Silvio Pellico* (Turin, 1954).

146. See V. Bromberg, *The Romantic Prison: The French Tradition* (Princeton, 1978), 62–87.

147. For the period context and some further representations, see *Daumier, 1808–1879* (Ottawa: National Gallery of Canada), 170–181.

148. Letter to Jeanron, 8 October 1832, reproduced in A. Alexandre, *Honoré Daumier, l'Homme et l'Oeuvre* (Paris, 1888), 54.

149. *Système Pénitentiaire*, 167–168.

150. T. Hopkins, *The Dungeons of Old Paris* (New York, 1897), 132 and following for an entertaining account.

151. G. Bonneron, *Les Prisons de Paris* (Paris, 1897), 248.

152. Émile Couret, *Le Pavillon des Princes: Histoire Complète de la Prison Politique de Sainte-Pélagie* (Paris, n.d. [1895]).

153. Deymès, *Contrainte par corps*, 68–70.

154. Ibid., 70–71.

155. The regime of the Restoration had declined to prosecute dueling as a crime.

156. See Nye, *Masculinity and Male Codes of Honor*, 134–135.

157. Beaumont and Tocqueville, *Du Système Pénitentiaire*, 31.

158. Ibid., 32.

159. Ibid., 75–83.

160. Ibid., 81–82.

161. Ibid., 82. On this aspect of Tocqueville and Beaumont's report, see Perrot, "Alexis de Tocqueville et les Prisons," 105.

162. Beaumont and Tocqueville, *Du Système Pénitentiaire*, 33–34, 168.

163. Ibid.,161–62.

164. Ibid., 167–168.

165. Ibid.,69.

166. Ibid., 92.

167. To Bérenger, writing in 1873, cellular imprisonment was "facilement accepté par l'homme dont l'esprit a quelque culture et le coeur quelque élévation," but the same treatment would be effectively harsh on lower-status persons. Quoted in Badinter, *La Prison Républicaine*, 42.

168. Perrot, "Tocqueville et les Prisons," 105–106.

169. Tocqueville, *De la Démocratie en Amérique*, 2:209

170. Vingtrinier, *Des Prisons et de Prisonniers* (Versailles, 1840), 238.

171. Described by Vimont, *Prison Politique*, 402–436.

172. Ibid., 431.

173. For the reforms of 1848, see E.g., Bérenger, *De la Répression Pénale, de ses Formes et de ses Effets* (Paris, 1855), 1:218.

174. E.g., J. E. Boitard, *Leçons sur les Codes Pénal et d'Instruction Criminelle* (Paris, 1851), 54–57; Bonnéville de Marsangy, *De l'Amélioration de la Loi Criminelle* (Paris, 1864), 432–466.

175. Deymès, *Contrainte par corps*, 72–75.

176. M. Pierre, "La Transportation (1848–1938)," in Petit et al., *Histoire des Galères, Bagnes et Prisons*, 231–259; and especially the detailed discussion in Badinter, *La Prison Républicaine*, 125–179. Badinter observes that French republicans justified this through the "mythe de la transportation régéneratrice," according to which life in the colonies would benefit convicts. See ibid., 133.

177. Pierre, "La Transportation," 237, 249 (case of Dreyfus).

178. Ibid., 244–246 (Communards); 254.

179. For continuing de facto cruelty as of 1872, see Petit, "Politiques, modèles et imaginaires," 149.

180. Rocher, *le Droit*, 27 Février 1853, Quoted in Deymès, *Contrainte par corps*, 82 n. 2.

181. Generally Couret, *Pavillon des Princes*.

182. J. Fabre, *De la Contrainte par Corps* (Toulouse, 1933), 14–15. This period of French reform also inspired some German literature. See H. Lüders, *Die Aufhebung des jetzigen Systems der Personal-Schuldhaft* (Berlin, 1865).

183. See E.g., A. Signoret, *De la Contrainte par Corps* (Montpellier, 1905), 2, for the "frequent" character of imprisonment for debt. For debtors in prison over the second half of the century, see M. Perrot, "1848: Révolution et Prison," in M. Perrot, ed.,

L'Impossible Prison: Recherches sur le Système Pénitentiaire au XIXe Siècle (Paris, 1980), 281; Bonneron, *Les Prisons de Paris*, 248.

184. See Badinter, *La Prison Républicaine*, 44–45.

185. Quoted in ibid., 219–220.

186. See *Code Pénitentiaire* 14 (1890): 17–25.

187. See generally, Badinter, *La Prison Républicaine*, 218–223.

188. Poncela, *Droit de la peine*, 87.

189. For the transition to La Santé, see P. Montagnon, *42 Rue de la Santé. Une Prison Politique* (Paris, 1996), 35 and throughout for accounts of political prisoners there.

190. Poncela, *Droit de la peine*, 87.

191. Pedron, *La Prison sous Vichy*; and the discussion below.

192. Léauté, *Les Prisons*, 41–42; P. Novick, *The Resistance versus Vichy: The Purge of Collaborators in Liberated France* (New York, 1968). M. Koreman, *The Expectation of Justice: France, 1944–1946* (Durham, 1999), 92–147, shows how legal pursuit of collaborators displaced private vengeance-taking. For a description of the chaotic conditions of the time by the leading reformer of the time, who makes however no mention of the political circumstances, see P. Amor, "La Réforme pénitentiaire en France," *Revue de Science Criminelle et de droit pénal comparé* (1947): 6.

193. Frédéric Debove, "Libertés physiques du détenu et droit européen: ou l'histoire d'une Convention passe-muraille," *Revue pénitentiaire et de droit pénal* (1997): 49. "Dès la libération," the same author continues, "la dignité de l'homme et le respect de son intégrité physique apparaissent à nouveau comme les biens les plus précieux."

194. I take this from the catalogue entry at the Archives Nationale BB^{18} 7164^{2}.8. Haute Cour de Justice. Dossier 4. "Régime à accorder aux détenus. Refus de la commission d'instruction près de la haute cour de leur accorder le régime politique, 1944–45." I was not permitted to view the actual documents in this dossier.

195. The many ex-collaborators sentenced to "dégradation nationale," a "peine infamante perpétuelle," generally saw their punishment commuted to a "peine correctionelle à temps" in 1951, and were amnestied in 1953: See J. Copper-Royer, *L'Amnistie. Loi du 6 Août 1953* (Paris, 1954), 20–33; B. Phan, *La France de 1940 à 1958* (Paris, 1998), 73. For uprisings by political prisoners in the interval, notably in 1948, see C. Faugeron, "De la Libération à la Guerre d'Algérie," in Petit et al., *Histoire des Galères, Bagnes et Prisons*, 297.

196. This is the striking argument of S. Gottwald, *Das allgemeine Persönlichkeitsrecht. Ein zeitgeschichtliches Erklärungsmodell* (Berlin, 1996).

197. Léauté, *Les Prisons*, 44.

198. Generally J. Spire, "La Détention à Fresnes Durant la Guerre d'Algérie," in C. Carlier, J. Spire, and F. Wasserman, eds., *Fresnes La Prison. Les Établissements penitentiaries de Fresnes: 1895–1990* (Fresnes, 1991), 100–111.

199. Indeed, the government created a special, somewhat sinister, political court, the Cour de Sûreté de l'État.

200. Art. D 492–495. For an outline of events in this period, see Faugeron, "De la Libération à la Guerre d'Algérie," 315–316.

201. Poncela, *Droit de la Peine*, 100.

202. Foucault's first appearance on the public stage as a student and critic of prisons cast him, in fact, in a thoroughly traditional French role: he demanded that certain Maoist prisoners be accorded the old special regime. For a fuller account, see C. Faugeron, "Les Prisons de la Ve République," in Petit, et al., eds., *Histoire des Galères, Bagnes et Prisons*, 329–330.

203. Poncela, *Droit de la peine*, 88.

204. The shift from an emphasis on the rights of *politiques* to prisoners of the *droit commun* in this period is noted by M. Perrot, préface, in Petit et al., *Histoire des Galères, Bagnes et Prisons*, 8. Poncela, *Droit de la peine*, 88, simply observes that "certaines des règles prévues pour les politiques" were extended to prisoners of "droit commun." This understates the extent of the borrowing as seen in large historical perspective.

205. Faugeron, "Les Prisons de la Ve République," 330–334; M. Beauvois, "Bilan de la réforme de 1975 sur le régime pénitentiaire," *Revue Pénitentiare et de Droit Pénal* (1978): 159–181.

206. Described in Léauté, *Les Prisons*, 54–55.

207. Décret du 23 mai 1975. Similar terminological changes have continued, such as the shift, in 1996, from the term "cellule de punition" to "cellule disciplinaire." See Herzog-Evans, "La réforme du régime disciplinaire dans les établissements pénitentiaires," *Revue pénitentiare et de droit pénal* no. 1 (1997): 23; or the shift from the term "gardien" to "surveillant." See Léauté, *Les Prisons*, 84.

208. Léauté, *Les Prisons*, 59.

209. Ibid., 55–57.

210. Decree of 26 février 1982.

211. Some longer-term prisoners have also routinely found themselves in the *maisons d'arrêt*, a practice just as routinely denounced by French commentators.

212. Poncela, *Droit de la Peine*, 324.

213. Art. 131–1 NCP.

214. See the discussion of Amnesty International in Vimont, *La Prison Politique*, 1.

215. Evans, *Rituals of Retribution*, 223–224.

216. For regional differences in beheading at the beginning of the twentieth century, see A. Köhler, *Deutsches Strafrecht* (Leipzig, 1917), 578; and M. Ramlau, "Wie Wird im Deutschen Reiche die Enthauptung Vollstreckt?" Ph.D.diss., Rostock, 1890. The standard statement—"Die Todesstrafe ist durch Enthauptung zu vollstrecken", StGB §13—appeared unaltered in German drafts from 1871 onward.

217. For a survey of developments in prison discipline in the German states, see T. Eisenhardt, *Strafvollzug* (Stuttgart, 1978), 54–55. For examples treating low-status punishments in a matter-of-fact way, see E. Henke, *Handbuch des Criminalrechts und der Criminalpolitik* (Berlin/Stettin, 1823), 1:472–482; C. G. Wächter, *Lehrbuch des Römisch-Teutschen Straftrechts* (Stuttgart, 1825), 1:171–185; Martin, *Lehrbuch des Teutschen gemeinen Criminal-Rechts* (Heidelberg, 1829), 194–206; A. W. Heffter, *Lehrbuch des gemeinen deutschen Criminalrechts* (Halle, 1840), 116–117; T. Marezoll, *Das gemeine deutsche Criminalrecht* (Leipzig, 1847), 151–156 (showing some limited concern to limit infamy). For an 1861 example of an author trying to introduce largely foreign arguments to his German audience, see G. Geib, *Lehrbuch des deutschen Strafrechts* (Leipzig, 1861), 1:424–429.

218. Wahlberg, Die Strafmittel, in F. v. Holtzendorff, ed., *Handbuch des deutschen Strafrechts* (Berlin, 1871), 503.

219. Nietzsche, *Zur Genealogie der Moral. Eine Streitschrift*, Erste Abhandlung, Paragraph 15, in Nietzsche, *Kritische Studienausgabe*, eds. G. Colli and M. Montinari (Berlin, 1999), 5:257–289.

220. For a few examples, see Sigrid Weigel, *Und selbst im Kerker frei . . . ! Schreiben im Gefängnis. Zur Theorie und Gattungsgeschichte der Gefängnisliteratur (1750–1933)* (Marburg, 1982), 20–27. The Karzer in Heidelberg remains as a touristic

example of such a high-status prison. Eighteenth-century Germans did not yet however always use the term "fortress" for high-status prisoners: in both Prussia and Austria, for example, "fortresses" were used to house ordinary prisoners. Some German authors associated "fortress arrest" in particular with one special class of German aristocrats: military officers. L. v. Jagemann and W. Brauer, *Criminallexikon* (Erlangen, 1854), 288–290.

221. E.g., E. Schmidt, *Einführung in die Geschichte der deutschen Strafrechtspflege* (Göttingen, 1965), 346–352.

222. See generally Sontag, *Festungshaft*, 34, 49, 102, 115; Jagemann and Bauer, *Criminallexikon*, 289. In one important respect, German practice differed from French: German legislators, rather than eliminating forced labor for high-status prisoners, tended simply to require labor "appropriate" to their status. E.g., *Allgemeines Criminalrecht für die Preußischen Staaten* (Berlin, 1827) 1:201 (§550); cf. H. Hälschner, *Das gemeine deutsche Strafrecht* (Bonn, 1881) 1: 582. Sontag himself thought it was critical to spare high-status person "mechanical" labor. Ibid., 114. Some authors indeed rejected the idea of status-differentiation in punishment, while holding to the idea that persons of different "Bildung" should be assigned different types of forced labor. See J. F. H. Abegg, "Bemerkungen über das rechtliche Erforderniß verhältnißmässig gleicher Behandlung verschiedener Uebertreter desselben Strafgesetzes," in *Archiv des Criminalrechts*, n.f. (1835): 151–179. Another particular concern of German legislation was whether punishments where what early modern jurisprudence called "infaming in law": whether they excluded the offender from public offices and the like. See generally Sontag, *Festungshaft*, 149–150.

223. Weigel, *Und selbst im Kerker frei . . .!*, 31 (case of Friedrich Ludwig Weidig). Weidig was however treated more harshly later on, and indeed became a cause célèbre. See ibid., 33.

224. E.g., C. F. Roßhirt, *Lehrbuch des Criminalrechts* (Heidelberg, 1821), 143; Hälschner, *Das gemeine deutsche Strafrecht*, 1:586.

225. Sontag, *Festungshaft*, 25, summarizing Württemberg debates of 1839. For a post-1848 statement, see G. F. Fischer, *Über Gefängnisse, Strafarten, Strafsysteme und Strafanstalten* (Regensburg, 1852), 6–7 and often.

226. Offering privileged fortress confinement was a practice widely defended on the straightforward ground that "honorable" persons suffered from mere confinement in a way that "dishonorable" persons did not. E.g., Sontag, *Festungshaft*, 5, 18–19.

227. Ibid., 112–113. In any case, this author continued, the goal of modern imprisonment was *Besserung*, and it went without saying that that goal should be pursued with different means with respect to cultured persons. Ibid., 113.

228. For a general survey, ibid., 24, 72–73.

229. C. J. A. Mittermaier, "Der revidirte Entwurf des Strafgestzbuchs für das Königreich Baiern," in *Neues Archiv des Criminalrechts* 10 (1828): 159–160.

230. Berner, *Lehrbuch des deutschen Strafrechts*, 5th ed. (Leipzig, 1871), 218–219.

231. E.g., Kleinschrod, *Systematische Entwickelung der Grundbegriffe des peinlichen Rechts*, 2nd ed. (Erlangen, 1799) 2: §§ 42, 65–72. Some states, like Hannover, aimed to even things out by extending the terms of those permitted confinement in Festungshaft. See Sontag, *Festungshaft*, 31–33. For the debates in Hesse, which eventually eliminated any express reference to social status, see Sontag, *Festungshaft*, 35. For the Prussian argument, in the 1840s, that only acts and not persons were dishonorable, see ibid., 61.For a survey of the views of other leading jurists, see ibid., 87–94.

232. For an influential early statement of the idea that the deciding factor should

have to do with state of mind more than (though not to the exclusion of) status, see the Danish author A. S. Ørsted, *Über die Grundregeln der Strafgesetzgebung* (Copenhagen, 1818), 376–377.

233. Quoted in Sontag, *Festungshaft*, 43.

234. Württemberg, Gesetz von 13.08.1849, Art. 2. Cf., e.g., Bavarian Criminal Code of 1861, Art. 19 (die "Bildungsstufe oder [die] bürgerlichen Verhältnisse[ ] . . . sowie [die] besonderen Umständen der That oder [die] derselben zu Grunde gelegene[ ] Gesinnung")

235. E.g., Württemberg, Gesetz von 13.08.1849, Arts. 201–205; Bavarian Criminal Code of 1861, Arts. 162ff.

236. Summarized and discussed in Sontag, *Festungshaft*, 64–69. In Prussia in particular, where the influence of Rheinland jurists, and through them the influence of French law, was strong, there was movement in the direction of specifying *Festungshaft* for political offenders. Later in the nineteenth century we hear of special treatment for politicals much like that in France: "The Prussians had enough decency," wrote one 1849 prisoner, "to spare political prisoners chains and handcuffs when they were transported." That prisoner did not succeed in being formally classed as a political "detainee," but the warden of his prison accorded him special treatment anyway, more or less on the French model. Otto von Corvin, quoted and discussed in Weigel, *Und selbst im Kerker frei . . . !*, 36. Like some French politicals, this German prisoner too could not contain his disgust and contempt for the "common" criminals around him. Ibid., 43.

237. *Verhandlungen des dritten deutschen Juristentages*, 2 vols. (Berlin, 1862), 2:420–421, and generally 418–443.

238. §§ 87, 88a, 90. Sontag objected both to the use of *Festungshaft* for political offenders, and to its extension to cases of extenuating circumstances, which, in his view, robbed it of its character as "custodia honesta," honorable detention.

239. Köhler, *Deutsches Strafrecht*, 593.

240. This was part of the standard literature. See v. Holtzendorff and Jagemann, *Handbuch des Gefängniswesens*, 1: 419 ("Princip der Individualisirung").

241. Sontag, *Festungshaft*, 136.

242. §§ 14–16—actually four types: *Zuchthaus, Gefängniß, Festungshaft, Haft.*

243. §§95, 99, 103, 97, 101, 104, 107. It was also available as an alternative punishment for violations of § 130, the predecessor of the current *Volksverhetzung* paragraph, which was then aimed against rabble-rousing preachers (not to mention Catholics).

244. Weigel, *Und selbst im Kerker frei . . .!*, 49–50, 53 (John Most). Quoted passage on 50.

245. Ibid., 51.

246. Ibid., 73.

247. Ibid., 76.

248. Ibid., 77.

249. Toller, *Briefe aus dem Gefängnis, Gesammelte Werke*, ed. W. Frühwald and J. Spalek, (Munich, 1975), 5: 236. Quoted and discussed in Weigel, *Und selbst im Kerker frei . . . !*, 77.

250. Weigel, *Und selbst im Kerker frei . . . !*, 87–88, discussing case of Georg Fuchs.

251. Ibid., 93–94, discussing "Captivus."

252. Dahm, "Die Ehre im Strafrecht," *Deutsches Recht* 4 (1934): 419.

253. Quedenfeld, *Der Strafvollzug*, 20–21.

254. Quoted and discussed in Sofsky, *Die Ordnung des Terrors*, 11–12.

255. *Ratgeber für Gefangene* (Berlin, 1990), § 3.9.

256. §§ 172–175 StVollzG.

257. For a famous effort in this period to shift punishment practices away from its traditional focus on honor, see B. Freudenthal, "Der Strafvollzug als Rechtsverhältnis des öffentlichen Rechtes," in *Zeitschrift für die gesamte Strafrechtswissenschaft* 32 (1911): 222–248. Also from the reform literature of the time, see J. Heimberger, *Zur Reform des Strafvollzugs* (Leipzig, 1905).

258. See J. Herrnstadt, *Das Institut der bedingten Begnadigung. Ein Hilfsbuch* (Berlin, 1911), 9; H. Eyerich, *Die bedingte Strafaussetzung* (Würzburg, 1911), 17. Probation had an older history. See v. Holtzendorff and Jagemann, *Handbuch des Gefängniswesens*, 2:111–119.

259. E.g., H. Fischer, *Die bedingte Strafaussetzung* (Würzburg, 1927).

260. E.g., Schmidt, *Einführung in die geschichte der deutschen Strafrechtspflege*, 420–424.

261. *Vorentwurf zu einem Deutschen Strafgesetzbuch* (Berlin, 1909), 4–5.

262. *Entwurf eines Strafvollzugsgesetzes* (Berlin, 1927), 4, 49. For similar earlier efforts, see W. Schubert, ed., *Entwürfe der Strafrechtskommission zu einem deutschen Strafgesetzbuch und zu einem Einführungsgesetz (1911–1914)* (Frankfurt a. M., 1990), 19–20; *Vorentwurf zu einem deutschen Strafgesetzbuch* (Berlin, 1909), 4–5, 51–82.

263. H. Ellger, "Der Strafvollzug in Stufen," in *Preußisches Justizministerium. Strafvollzug in Preußen* (Mannheim/Berlin/Leipzig, 1928), 110.

264. For its antecedents within and without Germany, see Bernd Koch, "Das System des Stufenstrafvollzugs in Deutschland unter besonderer Berücksichtigung seiner Entwicklungsgeschichte," Ph.D diss., Freiburg, 1972. A similar system was tentatively introduced in France in 1938, and generalized in the 1950s. See Faugeron, "De la Libération à la Guerre d'Algérie," 298–300.

265. M. Liepmann, *Die neuen 'Grundsätze über den Vollzug von Freiheitsstrafen' in Deutschland* (Berlin, 1924), 4–5, 14–19. Radbruch himself saw the issue differently, as this text observes.

266. Ibid., 111.

267. Dr. Finkelnberg, "Die Psychologie des Gefangenen," in *Preußisches Justizministerium. Strafvollzug in Preußen* (Mannheim, 1928), 73–82.

268. Goffman too analyzes such stage systems as gradually admitting inmates to less degrading treatment. See Goffman, *Asylums*, 53.

269. For Hitler's life in the fortress Landsberg, led in the refined fashion of political prisoners for generations, see J. Fest, Hitler. *Eine Biographie* (Frankfurt/M., 1973), 287–290; and the detailed account in H. Kallenbach, *Mit Adolf Hitler auf Festung Landsberg* (Munich, 1939).

270. *Haushaltsrechtliche Bestimmugen für die Justizverwaltung. Sonderbestimmungen für die Strafvollzugsverwaltung* (n.p., 1941), 71–74; "Kosten der Unfruchtbarmachung, der Entmannung und der kriminalbiologischen Untersuchung Gefangener," etc.

271. RGBl. 1934, I, § 49. Quoted and discussed in H. Müller, "Strafvollzug," in Adalbert Erler et al., eds., *Handwörterbuch zur Deutschen Rechtsgeschichte*, 5: 15.

272. See Pedron, *La Prison sous Vichy*, 61–97.

273. Whitman, "On Nazi 'Honour' and the New European 'Dignity,' " forthcoming in *The Darker Legacy of European Law*, eds. Joerges and Ghaleigh.

274. Otto August Schoetensack, Rudolf Christians, Hans Eichler, and Friedrich Oetker, *Grundzüge eines Deutschen Strafvollstreckungsrechts. Denkschrift des Aus-*

schusses für Strafvollstreckungsrechts der Strafrechtsabteilung der Akademie für deutsches Recht (Berlin, 1935), 63. Cf. E.g., W. Hofmann, "Der Strafvollzug in Stufen in Deutschland in Geschichte und Gegenwart," Ph.D diss., Würzburg, 1936, 60: "Ehrgefühl" instead of "Genußsucht."

275. Schoetensack et al., *Grundzüge*, 63.

276. Ibid., 69.

277. See Drittes Strafänderungsgesetz, vom. 4. August 1953, in BGBl I (1953), 736; *Strafgesetzbuch* (Leipziger Kommentar) (Berlin, 1957), 124 (Rdn. 1, § 17).

278. E.g., H. Schüler-Springorum, *Strafvollzug im Übergang. Studien zum Stand der Vollzugsrechtslehre* (Göttingen, 1969), 246.

279. The sensibility that attached a ritual dishonorability to confinement in *Zuchthaus* survived in German culture too, as expressed in such literature as Hans Fallada's *Wer einmal aus dem Blechnapf Frißt* (Hamburg, 1991). As the title of this novel suggests, to have been subjected to *Zuchthaus* life was to be permanently dishonored.

280. For this drift in the reforms, see H.-H. Jescheck et al., *Strafgesetzbuch. Leipziger Kommentar* (Berlin, 1985), 2: (18) (Vorb. 23, § 38).

281. See Roxin, *Strafrecht*, 87. It deserves emphasis that this is not a new ambition among German reformers. For an early statement, see F. Noellner, *Criminal-Psychologische Denkwürdigkeiten* (Stuttgart/Hamburg, 1858), 117.

282. Though in practice the distinctions are somewhat finer. See Laubenthal, *Strafvollug*, 142.

283. § 10, Abs. 1 StVollzG.

284. In 1998 there were about four times as many inmates in Geschlosssener Vollzug as in Offener Vollzug. See Statistisches Bundesamt Deutschland. Rechtspflege. At http://www.statistik-bund.de/basis/d/recht/rechts6.htm. For more figures and further discussion, see Laubenthal, *Strafvollug*, 147.

285. See chapter 3.

286. Bl.Comm. 4: 397–398.

287. J. Foviaux, *La Rémission des Peines et des Condamnations. Droit Monarchique et Droit Moderne* (Paris, 1970), 49–51, 70–76; and for a well-known study of an earlier period, N. Z. Davis, *Fiction in the Archives: Pardon Tales and their Tellers in Sixteenth-Century France* (Stanford, 1987).

288. R. M. Andrews, *Law, Magistracy and Crime in Old Regime Paris, 1735–1789* (Cambridge, 1994), 394–395.

289. Foviaux, *La Rémission des Peines*, 51–69.

290. See François Serpillon, *Code Criminel ou Commentaire sur l'Ordonnance de 1670* (Lyon, 1767), 793–796.

291. E.g., Andrews, *Law, Magistracy and Crime*, 398.

292. Thus Serpillon's discussion in the Code Criminel devotes many pages to pardons for "Gentilshommes," 778–783.

293. Again Serpillon, *Code Criminel*, 793–796.

294. Foviaux, *La Rémission des Peines*, 76; Andrews, *Law, Magistracy and Crime*, 400.

295. Andrews, *Law, Magistracy and Crime*, 408.

296. Ibid., 398. Andrews also notes that petitions were sometimes accompanied by letters from "entire parishes."

297. Montesquieu, *L'Esprit des Lois*, 206 (Bk. VI, Chap. V).

298. Though Kant's views were in fact more nuanced than the most famous passages suggest. See J. Murphy, "Does Kant have a Theory of Punishment?" *Columbia Law Review* 87 (1987): 509–532.

299. Code Pénal du 25 Septembre 1791, Pt 1, Tit. VII, art. 13. For a detailed account, see J. Viaud, *Le Droit de Grâce à la Fin de l'Ancien Régime, et son Abolition pendant la Révolution* (Paris, 1906). Political amnesties however were not rejected by the revolutionaries, who voted one two weeks earlier: Loi du 14 Septembre 1791. Subsequent years saw further political amnesties as well: 11 Février 1793; 12 Frimaire an III (1794); 29 Nivôse an III (1795). For discussion of a particularly famous nineteenth-century instance, see A. Dalotel, "Deux amnisties pour oublier la Commune," in P. Vigier et al., *Repression et Prisons Politiques en France et en Europe au XIXe siècle* (Paris, 1990), 171–185.

300. Reintroduced by Sénat-Consulte du 16 Thermidor An X (1802). For the general history, see J. Monteil, *La Grâce en Droit Français Moderne* (Paris, 1959), 14–25.

301. F. N. Bavoux, *Leçons Préliminaires sur le Code Pénal* (Paris, 1821), 621. Bavoux argued for allowing judges and juries to recommend that the king exercise his still exclusive power of grace.

302. Desmaze, *Les Pénalités Anciennes*, 4. For pardons as a means of managing the prison population (as in the U.S., see chapter 5): Petit, *Ces Peines Obscures*, 536–541; for the general nineteenth-century history, Foviaux, *La Rémission des Peines*, 92–97.

303. J. Legoux, *Du Droit de Grâce en France* (Paris, 1865), 18.

304. J.-G. Schätzler, *Handbuch des Gnadenrechts*, 2d ed. (Munich, 1992), 10.

305. For complaints that special statutory provisions for *Festungshaft* trenched upon the power of *Begnadigung*, see Sontag, *Festungshaft*, 35 (Hessen). In Baden, only *Gnade* could provide privileged punishment until 1845. See ibid., 37–38; and in Saxony this remained the exclusive resort, including for duelists, right through the making of 1855 Criminal Code. Ibid., 45–47. Thüringen followed the same rule. Ibid., 47–48.

306. E.g., United Nations Department of Social Affairs, Probation and Related Measures (New York, 1951), 67.

307. Generally A. Kurz, *Demokratische Diktatur? Auslegung und Handhabung des Art. 48 der Weimarer Verfassung 1919–1925* (Berlin, 1992).

308. J. McCormick, "The Dilemmas of Dictatorship: Carl Schmitt and Constitutional Emergency Powers," in D. Dyzenhaus, ed., *Law as Politics: Carl Schmitt's Critique of Liberalism* (Durham, 1998), 230–236.

309. E.g., R. Osgood, Book Review, *Cornell International Law Review* 28 (1995): 461, 463 n.27.

310. W. Heiman, "Die Begnadigung. Eine grundlegende Betrachtung," Ph.D. diss., Heidelberg, 1931, 15–S30.

311. Radbruch, *Rechtsphilosophie*, 8th ed. (Stuttgart, 1973), 272–275.

312. F. Mess, *Nietzsche der Gesetzgeber* (Leipzig, 1930), 28. For Schmitt's approach, treating grace as a form of decisionism, see C. Schmitt, *Über die Drei Arten des rechtswissenschaftlichen Denkens* (Hamburg, 1934), 26–27.

313. Gay, *Dramatic Works*, ed. Fuller (Oxford, 1983), 2:64.

314. Kurt Weill, *Die Dreigroschenoper: Klavierauszug* (Vienna, 1956), 71–72.

315. See U. Kuss, *Die materielle Problematik der politischen Reichsamnestien. 1918/1933* (Breslau/Neukirch, 1934); J. Christoph, *Die politischen Reichsamnestien. 1918–1933* (Frankfurt a. M., 1988).

316. These were treated as continuous with Weimar practice. See E.g., E. Uhle, *Die Amnestie nach altem und neuem Gnadenrecht* (Breslau/Neukirch, 1935), 22–29

317. Schätzler, *Handbuch des Gnadenrechts*, 13–15.

318. See *Gnadenordnung*, §§ 20–33. For the relatively more rulelike regulation of grace in this statute, by contrast with the standardlike approach that preceded it, con-

trast F. Grau and K. Schäfer, *Das Preußische Gnadenrecht* (Berlin, 1931), 30–40 with F. Grau and K. Schäfer, *Das deutsche Gnadenrecht* (Berlin, 1939), 28–57. The newly elaborate Nazi regulation of probation gave rise to a literature of guidebooks and forms: See W. Menschell, *Das Gnadengesuch* (Berlin, 1941); A. Röschel and E. Blaese, *Die Strafvollstreckung* (Berlin, 1944), 150–153. For the authorization of courts to issue orders of probation, see the 1939 edition of Grau and Schäfer, *Gnadenrecht*, 38.

319. For this discomfort, and the effective admission of routinization, see Uhle, *Amnestie*, 40–41.

320. Though for an important exception, see Jescheck et al., eds., *Strafgesetzbuch. Leipziger Kommentar*, vor § 56, 2.

321. E.g, Justizminister Amelunxen, quoted in Anon., *Vierzigster Deutscher Juristentag in Hamburg*, in *Deutsche Richterzeitung* (1953): 148. Inevitably, the German Länder continued to model their newly reacquired power of grace on the regulations of the Nazi *Gnadenordnung*. See *Strafvollstreckung-Strafregister-Gnadenwesen*, 2d ed. (Munich/Berlin, 1954), 259–267 (text of Gnadenordnung); 305–309 (Hessen); 323–331 (Nordrhein-Westfalen).

322. H. E. Egner, "Strafaussetzung zur Bewährung und Gnadenrecht," *Neue Juristische Wochenschrift* (1953): 1859–1860.

323. See K. Bunge, *Italienischer Vorentwurf zu einem neuen Strafgesetzbuch (Progetto di un nuovo codice Penale)* (Berlin, 1928), 48–49, Arts. 165–167.

324. Barthélemy, *Cours de Droit Constitutionel Comparé, rédigé d'après la sténographie et avec l'autorisation* (Paris, 1944), 243–347. This was an old specialty for him. See Barthélemy, *L'Amnistie* (Paris, 1920).

325. J. Barthélemy, *Ministre de la Justice. Vichy 1941–43* (Paris, 1989), 269–271.

Chapter 5

1. For Kropotkin at Clairvaux, and for his attacks on some aspects of French imprisonment, see Badinter, *La Prison Républicaine*, 219.

2. Kropotkin, *Memoirs of a Revolutionist*, ed. N. Walter (New York, 1971), 462.

3. In the U.K., the Criminal Justice Act of 1948 abolished flogging as a judicial punishment. For a description of the end of flogging as a judicial punishment in the U.K., see "Backlashes of History," *The Guardian* (London), April 19, 1994, at 15. Note that the practice of birching continued on the Isle of Man until 1976: "Behind the Times," *The Scotsman*, April 6, 1994. For the end of flogging in Canada, see Daniel Hall, "When Caning Meets the Eighth Amendment: Whipping Offenders in the United States," *Widener Journal of Public Law* 4 (1995): 403, 449. In Delaware, one crime, that of defacing or destroying a bill or act of the General Assembly, carried the punishment of whipping until 1986: Hall, "When Caning Meets the Eighth Amendment, 425–427 (1995).

4. For attempts to reintroduce flogging in the United States, see Curtis Wilkie, "Mississippi Flogging Debate Opens Old Wounds," *The Boston Globe*, February 21, 1995, 1; and Mark Hosenball, "Drug Traffickers Face the Lash," Delaware, *Times Newspapers Limited*, March 5, 1989, Issue 8586. For recent British support for the reintroduction of flogging, see "Fox Rapped on 'Flogging Comment,'" *Western Daily Press*, WDP First/Somerset Edition, July 9, 1998, 4; and Roy Hattersley, "Whipping Some Life into a Dying Government," *The Guardian* (London), November 11, 1996, 12.

5. For late-nineteenth-century practices in English prisons, see Sellin, *Slavery and*

the Penal System, 104–105; for the treadwheel, ibid., 106–109; and for oakum-picking, 112. This was often noted by continental observers: E.g., v. Holtzendorff and Jagemann, *Handbuch des Gefängniswesens*, 2: 231.

6. Bl. Comm. 4:370–371.

7. For trial by the House of Lords for peers accused of treason or felony, see, e.g., William Holdsworth, *A History of English Law*, Vol. 2 (London: Methuen, 1966), 196.

8. See ibid., Vol. 2, 453. For later developments based in the law of *scandalum magnatum*, see Mark P. Denbeaux, "The First Word of the First Amendment," *Northwestern University Law Review* 80 (1986): 1178–1187.

9. In this too, English developments simply anticipated continental ones. The same pattern would emerge in the treatment of "outrage" and "Majestätsbeleidigung" in the France and Germany of the nineteenth and twentieth centuries. See Whitman, "Enforcing Civility and Respect," 1279, 1305.

10. Holdsworth, *History of English Law*, 3:393.

11. See chapter 4.

12. J. M. Beattie, *Crime and the Courts in England, 1660–1800* (Princeton, 1986), 141–148, and here 142.

13. Ibid., 142.

14. Ibid., 490–92; Beattie, *Policing and Punishment in London, 1660–1750: Urban Crime and the Limits of Terror* (Oxford, 2001), 330–332.

15. Ibid., 143–144.

16. Selden, *Titles of Honor*, 3d ed. (London, 1672).

17. For a brief comparative discussion, see R. Brown and A. Gilman, "The Pronouns of Power and Solidarity," in T. Sebeok, ed., *Style in Language* (Cambridge, 1966): 253–276.

18. E.g., S. Writer, " 'Written naturally by the finger of God in our hearts': Leveller Politics, the English Revolution and the Natural Law Tradition," *Newcastle Law Review* 3 (1998): 52–54.

19. See J. P. Kenyon, ed., *The Stuart Constitution, 1603–1688*, 2d ed. (Cambridge, 1986), 105–106; E. P. Cheyney, "The Court of Star Chamber," *American Historical Review* 18 (1913): 747–748. T. G. Barnes shows that these punishments were rarely inflicted. Barnes, "Star Chamber Mythology," *American Journal of Legal History* 5 (1961): 6–7. This did not diminish their symbolic importance.

20. Fisher, "The Rise of Jury as Lie Detector," *Yale Law Journal* 107 (1997): 618. See also Beattie, *Crime and the Courts*, 456, focusing on the example of the duke of Devonshire, fined thirty thousand pounds in 1687.

21. *An Account of the Sentence which past upon Titus Oates* (*Upon Conviction of Horrid Perjuries*) (London: Printed for A. Banks, 1685).

22. Bl.Comm. 4: 138–139. See also Richard H. Underwood, "Perjury: An Anthology," *Arizona Journal of International and Comparative Law* 13 (1996): 307.

23. *The Doctor Degraded; Or the Reward of Deceit: Being an Account of the Right Perfidious and Perjury'd Titus Oates* (London: Printed by George Groom, 1685).

24. *The Little Infant Titus: or Oates Exalted Above his Brethren* (London: Printed by George Groom, 1685).

25. *The Tragick-Comedy of Titus Oates* (London: Printed by J. M., 1685).

26. *The Doctor Degraded.*

27. Anon., "A Letter to a gentleman at Brussels, containing an account of the causes of the peoples revolt from the crown" (London: n.p., 1689), 7.

28. The standard treatment, Granucci, "Nor Cruel and Unusual Punishments In-

flicted: The Original Meaning," *California Law Review* 57 (1969): 839, has effectively nothing to say about these questions of status. Status issues go similarly too little attended in L. Schwoerer, *The Declaration of Rights, 1689* (Baltimore, 1981).

29. Coke, *The Third Part of the Institutes of England*, 4th ed. (London, 1669), 211–212.

30. Pleas of the Crown 412.

31. More, *Utopia*, trans. C. Miller (New Haven, 2001), 72, 95–96; see also G. Winstanley, "The Law of Freedom in a Platform, or True Magistracy Restored," in G. Sabine, ed., *The Works of Gerrard Winstanley* (New York, 1965), 596–597.

32. R. Haines, *A Breviat of some Proposals* (London, 1679), 6; [S. Chidley]. *A Cry against a Crying Sinne* (London, 1652), 17.

33. Bl. Comm. 4: 398. For a sample list of the beheaded, see J. Laurence, *A History of Capital Punishment* (London, 1932), 29.

34. *A Foreign View of England in the Reigns of George I & George II: The Letters of Monsieur César de Saussure to his Family*, trans. and edited by Madame van Muyden (London, 1902), 126–127. For more on the horror of the gibbet, see Laurence, *A History of Capital Punishment*, 58–61.

35. Wilf, "Imagining Justice: Aesthetics and Public Executions in Late Eighteenth-Century England," *Yale Journal of Law and the Humanities* 5 (1993): 57–59.

36. Donna Andrew, "The Code of Honour and its Critics: The Opposition to Dueling in England, 1700–1850," *Social History* 5 (1980): 412–413.

37. For other private houses of confinement in England, see Spierenburg, *Prison Experience*, 250.

38. A. Borg, "The State Prison," in J. Charlton, ed., *The Tower of London: Its Buildings and Institutions* (London, 1978), 86–93; P. Fry, *The Tower of London, Cauldron of Britain's Past* (London, 1990), 140ff.

39. Beattie, *Crime and the Courts*, 290, 301. Beattie notes, at 290, that debtors in particular might receive such treatment. It is unclear whether this special treatment would have been afforded debtors because of their status rather than their (presumably impaired) ability to pay. For the difficulties in keeping felons separate from debtors in the English prisons of the day, see ibid., 570–571.

40. Ibid., 88.

41. Ibid., 463.

42. Hay, "Property, Authority and the Criminal Law," in Hay, Linebaugh, Rule, Thompson and Winslow, eds., *Albion's Fatal Tree: Crime and Society in Eighteenth-Century England* (New York, 1975), 33.

43. Hay, "Property, Authority," 34.

44. Wilf, "Imagining Justice," 51–78, 57.

45. As Wilf shows, the practice had grown of using a hearse as a coach, thus making the execution procession into a funeral procession—something that diminished its impact, as reformers saw it. Ibid., 57–59. Nevertheless, high-status offenders transported to the colonies did manage to have themselves brought in a coach. See R. Ekirch, *Bound for America: The Transportation of British Convicts to the Colonies* (Oxford, 1987), 92–93.

46. John Langbein's well-known and telling critique of Hay—"Albion's Fatal Flaws," in *Past and Present* 98 (1983): 96–120—is also, to my mind, a shade misleading. Langbein concludes, on p. 120: "men of the social élite . . . were treated with special courtesy and regard. . . . To seize upon that as the *raison d'être* of the criminal justice system is, however, to mistake the barnacles for the boat." This understates the significance of status questions.

47. L. Radzinowicz, *A History of English Criminal Law and its Administration from 1750* (New York, 1948), 1: 190.

48. Anon., *Genuine memoires of the life, family and behaviour of Laurence Shirley, Earl of Ferrers; who was executed at Tyburn, on Monday the fifth of May 1760 for the murder of his steward, Mr. Johnston* (London, [(1760]), 19, reports that dissections alternated between the viscera and muscles. Ferrers was subjected to a viscera dissection, done in relative privacy.

49. For the slow decline of low-status punishments such as branding in Essex, see P. King, *Crime, Justice, and Discretion in England, 1740–1820* (Oxford, 2000), 272.

50. Beattie, *Crime and the Courts*, 78, and 79 n.10 for mutilation practices.

51. It is also striking that the rule of retreat had established itself in claims of self-defense in the eighteenth century, and that even defendants who came on their wives *in flagrante* could still be convicted, even if treated gently. Beattie, *Crime and the Courts*, 87, 95. Whether or not systems require persons attacked to retreat before defending themselves is an important measure of their attachment to norms of personal honor, as is their tendency to acquit cuckolded murderers outright.

52. Beattie, *Policing and Punishment*, 446.

53. Ibid., 447.

54. Beattie, *Crime and the Courts*, 89.

55. Ibid., 461–468, 544–546.

56. Ibid.; Beattie, *Policing and Punishment*, 438, 457.

57. Discussion in Andrews, *Law, Magistracy, and Crime*, 410 n.1.

58. On the hulks, Beattie, *Crime and the Courts*, 565–569; for the continental comparison, Langbein, *Torture and the Law of Proof*. For early eighteenth-century interest in forced labor as a punishment, see Beattie, *Crime and the Courts*, 295–296, 492–500. Fines were also not uncommon, especially for assaults. These could be quite heavy, however, especially where a low-status person had assaulted a high-status one. See ibid., 456–458.

59. See below, note 203.

60. James Fitzjames Stephen, *A History of the Criminal Law of England* (London, 1883), 1:490.

61. Adam Jay Hirsch, *The Rise of the Penitentiary: Prisons and Punishment in Early America* (New Haven, 1992), 74 and 200 nn. 46 and 47. For mid- and late-eighteenth-century ideas, Beattie, *Crime and the Courts*, 521–525, 548–553.

62. Ibid., 297–298.

63. E.g., Muyart de Vouglans, *Les Loix Criminelles de la France, dans leur ordre naturel* (Paris, 1783), 40 and 44, and esp. his "Mémoire sur les Peines Infamantes," in ibid., 837, a comparatively reformist text that nevertheless insisted on status-differentiation. Muyart's text is reproduced, with a fine commentary, by M. Porret, "Atténuer le mal de l'infamie: Le Réformisme conservateur de Pierre-François Muyart de Vouglans," in *Crime, Histoire et Sociétés* 4 (2000): 95–120. For further examples of status-differentiation, see Jousse, *Traité de la Justice Criminelle de France*, 4 vols. (Paris, 1771), 1:42; Prosper Farinaccius, *Praxis et Theorica Criminalis Amplissima* (Venice, 1603), 322–329; Julius Clarus, *Opera Omnia, sive Practica Civilis et Criminalis* (Geneva, 1739), 473 (= Lib. V., q. 60, no. 95), surveying learned opinion; and the classic discussion of Tiraqueau, now in A. Laingui, ed., *Le "De Poenis Temperandis" de Tiraqueau* (1559) (Paris, 1986), 169–184.

64. E.g., Muyart de Vouglans, *Loix Criminelles*, 10.

65. *Commentaries*, 4:15.

66. R. MacMullen, "Judicial Savagery," 204.

67. [Henry Dagge], *Considerations on Criminal Law* (London, 1772), 164–179, making no mention of status questions.

68. J. M. Beattie, *Crime and the Courts*, 21.

69. See Voltaire's 1766 Commentary in *Des délits et des peines* (Paris: Brière, 1822), 277–358.

70. See Muyart de Vouglans, texts cited above; [Jousse], *Nouveau Commentaire sur l'Ordonnance Criminelle du Mois d'Août 1670* (Paris, 1772), 1:181–182; Jousse, *Traité de la Justice Criminelle de France*.

71. Muyart de Vouglans, "Réfutation du Traité des Délits et Peines, etc.," in *Loix Criminelles*, 811–831 (orig. 1766).

72. See C. Blamires, "Beccaria et l'Angleterre," in M. Porret, ed., *Beccaria et la Culture Juridique des Lumières* (Geneva, 1997), 69–81.

73. E.g., 4:18; and generally, Beattie, *Crime and the Courts*, 556–557.

74. There were arguably other differences, too, in the speculative English literature on punishment. Almost every speculative continental writer whose work I have found believed that "infamy" or "reputation" or "honor" should somehow remain at the core of the system of punishment. For a typical example, see Dufriche de Valazé, *Loix Pénales* (Alençon, 1784), 312–313. Further examples in Whitman, "What is Wrong with Inflicting Shame Sanctions?" 1072 n.80. The idea that punishments should somehow revolve around questions of honor or status was by no means wholly alien to English speculative writings. See e.g, [William Eden Auckland], *Principles of Penal Law*, 2d ed. (London, 1771), 57, 59. Nevertheless I have the impression that English authors simply thought less in such terms than did continental ones.

75. See chapter 4.

76. Bl.Comm. 4:445–446: "In democracies . . . this power of pardon can never subsist, for there nothing higher is acknowledged than the magistrate who administers the law"; also 4: 397–398.

77. Fielding, "An Enquiry into the Cause of the Increase of Robbers," in Fielding, *Complete Works*, ed. Henley (New York, 1902), 121.

78. Bentham, *Principles of Penal Law*, in *The Works of Jeremy Bentham*, ed. J. Bowring, 11 vols. (Edinburgh: William Tait, 1843), 1:530. Bentham also associated pardons with despotism. Cf. Bentham, *The Constitutional Code*, in Bentham, *Works*, 9: 37.

79. Beattie, *Policing and Punishment in London*, 346–362.

80. Beattie, *Crime and the Courts*.

81. Radzinowicz, 1:107. Pardoning had been contested earlier on English history. For a summary, see C. Jensen, *The Pardoning Power in the American States* (Chicago, 1922), 2–3.

82. See, for example, the 1728 case discussed in Beattie, *Crime and the Courts*, 118.

83. Ibid., 444–445.

84. Ibid., 432.

85. See King's count for the years 1787–90, and his tentative assessment, in King, *Crime, Justice and Discretion*, 299–300, 307–310. The impression given by Beattie's account of the process a century and three quarters of a century earlier is that connections at that stage counted for more. See Beattie, *Policing and Punishment*, 357–358, 454. No scientific comparison of these two accounts is possible, though.

86. Beattie, *Crime and the Courts*, 442–444.

87. Ibid., 432.

88. Ibid., 582–83. See further P. J. R. King, "Decision-Makers and Decision-Making in English Criminal Law, 1750–1800," in *Historical Journal* 27 (1984): 25–58.

89. King, *Crime, Justice and Discretion*, 317–318.

90. Andrews, *Law, Magistracy and Crime*, 398.

91. Both King and Beattie resist drawing firm conclusions in their new books.

92. For King's negative assessment of Hay's arguments, see ibid., 326, 332; Beattie, *Policing and Punishment*, 347–348.

93. Beattie, *Crime and the Courts*, 409, 413–414. Bacon was already defending the idea that judges should dispense mercy in the early seventeenth century. The contrast with France is again revealing: While the pressures of the management of justice were such that some delegation was necessary, the delegation was technically not to judges, but to "petites chancelleries"—representatives of the royal power attached to the courts. See Foviaux, *La Rémission des Peines*, 42–43, 76. French law was always careful to express the sovereignty of the king in matters of grace.

94. Beattie, *Crime and the Courts*, 424–425; King, *Crime, Justice and Discretion*, 238–239. For the views of Blackstone and Eden, see T. Green, *Verdict According to Conscience: Perspectives on the English Criminal Jury Trial, 1200–1800* (Chicago, 1985), 295, 298.

95. Juries also simply acquitted or convicted of a lesser offense, and prosecutors played the same game. See Beattie, *Crime and the Courts*, 410–412, 419–423, 286, 333.

96. Cf. Friedman, *Crime and Punishment in American History* (New York, 1993), 30–31.

97. D. Fisher, *Albion's Seed: Four British Folkways in America* (Oxford, 1989).

98. For a brief survey, see Friedman, *Crime and Punishment*, 36–44.

99. See Kathryn Preyer, "Penal Measures in the American Colonies: An Overview," *American Journal of Legal History* 26 (1982): 335–336; for public display in punishment in Pennsylvania, see M. Meranze, *Laboratories of Virtue: Punishment, Revolution, and Authority in Philadelphia, 1760–1835* (Chapel Hill, 1996), 19–127.

100. For a mid-eighteenth-century example, see S. Wilf, "Placing Blame: Criminal Law and Constitutional Narratives in Revolutionary Boston," *Crime, Histoire et Sociétés* 4 (2000): 47.

101. D. Rothman, *The Discovery of the Asylum: Social Order and Disorder in the New Republic* (Boston, 1971), 50. Donna Spindel, *Crime and Society in North Carolina, 1663–1776* (Baton Rouge, 1989), 117, finds little banishment in her period. Fines (over 75 percent of penalties) and whipping (10 percent) dominate in her sample, from 1663–1776. Ibid., 126–227. For the importance of whipping, see also Preyer, "Penal Measures in the American Colonies," 349.

102. Hirsch, *Rise of the Penitentiary*.

103. C. MacLachlan, *Criminal Justice in Eighteenth-Century Mexico: A Study of the Tribunal of the Acordada* (Berkeley, 1974), 21–28, 31.

104. Preyer, "Penal Measures in the American Colonies," 351. This was rare in North Carolina. Spindel, *Crime and Society in North Carolina*, 126.

105. M. P. Baumgartner, "Law and Social Status in Colonial New Haven, 1639–1665," *Research in Law and Sociology* 1 (1978): 168–170; B. Chapin, *Criminal Justice in Colonial America, 1606–1660* (Athens, 1983), 53; D. Greenberg, "Crime, Law Enforcement, and Social Control in Colonial America," 298.

106. Preyer, "Penal Measures in the American Colonies," 334, 331. Virginia, close in social spirit to metropolitan England, was the scene of a protests over the application of infaming punishments to colonists who regarded themselves as persons of high status in the 1630s, at the same time that Star Chamber raised English hackles by applying low-status punishments to members of the gentry. See D. Konig, "'Dale's Laws'

and the Non-Common Law Origins of Criminal Justice in Virginia," *American Journal of Legal History* 26 (1982): 368–375.

107. Spindel, *Crime and Society in North Carolina*, 123, 125–126.

108. See the account of one case in Douglas Greenberg, *Crime and Law Enforcement in the Colony of New York, 1691–1776* (Ithaca, 1974), 101.

109. A. G. Roeber, "Authority, Law and Custom: The Rituals of Court Day in Tidewater Virginia, 1720–1750," *William and Mary Quarterly*, 3d Series, 37 (1980): 29–52.

110. Spindel, *Crime and Society in North Carolina*, 131.

111. Ibid., 125–126.

112. Blacks were treated much more harshly, in ways that included mutilation. Ibid., 133–137. Perhaps we can speculate that the decline of mutilation for low-status white offenders in North Carolina reflected precisely the fact that this historically degrading treatment was reserved to an even lowlier class of persons.

113. Greenberg, *Crime and Law Enforcement*, 114.

114. On slaves: A. Leon Higginbotham and A. Jacobs, "The 'Law Only as an Enemy': The Legitimatization of Racial Powerlessness through the Colonial and Antebellum Criminal Laws of Virginia," *North Carolina Law Review* 70 (1992): 1038–1039; Preyer, "Penal Measures in the American Colonies," 341.

115. For this pattern, see J. Goebel and T. R. Naughton, *Law Enforcement in Colonial New York, 1664–1776* (New York, 1944), 591–597; Greenberg, *Crime and Law Enforcement*, 71.

116. Hirsch, *Rise of the Penitentiary*; also, e.g., Friedman, *Crime and Punishment*.

117. I have raised some doubts about this analysis in Whitman, "What is Wrong with Inflicting Shame Sanctions?"

118. Rothman, *Discovery of the Asylum*, 46.

119. Ibid., 53; Greenberg, *Crime and Law Enforcement*, 125.

120. Rothman, *Discovery of the Asylum*, 26.

121. See below, n.211; W. Winthrop, *Military Law* (Washington, 1886), 1:595 n.1. Even within the military, confinement within a military fort was discontinued as a standard punishment after the Civil War, with the establishment of Fort Leavenworth as a general military prison. See ibid., 1:599.

122. Rothman, *Discovery of the Asylum*, 55; Spierenburg, *Prison Experience*, 105–134.

123. Rothman, *Discovery of the Asylum*, 247.

124. Greenberg, *Crime and Law Enforcement*, 125–26.

125. Rothman, *Discovery of the Asylum*, 56; Friedman, *Crime and Punishment*, 50.

126. See Goebel and Naughton, *Law Enforcement in Colonial New York*, 675; P. Hoffer and W. Scott, Introduction, in Hoffer and Scott, eds., *Criminal Proceedings in Colonial Virginia* (Athens, 1984), liv.

127. Spindel, *Crime and Society in North Carolina*, 116; Greenberg, *Crime and Law Enforcement*, 113.

128. Generally Friedman, *Crime and Punishment*, 42. For Pennsylvania, see Meranze, *Laboratories of Virtue*, 29 and 29 n.19; for New York, Greenberg, *Crime and Law Enforcement*, 127–132.

129. Goebel and Naughton, *Law Enforcement*, 702–05; cf. Greenberg, *Crime and Law Enforcement*, 130–131.

130. Greenberg, *Crime and Law Enforcement*, 127–30.

131. Meranze, *Laboratories of Virtue*, 36.

132. For these two classes of pardons, see Greenberg, *Crime and Law Enforcement*, 129.

133. Spindel, *Crime and Society in North Carolina*, 124.

134. Greenberg, *Crime and Law Enforcement*, 132.

135. For Pennsylvania, Meranze, *Laboratories of Virtue*, 79, 81. On James Wilson, ibid., 66.

136. Meranze, *Laboratories of Virtue*, 81. For Beccarianism in eighteenth-century America, see also Rothman, *Discovery of the Asylum*, 60–62.

137. William Francis Kuntz, *Sentencing in Three Nineteenth-Century Cities: Social History of Punishment in New York, Boston, and Philadelphia, 1830–1880* (New York, 1988), 24–26.

138. Ibid., 42–44.

139. Ibid., 52–53.

140. Quoted and discussed in Meranze, *Laboratories of Virtue*, 41.

141. K. Moore, *Pardons: Justice, Mercy, and the Public Interest* (New York, 1989), 25.

142. Meranze, *Laboratories of Virtue*, 81, citing Hopkinson, *Miscellaneous Essays* (Philadelphia, 1792), 2:108,107.

143. G. Nash, *The Urban Crucible: Social Change, Political Consciousness, and the Origins of the American Revolution* (Cambridge, 1979), 408; S. Brobeck, "Revolutionary Change in Colonial Philadelphia: The Brief Life of the Proprietary Gentry," *William and Mary Quarterly* 3d ser. 33 (1976): 410–434; S. Rosswurm, *Arms, Country and Class: The Philadelphia Militia and the "Lower Sort" during the American Revolution* (Syracuse, 1975), 35–38.

144. G. Wood, *The Radicalism of the American Revolution* (New York, 1992), 6–7.

145. *Annals of Congress*, 435, 760

146. Other provisions of the Constitution also reflected old-world traditions of status. The Second Amendment, with its guarantee of the right to bear arms, represented something that can fairly be called a general extension of high status: the right to bear arms, we should remember, was restricted exclusively to the nobility in continental Europe.

147. See K. Preyer, "Crime, the Criminal Law, and Reform in Post-Revolutionary Virginia," *Law and History Review* (1983): 58–59.

148. Act of September 24, 1789, ch. 20, § 9; 1 Stat. 77.

149. Act of April 30, 1790, ch. 9; 1 Stat. 112–117.

150. See for example the discussion of Thomas Eddy in O. Lewis, *The Development of American Prisons and Prison Customs, 1776–1845* (repr. Montclair, 1967), 9.

151. B. Rush, *An Enquiry in the Effects of Public Punishment* (Philadelphia, 1787), 16. Rush's opposition to public punishment revolved in particular around its tendency to brutalize both the public and the offender. This was an argument common in Europe as well. See Whitman, "What is Wrong with Inflicting Shame Sanctions," 1073–1079. What is important to observe is Rush's comparative lack of interest in the questions of dishonor that mattered so much to European reformers.

152. See M. Hindus, *Prison and Plantation: Crime, Justice, and Authority in Massachusetts and South Carolina, 1767–1878* (Chapel Hill, 1980), 101–102.

153. Myra Glenn, *Campaigns Against Corporal Punishment: Prisoners, Sailors, Women, and Children in Antebellum America* (Albany, 1984), 54–59.

154. Friedman, *Crime and Punishment*, 74–75; and, for the change in sensibility, the acute account of Spierenburg, *The Spectacle of Suffering*.

155. Rothman, *Discovery of the Asylum*, 92, citing Caleb Lownes, *An Account of the Alteration and Present State of the Penal Law of Pennsylvania* (Philadelphia, 1793), 81–88; W. D. Lewis, *From Newgate to Dannemora: The Rise of the Penitentiary in New York, 1796–1848* (Ithaca, 1965), 46–47.

156. Penitentiary Act of 1779; Beattie, *Crime and the Courts*, 520–618.

157. M. Ignatieff, *A Just Measure of Pain: The Penitentiary in the Industrial Revolution, 1750–1850* (New York, 1978); Beattie, *Crime and the Courts*, 604, 617.

158. On this, see Meranze, *Laboratories of Virtue*, 55–86, esp. 63–68 for the influence of Beccaria.

159. Meranze, *Laboratories of Virtue*,131–213, tracing this and other experiments from 1790 onward.

160. For the Christian character, Meranze, *Laboratories of Virtue*, E.g., 173, 186; Walker, *Popular Justice*, 83–84. Adam Hirsch has taken issue with the traditional account of the Christian sources of the American penitentiary, and in particular of the Quaker strain in Pennsylvania. Hirsch, like Beattie, observes correctly that workhouses offered a familiar model for the new penitentiaries. This is certainly true; but it hardly means that prison reform was not driven by Christian sentiment. Indeed, it is misleading to view workhouses as somehow not "Christian": they too manifestly drew on Christian sentiment, as Hirsch would presumably agree.

161. Meranze, *Laboratories of Virtue*, 293–328.

162. Quoted and discussed in Meranze, *Laboratories of Virtue*, 1.

163. D. Lewis, *From Newgate to Dannemora*, 30.

164. Kuntz, *Sentencing in Three Nineteenth-Century Cities*, 50; cf. Lewis, *Development of American Prisons*, 58, 71–72.

165. Rothman, *Discovery of the Asylum*, 90–91.

166. Meranze, *Laboratories of Virtue*, 302–303.

167. Beaumont and Tocqueville, *Du Système Pénitentiaire*, 34 n. (1), describing branding, abolished in Massachusetts in 1829. For this, see Hindus, *Prison and Plantation*, 168.

168. See chapter 4.

169. G. F. Fischer, *Über Gefängnisse, Strafarten, Strafsysteme und Strafanstalten* (Regensburg, 1852), 37–38. Fischer's fears that German prisons would abandon corporal punishment proved unfounded, as new legislation came in during the 1850s. See the survey in T. Eisenhardt, *Strafvollzug* (Stuttgart, 1978), 54–55. Other Germans had other attitudes: Mittermaier, for example, shared Tocqueville's and Beaumont's view. See Mittermaier, "Neue Schriften über Gefängnisse," in *Archiv des Criminalrechts*, N.F. (1834): 148.

170. Lewis, *Development of American Prisons*, 61 and often.

171. Kuntz, *Sentencing in Three Nineteenth-Century Cities*, 38. Cf. Eddy, *An Account of the State Prison or Penitentiary House, in the City of New York By One of the Inspectors of the Prison* (New York, 1801); Hindus, *Prison and Plantation*, 171–173.

172. Kuntz, *Sentencing in Three Nineteenth-Century Cities*, 147; Lewis, *Development of American Prisons*, 94–98, 109, 221–224

173. Rothman, *Discovery of the Asylum*, 102, quoting an Auburn chaplain.

174. Thus the Auburn chaplain, quoted in ibid.

175. R. J. Turnbull, *A Visit to the Philadelphia Prison* (Philadelphia, 1796), 51, quoted and discussed in Meranze, *Laboratories of Virtue*, 187.

176. Ibid.

177. Rothman, *Discovery of the Asylum*, 93.

178. Kuntz, *Sentencing in Three Nineteenth-Century Cities*, 298.

179. Rothman, *Discovery of the Asylum*, 93.

180. For the continuing idea that idleness was the problem in Antebellum America, see Rothman, *Discovery of the Asylum*, 103.

181. Many references to early modern literature in Hirsch, *Rise of Penitentiary,* 199 n. 42

182. Sellin, *Slavery and the Penal System*; Hindus, *Prison and Plantation,* 125–181; Hirsch, *Rise of the Penitentiary,* 71–111.

183. Hirsch, *Rise of the Penitentiary,* 72.

184. Ibid., 73, quoting Gershom Powers, *A Brief Account of the Construction, Management, and Discipline . . . of the New York State Prison at Auburn* (Auburn, 1826), 3.

185. Quoted and discussed in Hindus, *Prison and Plantation,* 166.

186. See chapter 1.

187. Meranze, *Laboratories of Virtue,* 296, 298–299.

188. Hirsch, *Rise of the Penitentiary,* 71–111.

189. Ibid., 75–82.

190. Beaumont and Tocqueville, *Du Système Pénitentiaire,* 86–87.

191. See Hindus, *Prison and Plantation,* 168–171.

192. U.S. Constitution, Amendment 13.

193. See, "From Alabama's Past, Capitalism and Racism in a Cruel Partnership," *Wall Street Journal,* July 16, 2001, A1; and, for the historical background, Sellin, *Slavery and the Penal System,* 145–162.

194. For a brief account of the interpretation of this aspect of the Thirteenth Amendment, see Ira Robbins, "The Legal Dimensions of Private Incarceration," *American University Law Review* 38 (1989): 605–607.

195. 468 U.S. 517, 554–555 (1984). Sensitively discussed by Martha Nussbaum, *Poetic Justice: The Literary Imagination and Public Life* (Boston, 1995), 99–102.

196. Cf. B. Carpzov, *Practica Nova Imperialis Saxonica Rerum Criminalium* (Wittenberg: Mevius & Schumacher, 1677), 3:286 (q. 135, nu. 4). This passage treats the immunity to enslavement (reduction to "servus poenae"—that is to say, loss of a variety of civil rights for persons condemned to death), an immunity limited by Justinian to "bene nati," as applying "generaliter . . . de omnibus Reis condemnatis."

197. Zysberg, "Le Modèle des travaux forcés," in Petit et al., *Histoire des Galères, Bagnes et Prisons,* 228–229.

198. Sellin, *Slavery and the Penal System,* 85–86.

199. Bonnéville de Marsangy, *De l'Amélioration de la Loi Criminelle* (Paris, 1864), 432.

200. Desmazes, *Les Pénalités Anciennes,* 314. Desmazes's preface is dated September 1865. Desmazes was picking up some odd information: he was convinced that blacks were being systematically employed as guards over whites in the aftermath of the Civil War. Ibid., 315.

201. Ibid., 316.

202. Cf. Petit, *Politiques, modèles et imaginaires,* 149.

203. D. Taylor, *Crime, Policing, and Punishment in England, 1750–1914* (New York, 1998), 153 and generally 150–156; C. Emsley, *Crime and Society in England, 1750–1900,* 2d ed. (London, 1996), 276–286; M. Heather Tomlinson, "Penal Servitude, 1846–1865: A System in Evolution," in V. Bailey, ed., *Policing and Punishment in Nineteenth Century Britain* (London, 1981), 126–149.

204. H. E. Barnes, *The Story of Punishment* (repr. Montclair, 1972) (orig. 1930), 57. For a failed nineteenth-century reform effort, see S. McConville, *English Local Prisons, 1860–1900: Next Only to Death* (London, 1995), 741–742. The abolition was made by the Criminal Justice Act of 1948.

205. For a survey, see Ma, "The European Court of Human Rights and the Protection of the Rights of Prisoners and Criminal Defendants," 56–62.

206. Rothman, *Discovery of the Asylum*, 253.

207. Kuntz, *Sentencing in Three Nineteenth-Century Cities*, 385.

208. Rothman, *Discovery of the Asylum*, 254.

209. Tocqueville, *De la Démocratie en Amérique*, 2:209.

210. For their treatment, indistinguishable from the "special regime" in Europe, see Edward Livingston, *Criminal Jurisprudence* (New York, 1873), 2: 562–564.

211. Quoted in *Ex Parte Milligan*, 71 U.S. 2, 24 (1866).

212. For the English rejection of the category, see Radzinowicz, *A History of English Criminal Law and its Administration from 1750* (London, 1986), 1:401–461.

213. Meranze, *Laboratories of Virtue*, 177–178; Lewis, *Development of American Prisons*, 16–17. Still the colonies were already easier on debtors than metropolitan England. See P. Coleman, *Debtors and Creditors in America: Insolvency, Imprisonment for Debt, and Bankruptcy, 1607–1900* (Madison, 1974), 11–12.

214. Coleman, *Debtors and Creditors*, 41, 106–107.

215. *Du Système Pénitentiaire*, 314. Their general account, at 313–315, was broadly accurate, though.

216. See. E. Randall, "Imprisonment for Debt in America: Fact and Fiction," *Mississippi Valley Historical Review* 39 (1952): 89–102; Coleman, *Debtors and Creditors*, 43–45, 62, 73, 103, 116–123, 139–140, 148–154, 186, 202–203, 223–227, 235, 243, and generally 256–258. Rhode Island and Delaware were exceptions. Coleman, *Debtors and Creditors*, 89–90, 213, and in the South reform came more slowly than in the North. Ibid., 159–160.

217. Kuntz, *Sentencing in Three Nineteenth-Century Cities*, 125 (discussing Massachusetts).

218. South Carolina, it is worth noting, did have the bounds system for all prisoners—a fact that perhaps reflects that racial status hierarchy of the state. White prisoners there were definitionally high-status. See Friedman, *Crime and Punishment*, 81 n.

219. *Wilkerson v. Utah*, 99 U.S. 130 (1878).

220. *Du Système Pénitentiaire*, 163.

221. See e.g., Badinter, *La Prison Républicaine*, 31.

222. Wood, *Radicalism of the American Revolution*, 6–7.

223. Appendix II in *Notes on the State of Virginia*, ed. W. Peden (Chapel Hill, 1955), 214.

224. Jensen, *Pardoning Power in the American States*, 10.

225. Ibid.

226. See discussion of Moore, *Pardons*, 26–27; United States Constitution, Art. II, Sect. 2, granting the president "power to grant Reprieve and Pardons for offenses against the United States, except in cases of impeachment."

227. Moore, *Pardons*, 27.

228. Ibid., 51.

229. Ibid., 63.

230. Kuntz, *Sentencing in Three Nineteenth-Century Cities*, 28.

231. Ibid., 37–38.

232. William Crawford, *Report on the Penitentiaries of the United States, Addressed to His Majesty's Principal Secretary of State for the Home Department* (London, 1835), 6–8. Cited and discussed in Kuntz, *Sentencing in Three Nineteenth-Century Cities*, 36.

233. Ibid., 149.

234. Meranze, *Laboratories of Virtue*, 203–204.

235. Quoted and discussed in Kuntz, *Sentencing in Three Nineteenth-Century Cities*, 176.

236. Ibid., 191.

237. Ibid., 177–178.

238. Ibid., 28.

239. Ibid., 299, 322.

240. Hindus, *Prison and Plantation*, 111; E. Ayers, *Vengeance and Justice: Crime and Punishment in the 19th-Century South* (New York, 1984), 63; Walker, *Popular Justice*, 102.

241. Moore, *Pardons*, 53. On the modern history, see generally Moore's book and P. S. Ruckman, "Executive Clemency in the United States: Origins, Development and Analysis (1900–1993)," *Presidential Studies Quarterly* 27 (1997): 251–271.

242. Friedman, *Crime and Punishment*, 261–62.

243. Moore, *Pardons*, 62.

244. Ibid., 56.

245. Ibid., 55–56.

246. M. Zalman, "The Rise and Fall of the Indeterminate Sentence," *Wayne State Law Review* 24 (1977): 55–58.The tale in Michigan is particularly interesting: there the introduction of parole was challenged on the grounds that the power was constitutionally part of the pardoning power. *People v. Cummings*, 88 Mich. 249 (1891). Only a constitutional amendment made the transformation of pardoning into paroling possible

247. Rothman, *Discovery of the Asylum*, 244–245, 252.

248. Walker, *Popular Justice*, 93–95. Augustus was in fact not the originator of probation. See G. Fisher, "Plea Bargaining's Triumph," *Yale Law Journal* 109 (2000): 857. Nevertheless, the Christian associations that he gave the practice are of obvious importance for American legal culture.

249. Kuntz, *Sentencing in Three Nineteenth-Century Cities*, 284–285, 288–289.

250. Ibid., 315, 321.

251. Ibid., 346–351.

252. Jensen, *Pardoning Power in the American States*, 11.

253. Ibid., 27.

254. Bradford, "Enquiry into the Nature of Punishment," quoted in ibid., 27–28.

255. F. Lieber, *On Civil Liberty and Self-Government* (repr. Union, N.J., 2001), 439.

256. Smithers and Thorn, *Executive Clemency in Pennsylvania*, 35. Quoted and discussed in Jensen, *Pardoning Power*, 26.

257. For an example from the early years of the French Revolution, in which this egalitarian argument was made by a reformer who nevertheless did not believe that pardon should be entirely abolished, see the discussion of Goujon in Vimont, *Punir Autrement*, 39.

258. Quoted and discussed in Kuntz, *Sentencing in Three Nineteenth-Century Cities*, 151.

259. Ibid., 152.

260. Walker, *Popular Justice*, 101–102, summarizing this view perhaps a shade uncritically.

261. Quoted and discussed in Kuntz, *Sentencing in Three Nineteenth-Century Cities*, 83. For race riots in Philadelphia in this period, see A. Steinberg, *The Transformation of Criminal Justice: Philadelphia, 1800–1880* (Chapel Hill, 1989), 140–149.

262. Jensen, *Pardoning Power*, 25.

263. Quoted and discussed in ibid.

264. Kuntz, *Sentencing in Three Nineteenth-Century Cities,* 174–75.

265. Ibid., 233–34, on Massachusetts.

266. Jensen, *Pardoning Power,* 23–25; Hindus, *Prison and Plantation,* 111–121.

267. C. Bonaparte, "The Pardoning Power," *Yale Law Journal* 19 (1910): 603. Discussed in Moore, *Pardons,* 63.

268. W. Smithers, "Nature and Limits of the Pardoning Power," *Journal of Criminal Law* 1 (1910): 549. Discussed in Moore, *Pardons,* 64.

269. Lewis, *Development of American Prisons,* 38–39, 57.

270. *U.S. v. Wilson,* 32 U.S. 152, 158, 160 (1833).

271. U.S. 90 (1915).

272. *Biddle v. Perovich,* 274 U.S. 486 (1927).

273. *Ex parte Wilson,* 114 U.S. 417 (1885). This is still more or less standard jurisprudence. See *Wharton's Criminal Law,* 15th ed. (Deerfield, 1993), 1:117–122.

274. *Mackin v. United States,* 117 U.S. 348 (1886).

275. 163 U.S. 228 (1896).

276. *Trop v. Dulles,* 356 U.S. 86,101 (1958). See also, *Gregg v. Georgia,* 428 U.S. 153, 172–3 (1976).

277. *Talley v. Stephens,* 247 F. Supp 683, 687–689 (E.D. Ark 1965).

278. F.2d 571 (8th Cir. 1968).

279. See the intelligent discussion of this decision in Hall, "When Caning Meets the Eighth Amendment," 446–447.

280. *Balser v. State,* 195 A.2d 757 (Del. 1963); *State v. Cannon,* 190 A.2d 514 (Del. 1963).

281. Del. Code Ann. tit. 11, § 631, 3905–3908 (repealed 1973).

282. Antonin Scalia, *"Originalism: The Lesser Evil,"* University of Cincinnati Law Review *57 (1989): 849.* Discussed in Lawrence Lessig, "Fidelity in Translation," *Texas Law Review* 71 (1993): 1165, 1187.

283. 18 F.3d 662, 702 (9th Cir. 1994).

Conclusion

1. See chapter 4.

2. *Démocratie en Amérique,* 1:85.

3. *Démocratie en Amérique,* 1:114; Lipset, *It Didn't Happen Here,* 28–31; Hartz, *The Liberal Tradition in America.*

4. Heine, "Englische Fragmente," in *Historisch-Kritisch Gesamtausgabe der Werke,* ed. M. Windfuhr, 16 vols. (Hamburg, 1973–1997) 7/1:210: "[W]enn die Canaille roturière sich die Freiheit nahm, jene hohe Noblesse zu köpfen, so geschah dieses vielleicht weniger um ihre Güter als ihre Ahnen zu erben, und statt der bürgerlichen Ungleichheit eine adlige Gleichheit einzuführen." For a converse view of the same phenomenon, see Cottu, *De l'Administration de la Justice Criminelle en Angleterre et de l'Ésprit du Gouvernement Anglais,* 2d ed. (Paris, 1822), 246: In order for "la noblesse" to preserve itself, "il est indispensable . . . qu'elle soit accessible à tous les citoyens pour devenir le but de leur noble ambition."

5. Montesquieu, *Ésprit des Lois,* 1:149 (Bk. III, Ch. 7).

6. Tocqueville, *Démocratie en Amérique,* 1: 115.

7. For Tocqueville's unsuccessful attempt to address this problem, see Lamberti, *Tocqueville et les deux Démocraties,* 25–26.

8. *Wilkerson v. Utah,* 99 U.S. 130, 135 (1878).

9. Allen, *The Decline of the Rehabilitative Ideal*; S. Cohen, *Visions of Social Control* (Cambridge, 1985).

10. Described in Walker, *Popular Justice*, 208–210.

11. Durkheim, *The Division of Labor in Society*, trans. Halls (London, 1984), 44; Durkheim, *Two Laws of Penal Evolution*, trans. T. A. Jones and A. Scull, in M. Gane, ed., *The Radical Sociology of Durkheim and Mauss* (London, 1992), 21–49. Usefully summarized in Garland, *Punishment and Modern Society*, 29–41. For a survey of objections, and an attempt to salvage some of Durkheim's claims, see R. Cotterell, *Emile Durkheim: Law in a Moral Domain* (Stanford, 1999), 78–94.

12. This is true not only in American contract law, which shows a more deep-seated commitment to freedom of contract than French or German contract law does. It is also true in American corporate law, in American labor law, and more. Not least, it is true in the American law of punishment, for Beccarian act-egalitarianism of the kind that prevails in America today has, as I have suggested above, a close, if somewhat elusive, kinship with contractarian ways of thinking.

13. T. H. Marshall and Tom Bottomore, *Citizenship and Social Class*, 33.

14. Wood, *Radicalism of the American Revolution*, 6–7.

15. See Calliess and Müller-Dietz, *Strafvollzugsgesetz*, 115, and the discussion in chapter 3.

16. Tocqueville, *Démocratie en Amérique*, 2:209.

17. Bentham, *Principles of Penal Law*, 401.

18. "At a Slaughterhouse, Some Things Never Die," *New York Times*, June 16, 2000.

19. While Judge Henley did invalidate forced labor, he did so under the Eighth Amendment, holding it unconstitutional for the state to compel labor in order to gain profit. See Feeley and Rubin, *Judicial Policy Making*, 63. For the history of Arkansas prisons as assuming the place of what had been plantation punishment for slaves, see ibid., 52.

20. 468 U.S. 517, 554–555 (1984).

21. Compare the fine effort of David Garland to restate Durkheim's claims in Garland, *Punishment and Modern Society*, 54.

22. Schlosser, *The Prison-Industrial Complex*, 7–8.

23. Garland, *Culture of Control*, 9, 13–14.

24. Walker, *Popular Justice*.

25. Zimring, "Populism, Democratic Government, and the Decline of Expert Authority," 243.

26. Ibid., 9, and 111–112 for contrast between attitudes of "politician" and "administrator." Garland, *Culture of Contr*ol, 41, attributes this taboo to the impact of the "civilizing process" as described by Elias. Whether this explanation is reconcilable with my emphasis on bureaucratization is a question I leave to the side.

27. See Pillsbury, "Why are We Ignored? The Peculiar Place of Experts in the Current Debate about Crime and Justice," in *Criminal Law Bulletin* (July/August 1995): 305–336.

28. Ibid.

29. Cf. the excellent discussion in Garland, *Punishment and Modern Society*, 182–183, and generally 177–191 on the "rationalization of punishment" and the bureaucratic mentality; Cohen, *Visions of Social Control*.

30. Zimring and Hawkins, *Capital Punishment and the American Agenda*, 3, 21–22. I do think the strength of religious sentiment in the United States is also of critical importance: Christianity continues to give death meaning for Americans, which means

that the death penalty has meaning for them as well. Cf. Camus, "Réflexions sur la Guillotine" and my discussion above. This is not inconsistent with the argument of Zimring and Hawkins, though. It implies only that the bureaucratic abolitionist mentality is in part a secularized mentality.

31. Mitsch, *Ordnungswidrigkeiten*, 1.

32. There is a paradox here that deserves elaboration, if only in a footnote. Let us assume that a truly liberal state can only forbid conduct that is evil, that is *malum in se*; anything else would exceed its limited powers. If this is so, then the liberal state has not only the right, but the imperative duty to forbid such acts, since they are by hypothesis evil. If it has such a duty, though, it cannot be bound by doctrines of mildness in punishment such as the ban on retroactivity. Evils must be punished even if the state has neglected formally to prohibit them. The paradox in this argument, which was famously made by Binding in the 1880s, is that beginning from liberal premises it arrives at harsh doctrines of punishment. Something exactly of that sort has happened in the United States.

33. Rothman, *Discovery of the Asylum*, 15.

34. Garland's excellent neo-Durkheimian discussion in Garland, *Punishment and Modern Society*, 69–81; and Mead, The Psychology of Punitive Justice," *American Journal of Sociology* 23 (1918): 591. If I have a quarrel with this approach, it is only in its arguable neglect of the importance of degradation in stirring collective emotions—hinted at in Garland's discussion of Nietzsche in ibid., 63, but not explored in any detail.

35. See e.g., the observations of Spierenburg in his "Masculinity, Violence and Honor: An Introduction," in P. Spierenburg, ed., *Men and Violence: Gender, Honor and Rituals in Modern Europe and America* (Columbus, 1998), 1–29.

36. Whitman, "Enforcing Civility and Respect," 1391–1394.

37. I am not even making any general claim about Europe, or about the West. Developments in contemporary Denmark or Holland or Italy or Canada, for example, are not well captured by the tendencies I have identified either in France and Germany in the United States. England too presents distinctive patterns. Thus even David Garland, who insists on the close parallelism of American and English developments, is regularly compelled to concede that England looks rather different. See *Culture of Control* at, e.g., 9, 14, 168 and often. There are reasons for this: the United States, France, and Germany are countries with *revolutionary* traditions, countries in which the old status structures were broken down by force. This is not equally true, or true in the same way, elsewhere, and it is inevitable that political traditions and patterns of punishment elsewhere should differ. Moreover, the United States, France, and Germany are quite distinctive in having relatively insular and autonomous legal cultures, which resist outside influences. Countries like Canada or Italy, by contrast, are far more receptive to foreign influence—a fact that deeply complicates any effort to extend analyses of the more autonomous legal cultures to them

38. Damaska, *The Faces of Justice and State Authority: A Comparative Approach to the Legal Process* (New Haven, 1986).

39. Friedman, *The Horizontal Society* (New Haven, 1999).

40. *Du Système Pénitentiaire*, 163.

41. See chapter 1.

42. Muyart de Vouglans, *Institutes au Droit Criminel ou Principes Généraux sur ces Matières* (Paris, 1768), 281.

Bibliography

Abegg, Julius Friedrich Heinrich. "Bemerkungen über das rechtliche Erforderniß verhältnißmässig gleicher Behandlung verschiedener Uebertreter desselben Strafgesetzes." *Archiv des Criminalrechts, N.F.* 2 (1835): 151–179.

Abou El Fadl, Khaled M. *And God Knows the Soldiers: The Authoritative and Authoritarian in Islamic Discourses.* Lanham, Md.: University Press of America, 2001.

An Account of the Sentence which past upon Titus Oates (Upon Conviction of Horrid Perjuries). London: Printed for A. Banks, 1685.

Alexandre, Arsène. *Honoré Daumier, l'Homme et l'Oeuvre.* Paris: H. Laurens, 1888.

Alhoy, Maurice. *Les bagnes: Histoire, types, moeurs, mystères.* Paris: G. Havard, 1845.

Allen, Danielle S. *The World of Prometheus: The Politics of Punishing in Democratic Athens.* Princeton: Princeton University Press, 2000.

Allen, Francis A. *The Decline of the Rehabilitative Ideal: Penal Policy and Social Purpose.* New Haven: Yale University Press, 1981.

Alschuler, Albert W. "The Failure of Sentencing Guidelines: A Plea for Less Aggregation." *University of Chicago Law Review* 58 (1991): 901–951.

American Friends Service Committee. *The Struggle for Justice: A Report on Crime and Punishment in America.* New York: Hill & Wang, 1971.

Amor, Paul. "La réforme pénitentiaire en France." *Revue de science criminelle et de droit pénal comparé* 1 (Jan.–March 1947): 1–30.

Andrew, Donna T. "The Code of Honour and its Critics: The Opposition to Duelling in England, 1700–1850." *Social History* 5 (1980): 409–434.

Andrews, Richard Mowery. *Law, Magistracy, and Crime in Old Regime Paris, 1735–1789.* Cambridge: Cambridge University Press, 1994.

Arasse, Daniel. *La guillotine et l'imaginaire de la Terreur.* Paris: Flammarion, 1987.

Arlen, Jennifer. "The Potentially Perverse Effects of Corporate Criminal Liability." *Journal of Legal Studies* 23 (1994): 833–867.

Arnold, Eric A., Jr., ed., *A Documentary Survey of Napoleonic France*. Trans. Eric A. Arnold, Jr. Lanham, Md.: University Press of America, 1994.

Arret de la cour de Parlement, qui condamne Augustin-Jean Agasse & Anne-Jean-Baptiste Agasse à etre pendus & étranglés. Paris: Nyon, 1790.

Arvanides, Thomas. "Increasing Imprisonment: A Function of Crime or Socioeconomic Factors?" *American Journal of Criminal Justice* 17 (1992): 19–38.

Augustine. "Epistle 133." In *Patrologia Latina*, ed. Jacques-Paul Migne. Vol. 33, cols. 509–510. Reprint, Turnhout: Brepols, 1983.

Ayers, Edward L. *Vengeance and Justice: Crime and Punishment in the 19th Century American South*. New York: Oxford University Press, 1984.

Badinter, Robert. "Beccaria, l'abolition de la peine de mort et la Révolution française." *Revue de science criminelle et de droit pénal* (1989): 235–251.

———. *La prison républicaine (1871–1914)*. Paris: Fayard, 1992.

Bancaud, Alain. "La magistrature et la répression politique de Vichy ou l'histoire d'un demi-échec." *Droit et société* 34 (1996): 557–574.

Barnes, Harry Elmer. *The Story of Punishment: A Record of Man's Inhumanity to Man*. 2d ed., rev. Montclair, N.J.: Patterson Smith, 1972.

Barnes, Thomas G. "Star Chamber Mythology." *American Journal of Legal History* 5 (1961): 1–11.

Barthélemy, Joseph. *L'amnistie*. Paris: M. Giard & E. Brière, 1920.

———. *Cours de droit constitutionel comparé, rédigé d'après la sténographie et avec l'autorisation*. Paris: Les cours de droit, 1944.

———. *Ministre de la Justice: Vichy 1941–1943: Mémoires*. Paris: Pygmalion/Gérard Watelet, 1989.

Baumann, Jürgen, ed. *Alternativ-Entwurf eines Strafvollzugsgesetzes*. Tübingen: J. C. B. Mohr, 1973.

Baumgartner, M.P. "Law and Social Status in Colonial New Haven, 1639–1665." *Research in Law and Sociology* 1 (1978): 153–174.

Bavoux, François Nicolas. *Leçons préliminaires sur le Code pénal, ou examen de la législation criminelle*. Paris: A. Bavoux, 1821.

Beardsley, Elizabeth Lane. "A Plea for Deserts." *American Philosophical Quarterly* 6 (1969): 33–42.

Beattie, J. M. *Crime and the Courts in England, 1660–1800*. Princeton: Princeton University Press, 1986.

———. *Policing and Punishment in London, 1660–1750: Urban Crime and the Limits of Terror*. Oxford: Oxford University Press, 2001.

Beaud, Olivier. *Le sang contaminé: Essai critique sur la criminalisation de la responsabilité des gouvernants*. Paris: Presses Universitaires de France, 1999.

Beaumont, G. de, and A. de Tocqueville. *Du système pénitentiaire aux États-Unis, et de son application en France*. Paris: H. Fournier jeune, 1833.

Beauvois, M. "Bilan de la réforme de 1975 sur le régime pénitentiaire." *Revue pénitentiare et de droit pénal* (1978): 159–181.

Beccaria, Cesare. "Dei delitti e delle pene." In *Edizione nazionale delle opere di Cesare Beccaria*, ed. Luigi Firpo. Vol. 1. Milan: Mediobanca, 1984.

———. *Des délits et des peines*. Trans. Colin de Plancy. Paris: Brière, 1822.

Bentham, Jeremy. *The Works of Jeremy Bentham*, ed. John Bowring. Vol. 9. *The Constitutional Code*. Edinburgh: William Tait, 1843.

———. "Principles of Penal Law." *The Works of Jeremy Bentham*, ed. John Bowring. Vol. 1, 365–580. Edinburgh: William Tait, 1843.

Bérenger, Alphonse Marie Marcellin Thomas. *De la répression pénale, de ses formes et de ses effets: Rapports faits à l'Académie des sciences morales et politiques*. Paris: Cosse, 1855.

Beres, Linda S., and Thomas D. Griffith. "Do Three Strikes Laws Make Sense? Habitual Offender Statutes and Criminal Incapacitation." *Georgetown Law Journal* 87 (1998): 103–138.

Berner, Albert Friedrich. *Die Strafgesetzgebung in Deutschland vom Jahre 1751 bis zur Gegenwart*. Reprint, Aalen: Scientia, 1978.

———. *Lehrbuch des deutschen Strafrechts*. 5th ed. Leipzig: Tauchnitz, 1871.

Bernstein, Ilene Nagel, William R. Kelly, and Patricia A. Doyle. "Social Reaction to Deviants: The Case of Criminal Defendants." *American Sociological Review* 42 (Oct. 1977): 743–755.

Bertram, Claus, ed. *Kommentar zum Strafvollzugsgesetz*. 3d ed. Neuwied: Luchterhand, 1990.

Blechet, Françoise, ed. *Voltaire et l'Europe: Exposition Bibliothèque Nationale de France, Monnaie de Paris*. Paris: Bibliothèque Nationale de France, 1994.

Billacois, François. *Le duel dans la société française des XVIe–XVIIe siècles: Essai de psychosociologie historique*. Paris: Éditions de l'École des hautes etudes en sciences sociales, 1986.

Blackstone, William. *Commentaries on the Laws of England*. 4 vols. Chicago: University of Chicago Press, 1979.

Blamires, Cyprian. "Beccaria et l'Angleterre." In *Beccaria et la culture juridique des Lumières*, ed. Michel Porret, 69–81. Geneva: Droz, 1997.

Blumstein, Alfred, and Allen J. Beck. "Population Growth in U.S. Prisons, 1980–1996." *Crime and Justice: A Review of Research* 26, *Prisons*, ed. Michael Tonry and Joan Petersilia (1999): 17–61.

Bodde, Derk, and Clarence Morris. *Law in Imperial China*. Cambridge: Harvard University Press, 1967.

Body-Gendriot, S. "La politisation du thème de la criminalité aux États-Unis." *Déviance et société* 23 (1999): 75–89.

Boitard, Joseph Édouard. *Leçons sur les Codes Pénal et d'Instruction Criminelle*. 5th ed. Paris: Cotillon, 1851.

Bonaparte, Charles J. "The Pardoning Power." *Yale Law Journal* 19 (1910): 603–608.

Bonneron, Georges. *Les Prisons de Paris*. Paris: Firmin-Didot, 1897.

Bonnéville de Marsangy. *De l'amélioration de la loi criminelle en vue d'une justice plus prompte, plus efficace, plus généreuse, et plus moralisante*. Paris: Cotillon, 1864.

Book, Aaron S. "Shame on You: An Analysis of Modern Shame Punishment as an Alternative to Incarceration." *William and Mary Law Review* 40 (1999): 653–686.

Borg, A. C. N. "The State Prison." In *The Tower of London: Its Buildings and Institutions*, ed. John Charlton, 86–93. London: Department of the Environment, H. M. Stationery Office, 1978.

Bottoms, Anthony E. "Interpersonal Violence and Social Order in Prisons." *Crime and Justice: A Review of Research* 26, *Prisons*, ed. Michael Tonry and Joan Petersilia (1999): 205–281.

Bourdieu, Pierre. *La distinction: Critique sociale du jugement*. Paris: Éditions de Minuit, 1979.

Bradley, K. R. *Slavery and Society at Rome*. Cambridge: Cambridge University Press, 1994.

Braithwaite, John. *Crime, Shame, and Reintegration*. Cambridge: Cambridge University Press, 1989.

———. "White Collar Crime." *Annual Review of Sociology* 11 (1985): 1–25.

Braithwaite, John, and Philip Pettit. *Not Just Deserts: A Republican Theory of Criminal Justice*. Oxford: Clarendon Press, 1990.

Brobeck, Stephen. "Revolutionary Change in Colonial Philadelphia: The Brief Life of the Proprietary Gentry." *William and Mary Quarterly* 33 (1976): 410–434.

Brockway, Zebulon. "The Idea of a True Prison System for a State." In *Transactions of the National Congress on Penitentiary and Reformatory Discipline*, ed. Enoch Cobbs Wines, 38–65. Albany: Weed, Parson, 1871.

Brodersen, K. "Das Strafänderungsgesetz 1999." *Neue Juristische Wochenschrift* (2000): 2536–2542.

Brombert, Victor. *The Romantic Prison: The French Tradition*. Princeton: Princeton University Press, 1978.

Broszat, Martin. "Nationalsozialistische Konzentrationslager, 1933–1945." In *Anatomie des SS-Staates*, ed. H. Buchheim et al., Vol. 2, 9–160. 2 vols. Olten: Walter-Verlag, 1965.

Brown, Jodi M., and Patrick A. Langan. *Felony Sentences in the United States, 1996*. Washington, D.C.: U.S. Department of Justice, Office of Justice Programs, Bureau of Justice Statistics, 1999.

Brown, Roger, and Albert Gilman. "The Pronouns of Power and Solidarity." In *Style in Language*, ed. Thomas Sebeok, 253-276. Cambridge: M.I.T. Press, 1966.

Bryden, David P., and Sonja Lengnick. "Rape in the Criminal Justice System." *Journal of Criminal Law and Criminology* 87 (1997): 1194–1294.

Bunge, K. *Italienischer Vorentwurf zu einem neuen Strafgesetzbuch (Progetto di un nuovo codice Penale)*. Berlin: De Gruyter, 1928.

Bundesrepublik Deutschland. Statistisches Bundesamt. *Rechtspflege*. Rev. November 7, 2001. Online. Available: http://www.statistik-bund.de/basis/d/recht/rechts6htm.

Burley, Lynn M. "History Repeats Itself in the Resurrection of Prisoner Chain Gangs: Alabama's Experience Raises Eighth Amendment Concerns." *Law and Inequality* 15 (1997): 127–155.

Burns, James B., Barry Rand Elden, and Brian W. Blanchard. "We Make the Better Target (But the Guidelines Shifted Power from the Judiciary to Congress, not from the Judiciary to the Prosecution)." *Northwestern University Law Review* 91 (1997): 1317–1335.

Byrne, James A., Arthur Lurigio, and Christopher Baird. "The Effectiveness of the New Intensive Supervision Programs." *Research in Corrections* 2 (1989): 1–48.

Caballero, Francis, and Yann Bisiou. *Droit de la Drogue*. 2d ed. Paris: Dalloz, 2000.

Calliess, Rolf-Peter. "Die Neuregelung des Arbeitsentgelts im Strafvollzug." *Neue Juristische Wochenschrift* (2001): 1692–1694.

Calliess, Rolf-Peter, and Heinz Müller-Dietz. *Strafvollzugsgesetz*. 9th ed. Munich: Beck, 2002.

Calonius, Matthias. "Dissertatio Juridica de Delinquentium ad Publicam Ignominiam Expositione." In *Opera Omnia*, ed. Adophus Iwarus Arwidsson. 2 vols. Holm: Norstedt, 1829–1830.

Camus, Albert. "Réflexions sur la guillotine." In Albert Camus and Arthur Koestler, *Réflexions sur la peine capitale*, 119–170. Paris: Calmann-Lévy, 1957.

Cantarella, Eva. "Per una Preistoria del Castigo." *Collection de l'École Française de Rome 79, Du châtiment dans la cité: Supplices corporals et peine de mort dans le monde antique* (1984): 37–73. Rome: École Française de Rome, 1984.

Carbasse, Jean-Marie. *Introduction historique au droit pénal.* Paris: Presses Universitaires de France, 1990.

Carpzov, Benedict. *Practica Nova Imperialis Saxonica Rerum Criminalium.* Wittenberg: Mevius & Schumacher, 1677.

———. *Practica Nova Rerum Criminalium cum Observationibus Boehmerii.* Frankfurt: Varrentrapp, 1758.

Castan, Nicole. "Le Régime des Prisons au XVIIIe siècle." In *La prison, le bagne, et l'histoire*, ed. Jacques G. Petit, 31–42. Geneva: Médicine et Hygiène, 1984.

———. "Du grand Renfermement à la Révolution." In *Histoire des galères, bagnes et prisons, XIIIe—XXe siècles*, ed. Jacques-Guy Petit et al., 45–77. Toulouse: Bibliothèque Historique Privat, 1991.

Chapin, Bradley. *Criminal Justice in Colonial America, 1606–1660.* Athens, Ga.: University of Georgia Press, 1983.

Charles, Raymond. *Histoire du droit pénal.* Paris: Presses Universitaires de France, 1976.

Chauveau, Adolphe, ed. *Code pénal progressif: Commentaire sur la loi modificative du Code pénal.* Paris: L'Éditeur, 1832.

Chauveau, Adolphe, and Faustin Hélie. *Théorie du Code pénal.* 8 vols. Paris: Gobelet, 1836–1842.

Cheyney, Edward Potts. "The Court of Star Chamber." *American Historical Review* 18 (1913): 727–750.

[Chidley, Samuel]. *A Cry against a Crying Sinne.* London: Samuel Chidley, 1652.

Chiffoleau, Jacques. *Les justices du Pape: Délinquance et criminalité dans la région d'Avignon au quatorzième siècle.* Paris: Publications de la Sorbonne, 1984.

Chilton, Bradley Stewart. *Prisons under the Gavel: The Federal Court Takeover of Georgia Prisons.* Columbus: Ohio State University Press, 1991.

Chiricos, Theodore G., and Miriam A. Delone. "Labor Surplus and Punishment." *Social Problems* 39 (1992): 421–446.

Chomienne, Christian. "Juger les juges?" In *Juger sous Vichy*, 9–16. Paris: Seuil, 1994.

Christoph, Jürgen. *Die politischen Reichsamnestien 1918–1933.* Frankfurt a. M.: Lang, 1988.

Clark, John, James Austin, and D. Alan Henry. *"Three Strikes and You're Out": A Review of State Legislation.* [Washington, D.C.]: U.S. Department of Justice, Office of Justice Programs, National Institute of Justice, 1997.

Clarus, Julius. *Opera Omnia, sive Practica Civilis et Criminalis.* Geneva: Cramer and Philibert, 1739.

Clement of Alexandria. *Miscellanies, Book VII*, ed. Fenton John Anthony Hort and Joseph B. Mayor. New York: Garland, 1987.

Cohen, Stanley. *Visions of Social Control: Crime, Punishment, and Classification.* Cambridge: Polity Press, 1985.

Coke, Sir Edward. *The Third Part of the Institutes of the Laws of England.* 4th ed. London: Printed for A. Cooke, 1669.

Coleman, James W. *The Criminal Elite: The Sociology of White Collar Crime.* New York: St. Martin's Press, 1985.

Coleman, Peter J. *Debtors and Creditors in America: Insolvency, Imprisonment for Debt, and Bankruptcy, 1607–1900.* Madison: State Historical Society of Wisconsin, 1974.

Colvin, Mark. *Penitentiaries, Reformatories, and Chain Gangs: Social Theory and the History of Punishment in Nineteenth-Century America*. New York: St. Martin's Press, 1997.

Commission Nationale Consultative des Droits de l'Homme. *[Avis] Portant sur le Régime Disciplinaire des Détenus*. Adopted: June 17, 1999.

Commune de Paris. District de Saint-Jacques-l'Hôpital. *Comité civil permanent, séance du Lundi 1er Février 1790. Déliberation relative à Messieurs Agasse*. [Paris: Cailleau, 1790].

Conaboy, Richard P. "The United States Sentencing Commission: A New Component in the Federal Criminal Justice System." *Federal Probation* 61 (March 1997): 58–62.

Cooter, Robert. "Prices and Sanctions." *Columbia Law Review* 84 (1984): 1523–1560.

Copper-Royer, Jean. *L'amnistie: Loi du 6 août 1953*. Paris: Dalloz, 1954.

Cotterrell, Roger. *Emile Durkheim: Law in a Moral Domain*. Stanford: Stanford University Press, 1999.

Cottret, Monique. *La Bastille à prendre: Histoire et mythe de la forteresse royale*. Paris: Presses Universitaires de France, 1986.

Cottu, Charles. *De l'administration de la justice criminelle en Angleterre et de l'ésprit du gouvernement anglais*. 2d ed. Paris: Gosselin, 1822.

Couret, Émile. *Le Pavillon des Princes: Histoire complète de la prison politique de Sainte-Pélagie*. Paris: Flammarion, n.d. [1895].

Crouch, Ben M., and James W. Marquart. "Resolving the Paradox of Reform: Litigation, Prisoner Violence, and Perceptions of Risk." *Justice Quarterly* 7 (1990): 103–123.

[Dagge, Henry]. *Considerations on Criminal Law*. London: T. Cadell, 1772.

Dahm, Georg. "Die Ehre im Strafrecht." *Deutsches Recht* 4 (1934): 417–419.

Dalotel, Alain. "Deux amnisties pour oublier la Commune." In *Répression et Prisons Politiques en France et en Europe au XIXe siècle*, ed. Philippe Vigier et al., 171–185. Paris: Créaphis, 1990.

Damaska, Mirjan R. *The Faces of Justice and State Authority: A Comparative Approach to the Legal Process*. New Haven: Yale University Press, 1986.

Daumier, Honoré. *Daumier, 1808–1879*. Ottawa: National Gallery of Canada, 1999.

Davies, W. "Violence in Prisons." In *Developments in the Study of Criminal Behavior*, ed. Philip Feldman. Vol. 2. Chichester: J. Wiley, 1982.

Davis, Natalie Zemon. *Fiction in the Archives: Pardon Tales and Their Tellers in Sixteenth-Century France*. Stanford: Stanford University Press, 1987.

Debove, Frédéric. "Libertés physiques du détenu et droit européen: ou l'histoire d'une Convention passe-muraille." *Revue pénitentiaire et de droit penal* 1 (1997), 49–61.

Delmas-Marty, Mireille, and Geneviève Giudicelli-Delage. *Droit pénal des affaires*. 4th ed. Paris: Presses Universitaires de France, 2000.

Demleitner, Nora V. "Continuing Payment on One's Debt to Society: The German Model of Felon Disenfranchisement as an Alternative." *Minnesota Law Review* 84 (2000): 753–804.

Denbeaux, Mark P. "The First Word of the First Amendment." *Northwestern University Law Review* 80 (1986): 1156–1220.

Dershowitz, Alan M. "Indeterminate Confinement: Letting the Therapy Fit the Harm." *University of Pennsylvania Law Review* 123 (1974): 297-339.

Desmaze, Charles. *Les pénalités anciennes: Supplices, prisons et grâces en France*. Paris: H. Plon, 1866.

Desmoulins, Camille. *Révolutions de France et de Brabant*. Vol. 14. 4th ed. Paris: Garnéry, 1790.

Des Pres, Terrence. *The Survivor: An Anatomy of Life in the Death Camps*. New York: Oxford University Press, 1976.

Dessent, Michael H. "Weapons to Fight Insider Trading in the 21st Century: A Call for the Repeal of Section 16(b)." *Akron Law Review* 33 (2000): 481–522.

Deutscher Juristentag. *Verhandlungen des dritten deutschen Juristentages*. Vol. 1. Berlin: Jansen, 1862.

Deymès, Louis. *L'évolution de la nature juridique de la contrainte par corps*. Lavaur: Bonnafous, 1942.

DiIulio, Jr., John J., ed. *Courts, Corrections, and the Constitution: The Impact of Judicial Intervention on Prisons and Jails*. New York: Oxford University Press, 1990.

Dindorf, Wilhelm, ed. *Scholia Graeca in Homeri Odysseam*. Amsterdam: A. M. Hakkert, 1962.

The Doctor Degraded; Or the Reward of Deceit: Being an Account of the Right Perfidious and Perjury'd Titus Oates. London: Printed by George Groom, 1685.

Döpler, Jacob. *Theatrum Poenarum, Suppliciorum et Executionum Criminalium, oder Schau-Platz derer Leibes- und Lebensstraffen*. 2 vols. Sondershausen: In Verlegung des Autoris, 1693–1697.

Douglas, Mary. *Purity and Danger: An Analysis of Concepts of Pollution and Taboo*. London: Routledge & Kegan Paul, 1978.

Dover, Kenneth J. "Fathers, Sons and Forgiveness." *Illinois Classical Studies* 16 (1991): 173–182.

Downes, David. *Contrasts in Tolerance: Post-War Penal Policy in the Netherlands and England and Wales*. Oxford: Clarendon Press, 1988.

Dubber, Markus Dirk. "Recidivist Statutes as Arational Punishment." *Buffalo Law Review* 43 (1996): 689–724.

Dufriche de Valazé. *Loix pénales*. Alençon: Imprimerie de Malassis le jeune, 1784.

Dülmen, Richard van. *Der Ehrlose Mensch: Unehrlichkeit und soziale Ausgrenzung in der frühen Neuzeit*. Cologne: Bohlau, 1999.

———. *Theatre of Horror: Crime and Punishment in Early Modern Germany*. Trans Elisabeth Neu. Cambridge: Polity Press, 1990.

Dumont, Louis. *Homo hierarchicus: Le système des castes et ses implications*. Paris: Gallimard, 1979.

Duncan, Martha Grace. *Romantic Outlaws, Beloved Prisons: The Unconscious Meanings of Crime and Punishment*. New York: New York University Press, 1996.

Duquesnoy, Adrien-Cyprien. *Journal d'Adrien Duquesnoy, deputé du Tiers état de Bar-le-Duc, sur l'Assemblée constituante: 3 mai 1789–3 avril 1790*. Paris: A. Picard, 1894.

Durkheim, Emile. *The Division of Labor in Society*. Trans. W. D. Halls. New York: Free Press, 1984.

———. "Two Laws of Penal Evolution." In *The Radical Sociology of Durkheim and Mauss*, ed. Mike Gane, 21–49. London: Routledge, 1992.

Eclavea, Romualdo P. "Imposition of Enhanced Sentence under Recidivist Statute as Cruel and Unusual Punishment." *American Law Reports Federal* 27 (1976): 110–139.

Eddy, Thomas. *An Account of the State Prison or Penitentiary House, in the City of New-York: By One of the Inspectors of the Prison*. New York: Printed by Isaac Collins and son, 1801.

Eden, William, Baron Auckland. *Principles of Penal Law*. 2d ed. London: B. White and T. Cadell, 1771.

Egner, H. E. "Strafaussetzung zur Bewährung und Gnadenrecht." *Neue Juristische Wochenschrift* (1953): 1859–1860.

Eisenhardt, Thilo. *Strafvollzug*. Stuttgart: Kohlhammer, 1978.

Ekirch, A. Roger. *Bound for America: The Transportation of British Convicts to the Colonies, 1718–1775*. Oxford: Clarendon Press, 1987.

Elias, Norbert. *Über den Prozess der Zivilisation. Soziogenetische und Psychogenetische Untersuchungen*. 2 vols. Frankfurt a. M.: Suhrkamp, 1997.

Elikann, Peter. *Superpredators: The Demonization of Our Children by the Law*. New York: Insight Books, 1999.

Ellger, H. "Der Strafvollzug in Stufen." In *Preußisches Justizministerium. Strafvollzug in Preußen*. Mannheim: Bernheimer, 1928.

Emsley, Clive. *Crime and Society in England, 1750–1900*. 2d ed. London: Longman, 1996.

Entwurf eines Strafvollzugsgesetzes. Berlin: Heymann, 1927.

Evans, Richard J. *Rituals of Retribution: Capital Punishment in Germany, 1600–1987*. Oxford: Oxford University Press, 1996.

Eyerich, Heinz. "Die bedingte Strafaussetzung." Diss., Würzburg, 1911.

Fabre, Jean. *De la contrainte par corps*. Toulouse: Librairie Générale, 1933.

Fallada, Hans. *Wer einmal aus dem Blechnapf Frißt*. Hamburg: Rowohlt, 1991.

Farabee, Lisa M. "Disparate Departures Under the Federal Sentencing Guidelines: A Tale of Two Districts." *Connecticut Law Review* 30 (1998): 569–646.

Farinaccius, Prosper. *Praxis et Theorica Criminalis Amplissima*. Venice: Apud Georgium Variscum, 1603.

———. *Tractatus Integer de Testibus*. Osnabrück: Schwänder, 1677.

Faugeron, Claude. "De la libération à la guerre d'Algérie." In *Histoire des galères, bagnes et prisons, XIIIe—XXe siècles*, ed. Jacques-Guy Petit et al., 289–317. Toulouse: Bibliothèque Historique Privat, 1991.

———. "Les prisons de la Ve République." In *Histoire des galères, bagnes et prisons, XIIIe—XXe siècles*, ed. Jacques-Guy Petit et al., 319–343. Toulouse: Bibliothèque Historique Privat, 1991.

Feeley, Malcolm. "The Significance of Prisons Conditions Cases: Budgets and Regions." *Law and Society Review* 23 (1989): 273–282.

Feeley, Malcolm M., and Edward L. Rubin. *Judicial Policy Making and the Modern State: How the Courts Reformed America's Prisons*. Cambridge: Cambridge University Press, 1998.

Feeney, Floyd. *German and American Prosecutions: An Approach to Statistical Comparison*. Washington, D.C.: U.S. Department of Justice, Office of Justice Programs, 1998.

Feinberg, Joel. *Doing and Deserving: Essays in the Theory of Responsibility*. Princeton: Princeton University Press, 1970.

Feld, Barry C. "Criminalizing the American Juvenile Court." *Crime and Justice: A Review of Research* 17 (1993): 197–280.

———. "The Juvenile Court Meets the Principle of Offense: Punishment, Treatment, and the Difference It Makes." *Boston University Law Review* 68 (1988): 821–915.

Fest, Joachim C. *Hitler: Eine Biographie*. Frankfurt/Main: Ullstein, 1973.

Fielding, Henry. "An Enquiry into the Cause of the Increase of Robbers." In Henry Fielding, *The Complete Works of Henry Fielding*, ed. William Ernest Henley. Vol. 13. London: W. Heinemann, 1903.

Finkelnberg. "Die Psychologie des Gefangenen." In *Preußisches Justizministerium, Strafvollzug in Preußen*, 73–82. Mannheim: Bernheimer, 1928.

Finnis, John. "The Restoration of Retributivism." *Analysis* 32 (1972): 131–135.
Fischer, David Hackett. *Albion's Seed: Four British Folkways in America*. New York: Oxford University Press, 1989.
Fischer, G. F. *Über Gefängnisse, Strafarten, Strafsysteme und Strafanstalten*. Regensburg: Manz, 1852.
Fischer, Heinrich. *Die bedingte Strafaussetzung*. Würzburg: n.p., 1927.
Fisher, George. "The Jury's Rise as Lie Detector." *Yale Law Journal* 107 (1997): 575–713.
———. "Plea Bargaining's Triumph." *Yale Law Journal* 109 (2000): 857–1086.
Foote, Daniel H. "The Benevolent Paternalism of Japanese Criminal Justice." *California Law Review* 80 (March 1992): 317–390.
Foucault, Michel. *Surveiller et punir: Naissance de la prison*. Paris: Gallimard, 1975.
Foviaux, Jacques. *La rémission des peines et des condamnations: Droit monarchique et droit moderne*. Paris: Presses Universitaires de France, 1970.
France, Assemblée Nationale. *La France face à ses prisons: Rapport de lAssemblée Nationale no. 2521*. n.p.: 2000.
France, Ministère de la Justice. *Direction de l'Administration pénitentiaire: Les chiffres clés de l'administration pénitentiaire*. n.p.: 2000.
France, Sénat. *Les Prisons: Une Humiliation pour la République: Rapport du Sénat no. 449*. n.p., 2000.
Frankel, Marvin E. *Criminal Sentences: Law without Order*. New York: Hill & Wang, 1973.
Frase, Richard S. "Comparative Criminal Justice as a Guide to American Law Reform: How Do the French Do It, How Can We Find Out, and Why Should We Care?" *California Law Review* 78 (May 1990): 539–683.
Freudenthal, Berthold. "Der Strafvollzug als Rechtsverhältnis des öffentlichen Rechtes." *Zeitschrift für die gesamte Strafrechtswissenschaft* 32 (1911): 222–248.
Friedländer, Ludwig. *Roman Life and Manners under the Early Empire*. Trans. Leonard Magnus. 4 vols. New York: Barnes and Noble, 1965.
Friedman, Gary M. Comment, "The West German Day-Fine System: A Possibility for the United States?" *University of Chicago Law Review* 50 (1983): 281–304.
Friedman, Lawrence M. *Crime and Punishment in American History*. New York: Basic Books, 1993.
———. "Dead Hands: Past and Present in Criminal Justice Policy." *Cumberland Law Review* 27 (1996): 903–926.
———. *The Horizontal Society*. New Haven: Yale University Press, 1999.
Froment, Jean-Charles. "Vers une 'prison de droit'?" *Revue de science criminelle et de droit comparé* 3 (July-Sept. 1997): 537–560.
Fry, Plantagenet Somerset. *The Tower of London: Cauldron of Britain's Past*. London: Quiller, 1990.
Galen, Margarete von. "Prostitution and the Law in Germany." *Cardozo Women's Law Journal* 3 (1996): 349–376.
Garfinkel, Harold. "Conditions of Successful Degradation Ceremonies." *American Journal of Sociology* 61 (March 1956): 420–24.
Garland, David. *The Culture of Control: Crime and Social Order in Contemporary Society*. Chicago: University of Chicago Press, 2001.
———. "Philosophical Argument and Ideological Effect: An Essay Review." *Contemporary Crises* 7 (1983): 79–85.
———. *Punishment and Modern Society: A Study in Social Theory*. Chicago: University of Chicago Press, 1990.

Garnsey, Peter. "Why Penalties Become Harsher: The Roman Case, Late Republic to Fourth Century Empire." *Natural Law Forum* 13 (1968): 141–162.

Garvey, Stephen P. "Can Shaming Punishments Educate?" *University of Chicago Law Review* 65 (1998): 733–794.

Fuller, John, ed. *John Gay, Dramatic Works*. Oxford: Clarendon Press, 1983.

Geib, Karl Gustave. *Lehrbuch des deutschen Strafrechts*. Leipzig: n.p., 1861.

Gendin, Sidney. "A Plausible Theory of Retribution." *Journal of Value Inquiry* 5 (1970): 1–16.

Genscher, Norbert. *Boot Camp-Programme in den USA : ein Fallbeispiel zum Formenwandel in der amerikanischen Kriminalpolitik*. Mönchengladbach: Forum-Verlag, 1998.

Genuine memoires of the life, family and behaviour of Laurence Shirley, Earl of Ferrers; who was executed at Tyburn, on Monday the fifth of May 1760 for the murder of his steward, Mr. Johnston. London: T. Bailey, [1760].

Germain, Charles. "Le sursis et la probation." *Revue de Science Criminelle et de droit pénal comparé* (1954): 629–652.

Gernet, Jacques. *A History of Chinese Civilization*. Trans. J. R. Foster and Charles Hartman. 2d ed. Cambridge: Cambridge University Press, 1996.

Giraud, Pierre. *Observations sommaires sur toutes les prisons du Département de Paris*. n.p., 1793.

Glasser, Ira. "American Drug Laws: The New Jim Crow." *Albany Law Review* 63 (2000): 703–724.

Glenn, Myra C. *Campaigns Against Corporal Punishment: Prisoners, Sailors, Women, and Children in Antebellum America*. Albany: State University of New York Press, 1984.

Godechot, Jacques. *Regards sur l'époque révolutionnaire*. Toulouse: Privat, 1980.

Goebel, Jr., Julius, and T. Raymond Naughton, *Law Enforcement in Colonial New York: A Study in Criminal Procedure (1664–1776)*. New York: Commonwealth Fund, 1944.

Goffman, Erving. *Asylums: Essays on the Social Situation of Mental Patients and Other Inmates*. Garden City, N.Y.: Anchor Books, 1961.

———. *The Presentation of Self in Everyday Life*. Woodstock, N.Y.: New York Overlook Press, 1973.

Gottwald, Stefan. *Das allgemeine Persönlichkeitsrecht. Ein zeitgeschichtliches Erklärungsmodell*. Berlin: Spitz, 1996.

Granucci, Anthony F. "'Nor Cruel and Unusual Punishments Inflicted:' The Original Meaning." *California Law Review* 57 (Oct. 1969): 839–865.

Grau, Fritz, and Karl Schäfer. *Das deutsche Gnadenrecht*. Berlin: De Gruyter, 1939.

———. *Das Preußische Gnadenrecht*. Berlin: Stilke, 1931.

Gray, James P. *Why Our Drug Laws Have Failed and What We Can Do About It: A Judicial Indictment of the War on Drugs*. Philadelphia: Temple University Press, 2001.

Green, Thomas Andrew. *Verdict According to Conscience: Perspectives on the English Criminal Trial Jury, 1200–1800*. Chicago: University of Chicago Press, 1985.

Greenberg, Douglas. *Crime and Law Enforcement in the Colony of New York, 1691–1776*. Ithaca: Cornell University Press, 1976.

———. "Crime, Law Enforcement, and Social Control in Colonial America." *American Journal of Legal History* 26 (1982): 293–325.

Griset, Pamela L. *Determinate Sentencing: The Promise and the Reality of Retributive Justice*. Albany: State University of New York Press, 1991.

Grodzynski, Denise. "Tortures Mortelles et Catégories Sociales." *Collection de l'École Française de Rome* 79, *Du châtiment dans la cité: Supplices corporals et peine de mort dans le monde antique* (1984): 361–403. Rome: École Française de Rome, 1984.

Guarino-Ghezzi, Susan, and Edward J. Loughran. *Balancing Juvenile Justice*. New Brunswick, N.J.: Transaction Publishers, 1996.

Guilland, Rodolphe. *Recherches sur les institutions Byzantines*. Berlin: Akademie-Verlag, 1967.

Guillaume, Louis Marie. *Addition à la Motion de M. Guillotin, sur les Loix Criminelles*. n.p., [1789].

Guizot, François. *De la peine de mort en matière politique*. 1821. Reprint, Paris: Fayard, 1984.

Hälschner, Hugo. *Das gemeine deutsche Strafrecht*. Bonn: A. Marcus, 1881–1887.

Haines, R. *A Breviat of some Proposals*. London: Printed for Langley Curtis, 1679.

Haines, Jr., Roger W., Frank O. Bowman III, and Jennifer C. Woll. *Federal Sentencing Guidelines Handbook*. November 1999 ed. St. Paul, Minn.: West Group, 1999.

Hall, Daniel E. "When Caning Meets the Eighth Amendment: Whipping Offenders in the United States." *Widener Journal of Public Law* 4 (1995): 403–460.

Hall, Margaretha. "Sanctions in Athens." In *Greek Law in its Political Setting: Justifications Not Justice*, ed. L. Foxhall and A. D. E. Lewis, 73–89. Oxford: Clarendon Press, 1996.

Halm-Tisserant, Monique. *Réalités et imaginaire des supplices en Grèce ancienne*. Paris: Belles Lettres, 1998.

Hampton, Jean. "An Expressive Theory of Retribution." In *Retributivism and its Critics*, ed. Wesley Cragg. Stuttgart: F. Steiner, 1992.

Haney, Craig. "Riding the Punishment Wave: On the Origins of Our Devolving Standards of Decency." *Hastings Women's Law Journal* 9 (1998): 27–78.

Hanson, Roger A., and Henry W. K. Daley. *Challenging the Conditions of Prisons and Jails: A Report on Section 1983 Litigation*. Washington, D.C.: U.S. Department of Justice, Office of Justice Programs, Bureau of Justice Statistics, 1995.

Harcourt, Bernard E. "Reflecting on the Subject: A Critique of the Social Influence Conception of Deterrence, the Broken Windows Theory, and Order-Maintenance Policing New York Style." *Michigan Law Review* 97 (Nov. 1998): 291–389.

Hart, H. L. A. *Punishment and Responsibility: Essays in the Philosophy of Law*. New York: Oxford University Press, 1968.

———. "Social Solidarity and Morality." In H. L. A. Hart, *Essays in Jurisprudence and Philosophy*, 248–262. Oxford: Clarendon Press, 1983.

Hartz, Louis. *The Liberal Tradition in America: An Interpretation of American Political Thought Since the Revolution*. New York: Harcourt, Brace, 1955.

Hasday, Jill Elaine. "Contest and Consent: A Legal History of Marital Rape." *California Law Review* 88 (2000): 1373–1505.

Hauch, Jeanne M. "Protecting Private Facts in France: The Warren & Brandeis Tort is Alive and Well and Flourishing in Paris." *Tulane Law Review* 68 (1994): 1219–1301.

Hay, Douglas. "Property, Authority and the Criminal Law." In *Albion's Fatal Tree: Crime and Society in Eighteenth-Century England*, eds. Douglas Hay et al., 17–63. New York: Pantheon Books, 1975.

Heaney, Gerald W. "The Reality of Guidelines Sentencing: No End to Disparity," *American Criminal Law Review* 28 (1991): 161–232.

Heffter, August Wilhelm. *Lehrbuch des gemeinen deutschen Criminalrechts*. 2d ed. Halle: Schwetschke, 1840.

Heiman, Wolfgang. *Die Begnadigung: Eine grundlegende Betrachtung*. Berlin: H. S. Hermann, 1931.

Heimberger, Joseph. *Zur Reform des Strafvollzugs*. Leipzig: Deichert, 1905.

Heine, Heinrich. "Englische Fragmente." In Heinrich Heine, *Historisch-Kritische Gesamtausgabe der Werke*, ed. Manfred Windfuhr, vol. 7, 207–273. 16 vols. Hamburg: Hoffman and Campe, 1973–1997.

Helmholz, Richard H. "The Privilege and the *Ius Commune*: The Middle Ages to the Seventeenth Century." In *The Privilege Against Self-Incrimination: Its Origins and Development*, ed. Richard H. Helmholz et al., 17–46. Chicago: University of Chicago Press, 1997.

Henke, Eduard. *Handbuch des Criminalrechts und der Criminalpolitik*. 4 vols. Berlin/Stettin: Nicolai, 1823.

Henrion de Pansey, Pierre-Paul-Nicolas. *Dissertations féodales*. 2 vols. Paris: T. Barrois, 1789.

Hentig, Hans von. *Die Strafe*. Berlin: Springer, 1954–1955.

Herrnstadt, Ignaz. *Das Institut der bedingten Begnadigung*. Berlin: J. Guttentag, 1912.

Herzog-Evans, Martine. "La réforme du régime disciplinaire dans les établissements pénitentiaires: Un plagiat incomplet du droit pénal." *Revue pénitentiare et de droit pénal* (1997): 9–47.

———. "Vers une Prison Normative?" In *La Prison en Changement*, ed. Claude Veil and Dominique Lhuilier, 43–67. Ramonville-Saint-Agne: Éditions Érès, 2000.

Heusch, Luc de. "Préface." In Mary Douglas. *De la souillure: Essais sur les notions de pollution et de tabou*. Trans. Anne Guérin. Paris: La Découverte & Syros, 2001.

Higginbotham, Jr., A. Leon, and Anne F. Jacobs. "The 'Law Only as an Enemy': The Legitimatization of Racial Powerlessness through the Colonial and Antebellum Criminal Laws of Virginia." *North Carolina Law Review* 70 (1992): 969–1070.

Hindus, Michael Stephen. *Prison and Plantation: Crime, Justice, and Authority in Massachusetts and South Carolina, 1767–1878*. Chapel Hill: University of North Carolina Press, 1980.

Hirsch, Adam Jay. *The Rise of the Penitentiary: Prisons and Punishment in Early America*. New Haven: Yale University Press, 1992.

Hoffer, Peter Charles, and William B. Scott, "Introduction." In *Criminal Proceedings in Colonial Virginia*, ed. Peter Charles Hoffer and William B. Scott, ix–lxxii. Athens, Ga.: University of Georgia Press, 1984.

Hofmann, Wilhelm. *Der Strafvollzug in Stufen in Deutschland in Geschichte und Gegenwart*. Würzburg: Mayr, 1936.

Holdsworth, William. *A History of English Law*. 17 vols. London: Methuen & Co., 1903–1972.

Holtzendorff, Franz v., and Eugene v. Jagemann, eds. *Handbuch des Gefängniswesens in einzelbeiträgen*. Hamburg: J. F. Richter, 1888.

Hopkins, Tighe. *The Dungeons of Old Paris: Being the Story and Romance of the Most Celebrated Prisons of the Monarchy and the Revolution*. New York: G. P. Putnam's Sons, 1897.

Hould, Claudette. *L'image de la Révolution française*. Quebec: Musée du Québec/Les Publications du Québec, 1989.

Huber, Ulrich. *Eunomia Romana, sive Censura Censurae Juris Justinianaei*, ed. Zacharias Huber. Franeker: Strickius, 1700.

Hulsewé, A.F.P. *Remnants of Ch'in Law*. Leiden: Brill, 1985.

———. *Remnants of Han Law*. Leiden: E. J. Brill, 1955.

Husak, Douglas N. *Drugs and Rights*. Cambridge: Cambridge University Press, 1992.

Ignatieff, Michael. *A Just Measure of Pain: The Penitentiary in the Industrial Revolution, 1750–1850*. New York: Pantheon Books, 1978.

Imbert, Jean. "La Peine de Mort et L'Opinion au XVIIIe Siècle." *Revue de science criminelle et de droit pénal, n.f.* 19 (1964): 509–525.

International Centre for Prison Studies. [*Homepage*]. Rev. February 4, 2002. Online. Available: http://www.prisonstudies.org/. March 18, 2002.

Jagemann Ludwig v., and Wilhelm Brauer. *Criminallexikon*. Erlangen: Enke, 1854.

Jahangir, Asma, and Hina Jilani. *The Hudood Ordinances: A Divine Sanction?* Lahore: Rhotas Books, 1990.

[Janinet, Jean-François.] *Gravures historiques des principaux evénémens depuis l'ouverture des États généraux de 1789. Tome Premier*. Paris: Janinet, 1789[–1791].

Jefferson, Thomas. *Notes on the State of Virginia*. Ed. William Peden. Chapel Hill: University of North Carolina Press, 1955.

Jensen, Christen. *The Pardoning Power in the American States*. Chicago: University of Chicago Press, 1922.

Jescheck, Hans-Heinrich, et al., eds. *Strafgesetzbuch. Leipziger Kommentar*. Berlin: De Gruyter, 1985.

Jhering, Rudolf v. *Der Zweck im Recht*. 2 vols. Reprint, Hildesheim: Ohms, 1970.

Jordan, Carol E., et al. "Stalking: Cultural, Clinical and Legal Considerations." *Brandeis Law Journal* 38 (2000): 513–579.

Josephs, Hilary K. "The Upright and the Low-Down: An Examination of Official Corruption in the United States and the People's Republic of China." *Syracuse Journal of International Law and Commerce* 27 (2000): 269–302.

Jousse, [Daniel]. *Nouveau commentaire sur l'ordonnance criminelle du mois d'août 1670*. Paris: Debure père, 1771.

———. *Traité de la justice criminelle de France*. 4 vols. Paris: Debure père, 1771.

Kahan, Dan M. "What do Alternative Sanctions Mean?" *University of Chicago Law Review* 63 (1996): 591–653.

Kaiser, Günter, Hans-Jürgen Kerner, and Heinz Schöch. *Strafvollzug. Eine Einführung in die Grundlagen*. Heidelberg: Müller, 1991.

Kallenbach, Hans. *Mit Adolf Hitler auf Festung Landsberg*. Munich: Kress & Hornung, 1939.

Kant, Immanuel. *Metaphysische Angfangsgründe der Rechtslehre*. Ed. Bernd Ludwig. 2d ed. Hamburg: Meiner, 1998.

Kenyon, J. P., ed., *The Stuart Constitution, 1603–1688*. 2d ed. Cambridge: Cambridge University Press, 1986.

Kessler, Amalia. "From Virtue to Commerce: The Parisian Merchant Court and the Rise of Commercial Society in Eighteenth-Century France." Ph.D. diss., Stanford University, 2001.

Kilchling, Michael. "Tatproportionalität in den theoretischen und empirischen Grundlagen der Strafzumessung." *Monatsschrift für Kriminologie und Strafrechtsreform* 83 (2000): 30–35.

King, Peter. *Crime, Justice, and Discretion in England, 1740–1820*. Oxford: Oxford University Press, 2000.

———. "Decision-Makers and Decision-Making in the English Criminal Law, 1750–1800." *Historical Journal* 27 (1984): 25–58.

Klein, Alexander. *Die Vorschriften über Verwaltung und Strafvollzug in den Preußischen Justizgefängnissen*. Berlin: Vahlen, 1905.

Kleinschrod, Gallus Aloys Kaspar. *Systematische Entwickelung der Grundbegriffe des peinlichen Rechts*. 2 vols. 2d ed. Erlangen: Palm, 1799.

Koch, Bernd. "Das System des Stufenstrafvollzugs in Deutschland unter besonderer Berücksichtigung seiner Entwicklungsgeschichte." Ph.D. diss., Freiburg, 1972.

Koch Crime Institute. *Juvenile Boot Camps and Military Structured Youth Programs: 2000 Directory*. Topeka, Kans.: Koch Crime Institute, 2000.

Köhler, August. *Deutsches Strafrecht. Allgemeiner Teil*. Leipzig: Veit, 1917.

Konig, David Thomas. "'Dale's Laws' and the Non-Common Law Origins of Criminal Justice in Virginia." *American Journal of Legal History* 26 (1982): 354–375.

Koreman, Megan. *The Expectation of Justice: France, 1944–1946*. Durham, N.C.: Duke University Press, 1999.

Körner, Harald Hans, ed. *Betäubungsmittelgesetz*. 5th ed. Munich: Beck, 2001.

Krebs, Albert. "Entwicklung der Persönlichkeitserforschung im deutschen Gefängniswesen." *Zeitschrift für Strafvollzug* 4 (1954): 241–252.

Krekeler, Wilhelm, et al., eds., *Handwörterbuch des Wirtschafts- und Steuerstrafrechts*. [Heidelberg]: Deubner, 1990.

Kropotkin, Petr. *Memoirs of a Revolutionist*, ed. Nicolas Walter. New York: Dover, 1971.

Kuntz II, William Francis. *Criminal Sentencing in Three Nineteenth-Century Cities: Social History of Punishment in New York, Boston, and Philadelphia, 1830–1880*. New York: Garland, 1988.

Kurz, Achim. *Demokratische Diktatur? Auslegung und Handhabung des Artikels 48 der Weimarer Verfassung 1919–1925*. Berlin: Duncker & Humblot, 1992.

Kuss, Ulrich. *Die materielle Problematik der politischen Reichsamnestien 1918/1933*. Breslau/Neukirch: A. Kurtze, 1934.

Lacey, Nicola. *State Punishment: Political Principles and Community Values*. London: Routledge, 1988.

Laingui, André, ed., *Le "De Poenis Temperandis" de Tiraqueneau* (1559). Paris: Economica, 1986.

Laingui, André, and Arlette Lebigre. *Histoire du droit pénal*. Paris: Cujas, 1979.

Lambert, Christophe. *Derrière les barreaux: Document*. Paris: Michalon, 1999.

Lamberti, Jean-Claude. *Tocqueville et les deux démocraties*. Paris: Presses Universitaires de France, 1983.

Lameyre, Xavier. "Pour une éthique des soins pénalement obligés." *Médecine et Droit* 34 (2000): 1–23.

Langan, Patrick A., and Jodi M. Brown. *Felony Sentences in State Courts, 1994*. Washington, D.C.: U.S. Department of Justice, Office of Justice Programs, Bureau of Justice Statistics, 1997.

Langbein, John H. *Torture and the Law of Proof: Europe and England in the Ancien Régime*. Chicago: University of Chicago Press, 1977.

———. "Albion's Fatal Flaws." *Past and Present* 98 (1983): 96–120.

Larguier, Jean, and Philippe Comte. *Droit pénal des affaires*. 10th ed. Paris: Armand Colin/ Dalloz, 2001.

Lascoumes, Pierre, Pierrette Poncela, and Pierre Lenoël. *Au Nom de l'Ordre: Une Histoire Politique du Code Pénal*. Paris: Hachette, 1989.

Laubenthal, Klaus. *Strafvollzug*. 2d ed. Berlin: Springer, 1998.

Laurence, John. *A History of Capital Punishment, With Special Reference to Capital Punishment in Great Britain*. London: S. Low, Marston & Co., 1932.

Léauté, Jacques. *Les Prisons*. 2d ed. Paris: Presses Universitaires de France, 1990.

Legoux, J[ules]. *Du Droit de Grâce en France*. Paris: Cotillon, 1865.

Lenski, Gerhard E. "Status Crystallization: A Non-Vertical Dimension of Social Status." *American Sociological Review* 19, no. 4 (1954): 405–413.

Le Roy Ladurie, Emmanuel. *Saint-Simon and the Court of Louis XIV*. Trans. Arthur Goldhammer. Chicago: University of Chicago Press, 2001.

Lessig, Lawrence. "Fidelity in Translation." *Texas Law Review* 71 (1993): 1165–1268.

A letter to a gentleman at Brussels, containing an account of the causes of the peoples revolt from the crown. London: n.p., 1689.

Levin, David J., Patrick A. Langan, and Jodi M. Brown. *State Court Sentencing of Convicted Felons, 1996*. Washington, D.C.: U.S. Department of Justice, Office of Justice Programs, Bureau of Justice Statistics, 2000.

Lewis, Orlando F. *The Development of American Prisons and Prison Customs, 1776–1845*. Montclair, N.J.: Patterson Smith, 1967.

Lewis, W. David. *From Newgate to Dannemora: The Rise of the Penitentiary in New York, 1796–1848*. Ithaca: Cornell University Press, 1965.

Lezin, Katya. "Life at Lorton: An Examination of Prisoners' Rights at the District of Columbia Correctional Facilities." *Boston University Public Interest Law Journal* 5 (1996): 165–211.

Liang, Bryan A., and Wendy L. Macfarlane. "Murder by Omission: Child Abuse and the Passive Parent." *Harvard Journal on Legislation* 36 (1999): 397–450.

Lieber, Francis. *On Civil Liberty and Self-Government*. Reprint, Union, N.J.: Lawbook Exchange, 2001.

Liepmann, Moritz. *Die neuen 'Grundsätze über den Vollzug von Freiheitsstrafen' in Deutschland*. Berlin: De Gruyter, 1924.

Lipset, Seymour Martin, and Gary Marks. *It Didn't Happen Here: Why Socialism Failed in the United States*. New York: W.W. Norton, 2000.

Liszt, Franz v. *Lehrbuch des deutschen Strafrechts*. 20th ed. Berlin: J. Guttentag, 1914.

The Little Infant Titus: or Oates Exalted above his Brethren. London: Printed by George Groom, 1685.

Livingston, Edward. *The Complete Works of Edward Livingston on Criminal Jurisprudence*. New York: National Prison Association of the United States of America, 1873.

Loraux, Nicole. "Le corps étranglé." *Collection de l'École Française de Rome* 79, *Du châtiment dans la cité: Supplices corporals et peine de mort dans le monde antique* (1984): 195–224. Rome: École Française de Rome, 1984.

Loschelder, Wolfgang. "Staatseingliederung als Institutionalisierungsproblem. Zur Entwicklung und Krise des besonderen Gewaltverhältnisses." In *Das besondere Gewaltverhältnis*, ed. Detlef Merten, 9–32. Berlin: Duncker und Humblot, 1985.

Love, Margaret Colgate. "Of Pardons, Politics and Collar Buttons: Reflections on the President's Duty to Be Merciful." *Fordham Urban Law Journal* 27 (June 2000): 1483–1513.

Lüders, Heinrich. *Die Aufhebung des jetzigen Systems der Personal-Schuldhaft: eine forderung des rechts, der moral und des socialen fortschritts*. Berlin: n.p., 1865.

Lynch, James P. "A Comparison of Prison Use in England, Canada, West Germany, and the United States: A Limited Test of the Punitive Hypothesis." *Journal of Criminal Law and Criminology* 79 (1988): 180–217.

Ma, Yue. "The European Court of Human Rights and the Protection of the Rights of Prisoners and Criminal Defendants under the European Convention on Human Rights." *International Criminal Justice Review* 10 (2000): 54–80.

McConville, Sean. *English Local Prisons, 1860–1900: Next Only to Death*. London: Routledge, 1995.

MacCormack, Geoffrey. *The Spirit of Traditional Chinese Law*. Athens, Ga.: University of Georgia Press, 1996.

McCormick, John. "The Dilemmas of Dictatorship: Carl Schmitt and Constitutional Emergency Powers." in David Dyzenhaus, ed., *Law as Politics: Carl Schmitt's Critique of Liberalism*. Durham: Duke University Press, 1998, 230–236.

McDonald, Douglas C. "Medical Care in Prisons." *Crime and Justice: A Review of Research* 26, *Prisons*, ed. Michael Tonry and Joan Petersilia (1999): 427–478.

Mackenzie, Mary Margaret. *Plato on Punishment*. Berkeley: University of California Press, 1981.

MacLachlan, Colin M. *Criminal Justice in Eighteenth-Century Mexico: A Study of the Tribunal of the Acordada*. Berkeley: University of California Press, 1974.

MacMullen, Ramsay. "Judicial Savagery in the Roman Empire." In Ramsay MacMullen, *Changes in the Roman Empire: Essays in the Ordinary*, 204–217. Princeton: Princeton University Press, 1990.

Maestro, Marcello T. *Voltaire and Beccaria as Reformers of Criminal Law*. New York: Columbia University Press, 1942.

Marezoll, Theodor. *Das gemeine deutsche Criminalrecht als Grundlage der neueren Strafgesetzgebungen*. Leipzig: J. A. Barth, 1847.

Mariner, Joanne. *No Escape: Male Rape in U.S. Prisons*. New York: Human Rights Watch, 2001.

Marini, Philippe. *La modernisation du droit des sociétés: Rapport au Premier Ministre*. Paris: Documentation française, 1996.

Marquet-Vasselot, L.-A.-A. *École des condamnés: Conférence sur la moralité des lois pénales*. Paris: Joubert, 1837.

Marshall, T. H., and Tom Bottomore. *Citizenship and Social Class*. London: Pluto Press, 1992.

Martin, [Christoph Reinhard Dietrich]. *Lehrbuch des Teutschen gemeinen Criminal-Rechts*. Heidelberg: C. F. Winter, 1829.

Mead, George H. "The Psychology of Punitive Justice." *American Journal of Sociology* 23 (1918): 577–602.

Meeks, Wayne A. *The Origins of Christian Morality: The First Two Centuries*. New Haven: Yale University Press, 1993.

Meier, Bernd-Dieter. *Strafrechtliche Sanktionen*. Berlin: Springer, 2001.

Melossi, Dario, and Massimo Pavarini. *Carcere e fabbrica : alle origini del sistema penitenziario (XVI–XIX secolo)*. 3d ed. Bologna: Il Mulino, 1982.

Menschell, Wolfgang. *Das Gnadengesuch*. Berlin: Deutscher Rechtsverlag, 1941.

Meranze, Michael. *Laboratories of Virtue: Punishment, Revolution, and Authority in Philadelphia, 1760–1835*. Chapel Hill, N.C.: University of North Carolina Press, 1996.

Mess, Friedrich. *Nietzsche der Gesetzgeber*. Leipzig: F. Meiner, 1930.

Messner, Claudius, and Vincenzo Ruggiero. "Germany: The Penal System between Past and Future." In *Western European Penal Systems: A Critical Anatomy*, ed. Vincenzo Ruggiero, Mick Ryan, and Joe Sim, 128–148. London: SAGE Publications, 1995.

Michon, Georges. *Essai sur l'histoire du parti feuillant: Adrien Duport*. Paris: Payot, 1924.

Miller, William Ian. *The Anatomy of Disgust*. Cambridge: Harvard University Press, 1997.

Minow, Martha. "What Ever Happened to Children's Rights?" *Minnesota Law Review* 80 (1995): 267–298.

Mitsch, Wolfgang. *Recht der Ordnungswidrigkeiten*. Berlin: Springer, 1995.

Mittermaier, Carl Joseph Anton. "Neue Schriften über Gefängnisse." *Archiv des Criminalrechts*, N.F. (1834): 132–148.

———. "Der revidirte Entwurf des Strafgesetzbuchs für das Königreich Baiern." *Neues Archiv des Criminalrechts* 10 (1828): 144–170.

———. *Über den neuesten Zustand der Criminalgesetzgebung in Deutschland*. Heidelberg: Engelmann, 1825.

Molènes, Alexandre Jacques Denis Gaschon de. *De l'Humanité dans les Lois Criminelles et de la Jurisprudence sur Quelques-unes des Questions que ces Lois Font Naître*. Paris: Locquin, 1830.

Montagnon, Pierre. *42, rue de la santé: Une prison politique, 1867–1968*. Paris: Pygmalion/G. Watelet, 1996.

Monteil, Jacques. *La grâce en droit français moderne*. Paris: Librairies techniques, 1959.

Montesquieu, Charles de Secondat, Baron de. *De L'Esprit des Lois*. 2 vols. Paris: Flammarion, 1979.

Moore, Kathleen Dean. *Pardons: Justice, Mercy, and the Public Interest*. New York: Oxford University Press, 1989.

More, Thomas. *Utopia*. Trans. Clarence H. Miller. New Haven: Yale University Press, 2001.

Morris, Norval, and Michael Tonry. *Between Prison and Probation: Intermediate Punishments in a Rational Sentencing Structure*. New York: Oxford University Press, 1990.

Mote, F. W. *Imperial China, 900–1800*. Cambridge: Harvard University Press, 1999.

Mousnier, Roland. *Les institutions de la France sous la monarchie absolue, 1589–1789*. Paris: Presses Universitaires de France, 1974–1980.

Muchembled, Robert. *Le Temps des Supplices: de l'obéissance sous les rois absolus, XVe–XVIIIe siècle*. Paris: A. Colin, 1992.

Müller, H. "Strafvollzug." In *Handwörterbuch zur Deutschen Rechtsgeschichte*, ed. Adalbert Erler et al., vol. 5, 10–17. 5 vols. Berlin: Schmidt, 1964–1988.

Murphy, Jeffrie G. "Does Kant Have a Theory of Punishment?" *Columbia Law Review* 87 (1987): 509–532.

———. "Cruel and Unusual Punishments." In Jeffrie G. Murphy, *Retribution, Justice and Therapy*, 223–249. Dordrecht: D. Reidel Publishing, 1979.

Murphy, Jeffrie G., and Jean Hampton. *Forgiveness and Mercy*. Cambridge: Cambridge University Press, 1988.

Mushlin, Michael B. *Rights of Prisoners*. Ed. Donald T. Kramer. 2d ed. Colorado Springs, Colo.: Shepard's/McGraw-Hill, 1993.

Mustard, David B. "Racial, Ethnic, and Gender Disparities in Sentencing: Evidence from the U.S. Federal Courts." *Journal of Law and Economics* 44 (April 2001): 285–314.

Musto, David F. *The American Disease: Origins of Narcotic Control*. 3d. ed. New York: Oxford University Press, 1999.

Muyart de Vouglans, Pierre François. *Institutes au droit criminel, ou Principes généraux sur ces matières*. Paris: Le Breton, 1768.

———. *Les loix criminelles de la France, dans leur ordre naturel*. Paris: Barrois, Laporte, 1783.

Nash, Gary B. *The Urban Crucible: Social Change, Political Consciousness, and the Origins of the American Revolution*. Cambridge: Harvard University Press, 1979.

Nelken, David. "Whom Can You Trust? The Future of Comparative Criminology." In

The Futures of Criminology, ed. David Nelkin, 220–243. London/Thousand Oaks: Sage, 1994.

Neubauer, David W. *America's Courts and the Criminal Justice System*. 6th ed. Belmont, CA: West/Wadsworth, 1999.

Nietzsche, Friedrich. *Der Wille zur Macht. Versuch einer Umwertung aller Werte*. In Friederich Nietzsche, *Sämtliche Werke in Zwölf Bänden*, eds. P. Gast and E. Förster-Nietzsche, vol. 9. Stuttgart: Kröner, 1964.

———. *Zur Genealogie der Moral: Eine Streitschrift*. In Friedrich Nietzsche, *Kritische Studienausgabe*, eds. Giorgio Colli and Mazzino Montinari, vol. 5. Munich: Deutscher Taschenbuch Verlag, 1999.

Noellner, Friedrich. *Criminal-Psychologische Denkwürdigkeiten, für gebildete aller stände*. Stuttgart/Augsburg: Cotta, 1858.

Novick, Peter. *The Resistance versus Vichy: The Purge of Collaborators in Liberated France*. New York: Columbia University Press, 1968.

Nussbaum, Martha C. *Poetic Justice: The Literary Imagination and Public Life*. Boston: Beacon Press, 1995.

Nye, Robert A. *Masculinity and Male Codes of Honor in Modern France*. New York: Oxford University Press, 1993.

Obermaier, Otto, and Robert Morvillo. *White Collar Crime: Business and Regulatory Offenses*. New York: Law Journal Seminars-Press, 1990.

Observatoire internationale des prisons. *Le nouveau guide du prisonnier*. Paris: Éditions de l'Atelier, 2000.

Observatoire international des prisons, section française. *Prisons: Un état des lieux*. Paris: L'esprit frappeur, 2000.

Oikonomides, Nicolas. *Les listes de préséance byzantines du IXe et Xe siècles*. Paris: Éditions du Centre nationale de la recherche scientifique, 1972.

Ørsted, A. S. *Ueber die Grundregeln der Strafgesetzgebung*. Copenhagen: in der Gyldendalschen Buchhandlung, 1818.

Osgood, Russell K. Review of *Hitler's Justice: The Courts of the Third Reich*, by Ingo Muller. *Cornell International Law Review* 28 (1995): 461–467.

Pack, Roger A. "Artemidorus and his Waking World." *Transactions of the American Philological Association* 86 (1955): 280–290.

Paganel, Pierre. *Rapport sur les Prisons, maisons d'arrêt ou de police, de répression, de détention, & sur les hospices de santé*. [Paris: Imprimerie Nationale, An III (1795)].

Parent, Dale, et al. *Key Legislative Issues in Criminal Justice: Intermediate Sanctions*. [Washington, D.C.]: U.S. Department of Justice, Office of Justice Programs, National Institute of Justice, 1997.

Pashukanis, Evgenii. *La Théorie Générale du Droit et le Marxisme*. Trans. J.-M. Brohm. Paris: Études et documentation internationales, 1970.

Patin, Maurice. "Du sursis et des circonstances atténuantes." *Revue de science criminelle et de droit pénal comparé* (1947): 341–347.

Pauli, Gerhard. *Die Rechtsprechung des Reichsgerichts in Strafsachen zwischen 1933 und 1945 und ihre Fortwirkung in der Rechtsprechung des Bundesgerichtshofes*. Berlin: Walter de Gruyter, 1992.

Payne, A. Abigail. "Does Inter-Judge Disparity Really Matter? An Analysis of the Effects of Sentencing Reforms in Three Federal District Courts." *International Review of Law and Economics* 17 (Sept. 1997): 337–358.

Pedron, Pierre. *La Prison sous Vichy*. Paris: Éditions de l'Atelier/Éditions ouvrières, 1993.

Perrot, Michelle. "Alexis de Tocqueville et les Prisons." In *La prison, le bagne, et l'histoire*, ed. Jacques-Guy Petit, 103–113. Geneva: Médicine et Hygiène, 1984.

———. "1848: Révolution et Prison." In *L'impossible prison: Recherches sur le système pénitentiaire au XIXe siècle*, ed. Michelle Perrot, 277–312. Paris: Éditions du Seuil, 1980.

———. "Préface." In *Histoire des galères, bagnes et prisons, XIIIe—XXe siècles*, ed. Jacques-Guy Petit et al., 7–13. Toulouse: Bibliothèque Historique Privat, 1991.

Peterson, Paul E. "An Immodest Proposal." *Daedalus* 121, no. 4 (1992): 151–175.

Petit, Jacques-Guy. "Politiques, modèles et imaginaires de la prison (1790–1875)." In *Histoire des galères, bagnes et prisons, XIIIe—XXe siècles*, ed. Jacques-Guy Petit et al., 109–137. Toulouse: Bibliothèque Historique Privat, 1991.

———. *Ces Peines Obscures: La prison pénale en France (1780–1875)*. Paris: Fayard, 1990.

Phan, Bernard. *La France de 1940 à 1958: Vichy et la IVe République*. Paris: Armand Colin, 1998.

Pierre, M. "La Transportation (1848–1938)." In *Histoire des galères, bagnes et prisons, XIIIe—XXe siècles*, ed. Jacques-Guy Petit et al., 231–259. Toulouse: Bibliothèque Historique Privat, 1991.

Pillsbury, Samuel. "Why Are We Ignored? The Peculiar Place of Experts in the Current Debate about Crime and Justice." *Criminal Law Bulletin* 31 (July–Aug. 1995): 305–336.

Plato. "Gorgias." Trans. W. D. Woodhead. In *The Collected Dialogues of Plato*, ed. Edith Hamilton and Huntington Cairns, 229–307. Princeton: Princeton University Press, 1961.

Plawski, Stanislas. "Les droits de l'homme dans le procès et l'exécution des peines." *Revue pénitentiaire et de droit pénal* (1978): 203–228.

Poncela, Pierrette. *Droit de la peine*. 2d ed. Paris: Presses Universitaires de France, 2001.

Popitz, Heinrich. *Phänomene der Macht*. 2d. ed. Tübingen: J.C.B. Mohr (P. Siebeck), 1992.

Porret, Michel. "Atténuer le mal de l'infamie: Le réformisme conservateur de Pierre-François Muyart de Vouglans." *Crime, histoire et sociétés* 4 (2000): 95–120.

Poulos, Peter W. Comment, "Chicago's Ban on Gang Loitering: Making Sense of Vagueness and Overbreadth in Loitering Laws." *California Law Review* 83 (1995): 379–417.

Pradel, Jean. *Droit Pénal*. 6th ed. Paris: Cujas, 1987.

———. "Vers un retour à une plus grande certitude de la peine avec les lois du 9 septembre 1986." *Recueil Dalloz Sirey de doctrine, de jurisprudence et de législation* (1987): 5–10.

Preyer, Kathryn. "Crime, the Criminal Law and Reform in Post-Revolutionary Virginia." *Law and History Review* 1 (1983): 53–85.

———. "Penal Measures in the American Colonies: An Overview." *American Journal of Legal History* 26 (1982): 326–353.

Prittwitz, C. "Positive Generalprävention und 'Recht des Opfers auf Bestrafung des Täters'?" *Kritische Vierteljahresschrift für Gesetzgebung und Rechtswissenschaft. Sonderheft: Winfried Hassemer zum sechzigsten Geburtstag* (2000): 162–175.

Pyle, Kerry L. Note, "Prison Employment: A Long-Term Solution to the Overcrowding Crisis." *Boston University Law Review* 77 (1997): 151–180.

Quedenfeld, Hans Dietrich. *Der Strafvollzug in der Gesetzgebung des Reiches, des*

Bundes und der Länder: eine Untersuchung über die normative Grundlage des Strafvollzugs. Tübingen: Mohr, 1971.

Quétel, Claude. *De par le Roy: Essai sur les lettres de cachet*. Toulouse: Privat, 1981.

Radbruch, Gustav. *Rechtsphilosophie*. 8th ed. Stuttgart: K. F. Koehler, 1973.

———. "Stand und Strafrecht." *Schweizerische Zeitschrift für Strafrecht* 49 (1935): 17–30.

———. "Der Ursprung des Strafrechts aus dem Stande der Unfreien." In Gustav Radbruch, *Elegantiae Juris Criminalis: vierzehn Studien zur Geschichte des Strafrechts*. 2d ed. Basel: Verlag fur Recht und Gesellschaft, 1950.

Radzinowicz, Leon. *A History of English Criminal Law and its Administration from 1750*. New York: Macmillan, 1948.

Ramlau, Max. "Wie Wird im Deutschen Reiche die Enthauptung Vollstreckt?" Ph.D. diss., Rostock, 1890.

Randall, Edwin T. "Imprisonment for Debt in America: Fact and Fiction." *Mississippi Valley Historical Review* 39 (June 1952): 89–102.

Rassat, Michèle-Laure. *Droit pénal*. Paris: Presses Universitaires de Frances, 1987.

Ratgeber für Gefangene. Berlin: Schwarze Seele, 1990.

Ravello, Frederico. *Silvio Pellico*. Turin: Societa editrice internazionale, 1954.

Renaut, Marie-Hélène. "Le droit de grâce doit-il disparaître?" *Revue de science criminelle* 3 (July–Sept. 1996): 575–606.

Renucci, Jean-François, and Christine Courtin. *Le Droit Pénal des Mineurs*. 4th ed. Paris: Presses Universitaires de France, 2001.

Rhodes, Susan L. "Democratic Justice: The Responsiveness of Prison Population Size to Public Policy Preferences." *American Politics Quarterly* 18 (1990): 337–375.

Richter, Melvin. "The Uses of Theory: Tocqueville's Adaptation of Montesquieu." In *Essays in Theory and History: An Approach to the Social Sciences*, ed. Melvin Richter, 74–102. Cambridge: Harvard University Press, 1970.

Robbins, Ira P. "The Legal Dimensions of Private Incarceration." *American University Law Review* 38 (1989): 531–854.

Robert, Philippe, et al., eds. *Les Comptes du Crime*. 2d ed. Paris: L'Harmattan, 1994.

Roberts, Claire, ed. *Evolution & Revolution: Chinese Dress, 1700s–1900s*. Sydney: Powerhouse Pub., Museum of Applied Arts and Sciences, 1997.

Robespierre, Maximilien. "Discours sur les peines infamantes." In *Oeuvres Complètes*. Vol. 1, 20–47. Paris: Leroux, 1912.

Robinson, Paul H., and John M. Darley. "The Utility of Desert." *Northwestern University Law Review* 91 (1997): 453–499.

Roeber, A. Gregg. "Authority, Law and Custom: The Rituals of Court Day in Tidewater Virginia, 1720–1750." *William and Mary Quarterly*. 3d Series 37 (1980): 29–52.

Röschel, Alfred, and Ernst Blaese. *Die Strafvollstreckung: Durchführung der vollstreckung gerichtlicher strafen, mit beispielen*. Berlin: W. de Gruyter, 1944.

Roßhirt, Konrad Eugen Franz. *Lehrbuch des Criminalrechts*. Heidelberg: Mohr and Winter, 1821.

Rosswurm, Steven. *Arms, Country and Class: The Philadelphia Militia and the "Lower Sort" during the American Revolution*. New Brunswick: Rutgers University Press, 1987.

Rothman, David J. *The Discovery of the Asylum: Social Order and Disorder in the New Republic*. Boston: Little, Brown & Co., 1971.

Ruckman, P. S. "Executive Clemency in the United States: Origins, Development and Analysis (1900–1993)." *Presidential Studies Quarterly* 27 (1997): 251–271.

Rush, Benjamin. *An Enquiry in the Effects of Public Punishment*. Philadelphia: Joseph James, 1787.

Roxin, Claus. *Strafrecht. Allgemeiner Teil*. Munich: Beck, 1992.

Royer, Jean-Pierre. *Histoire de la justice en France: De la monarchie absolue à la République*. Paris: Presses Universitaires de France, 1995.

Rusche, Georg, and Otto Kirchheimer. *Punishment and Social Structure*. 1939. Reprint, New York: Russell & Russell, 1968.

Sagel-Grande, I. "Die Amnestie—ein Rechtsinstitut mit deutscher Zukunft? Überlegungen am Beispiel Frankreich." *Recht in Ost und West* 34 (1990): 293–298.

Saint-Edme, Edme Théodore Bourg. *Dictionnaire de la pénalité*. 5 vols. Paris: n.p., 1824–1828.

Saleilles, Raymond. *The Individualization of Punishment*. Trans. Rachel Szold Jastrow. Boston: Little, Brown, 1911.

Saller, Richard. "Corporal Authority, Punishment, Authority and Obedience in the Roman Household." In *Marriage, Divorce and Children in Ancient Rome*, ed. Beryl Rawson, 144–165. Canberra: Humanities Research Center, 1991.

Sanguez-Lovisi, Claire. *Contribution à l'étude de la peine de mort sous la république romaine (509–149 av. J.-C.)*. Paris: De Boccard, 1999.

Saussure, César de. *A Foreign View of England in the Reigns of George I. & George II.: The Letters of Monsieur César de Saussure to his Family*. Trans. and ed. Madame van Muyden. London: J. Murray, 1902.

Scalia, Antonin. Essay, "*Originalism: The Lesser Evil*." University of Cincinnati Law Review 57 (1989): 849–865.

Schätzler, Johann-Georg. *Handbuch des Gnadenrechts: Gnade, Amnestie, Bewährung*. 2d ed. Munich: Beck, 1992.

Schlosser, Eric. "The Prison-Industrial Complex." *The Atlantic Monthly* 282, no. 6 (Dec. 1998): Online. Available: http://www.theatlantic.com/issues/98dec/prisons.htm. March 18, 2002.

Schlothauer, Reinhold, and Hans-Joachim Weider. *Untersuchungshaft*. Heidelberg: Müller, 2001.

Schmidt, Eberhard. *Einführung in die Geschichte der deutschen Strafrechtspflege*. Göttingen: Vandenhoeck and Ruprecht, 1965.

Schmitt, Carl. *Über die Drei Arten des rechtswissenschaftlichen Denkens*. Hamburg: Hanseatische Verlagsanstalt, 1934.

Schnapper, Bernard. "Les systèmes repressifs français de 1789 à 1815." In *Révolutions et justice pénale en Europe: Modèles français et traditions nationales (1780–1830)*, eds. Xavier Rousseaux, Marie-Sylvie Dupont-Bouchat, and Claude Vael, 17–35. Paris: L'Harmattan, 1999.

Schoetensack, Otto August, Rudolf Christians, Hans Eichler, and Friedrich Oetke, *Grundzüge eines Deutschen Strafvollstreckungsrechts. Denkschrift des Ausschusses für Strafvollstreckungsrechts der Strafrechtsabteilung der Akademie für deutsches Recht*. Berlin: R. V. Decker, 1935.

Schubert, Werner, ed. *Entwürfe der Strafrechtskommission zu einem deutschen Strafgesetzbuch und zu einem Einführungsgesetz (1911–1914)*. Frankfurt a. M: Keip, 1990.

Schüler-Springorum, Horst. *Strafvollzug im Übergang: Studien zum Stand der Vollzugsrechtslehre*. Göttingen: Schwartz, 1969.

Schwartz, Benjamin I. *The World of Thought in Ancient China*. Cambridge: Belknap Press/Harvard University Press, 1985.

Schwind, Hans-Dieter. "Beccaria als Pionier moderner Kriminalpolitik." In *Cesare Bec-*

caria. Die Anfänge moderner Strafrechtspflege in Europa, ed. Gerhard Deimling, 7–10. Heidelberg: Kriminalistik Verlag, 1989.

Schwind, Hans-Dieter, and Alexander Böhm. *Strafvollzugsgesetz*. Berlin: W. de Gruyter, 1999.

Schwoerer, Lois G. *The Declaration of Rights, 1689*. Baltimore: Johns Hopkins Press, 1981.

Scott, Adolph Clarence. *Chinese Costume in Transition*. Singapore: D. Moore, 1958.

Selden, John. *Titles of Honor*. 3d ed. London: Tyler and Holt, 1672.

Sellin, J. Thorsten. *Slavery and the Penal System*. New York: Elsevier, 1976.

The Sentencing Project. *U.S. Surpasses Russia as World Leader in Rate of Incarceration*. Online. Available: http://www.sentencingproject.org/brief/usvsrus.pdf. March 18, 2002.

Serpillon, François. *Code criminel ou commentaire sur l'Ordonnance de 1670*. Lyon: Frères Perisse, 1767.

Shakespeare, William. *Measure for Measure*, ed. Brian Gibbons. Cambridge: Cambridge University Press, 1991.

Shapiro, Susan P. "Collaring the Crime, not the Criminal: Reconsidering the Concept of White-Collar Crime." *American Sociological Review* 55 (1990): 346–365.

Signoret, Albert. *De la contrainte par corps*. Montpellier: Jeanjean, 1905.

Simon, Jonathan. "Power without Parents: Juvenile Justice in a Postmodern Society." *Cardozo Law Review* 16 (1995): 1363–1426.

Smithers, William W. "Nature and Limits of the Pardoning Power." *Journal of Criminal Law and Criminology* 1 (1910): 549–562.

Société Générale des Prisons et de Législation Criminelle. "Séance du 13 mars 1982. Droits sociaux du détenu." *Revue Pénitentiaire et de Droit Pénal* (July–Sept. 1982): 267–283.

Sofsky, Wolfgang. *Die Ordnung des Terrors: Das Konzentrationslager*. Frankfurt am Main: S. Fischer, 1993.

Sontag, Karl Richard. *Die Festungshaft: Ein Beitrag zur Geschichte des deutschen Strafsystems und zur Erläuterung des Reichsstrafrechts*. Leipzig: Winter, 1872.

Sorokin, Pitirim. *Social and Culture Dynamics*. 4 vols. New York: Bedminster Press, 1962.

Soubiran, André. *The Good Doctor Guillotin and His Strange Device*, trans. Malcolm MacCraw. London: Souvenir Press, 1964.

Sowle, Stephen D. "A Regime of Social Death: Criminal Punishment in the Age of Prisons." *New York University Review of Law and Social Change* 21 (1995): 497–565.

Spierenburg, Pieter. *The Spectacle of Suffering: Executions and the Evolution of Repression: From a Preindustrial Metropolis to the European Experience*. Cambridge: Cambridge University Press, 1984.

———. *The Prison Experience: Disciplinary Institutions and Their Inmates in Early Modern Europe*. New Brunswick, N.J.: Rutgers University Press, 1991.

———. "Masculinity, Violence and Honor: An Introduction." In *Men and Violence: Gender, Honor and Rituals in Modern Europe and America*, ed. Pieter Spierenburg, 1–29. Columbus: Ohio State University Press, 1998.

Spies, Axel. *Amnestiemaßnahmen und deren Verfassungsmässigkeit in Frankreich und Deutschland*. Frankfurt am Main: P. Lang, 1991.

Spindel, Donna. *Crime and Society in North Carolina, 1663–1776*. Baton Rouge: Louisiana State University Press, 1989.

Spire, Juliette. "La Détention à Fresnes Durant la Guerre d'Algérie." In *Fresnes, la prison: Les établissements pénitentiaires de Fresnes: 1895–1990*, ed. Christian Carlier, Juliette Spire, and Françoise Wasserman, 100–111. Fresnes: Ecomusée, 1991.

Steinberg, Allen. *The Transformation of Criminal Justice: Philadelphia, 1800–1880.* Chapel Hill, N.C.: University of North Carolina Press, 1989.

Stephen, James Fitzjames. *A History of the Criminal Law of England.* London: Macmillan and Co., 1883.

Stewart, James B. *Den of Thieves.* New York: Simon & Schuster, 1991.

Stith, Kate, and José A. Cabranes. "Judging under the Federal Sentencing Guidelines." *Northwestern University Law Review* 91 (1997): 1247–1283.

———. *Fear of Judging: Sentencing Guidelines in the Federal Courts.* Chicago: University of Chicago Press, 1998.

Stith, Kate, and Steve Y. Koh. "The Politics of Sentencing Reform: The Legislative History of the Federal Sentencing Guidelines." *Wake Forest Law Review* 28 (1993): 223–290.

Strafvollstreckung-Strafregister-Gnadenwesen. 2d ed. Munich: Beck, 1954.

Strayer, Brian E. *Lettres de Cachet and Social Control in the Ancien Régime, 1659–1789.* New York: P. Lang, 1992.

Sutherland, Edwin H. "White-Collar Criminality." *American Sociological Review* 5 (Feb. 1940): 1–12.

Sutherland, Edwin H., and Donald R. Cressey, *Principles of Criminology.* 7th ed. Philadelphia: Lippincott, 1966.

Sutton, John R. "Imprisonment and Social Classification in Five Common-Law Democracies, 1955–1985." *American Journal of Sociology* 106 (Sept. 2000): 350–386.

Sykes, Gresham. *The Society of Captives: A Study of a Maximum-Security Prison.* Princeton: Princeton University Press, 1971.

Symons, Jr., Edward L., and James J. White. *Banking Law: Teaching Materials.* 3d ed. St. Paul, Minn.: West Pub., 1991.

Sypherd, Stephen S., and Gary M. Sypherd. Thirtieth Annual Review of Criminal Procedure, VI. Prisoners' Rights, "Substantive Rights Retained by Prisoners." *Georgetown Law Journal* 89 (2001): 1898–1938.

Szockyj, Elizabeth. *The Law and Insider Trading: In Search of a Level Playing Field.* Buffalo, N.Y.: W. S. Hein, 1993.

Taggart, William A. "Redefining the Power of the Federal Judiciary: The Impact of Court-Ordered Prison Reform on State Expenditures for Corrections." *Law and Society Review* 23 (1989): 241–271.

[Target, Guy Jean Baptiste], *Projet du Code Criminel, Correctionel et de Police.* n.p., 1802.

Taylor, David. *Crime, Policing, and Punishment in England, 1750–1914.* New York: St. Martin's Press, 1998.

Tiraqueau, André. *Le "De Poenis Temperandis" de Tiraqueau (1559).* Ed. André Laingui. Paris: Economica, 1986.

Tocqueville, Alexis de. *De la démocratie en Amérique.* 2 vols. Paris: Garnier-Flammarion, 1981.

Toller, Ernst. "Briefe aus dem Gefängnis." In *Gesammelte Werke*, ed. W. Frühwald and J. Spalek. Vol. 5. Munich: Hander, 1975.

Tomlinson, M. Heather. "Penal Servitude, 1846–1865: A System in Evolution." In *Policing and Punishment in Nineteenth Century Britain*, ed. Victor Bailey, 126–149. London: Croom Helm, 1981.

Tonry, Michael. "Preface." In *The Handbook of Crime and Punishment*, ed. Michael Tonry, v–vi. Oxford: Oxford University Press, 1998.

———. "Race and the War on Drugs." *University of Chicago Legal Forum 1994* (1994): 25–81.

———. *Sentencing Matters*. New York: Oxford University Press, 1996.

Tonry, Michael, and Kathleen Hatlestad, eds. *Sentencing Reform in Overcrowded Times: A Comparative Perspective*. New York: Oxford University Press, 1997.

Tonry, Michael, and Joan Petersilia. "American Prisons at the Beginning of the Twenty-First Century." *Crime and Justice: A Review of Research* 26, *Prisons*, ed. Michael Tonry and Joan Petersilia (1999): 1–16.

Torcia, Charles E. *Wharton's Criminal Law*. 15th ed. Deerfield, Ill.: Clark Boardman Callaghan, 1993.

The Tragick-Comedy of Titus Oates. London: Randal-Taylor, 1685.

Treiber, Hubert, and Heinz Steinert. *Die Fabrikation des zuverlässigen Menschen. Über die 'Wahlverwandschaft' von Kloster- und Fabrikdisziplin*. Munich: Moos, 1980.

Tulard, Jean, Jean-François Fayard, and Alfred Fierro. *Histoire et dictionnaire de la Révolution française, 1789–1799*. Paris: Robert Laffont 1987.

Turow, Scott. *Presumed Innocent*. New York: Farrar, Straus, Giroux, 1987.

Uhle, Edgar. *Die Amnestie nach altem und neuem Gnadenrecht*. Breslau/Neukirch: A. Kurtze, 1935.

Underwood, Richard H. "Perjury: An Anthology." *Arizona Journal of International and Comparative Law* 13 (1996): 307–379.

United Nations Department of Social Affairs. *Probation and Related Measures*. New York: [United Nations], 1951.

U.S. Congress. *Annals of Congress*, ed. Joseph Gales. Vol. 1. n.p., 1789.

U.S. Department of Justice, Bureau of Justice Assistance. *How to Use Structured Fines (Day Fines) as an Intermediate Sanction*. Washington, D.C.: The Bureau, 1996.

U.S. Department of Justice, Bureau of Justice Statistics. *Jail Statistics*. Rev. February 28, 2002. Online. Available: http://www.ojp.usdoj.gov/bjs/jails.htm. March 18, 2002.

U.S. Department of Justice, Office of Justice Programs, Violence Against Women Grants Office. *Stalking and Domestic Violence: The Third Annual Report to Congress Under the Violence Against Women Act*. July 1998. Online. Available: http://www.ojp.usdoj.gov/vawo/grants/stalk98/stalk98.pdf. March 18, 2002.

U.S. War Department. *A Manual for Courts-Martial*. Washington, D.C.: G. P. O., 1920.

Vasseur, Veronique. *Médecin-Chef à la Prison de la Santé*. Paris: Le Cherche Midi, 2000.

Velten, P. "Untreue durch Belastung mit Risiko zukünftiger Sanktionen am Beispiel bedeckter Parteienfinanzierung." *Neue Juristische Wochenschrift* (2000): 2852–2856.

Viaud, Jean. *Le droit de grâce à la fin de l'Ancien Régime, et son abolition pendant la Révolution*. Paris: Arthur Rousseau, 1906.

"Vierzigster Deutscher Juristentag in Hamburg." *Deutsche Richterzeitung* (1953): 146–149.

Vimont, Jean-Claude. "Enfermer les politiques: La mise en place progressive des 'régimes politiques' d'incarcération (1815–1848)." In Philippe Vigier et al. *Répression et Prisons Politiques en France et en Europe au XIXe siècle*, 189–203. Paris: Créaphis, 1990.

———. *La prison politique: Génèse d'une mode d'incarcération spécifique, XVIIIe—XXe siècles*. Paris: Anthropos: Diffusion, Economica, 1993.

———. *Punir autrement—Les prisons de Seine-Inférieure pendant la Révolution*. Mont-Saint-Aignan: C. R. D. P., 1989.

Vingtrinier, Artus Barthelemy. *Des prisons et de prisonniers*. Versailles: Klefer, 1840.

Vogelgesang, E. "Kleintierhaltung im Strafvollzug." *Zeitschrift für Strafvollzug* (1994): 67–68.

Vogler, Richard. *France: A Guide to the French Criminal Justice System*. London: Prisoners Abroad, 1989.

Von Hirsch, Andrew. *Doing Justice: The Choice of Punishments: Report of the Committee for the Study of Incarceration*. New York: Hill & Wang, 1976.

———. *Censure and Sanctions*. Oxford: Clarendon Press, 1993.

Von Hirsch, Andrew, and Uma Narayan. "Degradingness and Intrusiveness." In Andrew Von Hirsch, *Censure and Sanctions*, 80–87. New York: Oxford University Press, 1993.

Vorentwurf zu einem Deutschen Strafgesetzbuch. Berlin: Guttentag, 1909.

Wabnitz, Heinz-Bernd, and Thomas Janovsky. *Handbuch des Wirtschafts- und Steuerstrafrechts*. Munich: C. H. Beck, 2000.

Wacquant, Loic. *Les prisons de la misère*. Paris: Raisons d'agir, 1999.

Wächter, Carl Georg von. *Lehrbuch des Römisch-Teutschen Straftrechts*. 2 vols. Stuttgart: Metzler, 1825–1826.

Wahlberg, Wilhelm Emil v. "Die Strafmittel." In *Handbuch des deutschen Strafrechts*, ed. F. v. Holtzendorff, 429–511. Berlin: Lüderitz, 1871.

Waldeck, Sarah E. "Cops, Community Policing, and the Social Norms Approach to Crime Control: Should One Make Us More Comfortable with the Others?" *Georgia Law Review* 34 (2002): 1253–1310.

Walker, Samuel. *Popular Justice: A History of American Criminal Justice*. 2d ed. New York: Oxford University Press, 1998.

Ward, George E. Commentary, "Bennis and the War on Drugs." *Catholic University Law Review* 46 (1996): 109–118.

Weber, H. von. "Calvinismus und Strafrecht." In *Festschrift für Eberhard Schmidt zum 70. Geburstag*, ed. Paul Bocklemann and Wilhelm Gallas, 39–53. Göttingen: Vandenhoeck and Ruprecht, 1961.

Weigel, Sigrid. *"Und selbst im Kerker frei . . .!". Schreiben im Gefängnis. Zur Theorie und Gattungsgeschichte der Gefängnisliteratur (1750–1933)*. Marburg/Lahn: Guttandin & Hoppe, 1982.

Weigend, Thomas, and Hans-Jörg Albrecht. "West Germany." In *Sentencing Reform in Overcrowded Times: A Comparative Perspective*, ed. Michael Tonry and Kathleen Hatlestad, 177–187. New York: Oxford University Press, 1997.

Weiler, Joseph M. P. "Why Do We Punish? The Case for Retributive Justice." *University of British Columbia Law Review* 12 (1978): 295–319.

Weill, Kurt. *Die Dreigroschenoper: Klavierauszug*. Vienna: Universal Edition, 1956.

Weinstein, Jack B., and Fred A. Bernstein. "The Denigration of Mens Rea in Drug Sentencing." *Federal Sentencing Reporter* 7 (1994): 121–124.

Weis, Kurt. "Die Subkultur der Strafgefangenen." In *Strafvollzug in der Praxis*, ed. Hans-Dieter Schwind and Günter Blau, 239–255. 2d ed. Berlin: De Gruyter, 1988.

Weisburd, David, et al., *Crimes of the Middle Classes: White-Collar Offenders in the Federal Courts*. New Haven: Yale University Press, 1991.

Weld, Theodore Dwight. *American Slavery As It Is: Testimony of a Thousand Witnesses*. 1839. Reprint, New York: Arno Press, 1968.

Wetzell, Richard F. *Inventing the Criminal: A History of German Criminology, 1880–1945*. Chapel Hill, N.C.: University of North Carolina Press, 2000.

Wheeler, Stanton. Review of *Sentencing Matters*, by Michael Tonry. *Criminal Justice Ethics* 16, no. 2 (summer-fall 1997): 46–51.

Wheeler, Stanton, Kenneth Mann, and Austin Sarat. *Sitting in Judgment: The Sentencing of White-Collar Criminals*. New Haven: Yale University Press, 1988.

Whitman, James Q. "At the Origins of Law and the State: Supervision of Violence, Mutilation of Bodies, or Setting of Prices?" *Chicago-Kent Law Review* 71 (1995): 41–84.

———. "Enforcing Civility and Respect: Three Societies." *Yale Law Journal* 109 (2000): 1279–1398.

———."The Moral Menace of Roman Law and the Making of Commerce: Some Dutch Evidence." *Yale Law Journal* 105 (1996): 1841–1889.

———. "On Nazi 'Honour' and the New European 'Dignity.'" In *The Darker Legacy of European Law*, eds. Christian Joerges and Navraj Ghaleigh. Oxford: Hart, forthcoming.

———. "The Opposition to Public Punishment in Germany: The Christian Sources." In *Grundlagen des Rechts. Festschrift für Peter Landau*, ed. R. Helmholz et al., 759–776. Paderborn: Schoningh, 2000.

———. Essay, "What Is Wrong with Inflicting Shame Sanctions?" *Yale Law Journal* 107 (1998): 1055–1092.

Whittle, Shirley W. "New York's Property Clerk Forfeiture Act—Can They Do That?" *Washington University Journal of Law and Policy* 4 (2000): 361–376.

Wilf, Steven. "Imagining Justice: Aesthetics and Public Executions in Late Eighteenth-Century England." *Yale Journal of Law and the Humanities* 5 (1993): 51–78.

———. "Placing Blame: Criminal Law and Constitutional Narratives in Revolutionary Boston." *Crime, Histoire & Sociétés* 4 (2000): 31–61.

Wilson, James. *The Works of James Wilson*, ed. Robert Green McCloskey, vol. 1, *Lectures in Law*. 2 vols. Cambridge: Belknap Press/Harvard University Press, 1967.

Wilson, James Q. *Thinking about Crime*. New York: Basic Books, 1975.

Winstanley, Gerrard. "The Law of Freedom in a Platform, or True Magistracy Restored." In *The Works of Gerrard Winstanley*, ed. George H. Sabine. New York: Russell & Russell, 1965.

Winthrop, W[illiam]. *Military Law*. 2 vols. Washington, D.C.: W. H. Morrison, 1886.

Witkin, B. E., and Norman L. Epstein. *California Criminal Law*. 2d ed. San Francisco: Bancroft-Whitney, 1988–1989.

Wolfgang, Marvin. "Beccaria: Precursor of Modern Criminology." In *Beccaria als Wegbereiter der Kriminologie*, ed. D. Rössner and J.-M. Jehle, 27–35. Mönchengladbach: Forum, 2000.

Wood, Gordon S. *The Radicalism of the American Revolution*. New York: A. A. Knopf, 1992.

Writer, Simon. "'Written naturally by the finger of God in our hearts': Leveller Politics, the English Revolution and the Natural Law Tradition." *Newcastle Law Review* 3 (1998): 38–56.

Zalman, Marvin. "The Rise and Fall of the Indeterminate Sentence." *Wayne Law Review* 24 (1977): 45–94.

Ziegler, Kaspar. *In Hugonis Grotii de Jure Belli ac Pacis Libros Notae et Animadversiones*. 4th ed. Strasbourg: Dulssecker, 1706.

Zimring, Franklin E. *Capital Punishment and the American Agenda*. Cambridge: Cambridge University Press, 1986.

———. "Populism, Democratic Government, and the Decline of Expert Authority:

Some Reflections on 'Three Strikes' in California." *Pacific Law Journal* 28 (1996): 243–256.

Zimring, Franklin E., and Gordon Hawkins. *Crime Is Not the Problem: Lethal Violence in America*. New York: Oxford University Press, 1997.

Zysberg, A. "Le modèle des travaux forces." In *Histoire des galères, bagnes et prisons, XIIIe—XXe siècles*, ed. Jacques-Guy Petit et al., 199–229. Toulouse: Bibliothèque Historique Privat, 1991.

Index